T0265605

BLACKBOARDS
AND BOMB SHELTERS

BLACKBOARDS
AND BOMB SHELTERS

*The Perilous Journey of Americans
in China during World War II*

James P. Bevill

SCHIFFER MILITARY

4880 Lower Valley Road   Atglen, PA 19310

Published by Schiffer Publishing, Ltd.
4880 Lower Valley Road
Atglen, PA 19310
Phone: (610) 593-1777; Fax: (610) 593-2002
E-mail: Info@schifferbooks.com
Web: www.schifferbooks.com

For our complete selection of fine books on this
and related subjects, please visit our website at
www.schifferbooks.com. You may also write for a
free catalog.

Schiffer Publishing's titles are available at special
discounts for bulk purchases for sales promotions
or premiums. Special editions, including
personalized covers, corporate imprints, and
excerpts, can be created in large quantities for
special needs. For more information, contact the
publisher.

We are always looking for people to write books
on new and related subjects. If you have an
idea for a book, please contact us at proposals@
schifferbooks.com.

This work is dedicated to
my lovely and talented wife,
Jodie Springer Bevill. Without you,
this project would have never come to life.
For our grandchildren, Fox, Eleanor, Jamie, and Frederik—
you motivated me to preserve this story for future generations.

Contents

FOREWORD

James P. Bevill contacted us at the Yale-China Association a few years ago to share that he was writing a book about the wartime China experiences of three Yale-in-China bachelors. That book is now here, chronicling in colorful detail the true stories of courageous Americans and Chinese working together in central China amidst the vast sweep of World War II.

It's particularly wonderful that this book is being published in 2021 on the 120th anniversary of the Yale-China experiment. Twelve decades is an audacious act of survival, considering the great upheavals and transformations, partnerships and enmities that both China and the United States experienced between 1901 and 2021. This encompasses revolutions and world wars, political re-alignments and tumultuous separations, emotional reconnections and unimaginable modernization and techno-logical change. Yale-China's legacy of building famous institutions of education and medicine; nurturing a community of tens of thousands of professional people trained and motivated; and an unbroken devotion to bringing Americans and Chinese together and bridging the deepest of divides—these are historic accomplishments. The practice of bringing recent graduates of Yale like Paul Springer, Jim Elliott and Art Hopkins, (called "Bachelors" because of their bachelor degrees) to serve as teachers at Yale Union Middle School, usually for a two-year stint, began in 1918—is a tradition that still continues.

Bevill's detailed account of three Yale graduates arriving in China to teach during the Japanese occupation in the summer of 1941 is an engaging coming-of-age story. This charming book reminds us what a vast gulf existed between relatively sheltered American college graduates and the wider world, and how transformative such an immersive service experience was. Upon their arrival in Changsha, on their way to Yuanling, they were introduced to Dr. Winston Pettus, a young Yale-educated surgeon struggling to keep open the legendary Xiang-Ya (Hunan-Yale) Hospital. The book's level of detail takes us right into the homes, truck-rides, meals, friendships, class-rooms, dangers, mid-air dogfights, bombing runs, and operating rooms. Springer,

Elliott, and Hopkins embraced whatever came their way, starting with eight weeks of onerous travel to reach their sites, and then carrying out their wartime work under dangerous and inspiring conditions. Their openness to adventure and unpredictability, their sense of humor and devotion to service keep us turning the pages.

Bevill is uniquely qualified to bring the reader into an intimate relationship with the story. He knew Paul Springer, one of the central characters, meticulously organized his papers and those of his colleagues, then wove their journals together into a single narrative. He conducted extensive research on the people, the war, economics, politics, and diplomacy efforts during the period. The book is richly illustrated with historical images, some from private collections, and many from the archives of the Yale-China Association and Yale University Library.

Going beyond individual hardships and adventures, the book portrays the vast reach of the Japanese occupation of China, what changed when the United States entered the war, and how these fast-moving events impacted Americans on the ground who were suddenly no longer neutral. Many wartime histories focus on those at the highest levels of command; by contrast, this book illuminates the intimate experiences and insights of individual people caught up in the chaos. Yet the diverging paths of the protagonists also illustrate the broader political, diplomatic and military presence of the US and China during that period. This bigger picture—the vicious air war, the overtures by Chinese Communists soliciting military aid from the Americans, a Nationalist government trying to defend its homeland, with outsized characters and conflicting personalities—sets the narrative in its vivid historical context.

During this 120th anniversary year at the Yale-China Association, we are revisiting Yale-China's multitude of stories of brave, generous, remarkable people. Bevill's book is a welcome addition. The narrative reminds us that this community has carried on with collaboration, positivity, learning, mutual respect and pragmatic results through wars, turmoil and modernization, and that it can do so again in our own complicated century.

This book recounts a high-water mark moment of the Sino-American partnership and what it was like to be there among ordinary heroes in wartime China. May that spirit long endure.

David Youtz
President, Yale-China Association
New Haven, Spring 2021

ACKNOWLEDGMENTS

The scope of the Yale-in-China educational and medical mission in the mid-twentieth century is largely unknown outside the Yale-China Association and a few alumni groups. This story, by itself, needed to be brought to life for the widest possible audience. My passion for bringing history alive inspired me to write this true story once I recognized that I had a unique access to a treasure trove of primary-source documents relating to the period. These came from my wife, Jodie Springer Bevill. Her father, Paul Springer, began teaching at the Yali Middle School in Hunan Province of China in 1941. He left behind hundreds of pages of letters as well as documents, plane tickets, memos, and photos documenting his adventures. These letters included detailed descriptions of his experiences and life-changing events during the war. His papers also contain original essays by his Chinese students writing about family and friends who were tortured and killed by the Japanese.

I thank Jodie's grandmother, the late Audrey Coder Springer, who had the incredible foresight to save every scrap of paper that her well-traveled son sent her from around the world. I often imagined her gazing out her front window, eagerly awaiting the postman delivering an envelope affixed with Chinese stamps. She then carefully opened and read the latest update on Yale-in-China and her son Paul's work in the US State Department abroad during World War II. Amazingly, these papers stayed in the family, although they were not discovered by myself and Jodie until 2010.

It would have been impossible to write a book of this magnitude without the helpful suggestions and ongoing encouragement of Jodie Springer Bevill. Her insights and rewrites were invaluable. As I read and organized the materials and the story began to unfold, she encouraged me to move forward with the project. She critiqued the story lines, selected photographs, and narrowed down the final selection of images for the book cover. She was my first-line editor, my constructive critic, and closest advisor. She made a number of recommendations for the manuscript and encouraged me to bring out the human elements of the story. She recalled several stories her father relayed years ago about his experiences in China, which were worked into the book.

Thanks go to my dear friend and retired English teacher Penny Garcia, who helped edit the work for grammar, punctuation, and readability. After her suggestions were implemented, my sister-in-law, Sarah Springer, proofed the next draft of the manuscript. I thank her for her time and efforts. Frank Wang and Patricia Holmes each read the initial draft from their Chinese perspective and offered several helpful comments. Patricia took a personal interest in the story by translating Chinese documents, ID cards, driver's licenses, and other items into English. Frank was a high school student in Shanghai when the war broke out, and offered insightful commentary and personal observations from the period, confirming what personal travel was like in China during the war.Jodie then reviewed the final manuscript and helped with some finishing edits during the publishing process.

Nancy Chapman, author of *The Yale-China Association: A Centennial History*, remembered my father-in-law and led me to the Yale-China Association records at Yale University. Once I located them, I was able to obtain more information on his Yale-in-China colleagues, specifically Jim Elliott, Art Hopkins, and William Winston Pettus. Their writings greatly expanded the story. Nancy also referred me to David Youtz, president of the Yale-China Association. David took a keen interest in the manuscript and granted the approval for publication of photos from the Yale-China Association records at the Yale University Library. He referred me to David Elder and George Zhongze Li. David is the husband of Betty Jean Rugh, and the son-in-law of Dwight Rugh. Both of which figure prominently in the story. George, a true Yale-in-China scholar, reviewed a copy of the manuscript from his unique Chinese technical and historical perspectives, making corrections on names of Chinese cities and provinces and providing their modern-day Pinyin spellings. George took my literary detective work to new levels, telephoning the adult children and grandchildren of former Yale-in-China staff members in Changsha, China, to verify names, places, and the context behind some of the characters in the story. Their relatives worked with, lived with, or taught with the American teachers. I am forever grateful for his thoroughness and perseverance in his review. There are several instances in which George's efforts are referenced and noted throughout this book.

This literary project led me to new acquaintances from afar. Andrew Hicks is the author of *Jack Jones, a True Friend to China*, which is an engaging literary and visual documentary work on the Friends Ambulance Unit (FAU) China Convoy from 1945 to 1951. He helped me tremendously with research on the FAU, much of which is based on information he discovered in writing his own book. Andrew referred me to Michael Llewellyn, whose father served in the FAU during this time period, and who graciously furnished one of the line-drawn maps for use in the book. The email correspondence with Andrew led me to a compilation of photographs that were passed down from various FAU drivers, mechanics, and administrators, which I reference as the FAU Collection. Every effort has been made to trace the copyright holders and to obtain their permission for the use of any copyrighted material. The author would be grateful to be notified of any corrections that should be incorporated in future reprints or editions of this book. I would like to thank David Sobel, a Washington, DC, attorney, for his help in obtaining Paul Springer's US State Department files through a Freedom of Information Act (FOIA) request.

Collecting the photos to illustrate the story was a project in itself. Many of the pictures came from the Springer Family Collection, which currently resides in our home. David Elder and Nancy Greenfield kindly offered their personal family photos to help illustrate different parts of the story. I am grateful for their contributions. Nancy's pictures from her father's wartime experience in North Africa, particularly in Jerusalem, were simply unobtainable from any other source. My research assistant, Joan Cavanaugh, searched through dozens of folders at the Yale University Library and pulled out some absolute gems. A special thanks goes to Jessica Dooling and Jessica Becker at the Yale University Manuscripts and Archives Library, and Diana Sykes at the Hoover Institution at Stanford University. Their efforts in researching and guiding me through the selection and re-production process for the hundreds of pages of manuscript documents and dozens of archival photographs are greatly appreciated.

I thank Angela Vincent, my colleague at UBS, for her patience and understanding as I undertook this project over the last three years. To everyone at Schiffer Publishing, especially Bob Biondi, John Stone, and Carey Massimini, you did a fabulous job. Your gifts of creativity, design, technology, and relentless pursuit of perfection have helped make this book a tribute to the men and women who were a part of this incredible story. There are others not named here who helped me in other ways.

All who contributed to this work are so appreciated. Your support is priceless and your friendship will be treasured always. It has been an exciting journey for all of us.

James P. Bevill

THE GREAT CHANGSHA FIRE

It is mid-November 1938. The Sino-Japanese War has ravaged the Republic of China for well over a year. All the coastal cities and industrial areas were firmly in control of the invading Japanese. Hundreds of thousands had died. Food supplies were captured by the enemy, property was looted, and Chinese women were kidnapped and raped. Their homes were occupied by conquering troops and sometimes set up as brothels for the soldiers. In their push into the interior of China, the imperial Japanese forces had their sights set on capturing Changsha, the capital of Hunan Province.

A fanatical group of Chinese had so resented the fall of Wuhan and Canton to the Japanese in late October 1938 that they removed all firefighting equipment from Changsha. Rumors circulated in Changsha that the city was to be sacrificed rather than let it fall to the invading Japanese, who were then in nearby Yochow, less than fifty miles to the north. People were being urged to leave the city, and those who had relatives in the province were leaving to take shelter with them. Many were determined to see their illustrious city burn rather than have it fall to the Japanese. It was a scorched-earth policy in the most literal sense.

The people interpreted the news as a signal to flee. They formed gangs of about ten men each to take the responsibility for denying the city to the invaders. The garrison commander's office in Changsha had confused the names of Hsin Chang Ho and Hsin Ho from a telephone message identifying the advanced position of the Japanese. The former, a town near Yochou on Tung Ting Lake, was reasonably distant, whereas the latter was a village on Changsha's doorstep. The scorched-earth organization panicked, acted on the theory that the Japanese were on their doorstep, and rushed into action without orders from either the governor or the national headquarters of the Kuomintang.

Gangs of Chinese entered the houses of Changsha residents; threw the occupants' clothing, wooden chairs, and other flammable belongings on and underneath the stairs; dashed kerosene on them; and touched a match to the pile. As they moved from house to house, the arsonists' work quickly spread into a raging inferno that consumed parts of the city.

Two Yale-in-China employees, Frank Hutchins and Dr. Phil Greene, were having dinner at the temporary residence of Governor Chang outside the South Gate of the city. During the dinner they were assured by the governor that the rumors of a scorched-earth policy were entirely false. They were taken home around 11:00 p.m. via a military car in the circuitous route well east of the city in order to avoid the glut of people, most of them on foot but many utilizing cars, buses, trucks, wheelbarrows, and rickshaws. When the two men reached the Yale-in-China campus on the west end of the city, they went to sleep as they normally did. The campus was a collection of educational buildings, dormitories, a medical school, a nursing school, and Hsiang-Ya Hospital. Dr. Greene was fast asleep only to be awakened by Hutchins at about 4:00 a.m., to see the sky bright from dozens of blazes in the city.

Hutchins remained on the Yali campus; Dr. Greene went to Hsiang-Ya Hospital. Each spent his time putting out occasional firebombs being thrown over the walls, and, most importantly, dissuading the groups from setting fire to their buildings. Rats began to pour out of the city in what became a flood so dense that it seemed to cover the ground. Doors and windows had to be tightly secured. When the flood of rats was at its height after a period lasting about twelve hours, Dr. Greene found it difficult to get through a door without a dozen rats squeezing in.

The Changsha fire blazed intensely for about three days, the second day being the worst. As areas were burned out, follow-up gangs arrived to burn whatever was left standing. Around noon on the third day, a gang of about fifteen arrived to burn the hospital and medical school buildings. They concentrated on a small Chinese house at the northeast corner of the hospital compound, which was not owned by Yali, although its roof was continuous with the sheds where their fuel oil was usually stored. Dr. Greene had already moved most of this into the hospital cellar. Next to the steel shed were a number of temporary bamboo shacks that had been used as an isolation ward for cholera patients some weeks earlier.

The gang was determined to set fire to the Chinese house. If they succeeded, the adjacent structures would catch fire and pass the flames to the hospital itself and possibly to the entire compound. Dr. Phil Greene seized a heavy pole about fifteen feet long, took up a position in front of the Chinese house, and defied the gang. They argued a long time, the gang insisting the house was Chinese and none of Phil's business. Dr. Greene told them, "The hospital is my business, and anyone can see how fire in the small house would gravely endanger the hospital." As their mutual patience evaporated, Dr. Greene said that he would brain the first man to put fire to the Chinese house, adding that they would certainly have to kill him before they could get the fire going. Greene had a very erratic command of the Chinese language at best, and in that dramatic scene of unbridled passion, the chaos of his language must have created a Shakespearian intensity that got his message across. The gang consulted among themselves and told Dr. Greene that murder was not part of their mission, and they left.

Across the street on the Yali campus, Yale staffers and their servants were similarly active. One was told by a member of a fire gang that "the only people who deserve to be called Chinese now are the ones who are giving everything to fight the Japanese— their property, their strengths and lives." At one point when a nearby building with cases of ammunition was burning, shells went off in all directions, some whizzing into both the Hsiang-Ya and Yali compounds, where they mercifully did little damage. Each of the Yali properties was saved, but the city of Changsha itself was gutted in the frenzy. The Japanese army had not invaded—but large parts of the city were already destroyed.

After the Changsha fire of 1938, all of the hospital's Chinese doctors and nurses evacuated the city due to the imminent danger of a Japanese occupation of the city. The fire left Hsiang-Ya Hospital as the only functioning hospital in the city. It was now staffed with only two Americans, Dr. Phil Greene, a surgeon, and Edna Hutchinson, the dean of the nursing school. Dr. Greene recruited Phil Runnells, an English teacher, to assist him in managing the drug supplies and to help out in the operating room. Dr. Hsiao Yuan-ting of the regular staff soon returned, along with intermittent help from a Dr. Sheridan, stationed on a British gunboat in the river. These were soon joined by Winifred Galbraith, a strong-willed and energetic teacher who joined them as a nurse's aide, as did an elderly Chinese man, another missionary, and a Russian dentist. It was as modest a hospital staff as was ever assembled, but somehow they managed to keep Hsiang-Ya Hospital running, taking care of patients, producing meals, performing operations, and opening an outpatient clinic for about a hundred persons per day, once the imminent Japanese threat subsided and people returned to the city.[1] It was a long-term process for the Yale-in-China trustees to find and recruit a new doctor and nursing staff for their medical mission, as well as recruit new English teachers for their educational mission at the Yali Middle School, about 200 miles to the west by road.

Chapter 1
BEGINNINGS AT YALE

Yearning for Adventure

Paul Le Baron Springer was born on August 25, 1917, in Merchantville, New Jersey. The front page of the *New York Times* that morning featured a story about black Army troops rioting at Camp Logan in Houston, Texas.[1] The Great War was raging in Europe. Paul had four siblings: Ruth, Joe, Eleanore, and Victor. Their family was of modest means, with his mother, Audrey, supervising the household and raising the children, while her husband, Armand, pursued a military career in the US Army. He received his commission as a lieutenant in May 1916 in Philadelphia. There were long absences for the couple as the young father took positions where the Army assigned him. The family moved to Brooklawn, New Jersey, during 1921–22, after which they resided in Camden, New Jersey.

When the Great Depression gripped the country in the early 1930s, times were hard for many families, including this one. Paul later recalled their meager accommodations: "A hovel at 8th and Woodward, where we lived in one room all winter, had no bathrooms, miserable lighting facilities, etc. It still makes me shudder. Maybe we'll be able to look back someday with disdain on 2973 [Congress Rd.]."[2] The long, lean years of the Depression had a profound impact of instilling thriftiness on this family of seven. From a young age, Paul strived to apply himself to do better than the next student, while not forgetting to have fun.

Even as a young boy, Paul Springer had an adventurous streak for travel, as he recalled in an essay he wrote at the Camden High School in New Jersey, where he discussed a hitchhiking experience:

> My most interesting hitch hike (mostly hike) was a trip to a friend's aunt's in Delta, Pennsylvania, a distance of about 120 miles, the road running through Delaware and Maryland. Being young and inexperienced, we

expected to make the round trip in one day. Starting out the day after Thanksgiving, in a snow flurry, we managed to reach the jail at the Conowingo Dam by nightfall. Here a drowsy trooper, devouring a luscious apple (we had not eaten since 7 a.m., hence the adjective), said he would provide sleeping quarters for us. The cell, a la birdcage, was composed of a small metal box, barred on one side, with a single metal cot (no mattress).

To my disgust, my partner immediately fell into a deep sleep, as indicated by his healthy snore, which gave fair competition to that of the Negro in the adjoining cell. Incidentally, I found that the door of that cell was locked. No doubt the thieves were bad in this section, and our kindly host was troubled with the thought that we might be robbed as we slept. At 11:30 the following morning, two starving boys with the looks of martyrs (or murderers) in their eyes were liberated and led to the best meal they had ever eaten in their short lives. Late the same afternoon we arrived at our destination. After a brief glimpse of the farm, including the prize hogs, we partook of a good meal, moistened with warm, fresh milk (my first cow milk), and bidding our host a hasty farewell, we set out for home, sweet home.

After getting a sufficient distance to be considered well on our way, we decided to return as it was fast-growing dark, and we did not relish the idea of a night in the open. We reached the farm at midnight and were furnished with a feather-bed on which to spend the night. After another sleepless night (for me), and an early breakfast, we started out once more. We arrived in the old hometown about nine o'clock that Sunday night. I now found that, somehow, I experienced great difficulty in persuading myself to go home, perhaps due to the fact that I had not informed my parents where I was going. Finally, with my sunken willpower, I managed to drag myself home, and then, well—the preacher, two neighbors, and my parents took charge of me. Thus comes to a close a pathetic tale of romance on the open road. In a few years I shall again continue to hold my head high and probably return the scrutiny of my fellow countrymen.[3]

The fact that Paul had a penchant for travel into the unknown was somewhat of an understatement, even as a young boy. At Camden High School, Paul discovered a love of singing, where he took the lead in school musicals, including *The Pirates of Penzance*, by Gilbert and Sullivan. Football was his favorite spectator sport, especially in the glory days of 1933, when not a single touchdown was scored against the Camden

High School team.[4] Paul graduated from Camden in June 1934, when he was sixteen. In high school he won a scholarship to the College of South Jersey and completed the six-month course, after which he took a job at a bank, the Fidelity Philadelphia Trust Company, initially as a messenger and later as a clerk in the Real Estate Department, where he worked from 1934 to 1937. During this period, he took evening courses on scholarship at the College of South Jersey for half a year, then he relinquished the scholarship to study at the Pierce Business School, which was financed by the trust company on his behalf.

Paul learned of a competitive examination held for candidates in April 1937 for a full scholarship to Yale University. The examination was prepared by the College Board and was held at the University of Pennsylvania. Paul tested well. He was one of several successful candidates for a number of scholarships that Yale offered that year.[5] He accepted the scholarship in a letter to Yale University dated June 10, 1937. Admission to the freshman class was subject to his satisfactory completion of the college interest board examinations, which, of course, he did.

Admission to Yale was a life-changing event for him. He planned to enter Yale as a twenty-year-old freshman in September 1937, intending to study in the theological school and prepare for entrance into the Presbyterian ministry, a dream come true for the young man from Camden. This dream took him down an academic path that he found much more challenging than what he experienced at his high school. It also marked the beginning of a lifetime of letter writing to his mother, Audrey. These letters became a lifeline of communication for Paul to his family throughout his life.

Freshman Class

A peculiarity of the era was that none of the Yale freshman boys were expected to do their own laundry. The school provided a shipping service and boxes for the students to send their laundry home to their mothers. The moms, in turn, sent their clothing back to the students washed and folded. The laundry box was also a tool routinely used to ship a book, papers, or other small items that could not be sent in a letter-sized envelope. Once a common practice, this has long since disappeared from college campuses.

In Paul's first letter home, he outlined his class schedule and some of the extracurricular activities on campus. A singer during his youth days at church, Paul auditioned for the chapel choir, singing several scales despite a somewhat sore throat. He was running low on cash but announced his new job as a "full-fledged waiter, two meals old."[6] The new job provided him with a few dollars in his pocket each week. He was ready for all the social life that Yale had to offer. Within a few days he had tried out

Paul Springer at Yale University, 1937. In the background is Harkness Tower, serving as a symbol of Yale and New Haven since its completion in 1917. *Springer Family collection*

for and made the first-squad Yale Glee Club. This offered him a chance for travel with the club.

The glee club represented the full tradition of singing among Yale men—a tradition that runs richly through every class that has come to Yale.[7] The club offered an unparalleled blend of leadership, personnel, program selection, and musical artistry under the direction of Marshall Bartholomew, who took over the Yale Glee Club in 1921. Under his direction, the club's singing skills won the national intercollegiate contest in 1924 and 1925, maintaining high standards ever since. The tradition was responsible not only for the spontaneous and enthusiastic support of the alumni, but also for the exceptional personnel of the club. The concert squad that Paul joined was selected from over three hundred applicants who turned out for auditions at the beginning of the year. Its success and the rewards of membership made it the most popular of all the extracurricular activities at Yale University. That fall, the glee club visited several girl's colleges, and every four years the group made a trip to a foreign country.

Paul tried out for the drama club and also for a position as a Yale sports commentator, learning that the two selected finalists would be regular sports commentators on alternate nights, for which they would receive $10 per week throughout the year. His lack of funds put pressure on him to work to meet his expenses incurred while away from home. He worried that he would not have the money to buy a tuxedo for Yale Glee Club concerts. Paul quickly tired of waiting tables. As an alternative, he volunteered to usher (with free admission) at the 1937 Yale football games. The Yale Bulldogs' opponents were Pennsylvania, Army, Cornell, Dartmouth, Brown, Princeton, and Harvard. In a letter to his sister Eleanore, he conceded that he was no longer a high school football fan. "I guess Camden hasn't much of a team this year. If they didn't win this last Saturday, I do hereby formally disown them."[8]

At the time, Yale University was an all-male college. He wrote his sister about the dearth of women on campus: "You should hear the riot on the campus every time a girl passes through. You see, there is a big grass plot in the center surrounded on all sides by the dormitories and having crosswalks more or less open to the public. When the aforementioned girl passes through, the cry of 'Fire' is taken up by the first one beside her. Straightaway, windows are thrown open and heads thrust out all over the campus, each yelling 'Fire' at the top of his lungs, till the place fairly reverberates, and the girls, Crimson faced, beat a hasty retreat. Speaking of girls, they seem very scarce around here, and I haven't seen or spoken to an eligible one since my arrival."[9]

Reality set in within a month of the academic challenges of coursework at Yale. Because the majority of his classmates had attended elite prep schools in the northeastern United States, they were better prepared for the amount of study it took to bring good grades. By early November, Paul became frustrated with his low grades on exams in history and geology and was overwhelmed by the additional study in the assignments that he had to complete. This didn't stop him from enjoying his time in the glee club, where he developed camaraderie with the other students and put his academic worries behind him, at least for a few hours. By the time he received his midyear exam grades, he conceded to his mom: "The above looks to me like the final blasting of my scholarship hopes. Upon this question hinges my entire future."[10] He apologized to his mother for the poor marks and added that the subjects had grown "amazingly difficult," but stated that "I want to stick it out or die in the attempt."[11]

Boxing

In the spring semester of 1938, Paul was required to choose a sport. He announced to his mother that he was taking up boxing, and he attempted to secure a spot on the Yale boxing team, although he weighed in at only 152 pounds, a recent gain of 11 pounds. Ever the diplomat, he remarked that "it can't be the [Yale] food. I couldn't even eat the supper last night; its taste conveyed my idea of what human excrement would be like."[12] Paul was mentored in boxing by a recent University of Michigan graduate and football star named Gerald Ford.[13] Ford received offers from two professional football teams, the Detroit Lions and the Green Bay Packers, but chose instead to take the position as a boxing coach and assistant football coach at Yale, hoping to attend law school there. Coach Ford worked as an assistant on the team under varsity boxing coach Mose King, while Ford pursued a law degree at Yale. It was not until the following October that Paul boxed competitively for the first time.[14] Even though Paul was new to the sport, he held his own in his weight class against others and contended for the varsity positions. Yale continued to field a boxing team but dropped it as an intramural sport after the 1939 season. Coach Ford earned his LLB degree from Yale Law School in 1941, graduating in the top 25 percent of his class in spite of the time he had to devote to coaching duties. He is best known as the thirty-eighth president of the United States.

Paul's grades improved markedly that spring, a result of a dogged determination to keep his scholarship funds intact. His study habits changed, as did his test scores in history and Greek. He received a coveted spot as a bass soloist in the Yale Glee Club. He sold his car for $25 and bought a new suit, a white tuxedo shirt, and a new pair of shoes for the concerts. He had to dress the part for a concert the glee club was performing at Beaver College, an all-girls school in Jenkintown, Pennsylvania. Paul struck up a courtship with one of their students, Georgie Magargal, on his road trip for the show. When Georgie came to stay at a friend's home in nearby West Haven for a weekend, she made plans to visit Paul at Yale. On one visit he took her to the Yale-Dartmouth hockey game. Money was tight for him as he juggled odd jobs, glee club concerts, and an ever more difficult academic course load. On May 9, he wrote to his mother: "Beginning today I'm going to start an extensive preparation for examinations, allowing no time for recreation or idleness. I simply must pass everything, and with good marks too."[15] He planned to bring Georgie home to meet the family. He wrote his mother, "What would you say to my bringing Georgie over to dinner on the fourth? If you consent, don't be too elaborate, but make her aware of the cooking I'm used to."[16] Georgie wrote to Audrey Springer thanking her for the lovely dinner. She said, "It is easy to see where Paul gets his fine ideals and aspirations, with such a family for encouragement."[17] Over the summer, Paul resumed his job as a clerk in the real estate department at the Fidelity-Philadelphia Trust Company, where he returned in the summers of 1939 and 1940.[18]

Football Season

As the fall semester of 1938 rolled around, Paul took a job as a cashier at the dining hall. For him, no more dirty dishes and sloppy food to dish out! One night, all of New Haven was struck by a severe thunderstorm, and the entire town except Yale (the university had its own power plant) was without electricity.[19] After checking on some friends in New Haven, he learned that seven large trees had blown down on their block, including their beloved apple tree. Paul brought home a big bag of apples—the last of the crop that had littered the ground following the storm. His classwork became all-consuming. He was taking English, Greek, psychology, history, and French, which he began with great difficulty early in the semester. His frustration with the coursework was compounded by his "inability to grasp the most abominable of subjects—Greek."[20]

There were some bright spots that fall. He was singing in the chapel choir and grew more amazed as time went by that he made the cut. On October 20, Paul wrote, "This Saturday is the Michigan game, and 800 coeds are coming down in a special train. It's rumored that the freshmen will be ousted from the old campus to make room for them. The Yale lads are quite thrilled, not having seen a woman (most of them) since September 26."[21] Although Michigan won the game, 15–13, Paul surmised that Yale could have won if it were not for an unlucky break—a roughing-the-kicker penalty after Yale had held Michigan for three downs.[22] College football, singing, studies, and girls took up most of his attention. In regard to girls, he mentioned, "My roommate's sister was up for the Navy game. She's very nice, but a trifle too old to be eligible (about 25)."[23] Georgie came to New Haven for the Harvard game in November, staying in town with her great-aunt. The Bulldogs lost that game 7–0 on November 19. After Georgie's departure, Paul said that they had a grand time over the weekend in spite of the rain. It poured in bucketloads throughout the Harvard game, and for the rest of the day and night.[24] It had been a tough semester, and the worst football season that Yale had ever had. The nearest season to it was in 1915, when they lost five out of eight games. This season they had lost six of eight games. Paul reflected, "That's what Yale gets for de-emphasizing sports!"[25]

In the spring of 1939, Paul became more systematic in his studies. The additional effort began to pay off. He wrote his mother, "If this keeps up I'll actually begin to feel intelligent in a couple of years."[26] His grades included an 88 on the Greek exam; this put him over the top to making the dean's list. Shortly thereafter, Paul found out that he was accepted into Saybrook, a residential college on the campus, for the next two years, a step up for him. He would soon be saying goodbye to the common dorms. His friend Bob Crockett joined him at Saybrook as a roommate in his junior school and senior years.

Saybrook

Paul and Bob became the best of friends and were inseparable during their final two years at Yale. His brief romance with Georgie didn't last. Paul, having his tennis racket and balls sent up to the school, played in Saybrook's fall tennis tournament. He began work in the bursar's office, taking dictation and typing letters for Professor Calhoun as well as doing library work for him. He found the work interesting, much preferred to the cafeteria work. Additionally, his courses were tougher than ever since he changed his major to English literature. Football season and making Thanksgiving plans were also high on Paul's list of social priorities.

His roommate, Bob Crockett, took the train to his parent's house for Thanksgiving. Paul hitchhiked his way up to Pelham, New York, the next day to join him for dinner. Paul attended the Yale-Harvard game on November 25, with the Bulldogs coming out on top 20–7. Paul wrote his mother about it from the Crocketts' house: "The game Saturday was really worth watching and made up for our defeats this season. I assisted in the tearing down of the goal-posts and managed to get a sizable piece of one—over a foot long. We're going to paint the date and score on in blue letters today, and put it over our fireplace at school."[27] He had a sore jaw from boxing, having been smacked on the chin by another freshman who was out of his weight class. "Moral: Never lead with your chin!"[28] Despite the setback, he thought his chances were quite good at making the varsity team. The rest of the school year was filled with a Yale Glee Club concert at Smith College on December 8, studies, exams, and more studies. He was looking forward to the glee club trip to Florida during the spring recess of 1940, "but there is to be a big cut in January which I probably won't survive," he told his mom.[29] Paul proved to be a much-better singer than a boxer and never made the Yale varsity boxing team. His singing became a lifelong passion. He spent the Christmas holidays at home with his family in Camden, New Jersey, in 1939.

Yale Glee Club

Singing in the glee club became a bigger part of Paul's social life by mid-January 1940. They were singing in Riverdale, New York, on a Saturday night and at the New York Yale club on Sunday.[30] The glee club had a terrific repertoire of chanteys and spirituals. The following week they sang in Hartford and later gave a Finnish benefit concert at Woolsey Hall at Yale, followed by a concert at Carnegie Hall in New York. The glee club experience exposed Paul to another side of life he had yet to experience—affluence. Following that busy concert week in January, there was a reception for the glee club, which he described in a letter home, "We had dinner at E. W. Freeman's shack at Riverdale. It is only about a block long and overlooks the Hudson and the Palisades. I don't know how big the estate is. It's all surrounded by a 3' [foot] stone wall. The mansion is stone and has a couple of wings, each one about the size of Woodland Ave., Presby[terian] [his home church]. One of them was built especially to accommodate scads of old armor that the museum couldn't use. They have a whole crew of butlers and maids. . . . I found out later that Mr. Freeman is a J. P. Morgan partner. I stayed overnight at Mrs. Perkins' [Freeman's mother] where I had a decidedly palatial suite all to myself. So that's how the upper crust lives. I'm all for it."[31]

Chapter 2
CONFLICT IN CHINA

The Wars Overseas

Hostilities broke out in China on July 7, 1937, when a Japanese army battalion stationed in Wanping County, south of Peking, claimed one of its soldiers had gone missing during a training exercise.[1] At midnight, the Japanese demanded that they be allowed to search the Citadel, which housed the Wanping government. Artillery fire began pounding the area, destroying five buildings, killing two people, and wounding five others. The next few weeks saw sporadic fighting between Japanese and Chinese troops in Hebai and Chahar Provinces of China, which escalated during July. As a result, decades of tension between the two governments quickly spun out of control. When the Japanese launched a full-scale invasion of Shanghai in August, it was only the beginning of China's long and ultimately successful fight against the Japanese invaders. Two years later, in 1939, World War II began in Europe with the German invasion of Poland on September 1, drawing both Great Britain and France into the conflict in defense of Poland. The Soviet Union's invasion of eastern Poland on September 17, in accordance with a secret pact of the Soviet and German ministers Molotov and Ribbentrop, rendered any Allied plans to come to the defense of Poland obsolete.

The Yale students became keenly aware the possibility that the military conflict might spread, thereby involving the US. In February 1940, the Saybrook residential college hosted the French secretary, who gave a talk on the war in Europe and the aims of the French. In the next week the German ambassador came to Saybrook to tell his side of the story. "So you see, we have no opportunity to get propagandized by one side, like so many people I know," said Paul.[2] Not long afterward, beginning May 10, 1940, German forces invaded and took control over France, Belgium, Luxembourg, and the Netherlands, in a period of only six weeks. Even so, the war in Europe was separated from them by an ocean, as was the war in China. The feeling on the campus was one of apprehension, since it was widely felt that the US would soon be drawn into this increasingly global conflict.

Spring Break

The Yale Glee Club was in preparations for its spring trip—a series of concerts through Florida and the Deep South taking place over spring recess. The club made stops in Charleston, South Carolina; Hobe Sound, Palm Beach, Miami Beach, Clearwater, Mountlake, and Winter Park, Florida; and Savannah, Georgia. Having funded his education with a scholarship, student loans, and part-time jobs, Paul was without the money needed for the trip. When his family received the news that he had been accepted, he received contributions from his parents and his sister Eleanore, who made the travel experience possible.

The glee club sang outside in an open-air concert at the Biltmore Hotel in Palm Beach, Florida. They were in great shape musically and received good turnouts and applause. One evening, several of the boys, including Paul, were dining in Hobe Sound, Florida, where Paul met Gene Tunney, who held the world heavyweight boxing title from 1926 to 1928. Tunney had married a wealthy socialite, the former "Polly" Lauder, who accompanied him to hear the concert. During the buffet dinner, they chatted at some length not just about boxing, but about William Lyon Phelps, a famous American author, critic, and scholar. At a reception at the Belgian ambassador's house (literally a Spanish castle), the glee club was introduced to Brenda Frazier. She was a young socialite so well known that she appeared on the cover of *Life* magazine as a result of her extravagant 1938 debutante ball. Paul was charmed to meet the "Poor Little Rich Girl," as she had been dubbed by the media. The glee club sang in the finest homes in the South and found the hosts and hostesses to be welcoming and friendly, going out of their way to attend the performances with a number of houseguests. Paul remembered, "We ate four times yesterday—an eight course breakfast at the Jupiter Island Club, lunch at the Bath and Tennis Club (what a layout that was!) then again at the castle and finally at the hotel after the concert. This hotel cost $25 day, and we get it for nothing."[3]

Paul got his first real taste of affluence on this tour. There were several highlights of his trip, one of which was visiting a well-to-do family in Charleston, South Carolina, and meeting a young lady, Julia Ravenel. Paul was quite taken with her, and this began an on-again, off-again courtship, albeit a long-distance relationship, with Julia. Another standout of the trip was Mountain Lake, Florida, in the heart of the orange district of the state, and "the air was filled with a sweet perfume of their blossoms."[4] Paul stayed at the home of Mrs. Cox, whose home overlooked the lake. The grass was green (verses snow in New Haven), the lake was deep blue, and the roads were a brilliant orange red. There were several palm trees in the yard, beside orange and kumquat trees. A servant brought out orange juice while a valet took his tuxedo tails to get them pressed. The chauffeur took them (two of them stayed together there) in their new Cadillac to the Bok Singing Tower (for the concert) and then to a formal tea afterward. He found it to be the most charming spot in Florida. The Yale Glee Club experience opened his eyes to a world that he had previously only read about. Paul felt that he had finally "arrived."

Fall of 1940

When Paul returned to Yale, he resumed his classes and his work in the bursar's office, where he assisted with correspondence, composing and typing letters. On Saturday, April 6, 1940, he smashed his left index finger playing baseball. The finger was splintered as well as fractured, and the bone between the first and second knuckle was also fractured. The bandage, in addition to a splint, included a felt pad, which kept the finger straight. He reassured his mother: "It's in pretty good shape now and is receiving excellent care at the University health department. The most annoying thing about it is that I can't type, which is about all my bursary work consists of. I haven't told my boss yet . . . but I am already about nine hours behind. I'll have to make it up later—probably just about exam time."[5] Two weeks later, his index finger was still in a cast. Although the pain subsided, he described the finger as "unsightly and slightly annoying."[6] He was at least a week behind in his bursary work because of it and would have to make up for the time. His finger was crooked, and he worried that it may never be straight again. His junior school year at Yale was almost over. The war in Europe was far from over. The common knowledge on the campus was that the United States would become involved in the action before too long. Paul surmised that "Roosevelt will probably have quite a few of the boys in uniform after a while."[7]

As Paul neared graduation, he was making plans to tour South America with the glee club in the summer of 1941. It would be a two-month tour, with concerts in ten South American cities, one in Panama City, and one in Trinidad. The singing group was in full swing that fall, with a terrific squad. Paul felt good about his chances to stay in the club as a senior, since basses were in great demand.[8] Funding for the trip was still up in the air. A gift from the New York Yale Club to finance their travel had been proposed, but no commitment had been made. The trip was also contingent on the United States remaining neutral in the European war. This reality hit home in October 1940, when Paul and his roommate Bob Crockett both registered for the draft at Saybrook.[9] The on-campus registration for the selective service made sure that no one at Yale would be missed. Bob was worried that his number would be called among the first. Paul felt that his poor eyesight might exempt him even if he was called. He said, "I'd much rather stand the risk—or even the uncertainty and have good eyes."[10]

Lindbergh on Campus

On October 30, 1940, Charles Lindbergh spoke on campus at Woolsey Hall.[11] His appearance at Yale was one of many stops on a speaking tour that fall. Once the country's greatest aviator, Lindbergh had become a leader of the notorious antiwar movement and was urging his country to keep out of the fight against Hitler's Nazi Germany. Whenever "Lindy" spoke, America listened. This was the man who, only thirteen years earlier, had thrilled the world by flying nearly 4,000 miles nonstop from Long Island to Paris. Then in 1932, this tall, blond man and his family received waves of sympathy after his infant son was kidnapped and murdered. As he told his listeners in the autumn of 1940, when Britain was at its most vulnerable: "I [believe] that no outside influence could solve the problems of European nations, or bring them lasting peace. They must work out their destiny as we must work out ours. In the past we [America] have dealt with a Europe dominated by England and France. In future, we may have to deal with a Europe dominated by Germany."[12] Paul got within a foot or two of the famous aviator afterward and naively remarked in a letter, "His ideas about foreign policy are about identical mine, and his speech enabled me to more clearly define them."[13] In any event, he was quite moved by Lindbergh's speech. As his final semester came to a close, Paul focused on finishing his classes and securing his spot in the glee club's Christmas concert tour, which would begin December 20, 1940, and take him through the new year.

The glee club trip began with but a single step onto a train and became more than twice the distance that Confucius had in mind. Between New Haven, Connecticut, and St. Paul, Minnesota, the glee club made six stops, singing six concerts before Yale alumni and their guests.[14] The tour left New Haven on December 20 for concerts in Cleveland and Detroit. On Christmas night, the citizens of Chicago were entertained by the raucous boys in the Yale Glee Club. After performing in the Twin Cities, the club turned east to sing in Cincinnati before their final concert in Pittsburgh on December 30. It was Paul's last "hurrah" with his beloved Yale singing comrades.

Paul's postgraduate options also included a management offer from the Campbell Soup Company. He was discouraged from taking the South American trip by a letter from Marshall Bartholomew, the glee club director, who had taken a personal interest in him. He wrote, "I can see eye to eye with you in this situation because I was a self-supporting student myself, worked and paid my way through college and through a year of graduate study and I know what it is to have to count pennies and to have to deny oneself a number of things that hurt at the time. . . . Even if we raise for you the full sum of $400 it is going to cost you about $250 more than this plus the loss of whatever money you would earn if you stayed in the United States and worked this summer. This trip would undoubtedly be a pleasant and a profitable thing from a cultural standpoint. It is by no means essential and I want you to decide it realistically and in your own best interest."[15] Paul took note of this practical, candid, and heartfelt advice from the glee club director.

Yale-in-China

In March 1941, Paul was encouraged by one of his Yale professors, Stuart Clement, to apply for a teaching position at the Yali Middle School in Yuanling, in Hunan Province, China. It would be a prestigious appointment to an important Yale institution. Only three candidates were accepted every other year to fill teaching positions at the school.[16] Yale-in-China offered Paul the opportunity to partake in an important educational and humanitarian mission. He could see a part of the world that few Americans had seen or had given much notice to. He received word on March 20 that he was being considered for the position and was advised to seek a two-year deferment with his local draft board.[17] He found that the draft board appeal agent, Mr. Godshaw, was a graduate of Yale Law School, who knew of and was interested in the work of Yale-in-China. Paul was encouraged by his initial conversations and took the necessary steps needed to seek a deferral of his draft status.

Yale-in-China sponsored a cluster of educational and medical institutions, of which the Yali Middle School was one.[18] They had been established in the capital of Hunan Province by a group of young Yale graduates in the early twentieth century. The founders were eager to demonstrate Christian fellowship by serving as educators and doctors in Hunan, by setting examples for hard work and the betterment of their communities. This endeavor took place during a time that powerful economic, political, and social dislocation was leading prominent intellectuals to propose sweeping reforms to age-old institutions. China was especially open to and in need of the message of Christian educators, whose missionary influence was the key to this belief. The name "Yali" was one that rang in similarity with Yale University, but the Chinese characters for "Yali" were two words taken from a well-known quotation of Confucius. Although there is no exact translation for the quotation, any educated Chinese at the time knew what the two words meant—*ya* for elegance of expression and civility and *li* for propriety and right conduct.[19] It was the perfect name for a private school in Hunan, and it reflected both the blending of and the respect for the culture of the two countries.

Yale-in-China had its home office in New Haven, Connecticut. They raised funds in support of its institutions in China and recruited American personnel, chiefly for

A New Yale in the Far East. A map highlighting Changsha, in Hunan Province, the epicenter of Yale-in-China, and a key stop on the railroad running from Canton to Peking, ca. 1930s. *Yale-China Association Records, RU 232, Manuscripts and Archives, Yale University Library*

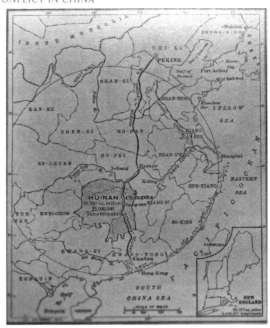

Hsiang-Ya Medical School and the Yali English Department. During the 1920s, Yale University began to recruit recent Yale graduates for a two-year teaching stint in China. It was referred to as the Bachelor program. These "Bachelors" were paid a modest teaching stipend along with their travel expenses to and from China. It was thought that having young male teachers would inspire and energize their younger Chinese students. The term "Bachelor" was used to indicate that each teacher was required to have a bachelor's degree, versus a master's or postgraduate degree. The selection of young male instructors did not always work out as planned. Some of the recent graduates were less committed to the mission of Yale-in-China than they were in escaping the implementation of Prohibition in the US, while getting a free trip around the world.[20] Over time, the Yale-in-China committee became much more selective in choosing the candidates, since the focus was on academics and the ability to work with the Yali staff in China.

The original Yale-in-China campus was located at the north end of Changsha, a city of about 500,000 people. Changsha is situated on the Hsiang River, about 350 miles north of the port city of Canton (present-day Guangdong). When a fledgling school and modest medical dispensary were established by Yale in the fall of 1906, these early institutions were hard to distinguish from the other shops inside the old walled city.[21] A former rice storehouse in the city center had been secured by early Yale missionaries and converted into classrooms, a small chapel, and student dormitories for the American staff and their growing families. The early appointees began

View of the Changsha campus of Yale-in-China, prior to the Japanese occupation. Buildings shown are the chapel, Science Building, Medical College, Recitation Building, and Hsiang-Ya Hospital. *Yale-China Association Records, RU 232, Manuscripts and Archives, Yale University Library*

language study with Chinese tutors and were told to be proficient in the Chinese language, even if it took years of study. Bulletins were posted around the city, announcing the aim of the school: "to broaden the learning of its students, build up character and train in loyalty to the Emperor and patriotism to the Nation."[22] In regard to the school's Christian orientation, it was decided that it would adopt a tolerant tone, with the teaching of Christianity and church services on Sundays, although students would have full liberty to follow their own religion. This makeshift cluster of educational facilities soon outgrew itself. In 1913, Yali representatives joined local Hunan officials in concluding the Hsiang-Ya Agreement, which laid the groundwork for a sprawling new campus on the north end of the city, including the funding and construction of a medical college and nursing school and the ongoing expenses. Yale-in-China, in turn, agreed to build a hospital, provide equipment, and fund the salaries of Western-trained doctors.

With the move to a new and modern campus, the next decade brought remarkable growth to all the Yale-in-China institutions. The Yali Middle School had become increasingly respected in the region as a top-notch preparatory school. The medical and nursing schools were also thriving, and many of their graduates found their skills in great demand, with some returning to teach and staff the hospital. By the 1930s, Yale-in-China had evolved into a cluster of five institutions on a spacious campus, a large staff, and ever increasing financial and administrative needs. These were the Yali Middle School, Hua Chung University, Hsiang-Ya Hospital, and a medical college and nursing school.[23] The Executive Committee in New Haven was replaced with a board of trustees, which oversaw broad policy and fiscal responsibility. A governing board comprising the deans and officers of the academic and medical departments was created to oversee local operations in Changsha. The global headquarters remained in New Haven.

The Sino-Japanese War

The Japanese military offensive, which ravaged many parts of China in 1937, took its toll on the city of Changsha. The Yale-in-China personnel were subjected to heavy Japanese bombings over a two-day period ending on Thanksgiving Day in 1937.[24] Although no Yali staff were killed during the raid, bombs had fallen on two small hotels filled with refugees from other cities. Tragically, over a hundred of these civilians were killed. The city of Nanking, the capital of Nationalist China, was overcome by panic and horror brought on by the invading Japanese army, which entered the city on December 13, 1937. After the initial military resistance was wiped out, tens of thousands of Chinese soldiers who surrendered in the city were summarily executed by the invaders. The Japanese commanders rewarded their troops by releasing them from any discipline during the occupation. The Japanese soldiers bullied, raped, and killed the inhabitants and burned and looted the city, in one of the most horrific war crimes that civilization has ever witnessed. In the aftermath of what became known as the "Rape of Nanking," Changsha suddenly found itself swollen with as many as 300,000 refugees from Nanking. This put an enormous strain on the city's resources. Faced with the imminent threat of Japanese occupation, parents began withdrawing their children from the Yali school. The student enrollment dwindled from over two hundred to only forty-nine, who finished their term in the last week of January 1938.[25] Although many students returned during the spring of 1938, the classes were often disrupted by air raids and warnings. Despite the challenges, the school stayed open and continued its mission. By September 1938, when confronted with possible invasion and military occupation, the Yali leadership decided to move the school from Changsha to refugee quarters in a remote and obscure river town, Yuanling, lying 200 miles west of Changsha (via dirt roads) in Hunan Province.[26] Yuanling was an inconspicuous town in a rural setting and deemed to be relatively safe. The senior school was combined with the middle school to form the Yali Union Middle School (a.k.a. Yali Middle School), a prominent boarding school for Chinese boys aged thirteen to eighteen. It was here, in Yuanling, that the newest group of Yale Bachelors was to begin teaching.[27]

Yale-in-China staff, about 1940. Preston Schoyer, Dwight Rugh (*with mouse*), Winifred Rugh, Brank Fulton, and unidentified man. There is no known explanation for the mouse climbing on Dr. Rugh's cheek. *Yale-China Association Records, RU 232, Manuscripts and Archives, Yale University Library*

Paul's Appointment

Paul received his appointment from the Yale-in-China trustees in the form of a letter on April 15, 1941, subject to his passing a medical examination. He would serve on the staff of the Yali Middle School for a two-year term beginning July 1, 1941, with plans to sail for China in early July. His two-year term as a teacher at the middle school would conclude on June 30, 1943, after which he would return to the United States. He was thrilled with his selection and proceeded posthaste for his medical exam, which he passed on April 22. His appointment included a travel allowance of $375 each way, with twenty-two months of service in China from September 1 of the year of his appointment to the close of the school sessions in the second year. His first-year teaching stipend was $33 per month, beginning on July 1.[28] The Yale-in-China Association also provided free medical care by its own physicians while the appointee was in China and within reach of its doctors.[29] The primary risks were considered to be tuberculosis, dysentery, and malaria. There were other obvious risks associated with working and teaching in a country that was at war. The Bachelors were told as clearly as possible of the risks involved in their travel and service before they were allowed to accept their appointment. The trustees did not wish anyone to enter the service of the association without full knowledge of the difficulties and dangers of travel to and from the Orient and life in China.

The chain of events progressed rapidly. Paul was introduced to Robert Ashton "Bob" Smith, the executive secretary of Yale-in-China, who helped him navigate the myriad of details regarding his appointment. These included mandatory inoculations, completing his passport application, and securing travel arrangements. John C. Tilson, an attorney and member of the board of trustees, assisted with obtaining permission from his local draft board to leave the country. All able young men were required to be registered in the Selective Service. The Yale appointees destined to travel to China for an educational and humanitarian mission were no exception. Already registered for the draft, they were required to get a special permit that allowed them a deferment before a passport could be issued to leave the country.[30] Rachel C. Dowd, the home office secretary, coordinated details among the various departments. Paul formally accepted the position via a letter to Bob Smith on June 11, 1941.[31]

Graduation

There were plenty of things for Paul to wrap up before leaving for China. Most importantly was his graduation from Yale University. His commencement exercises were scheduled for Sunday, June 15, 1941.[32] All graduating seniors of the undergraduate schools assembled in the courtyards of their colleges at 10:00 a.m., then formed a procession as directed by the college marshals. Paul wore his academic robe over a dark suit and black shoes. Once inside Woolsey Hall, all the baccalaureate candidates remained standing until the president, deans, and masters of the colleges were seated. After being seated, each candidate rose and put on their caps as their degree was announced. The Class of 1941 had been introduced. It was a joyous celebration with his family in attendance. Indeed, it was a weekend to celebrate.

On the same evening, Paul attended a reunion of the Yale-in-China group, which assembled for supper in the south wing of the Dwight Hall on the old Yale campus at 6:30 p.m.[33] A traditional Chinese dinner was served. Immediately following the dinner, Paul attended the annual meeting of the association held in Sprague Hall at 8:15 p.m. Paul was asked to be there at 8:00 p.m. to pass out programs and news bulletins as the people entered.[34] The room was packed with people at all levels of the organization. He and the other two Bachelors were to sit on the platform with the speakers. It was here that Paul and the other two Bachelors, Arthur "Art" Hopkins ('41) and James A. "Jim" Elliott ('40), were officially introduced to the Yale-in-China trustees.

Arthur H. "Art" Hopkins Jr. was born September 17, 1918, in Philadelphia but lived in Marion, Pennsylvania, from the age of five.[35] His father, Arthur Hopkins Sr., had a BS from Haverford College and an MD from the University of Pennsylvania. Art's preparatory education was at the Episcopal Academy in Philadelphia, which helped prepare him for his major in classical civilization at Yale. He was a member of the Branford College, Alpha Sigma Phi, and the Political Union on the Yale campus. A gifted runner, Art was on the freshman track team, the university track squad during his sophomore and junior school years, and the Branford football team his senior year.

James A. "Jim" Elliott was born in Greene, New York, on March 12, 1918.[36] He prepared for college at Green High School and had done departmental work in modern history. He was an Eagle Scout and a member of Saybrook College and the Political Union. In his freshman year, he was a scholar of the second rank, and in the following two years he received two additional academic scholarships, as well as an oration appointment. He wanted the opportunity to teach in a foreign land and feel that he was doing humanitarian and religious service at the same time.[37] He waited a year after his graduation for the coveted spot on the Yale-in-China teaching staff and was enrolled as a graduate student in Asian studies at the time of his appointment.[38] A prolific writer, he planned to keep a diary of his travels and write a detailed journal of his experiences in the service of this storied Yale institution.

The Yale-in-China trustees had high expectations for these three young men. All were gifted academically and yearned for the adventure that it offered them. The keynote speaker at the banquet that evening was Rear Adm. Harry E. Yarnell, formerly commander in chief of the American fleet in the Far Eastern waters.[39] Burton Rogers had just returned from his teaching assignment at the Yali Middle School in Yuanling. He and his wife were on hand for the meeting, undoubtedly briefing the new Bachelors on their recent experience in war-torn China. It had been a long and busy day for the newest crop of Yale graduates, 1941.

Following Paul's graduation, he took a trip to Charleston, South Carolina, to see his girlfriend, Julia Ravenel. He undoubtedly told her about his grand plans for adventure, his acceptance into the Yale-in-China program, and how much he would miss her while he was gone. When he returned to Camden, New Jersey, on June 23, he opened a letter from Bob Smith regarding his travel arrangements, a list of necessities in the way of clothing and equipment that he should pack, and the news that the deferment of his draft status had not been granted.[40] There had been a mix-up regarding his order number (i.e., draft number) with his local draft board. Compounding the problem, once the matter was cleared up and the draft deferral was issued, the local draft board inadvertently omitted the stamp that was needed for the issuance of his passport. This stamp was not added to his passport application until June 26.[41]

Paul was frustrated with the delay caused by these errors. He still had to show definitive arrangements for his travel to China for the passport to be issued. The Yale-in-China Association intervened on his behalf to expedite the process. Knowing that fellow Yali Bachelors Hopkins and Elliott had already finalized their travel, Bob Smith reassured Paul that Tilson's father, Colonel Tilson, would travel to Washington, DC, on Paul's behalf to make his case to the proper authorities that the issuance of Paul's deferral "will not seriously affect the operation of the Selective Service Act."[42] The permit was needed before Paul's passport could be issued. Tilson's efforts were successful. Paul received word from Rachel Dowd on June 30 that his passport would be issued on July 10 and sent to the Yale-in-China office.[43] From there it could be forwarded to Paul via special delivery for the necessary visas so that he sailed with the other men for the voyage to Hong Kong.[44] Paul was to arrive in San Francisco no later than July 19, when his first US passport would be waiting for him. In addition to his photograph and signature, on page 3 of his passport, under "Distinguishing marks or features," was the description "LEFT INDEX FINGER IRREGULAR," a reference to the baseball injury he sustained at Yale in April 1940. His finger would remain somewhat crooked the rest of his life.

Chapter 3
ACROSS THE PACIFIC

San Francisco

Springer said his goodbyes to family and friends and departed from Camden by train on July 9,1941, headed west toward Seattle, Washington. He arrived in San Francisco on Thursday, July 17. His fellow Bachelors, Jim Elliott, and Art Hopkins arrived that night, with Robert Ashton "Bob" Smith coming in on Friday morning.[1] Their ship was scheduled to depart on July 19 but was delayed to July 23. This gave them extra time to manage their affairs. Their top priority was a visit to the British consulate the next day, where they each received their visa to enter Hong Kong.[2] On the same day, the men visited the Chinese consulate for their visas to enter the Republic of China. Their six days in San Francisco proved to be delightful.

After checking into the Army and Navy YMCA on Friday afternoon, they went to Chinatown. It was an interesting place. They visited the Joss Temple, the first Chinese temple in America. After that, they wandered among the innumerable Chinese restaurants and shops. Jim Elliott ran into Bill Fager, Yale '39, whom he recognized as he stood talking with friends on the street. As it turned out, Bill and Art Hopkins were good friends, and Bill invited them to visit him in Berkeley on the following day. A good deal of their time was spent equipping themselves, repairing luggage, getting steamship tickets, and getting ready for their voyage.

They spent Saturday in Berkeley, across Oakland Bay from San Francisco. They split up into two parties. Paul and Art went first, with Bob and Jim following a half hour later.[3] They met Bill Fager at the library of the University of California, then explored the University of California campus, going to the top of the tower on the grounds, which gave them a stunning view. After dinner, Bob Smith called Miss Marie Moore, a friend of Rachel Dowd's, the Yale-in-China secretary. Marie was a delightful hostess and drove to San Francisco to meet them, taking them on a driving tour around the city. They stopped at Fisherman's Wharf, drove past Joe DiMaggio's restaurant and over the Golden Gate Bridge and then to downtown San Francisco. The next day, Marie spent the whole day entertaining them. The group left San Francisco about noon and drove south, over the Twin Peaks to the Big Basin State Park, where they saw their first redwood trees. After a leisurely stop at an apricot farm, they proceeded to Palo Alto. There they explored the Stanford University campus and stopped to visit a friend of Bob's. They traveled back to San Francisco via San Mateo. That night they topped off a splendid day with a Chinese dinner at Tao Tao's in Chinatown. Their layover in San Francisco provided the Bachelors with a world-class touring experience.

On Monday morning, Paul, Art, and Jim went down to the port to see SS *President Harrison*. They were not impressed. It seemed terribly small compared with *President Coolidge* (on which they were originally supposed to sail) and some of the other ships in the harbor. Art kept reminding them that *Harrison* was much inferior to *Kungsholm*, a Norwegian luxury liner on which he journeyed as a crew member to Havana on his last spring vacation. The three spent a couple of hours exploring the ship. That afternoon they met up again with Bob Smith and his friend who was teaching. They drove together all over San Francisco, to several parks, the beach, the Cliff House, and Lucca's Restaurant for an Italian dinner. Tuesday was consumed with last-minute shopping and packing. At 5:00 p.m., they all met at the YMCA, where Ed Lupton drove them to his home for dinner in San Mateo, eighteen miles from San Francisco. His wife, Dorothy, was the sister of Winifred Rugh, whose husband Dwight was the acting representative of the Yale-in-China trustees in China, as well as an instructor in religious education. Their son Bob had a motor scooter that the Bachelors found most interesting, and all gave it a try. The Lupton home was filled with Chinese art objects, which they found fascinating. Around 9:00 p.m., Lupton drove them back to San Francisco.

Slow Boat to China

On Wednesday, July 23, they boarded SS *President Harrison*, of the American President Lines, just before noon, only to learn that the sailing hour had been changed to 2:00 p.m.[4] After lunch on board, they were told the departure was postponed to 5:00 p.m.[5] So they spent the afternoon shopping in Chinatown, then back to the ship only to find the departure was now set for 10:00 p.m. They did not leave the ship again and had dinner on board. The ship finally set sail at 10:00 p.m. It was quite a thrill to pull away from the pier, backing into the bay, swinging around, and finally steaming under the Golden Gate Bridge and into the Pacific Ocean. Not until then could any of them think about going to bed, although all of them were dead tired from anticipation of the journey.

Paul Springer, Art Hopkins, and Jim Elliott on board SS *President Harrison,* July 1941. *Springer Family collection*

Bob, Jim, and Art roomed together on the boat, while Paul was assigned a room one deck below with two other men: Norman Hall, en route to Manila to work on defense-related measures, and George Small, en route to Chungking, China, for work at the US embassy.

Once under way, Jim and Art were fortunate enough not to have been afflicted with the dreaded malady of seasickness, due to the relatively small size of the ship. Paul and Bob did not fare so well, both falling victim on the first day. While Paul recovered after a couple of days, Bob felt somewhat below par during the entire length of the voyage.[6] Jim Elliott described their journey:

Life on board ship, although a novel experience, has been quite unexciting. In the first place, there are only about 140 passengers—you can see what a small boat it is. In the second place, there is an exasperating dearth of females. There are possibly twenty women aboard, at least half of whom are Chinese. Therefore, we have no dances. Therefore, the deck games are almost entirely masculine contests. Therefore, conversation tends to fall into the "bull-session" rut of college days. My time has been spent partly in conversation (one meets interesting people on the ship and it's very easy to strike up an acquaintance), partly in games, and partly in reading. Those three categories just about tell the story. About the only thing they fail to include is the [indoor] cinema. We have movies up on the top deck every two or three nights. The first time we had them was Saturday night and it was quite exciting—just the idea of movies on board ship in the middle of the ocean. Practically everybody turned out for them that night. It's really a very enjoyable setting for motion pictures though, clear blue sky, moon, stars, calm seas, clean fresh air.[7]

Honolulu

They approached Hawaii after a week at sea and watched the island of Oahu drawing nearer for almost two hours. They could hardly wait to go ashore and disembarked as soon as the boat docked.[8] The whole gang—Paul, Norman, George, Bob, Jim, and Art—set out for the US post office, where they deposited stacks of mail bound for home. They hoped their letters would catch the outgoing Clipper plane, but found that the plane they had just seen fly over as their ship put into port was the mail plane bound for the US mainland. The next one would not leave for six days. Disappointed, they still sent a good many letters airmail, heading back to the ship for breakfast, with Bob and Jim purchasing leis for the group on the way. Their unrelenting peer pressure forced Art to wear one, much against his will. "Dude" Hopkins was out of character for the moment, but not for long. Immediately after breakfast, he and Jim went on a shopping spree and bought the gayest Hawaiian shirts they could find, along with swimming trunks of brilliant patterns and hues. They now felt like 100% tourists and proceeded to Waikiki Beach, where they went swimming in the ocean in their new and brilliant Hawaiian digs.

Robert Ashton Smith, during their stop in Honolulu, Hawaii, 1941. *Yale-China Association Records, RU 232, Manuscripts and Archives, Yale University Library*

When the ship docked in Honolulu, Paul described his first view of Hawaii as hardly worth getting up for: "Waikiki Beach was about a block long and ten yards wide. One can walk way out in the surf, but the bottom is covered with rocks or coral which hurts the feet. Surf board riding is all right, I guess, if you know how. I tried it and practically broke my neck."[9] His companion, a Harvard man, got a bloody nose when his board hit him in the water. Paul described the water as beautiful and was in awe of the unusual vegetation. He saw hedges of bright red; shower trees of pink, yellow, and rainbow; flame trees of dazzling scarlet; and countless others. Palm trees were everywhere. He did some sightseeing and took in a grand view of the luscious green northeast coast of Oahu from Pali Mountain. The bright colors and vivid landscapes of Hawaii offered Paul a pleasant contrast to those of his native New Jersey.

After SS *President Harrison* sailed from Honolulu on the night of July 30, Jim Elliott reflected on their daylong respite from travel in this tropical paradise: "From the moment when we first stood on deck that morning, transfixed by the splendor that was Diamond Head rearing its proud eminence above the fog, beautifully illuminated by the glory of the early morning sun rising out of the Pacific, to the time of departure when we sadly tossed our much admired leis overboard into the waters of Pearl Harbor, and gazed back at the lights of Honolulu, we had had a day of perfect enjoyment."[10] The ship was headed for ports of call in the Far East, including Shanghai, Hong Kong, Manila, and Singapore. About one-half of the passengers were US Navy men en route to Manila.[11] Several others were civilians connected with the engineering branch of the army, also headed for the Philippines. Most of the others were missionaries. There were only a handful of teachers and businessmen. The ship made an average speed of about thirteen knots. Paul described the trip across the Pacific as almost without incident. To pass the time, in addition to the cinema and the chance to read, there were a number of tournaments on board. As a recreational tennis tournament among the passengers got under way, Paul recalled the following observation about his fellow Bachelor, Jim Elliott:

> He played only to win, and any means was worth that end. In the deck tennis tournament, he drew a woman as partner in what was to be just a friendly tournament. He immediately protested loudly to the committee, insisting that he should have a man partner, as any man was better than a woman at that or any game. Why should he have one of the few women on board as partner, when most of the contestants were men? Why, indeed. The news spread around the ship, and even the woman in question found out about it. His reputation sagged to a new low. He succeeded in obtaining an exchange with a Navy man on the ship who was quite willing to take a lady as a partner. The ideal termination of the whole affair would be for the woman in question and her partner to beat Jim and his partner in the finals, but it did not work out that way. Jim defeated the rejected woman in the semi-finals, but was beaten in the finals. However, he might have won the finals had he kept the woman partner, and she proved to be an excellent player, far better than his partner, who was responsible for his defeat in the finals. Naturally a great crowd of hostile people turned up to watch the matches, jeering at Jim and cheering his ex-partner and the team which stopped him in

the finals. Such was he, through and through. He seemed ignorant of the hostility aroused or if he was aware of it, treated it with contempt.[12]

Although Paul did not place in the tennis tournament, he finished as runner-up in both chess and checkers. He made some good friends on board, notably Capt. Albert H. Rooks of the US Navy, bound for Manila, whom he first met on the train from Seattle. Captain Rooks and his wife rode down together, and she accompanied him as far as Honolulu, where she was to wait out his assignment as he took command of the heavy cruiser USS *Houston* in Manila, the flagship of the US Asiatic Fleet. It was Rooks whom Paul went head to head with in the chess tournament, with Paul defeating him in the semifinals before losing to another man in the finals by what Paul called a "careless" move. Other new friends he met on the ship were George Barlow, traveling to Singapore as a freight agent, and Lt. Bob Fulton, also in the US Navy, who hailed from Charleston and was headed to Manila for service on the USS *Houston*. After some discussion, Paul and Bob Fulton determined that Fulton's wife was probably a friend of Julia Ravenel's in Charleston. Paul found a good buddy in George Small, with whom he shared a cabin on the voyage. Small was on his way to his job at the US embassy in Chungking, China, and invited Paul to come visit after getting settled.

On August 12, they passed several islands in the Japanese group and saw one of their active volcanoes. From Hawaii to Japan, they went almost two weeks without seeing land of any kind. The vastness of the ocean had become difficult for them to comprehend. They took note of schools of sharks that followed the boat, and remarked that flying fish could be seen all day, every day. These fish were the only type of marine life they had seen. Paul and Jim became fascinated by them. They were not the large type of flying fish they had imagined, but rather small, with two sets of fin-wings. They flew a considerable distance, as much as fifty yards, always close to the water, sometimes plunging into a wave, only to appear on the other side. Watching these fish was a pleasant diversion for them during the long, monotonous journey from Hawaii across the Pacific. As they approached the eastern coast of China, they saw several Japanese sampans in the surrounding waters, but none of them veered toward the ship. Judging from their daily news bulletins, they felt that the political situation between the US and Japan was increasingly tense. That was an understatement. Some seven months later, both Fulton and Rooks were killed aboard the USS *Houston* in the Battle of Java on March 1, 1942.[13]

Shanghai

SS *President Harrison* took a two-day stopover in Shanghai, where they arrived on the morning of Thursday, August 14. It was a great, swarming, cosmopolitan city of more than 3,500,000 people, although parts of it had been devastated during the Sino-Japanese War. The city was a market for perhaps one-tenth of the world's population before it fell under Japanese occupation in 1937.[14] The port was located thirteen miles up the Whangpoo (now Huangpu) River, within the neutral zone of the Shanghai International Settlement. This was a concession to the foreign powers of France, Great Britain, and the United States via treaty in exchange for their support in suppressing a rebellion on the Chinese mainland in 1853. Under this treaty, Shanghai was one of five "treaty ports" where foreign merchants could build warehouses and residences. In 1862, the French Concession dropped out of the arrangement, and in 1863 the British and American enclaves were formally united. It was these foreign settlements that expanded the port and its oceangoing commerce by tremendous proportions before the war. Thus, Shanghai was divided into three parts: the International Settlement, the French Concession, and the Chinese municipality of greater Shanghai, now under Japanese control. The International Settlement was considered politically neutral and supposedly safe, although it did sustain significant damage during the worst parts of the battle of Shanghai. The International Settlement and the French Concession formed an island, a sort of political oasis for 1,400,000 people, surrounded by the Japanese forces that occupied Shanghai and turned parts of this once-bustling Chinese city into a stark wilderness of destruction.[15]

Shanghai was their first stop in China, on their way to "Free China." Free China was a widely used term, which referred to that part of war-torn China still under the control of the Chinese Nationalist forces, headed by Gen. Chiang Kai-shek. Since the invasion by the Japanese in 1937, Chiang Kai-shek's Kuomintang, or Chinese Nationalist Party, had formed an uneasy military alliance with China's Communist Party (CCP), headed by Mao Tse-tung and Chou En-lai, to resist and repel their common enemy—the Japanese.[16] By the summer of 1941, the eastern part of China with its port cities and industrial areas was already lost to the Japanese. Also lost were the resulting customs revenue, its most fertile farming provinces, and the advanced infrastructure in its modern cities. These sections were referred to as "Occupied China." The vast swatches of the North and the Northwest of China were lightly populated. The CCP had made great inroads with the peasants in these regions. As a result, the guerrillas of Mao's Communist army had made it impossible for the Japanese to hold the areas deep in the countryside. The new center of resistance in the war, Chiang's "Free China," now referred to the southwestern provinces of

Szechuan, Hunan, Henan, Sichuan, and Yunnan. The new center of resistance to the Japanese had been moved to the wartime capital at Chungking.

The Bachelors' first impression of Shanghai was a city of considerable filth and squalor. The minute that *President Harrison* dropped anchor in the Whangpoo, it was surrounded by dozens of sampans, filled with wretched-looking humanity, from which they heard incessant pleas for "mo-nay, mo-nay, mo-nay."[17] They did not see anybody handing out money, but most of the passengers and crew complied to the extent of throwing over oranges and apples, soap, candy, and trinkets. All in all, the boat people looked tolerably happy: they were smiling and laughing, but they did not seem to have much to be happy about. Apparently, they lived on these boats and made a living from their begging. They were miserably dressed and largely exposed to the wind, sun, and rain. Those who survived looked pretty rugged, as one would expect. Jim Elliott guessed that "the mortality rate is terrific among the very young."[18] They seemed to be good-sized families: a mother, a father, three or four children, and a baby or two. They all had their appointed tasks: one would work the large oar in the rear, and another looked out after the bow, avoiding collisions with the other boats. It took three people to handle the long poles with nets attached on the ends, used to retrieve the prizes tossed to and handed from the boats. It was a team effort.

The four Yale men went ashore via a tender boat that left at 9:30 a.m., taking them three miles down the river to the customs jetty. Jim and Art spent the morning with Bob, or most of it, then went to the office of the Presbyterian mission, where they received some advice in regard to touring the city. They were told that if they went into the devastated (Japanese-occupied) areas, they were required to have their passports as well as cholera inoculation certificates. They decided to pass on seeing those areas that first day, opting to visit a chocolate shop, enjoy a good American meal for lunch, and have front seats in the upper story of a double-decker bus to tour much of Shanghai's busiest thoroughfares and principal business districts. One advantage of the sightseeing was they found Shanghai to be a wonderful place to buy books, buying almost any book they chose for practically nothing. All the latest bestsellers could be had for just about one-tenth of the US prices in Shanghai. Jim discovered the reason for the discount—there were no laws in Shanghai governing copyrights, royalties, etc. These books were pirated, printed on cheap paper with cheap covers, and sold cheaply. They did the same with magazines too. Only the limitation of space prevented Jim and Art from stocking up on reading material. While there, they picked up a book to help with their Chinese vocabulary. They met up again with Bob Smith that evening, when, upon landing, they accompanied him by rickshaw to the American Club, where arrangements were made for reservations at a cinema at which they saw a Humphrey Bogart film, *The Wagons Roll at Night*, at the grand theater. They were surprised that the recently released movie was playing in Shanghai.

The Bachelors found the Chinese money and the exchange rates fascinating. In the myriad of letters written by Paul, Jim, and Art, they universally referred to Chinese money as "Mex," a holdover term that referenced the once-prevalent silver-dollar-sized Mexican eight-real and one-peso coins. The Chinese were familiar with Mexican silver pesos since they were used extensively in China in the nineteenth and early twentieth centuries, including the decades leading up to the Sino-Japanese War. The local merchants readily accepted these. Today, the Chinese money is known as "renminbi." The "yuan," a unit of Chinese money, was often referred to as a Chinese dollar, as in $10 Chinese (ten yuan). Jim described the exchange of money as follows in a letter to the Yale-in-China office in New Haven:

> Our US dollars were worth about $21.50 each in terms of Chinese currency and we had to laugh at the "tremendous" prices we paid for everything. Our $7.00 luncheon is an example. Really, it was less than $.35 US or, as everybody out here would say, 35 cents gold. US money is always referred to as gold. Why, I don't understand. Practically 100% of the Chinese money is paper. They have bills of every denomination, right down to 10 cents—maybe even a penny (I've forgotten). There are a few 10 cent coins floating about but they're not at all prominent or desirable. One of our favorite sports was haggling with the money changers on the street, trying to get the most for our American dollars. They'll always increase their first offer which is often very low if they think you're a greenhorn. I understand they sometimes give tourists worthless money too, but fortunately that never happened to any of us. Imagine the raft of money about with prices what they are and money so very cheap. It was positively astounding.[19]

The quoted prices for goods in Shanghai seemed outrageous at first, since the Bachelors were not yet used to seeing prices quoted in yuan, yet they attempted to pay in US dollars. The Chinese nickname for US money as "gold" was a reference to the US paper money issued from 1922 to 1934 known as "gold certificates." The face of the 1928 gold certificates were identical to the more familiar federal reserve notes, except for a gold-colored seal and serial numbers on the face and the wording "IN GOLD COIN PAYABLE TO THE BEARER ON DEMAND." Because these bills were still circulating, the term "gold" became an often-used reference to nearly all US money in China during this time period.

Art and Jim did get into the Japanese-controlled part of town for a few hours on the following day, although not long enough to really see anything. They got by the Japanese sentries easily enough: they just showed their cholera inoculation certificates, which said "American President Lines." They apparently understood the "American" part of it and passed them through with no question. Most of what they saw in the occupied section was war-torn destruction. They enlisted a guide, "Shanghai Charlie," a referral from a friend on the ship who, when he discovered Art was an incurable curio seeker, proceeded to take them to shops that they later ascertained contained pure junk.[20] They did see some interesting things along the way, however, among which was a Buddhist temple replete with gold statues, incense burning, and monks with shaven heads reciting their prayers and reading their sutras. They went along a section of Soochow Creek where a great many boat people lived. "Most of the babies were naked, everybody was filthy, the majority had prominent sores and diseases, all looked wretched. It nearly turned my stomach," said Jim.[21] From there "Shanghai Charlie" had them board a bus that took them through much of the Chinese parts of the city, then back to the shore from where they started. They paid him $10 Mex each, the amount agreed upon, whereas he asked for $10 more for his friend who accompanied them. They "put their collective foot down, and flatly refused." Jim said, "Art and I had an especially difficult time of it the second afternoon when we were sight-seeing together."[22] They hired rickshaw men for the afternoon and rode all over the French Concession, the Russian areas, and part of the Chinese city and International Settlement. In regard to Shanghai, once one of the world's great cities, Jim noted: "It certainly doesn't have much to offer. It is purely and simply an industrial and commercial center. There is practically nothing in the way of museums, parks, good music, etc. It has no outstanding buildings, monuments, places of special interest to sightseers. It is extremely dirty. . . . I can't say that I cared a great deal for Shanghai, although I did enjoy my two-day stay there."[23]

It was the rickshaw coolies, rather than the Japanese, who made their life unpleasant while trying to tour Shanghai. There were thousands of them everywhere, all clamoring for Art and Jim to ride with them, ready to do anything to get a fare. Then when they arrived at their destination, they always argued about the fee. To make matters worse, and even more confusing, all the rickshaws were fitted with enamel plates that stated their fixed prices. The prices had gone up since the plates were affixed to the rickshaws and could not be depended on. Then naturally, if the customer paid too little, there was a terrific argument. On the other hand, if they paid him too much, the coolie started howling in hopes they would add another tip on top of the fee. They caught the 5:15 p.m. tender back to the boat for dinner and a bath, then changed for a night out on the town. That night, Jim frequented several cabarets with the rest of the gang—Paul, George, and Norman; that's what the rest of them had done the night before. Jim described the nightclub scene:

> Most of the nightclubs or cabarets in Shanghai are taxi-dance halls. The dance floor is always enclosed by a circle of taxi-dance girls who will join your table for drinks and extra dance tickets. There is no cover charge, drinks are cheap, and dance tickets are of varying prices. The drinks are usually between $3 and $4 Mex. (15 to 20 cents US). The tickets at one place were 15 for $4.65, at another 3 for $5.00. Even the latter are much cheaper than in the US, especially since in Shanghai the tickets are good for a full 3-minute dance. Incidentally, the Chinese girls dance just as well as American girls. That greatly surprised me for some reason or other. The higher-priced cabarets had only European girls (white Russians), but most of them employed Chinese girls as well—or only. The orchestras are often Filipino and play mostly American dance music, not badly. Everything is modern, soft lighting, air conditioning, etc. In a Shanghai cabaret, one finds it hard to believe he is actually in China.[24]

The Yale men left the club about midnight on Friday, August 15, and were about to order a taxi when some Marine MPs offered them a ride to the customs jetty in their truck. Accepting the offer, they had a good talk about their experience on the way down Nanking Road to the port. They took the 12:30 a.m. tender back to the boat and said their goodbyes to Shanghai. They started moving out of the port about 3:00 a.m. on Saturday. When they woke up the next morning, they found themselves lodged on a sandbar in the middle of the Yangtze River, where they remained until the next high tide swept *President Harrison* off at 3:00 p.m. that afternoon. Two days later, they arrived in Hong Kong, their final destination by sea.

Hong Kong

As they did in Honolulu and Shanghai, they steamed into port early in the morning. What a contrast Hong Kong harbor was from Shanghai! Beautiful, filled with clear green water, surrounded by sharp, rising mountains (much like Honolulu), filled with prosperous-looking junks. It looked cleaner and more inviting. They passed through a narrow channel, between several islands and the mainland, and finally tied up at Kowloon on the mainland opposite Hong Kong, about 8:30 a.m.

Hong Kong was a British colony and had been under the rule of the British Crown since 1841. It had been ceded to Great Britain by the Qing Dynasty of China after the first Opium War, 1839–1842. The Kowloon Peninsula was added to the colony after the second Opium War, 1856–1860. Both of these wars were fought by the Chinese against the British, who gained a substantial foothold in China as a result of the conflicts. In 1898, the British sought to extend their influence in Hong Kong for defense. After lengthy negotiations with Peking, the two powers agreed that it was no longer permissible to acquire outright sovereignty over any parcel of Chinese territory. The extension of British influence over Hong Kong took the form of a ninety-nine-year lease. The lease consisted of the island of Hong Kong, the Kowloon Peninsula, and the New Territories, which comprised much of the rural farmland, as well as over two hundred outlying islands. It was from Kowloon that the Bachelors traveled by airplane into "Free China."

After breakfast, the Bachelors packed, had their passport stamped with permission to enter Hong Kong, and disembarked about 10:00 a.m. on August 19. They had a lengthy wait before their storeroom baggage cleared customs, since all of it had to be opened and searched. Nothing in their bags was of interest to the customs officials, and they got through without delay. From there, they took a taxi over to the Phillips House (on the Kowloon side), where they found the rooms reserved for them. The lodge was established by an American couple named Phillips for the purpose of housing missionaries in transit. It had built up a reputation over the years for good meals and rooms at low cost. They found the price reasonable enough, but the place seemed to have slipped somewhat, especially the food, since Mr. and Mrs. Phillips had retired. Jim Elliott remarked, "It is now run entirely by Chinese and is running largely on its reputation."[25]

After they had been in Hong Kong for two days, they were told that all aliens had to register with the police immediately upon entering the colony. Sure enough, the next day, Bob Smith was informed that they should all report to the police. Surprisingly, they found the police polite and professional about the whole process, and nothing was said about their tardiness in registering. Everything in Hong Kong seemed much cleaner and more efficient than in Shanghai. One noticeable difference was in the behavior of the rickshaw coolies. In Shanghai, they had swarmed all over them. In Hong Kong, they were well organized, waited their turns in line, and were generally well behaved. Jim noticed that air raid shelters of cement blocks had been built all over Hong Kong, and they were told that they had been stocked with stores of food sufficient for a six-month siege. The government had been doing much in the way of volunteer civilian defense corps training, in the unlikely event that the Japanese would try to take control of the island—or doubted that they could if they wanted to, since the city did not seem particularly well fortified.

The Yale men were in Hong Kong twelve days. They had high hopes of getting a plane into the Chinese mainland on Monday, August 25, but were not able to secure a flight until Saturday, August 30. They made the most of their visit in those extra days. During the first week, they roomed with George Small for several days. He had a swanky suite in the expensive Gloucester Hotel on the island, with two beds. The group took turns sleeping in George's extra bed, with one on the couch and another in a makeshift bed on the floor. There was a big fan in his hotel room. They found it much more comfortable than their shared room in the Phillips House, where there were no fans in the rooms and the sweltering summer heat in Kowloon was unbearable.[26]

The greater part of their time (at least that of Paul, Art, and Jim) was spent in shopping and finally equipping and outfitting themselves for the next two years in China. Although they were staying in Kowloon, only one day passed that didn't take them to the Hong Kong side to buy something. Transportation was easy and inexpensive. Most all rickshaw rides were $.10 HK (about 2½ cents US). The ferry ride to Hong Kong was $.10 each way, and a ferry left about every five minutes. Buses were only five cents, and they rode for half an hour for $.10 each. It was easy for them to get around the city during their layover.

Jim and Art could barely pass a curio shop or retailer without stocking up on supplies. For the record, Jim Elliott felt compelled to list the items he found necessary or desirable to purchase in Hong Kong for the long stay in China:

> Straw slippers, cigarettes, pipe tobacco, a silk Chinese robe, a wool robe, khaki shorts and socks, airmail envelopes and stationery, a light wash suit, thermos bottle, nose drops, cough drops, soap, twine, aspirin, talcum powder, Chinese calling cards (very important—almost as important as a passport), cigarette lighter and fluid, flashlight batteries and bulbs, duplicate keys, wool socks, flannel shirts and pajamas (extremely difficult to find in hot Hong Kong), tennis shoes, rubber boots, rubber overshoes, citronella (anti-mosquito weapon), mosquito netting, iodine, bug powder, shaving soap, alcohol, chopsticks, padlock for duffel bag, oiled cloth for wrapping a box of books and other sundry uses, writing board, rice bowl and washbasin for traveling, violin strings and bridge, adhesive tape, shoe polish, bath towels, film, rain hat and rain pants, glue, rubber bands, ink, darning cotton, scotch tape, etc. ad infinitum. Cigarettes, pipe tobacco, the silk Chinese robe and cigarette lighter are the only items mentioned above that weren't pretty necessary.[27]

Treated like Royalty

Jim was well supplied for the trip, although during his time in Hong Kong he contracted malaria, the symptoms of which would not surface until he reached Changsha. When the Bachelors were not shopping, they were dining or being shown around the city. On their first meal out, Paul, Art, Jim, and Bob were invited to the Episcopal Church guesthouse in Hong Kong. There they met Bishop Hall, an influential man in Hong Kong and the Far East. Hall's assistant, Mr. Higgins, and his wife hosted them for lunch. After a fine meal, Higgins took Paul and Art on a driving tour around the city and invited them for a swim that afternoon at a private club on the Kowloon side. Paul and Art took a dip in the pool and enjoyed a respite from the summer heat. Later that afternoon, they were taken on a driving tour by a friend they met on the boat, a Mr. Udaram Shamdas, a young Indian man of about twenty-one who was in the import-and-export business with his father. He was returning from Gibraltar, where their company had a branch office. Hong Kong was their headquarters and also where they lived.

Two nights later, the Bachelors enjoyed one of the big treats during their stay in Hong Kong. Shamdas invited them to his home for an authentic Indian dinner. Upon arrival at his home, they found the exterior unassuming and quite ordinary for a middle-class house. Inside the house was quite a surprise. They found it odd that in the corner of the large room used as a dining room and living room was a glass china closet in which were, of all things, cans of Del Monte peaches, grapefruit, pineapple, etc. The family was obviously stocking up on canned goods in case the war raging on the Chinese mainland were to engulf Hong Kong. There were no rugs on the floor, and no books were to be seen, although they found the imported furniture to be quite comfortable. There was plenty of liquor in the house. They had radios and phonographs in every room. Jim found the family to be "people with considerable money but with rather strange tastes." They all enjoyed fine Indian cuisine. The Yale men were surprised—and rather relieved—that the curry was not as hot as what they experienced when dining on SS *President Harrison*. There was no beef served, since the cow was sacred in India. Jim Elliott wrote, "The Indians use their fingers much more than we do during their meals. They fry many things in deep fat. Some of the courses are absolutely delicious, others didn't appeal to us, but on the whole we thoroughly enjoyed the meal. Afterwards we listened to American dance music (on records), drank a little, and talked with Mr. Shamdas, his parents, and his two sisters and one brother (all younger). We left about 10:30 and Mr. Shamdas accompanied us back downtown. Incidentally, Bob wasn't with us that night; we told him he missed a real treat."[28]

Their Yale calling cards opened up the world to them. The three Bachelors were treated like royalty during their extended stay in Hong Kong. They were befriended by the Lis, a prominent Chinese family they met on *President Harrison*. George Li, a young Chinese of about twenty-six, and his wife, May, whom he married in California, had never been to China before. Pauline, his younger sister, was a very pretty girl of twenty-two who had graduated from Marquette University in 1938 and had just spent an additional two years in the US. Their father, Ping Li, was a wealthy man, undoubtedly a multimillionaire. On the evening that *President Harrison* docked in Hong Kong, Pauline threw a big party for about forty of the passengers, mostly Navy men. George, Art, Paul, and Jim joined them at the party for tea and "almost had a full meal" during their stay.[29] They met Pauline's mother and younger brother, although their father was away at one of their other mansions. The home they were at was a palace in itself, the highest of luxury. From the ferry they could see the Lis' other mammoth home, complete with tennis courts and a swimming pool.

The family invited them for dinner on Monday, August 25, 1941. It was Paul's twenty-fourth birthday. Paul, George, Art, and Jim arrived at the Lis' villa for dinner. Jim described the experience: "They made a special effort to serve us with all the exotic dishes for which China is known and we found them all palatable and some quite delicious. Notable among the endless stream of delicacies were birds nest soup (really not bad), sharks fins (again quite edible), 'gold coin' chicken livers (so called from their shape), Chinese rice wine and a transparent fungus imported from Szechuan province that was served in a very sweet sauce, the substance of the fungus being very like glycerin. After dinner we mostly listened to records, some Chinese, mostly American dance music. About 10:30 we took our leave, grateful for another fine evening, one long to be remembered."[30] That evening was a fond memory for the Bachelors, their last big soiree before they stepped foot into Nationalist China.

Chapter 4
THE JOURNEY TO YUANLING

Departing Kowloon

The Bachelors' layover in Hong Kong was extended due to numerous delays in securing a plane to the Chinese mainland. Their situation improved when they met up with Brank Fulton, a Yali colleague who arranged their plane reservations with the China National Aviation Corporation (CNAC). Springer described him as an "Old China Hand." Fulton graduated from Yale in 1932, after which he was given an appointment as a Yali Bachelor, teaching in Changsha.[1] On his return to the US, he entered the Union Seminary in New York, receiving his BD degree in 1938. He spent two years on the faculty at Yenching University in Peking (now Beijing). He was on his way to visit Yale-in-China institutions in Changsha when he met the incoming group of Bachelors. Fulton arranged their flights and departed two days ahead of them.

Early on the evening of August 30, Paul, Art, Jim, and Bob gathered at Kowloon Airport to be weighed in.[2] Their baggage had arrived the day before and was already packed away in the plane. The airport was not large, but several big silver biplanes were parked on the tarmac in preparation for flight. They learned that these were Condors. These planes originally did service in the US and then were reconditioned for freight service in

Robert "Brank" Fulton. *Yale-China Association Records, RU 232, Manuscripts and Archives, Yale University Library*

China, each plane carrying only two passengers. It was from here that they began their trip into the interior, their first introduction to the real China.

They left the Kai Tak airfield in Kowloon on August 30, flying at dusk by Condor freight plane to Namyung, some 200-odd miles inland.[3] Hopkins and Ellliott took the first plane at 8:10 p.m., followed by Smith and Springer in a second one at 8:20 p.m. They flew at an altitude of 14,000 feet, keeping a wary eye out for Japs, but saw no signs of them en route. The plane with Springer and Smith was caught in a severe electrical storm, but the pilot landed safely after diving through a hole in the clouds—temporarily deafening his passengers. They landed on a mysterious field at Namyung at 10:15 p.m., one and three-quarter hours after taking off. The field was well outlined with lights, and there was a small bamboo hut with a light on at the end of the field. Otherwise, everything was black, especially the surrounding hills.

The next leg of their travel, from Namyung to Changsha, was markedly different from that of the group of Bachelors who preceded them only four years before. An important rail line was completed in 1936 with service from Namyung to Canton, then continuing to Changsha. One of the most important arteries to central China, it was about 400 miles long, took a day and a half to cover, and at that time was the only practical means of traveling to Hunan. Three Bachelors had made the trip in 1937, despite fears that early Japanese air raids would cut the rail connection to Changsha.[4] Numerous bombings had taken place on the rail line since then, derailing trains, wreaking havoc, and causing dozens of casualties with each interruption. This current group of Bachelors, instead of traveling by train, used an antiquated system of roads that took them deep into the interior to the town of Shiukwan. Here, they would board a train for Siangtan, then a boat to Changsha. From there, they would travel by boat to Tauyuan, before making the final leg of the trip via a small bus.

Namyung

Namyung was the first taste of the real China for the three Bachelors. So far, it had been free from bombing. It was a small town and a beehive of trade. From the minute they got off the plane in Namyung, and from then on, they became acutely conscious of the war. Bob Smith wrote, "If it should get a pummeling from the sky, the results would be most disastrous."[5] Paul described their arrival and the next leg of their trip: "We landed in a drizzle and walked to a thatch hut, where our passports and calling cards were examined by a youthful group of soldiers, several of whom I am certain were not over 16. Then, we had coolies take our luggage to town, a distance of about two miles, and we followed in a crude-oil-burning truck. What a ride that was! The driver was apparently trying to show off, for he drove at break neck speed over a rough, narrow road, through tunnels which didn't leave an inch to spare, over rickety bridges, around sharp turns which looked like dead ends as you came up to them."[6]

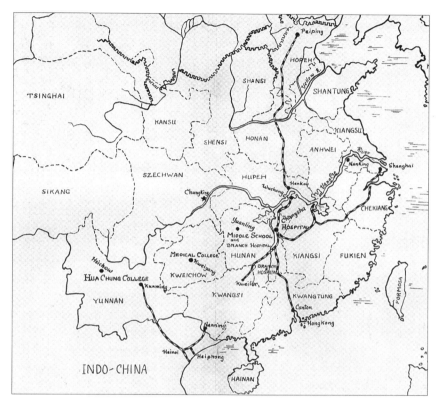

Map showing wartime locations of Yale-in-China institutions. *Courtesy of the Yale-China Association, reprinted from* The Yale-China Association: A Centennial History, *by Nancy E. Chapman and Jessica C. Plumb*

Paul sarcastically remembered, "There were a number of Chinese aboard, who seemed to enjoy the trip as much as we did. The swanky hotel where we stayed was up an alley (I can call it nothing more) about six feet wide. One look at the lavatories provided promptly constipated all of us for the next three days."[7] He speculated this may also have been brought about by the steady diet of tea and rice at irregular intervals. "Our rooms cost us a grand total of .35 gold, and were worth almost every penny of it. The mattress consisted of a board covered with a dirty cloth. Jim and I put a sleeping bag on top of ours, and it wasn't half bad, though I didn't sleep a wink.

We were assured by our English-after-a-fashion-speaking guide that there were no mosquitoes in town, but we took hastily to our nets when we heard the drone of their dive bombers. We were told that we might leave early in the morning by truck for Shiukwan, and were duly called at 6 [a.m.], only to find that we could not leave until 1 [p.m.]."[8] After sitting around and arguing with their Chinese counterparts for an hour or so about the delay, they decided to eat. They were ushered into the finest eating place in town. Paul consumed his customary gallon of tea, which he deemed to be safe because it was boiled, some rice a la chopstick, and a patch of watermelon seeds. Any biological urges he might have had were discouraged by one look at the privy, after which they returned to negotiate for another truck. A new Dodge truck finally pulled up (with a 1902 body built on it), and their luggage was moved out to the middle of the street by several coolies. Thinking that the luggage was about to be loaded aboard this truck, Paul watched helplessly as dozens of Chinese army trucks careened along the only route available through the town—at breakneck speeds. He recalled, "Now, before our eyes, the Dodge truck was entirely loaded with packages of paper bound for Shiukwan, and carried to the truck by coolie women, literally 9/10 of whom were in the last stages of pregnancy. A big argument arose of course, with our English, etc. speaking friend defending us, but to no avail, for the doors of the truck were closed and it drove away."[9] Their baggage was left in the street. They finally commandeered another truck, of ancient vintage, on which was loaded their baggage, the Yale men, and another load of paper. After due repairs and after much squabbling, they shoved off, crammed in the back of the truck with about ten Chinese, including one girl. "The ride to Shiukwan was a painful one, especially if one chose, as I did, to ride at the back end of a springless truck. My choice was not entirely foolish, however, as I did not quite suffocate, and was able to look out of the back. We stopped every five minutes to add water, and every ten minutes at barricades, to be examined by boy-soldiers. Fortunately, none of them got the bright idea of examining our luggage (800 lbs. in all)."[10]

The terrain was so pockmarked it might have easily been labeled as passable only for large enemy tanks. Paul was perched on top of a big pile of assorted baggage and miscellaneous cargo in the ancient wooden rear of the truck, amid a score of dirty Chinese, with his head about a half inch from the roof between bounces. "When it bounced, Ow!"[11] Every time the truck stopped, it could be started again only after much cranking and coaxing. En route they ran down a woman who failed to get out of the way when the driver shouted (the truck had no horn). A soldier riding on the fender grabbed her and threw her aside, causing her to fall under the rear wheel. The driver didn't bother to stop. "Life is cheap here, and only the fit and alert survive," wrote Paul.[12]

After five hours of this torturous ride, they arrived at Shiukwan at 7:30 p.m., expecting to be graciously received by Mr. Lockwood, who ran the YMCA in the town. However, he was away on vacation, and Brank Fulton, who was to have waited for them, had gone on ahead. This was their lowest ebb of the journey. They were told that this city was bombed several times daily and that all inhabitants must flee to the fields from 6:00 a.m. to 3:00 p.m. This was a frightful realization. They had seen much damage on the way to the "Y" and were anxious to ask Mr. Lockwood what they should do when the alarm sounded (none of the buildings were over two stories high, and none had cellars). They found an English-speaking attendant at the front desk of the YMCA who told them no rooms were available. The Bachelors had to sleep with their luggage on the floor of a damp room that would have made a pig sty look sumptuous and immaculate. The room was filled with the smell of excrement. They put their mosquito netting over some tables and tried to rest underneath. It was another sleepless night, all through which they burned incense to drown out the smell of shit. They had but one meal that day but were quite content without the usual gallon of tea.[13]

When Fulton departed Shiukwan two days ahead of them, he had arranged for Mr. Evison of the English Methodist mission to meet them upon their arrival and take them out for dinner. Paul recalled, "At nine the next day Mr. Evison, of the English Methodist mission, came to greet us and take care of us. Never were we so glad to see a white man before, and probably never will be again. He told us, contrary to our fearful report, that the town hadn't been bombed in a week, and there would be ample time to get to the fields if the alarm sounded. Incidentally, the Japs never bomb at night, except at Chungking. We ate at a big openair, thatch-roofed place across the river, our only meal for that day."[14] Then they went to the Evisons' home, which was in the same compound with a hospital. They were able to drink clean water and refill their thermos jugs with more after Evison boiled it for them. They relaxed in the afternoon and had tea, then were packed off to the railroad station, where they boarded the train for Siangtan.

It was a decent English train that departed on schedule. They moved on into China, north through Hengyang, although they didn't see much of anything because they were traveling by train at night. They were able to get a good night's sleep on board. As they approached their destination, the countryside appeared peaceful and beautiful in the warm morning sunlight. The train reached the end of the line in Siangtan, at 8:15 the next morning, some 260 miles north and not far from Changsha. The difference in the city's scenery was in stark contrast to the countryside. Destruction surrounded them on all sides. All through the summer, Siangtan had suffered from heavy bombardments by the Japanese. During the daylight hours, the city was deserted, as were most cities in the war area. It looked like a ghost town with its empty streets, buildings in shambles, and gaunt, mangy-looking dogs lurking about. Jim described the dogs as "the worst of all the moth-eaten 'wonks' we've seen in China," adding that they looked like "warmed up death."[15] The Bachelors traveled to a local mission via rickshaw, where their next host awaited them. Paul remembered, "This town had really been bombed, though Miss Woods' mission, where we went for lunch, had come through unscathed. Miss Woods gave us a nifty lunch, including coffee, an unheard of luxury. You'll never know how much that coffee was appreciated."[16] After lunch, the Bachelors shoved off again, this time by boat to Changsha, a three-hour trip on a boat laden to the gunwales. They rode on the top deck with the captain for a small additional sum and had quite a time when Jim played his fiddle and they sang along when he played. In due time the ruins of Changsha were in sight, and after the now-customary squabble with the Chinese crew, they disembarked at Changsha on September 2. A Yali servant in a bright-blue tunic was there to meet them, and in a few minutes they were introduced to Dr. Winston "Win" Pettus.

Dr. Winston Pettus (Yale '33, BA; Yale '37, MD). Professor of Surgery, Hsiang-Ya Hospital. *Yale-China Association Records, RU 232, Manuscripts and Archives, Yale University Library*

Dr. Winston "Win" Pettus

Win Pettus was a missionary surgeon, born in Shanghai, China, on February 25, 1912.[17] His Chinese name was P'ei Wen-t'an, a name he used throughout his life in addition to his American name, William Winston Pettus.[18] He entered Yale College in 1929 after attending the American School in Peking, where his father, William B. Pettus, was president of the College of Chinese Studies. After completing his undergraduate work in 1933, he enrolled at the Yale medical school, where he received his MD degree in 1937. That same year, he married Maude Miller, an attractive pediatric nurse from Inwood, West Virginia, and began a residency in surgery at the Presbyterian Hospital in New York City. In 1940, after completing his residency, Pettus received a Yale-in-China Association appointment as professor of surgery at Hsiang-Ya Hospital in Changsha, Hunan.[19] A small, slight man with dark hair and a

Hsiang-Ya Hospital building, Changsha, September 1941. *Yale-China Association Records, RU 232, Manuscripts and Archives, Yale University Library*

mustache, he exuded boundless energy and determination. He was very much at home in China and accomplished every task with vigor and enthusiasm.[20] Pettus was in his second year of a two-year appointment from Yale-in-China when the Bachelors arrived.[21] His wife, Maude (or Maudie), had continued her training as a surgical nurse and worked with him at Hsiang-Ya Hospital. She was a gentle, smiling young woman of medium height, with light-brown hair and capable hands. She specialized in operating-room techniques and was immediately loved by the staff.[22]

Hsiang-Ya Hospital was the most active unit on the Yale campus in Changsha.[23] It was a teaching hospital and had the best reputation in this section of Hunan Province. It was said that if the patient was not very sick and wanted a rest, he or she went to the Catholic hospital. If they were really ill and needed medical attention more than anything else, they went to Hsiang-Ya Hospital. At the time, they had very few private patients, fewer than thirty at that point in time. The rest of the hospital was full to capacity with ward patients, between 150 and 200. Bob Smith found it "most enlightening to watch this hospital at work; I do not believe I have ever had the opportunity to observe at such close hand the functioning of a large hospital. There are twenty-one doctors on the staff at this time and three interns loaned to other hospitals under the medical center plan, and fifteen graduate nurses."[24] As a testament to the Yale-in-China commitment toward medical education, nearly 100% of their Chinese medical personnel were recruited directly from their own Hsiang-Ya medical-educational institutions. The hospital was a busy place, employing a total of 159, which included medical staff, technicians, engineers, and attendants. It was a scene of tremendous medical activity and had exceeded all expectations of the Yale-in-China trustees.

Yali Campus in Changsha

Win Pettus and Brank Fulton came down from the Yali campus to greet the new arrivals. In another hour or so they were all eating a delicious meal around Maude Pettus's table. Pettus and Fulton showed their guests around the town, where they spent part of a day sightseeing and taking pictures. On September 3, Paul and Art went on a picnic on top of a mountain and visited a Taoist temple before lunching at Miss Davis's of the Presbyterian mission in Changsha. Jim was not feeling good after lunch and begged off the rest of the afternoon and went to bed, where he stayed for the next ten days. He was sick with malaria.

It did not take long for Springer and Hopkins to notice that they were a source of unending curiosity among the Chinese people. They came to feel like walking sideshows. Wherever they stopped in the street, crowds gathered and both young and old stared openly at them. When they walked down the street, people stopped their work to gawk at them and discuss the new arrivals. Springer mused that "I am afraid that I shall feel quite neglected when I get back into a country where one may pass completely unnoticed."[25] There were two air raid alarms that day, but no bombings in the vicinity. This first alarm, known as a "*chin-pao*" (as in *bow-wow*) told them that planes were in the province, but no one except the newcomers at the Yali campus and hospital seemed concerned about it.[26]

Air Raid Warning System

In 1934, Chiang Kai-shek appointed Tai Li as the director of a new Investigation Department, in charge of military intelligence in China.[27] Following a diligent search by the Chinese assistant military attaché in Washington, Tai brought in a bald American man from Queens, New York, Herbert Yardley. He was paid a salary of $10,000/year to work as an outside consultant for Tai Li in Chungking, the wartime capital. Yardley was the father of modern cryptography, the legendary code breaker of Japanese codes during the Paris Conference and the Washington Naval Conference immediately after World War I. The team recruited all the Japanese experts they could find in China to work under Yardley, who headed a deciphering endeavor geared toward Japanese radio interception. Before long, the operation had more than fifty interception stations and more than two hundred radio operators. During Yardley's tenure of over a year, the group (also known as the Black Chamber) intercepted 200,000 secret radio and telegram communications of the Japanese army, of which 20,000 were studied and evaluated. Finally, a major breakthrough came in mid-1939. The group succeeded in decoding the secret code system of the Japanese air force in China. This allowed China to establish an excellent air raid warning system against the ferocious air bombing by the Japanese.

This sophisticated warning system prevented numerous bombing disasters for China. It also facilitated more-effective evacuations before major Japanese air attacks. It was this development in military intelligence that triggered the widespread use of air raid sirens known as *chin-pao*s. There were three signals: the *chin-pao* (first alarm), the *chin chi chin pao* (urgent alarm), and the *kai chu* (release), all of which were given by a siren.[28] In parts of war-torn China, people sometimes shrugged off

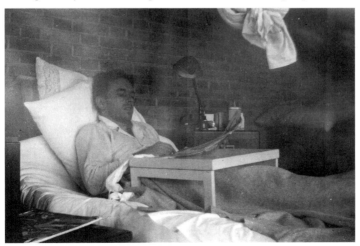

Jim Elliott recovering from malaria, Hsiang-Ya Hospital, Changsha, September 1941. *Yale-China Association Records, RU 232, Manuscripts and Archives, Yale University Library*

or ignored the *chin-pao*s, but they did pay attention to the *chin chi chin pao*s, which signaled an imminent attack. When that sounded, everyone scurried into the dugouts or for the hills, and most of them stayed there until the *kai chu* (guy-jew) was sounded.

Shells of Houses and Buildings

The buildings of the former Yali Middle School on this beautiful campus were devoid of students. The school was now housed in Yuanling, having been moved to these somewhat inadequate quarters in 1938. The Yale-in-China Association believed that the smaller campus was the best place for the safety of the students and staff. The great fire of three years before had ruined Changsha. Sporadic bombings since then had kept it in shambles.[29] The shops were continually being rebuilt of flimsy temporary materials. At first glance, the situation did not look so bad if one just walked down the street. But one peek behind the shop fronts, and the real state of affairs became apparent. Buildings that were once crowded with numerous business establishments had crumbling walls and vast open spaces. The desolate shells of houses revealed that it was a burned-out and battle-scarred city by the time the three newest Bachelors

Frances Scherrer and Marjorie Tooker, nurses at Hsiang-Ya Hospital. *Yale-China Association Records, RU 232, Manuscripts and Archives, Yale University Library*

arrived. Although the threat of a full-scale Japanese invasion seemed remote, the threat of a bombing was always looming in Changsha.

Jim Elliott had developed a full-blown case of malaria and was bedridden for ten days. By September 5, his fever was lower (down from 104), but his departure for Yuanling was delayed to give him time to respond to the multiple quinine treatments he received in Changsha. Bob Smith used his time during Elliott's recuperation to work on his evaluation of the conditions in Changsha for a report to the Yale-in-China office. A capable young executive, Smith was overwhelmed by the devastation in the city after the fires and frequent bombings. He attended meetings and interviewed the staff. He was entertained by missionaries and local officials and took excursions into the surrounding countryside. Most importantly, he inspected Hsiang-Ya Hospital in action and was impressed by a meeting of the Changsha International Relief Committee (IRC), held in one of the mission buildings. Their activities were entirely concerned with urgent relief: rice kitchens, refugee camps, schools, medical care, clothing, and individual as well as industrial rehabilitation. Yale-in-China took a leading role in this valuable community effort.[30]

Springer had caught a slight cold and developed a nasty blister on his foot from a long, arduous hike up the mountain. Fulton was down with tonsillitis but felt good enough to guide Springer and Hopkins to Yuanling. Fulton was the only one of the three who spoke Chinese. Elliott and Smith were to follow a few days later. It was difficult for the new Bachelors to depart for Yuanling after they had experienced Changsha, but they too began to grasp the dangers of bombing raids during their days on the former campus. They found their American hosts and staff to be most hospitable. Their stopover in Changsha ended with a buffet dinner at the Presbyterian mission, with all the local Americans and a few Chinese in attendance. It became a celebratory occasion for the young men, who gathered around the piano for a song fest, with a number of selections from Win Pettus's Yale songbook. Paul also met the father of an old friend, Jack Tootell, who had accompanied him on a cross-country road trip in a Packard from Tennessee to New Jersey in 1936. The senior Mr. Tootell was working with the mission in Changsha.

Marjorie Tooker, the head nurse at Changsha, packed a substantial lunch for them before they continued their journey. Born in China to medical missionaries, she studied in the US and was a graduate of Wellesley College, returning to China in 1939. She settled into her new position as superintendent of nurses at Hsiang-Ya Hospital in 1940. She was fond of each group of Yale Bachelors as they passed through, and this group was no exception. She did her best to make sure they had little fear of starving along the way. The Bachelors, who had made it to the interior of China in one piece, were surrounded by new friends on this third leg of their journey.

Riverboat Trip

Art, Brank, and Paul left Changsha on the night of September 6, only to find that the boat on which they had secured accommodations (and was to be their home for the next three nights) did not leave until 6:10 the next morning.[31] This greatly distressed Paul in particular, knowing that he could have had a clean bed in Changsha. One look at the boat assured him that he would not get a wink all night. He described the restless evening as follows:

My first view of the boat was filled with dismay. It was covered with Chinese like a piece of food left lying around is covered with ants. Most of them were asleep, and we had to wedge our feet in between them to get footing. I walked on dozens before we got to our quarters. The roof was covered, the floor was covered, the steps were covered, even the walls were covered with sleeping or sleepy figures in various stages of dishabille. Our passageway was so packed with soldiers at all hours that it was well nigh impossible to get in or out of our cabin, so we remained pretty well confined once we got in. And what a cabin! This was a first-class accommodation, costing us about 50 cents gold apiece for the entire trip. It contained three bunks, each of which was about 5½ feet long (Art and I are about the same height) and about 2½ feet wide. They occupied the three walls other than that on which the door opened, and left a space in the middle of the room about big enough for ten Chinese soldiers to sleep in. . . . Fourteen of our twenty pieces of luggage were dumped here, and we were left to shift for ourselves. We promptly tossed out our so-called mattresses, which had quite enough living creatures in them already, we thought, so why add one more?[32]

After a bit of fumigation and citronella to dispel the insects, Art, Brank, and Paul got out their sleeping bags and bedding. For protection, they went to bed fully clothed and sweltered through a sleepless night with only a few minor bites. A malaria mosquito dive-bomb squadron was effectively held at bay by their mosquito netting.

At 6:10 the next morning, with much shouting and squabbling, they finally got the show on the road, heading downstream with a strong current and the help of a chugging, sooty motorboat, which towed their vessel and another barge. They scarfed down the lunch that Miss Tooker sent with them. The three travelers also found fresh eggs on the boat, since they mistrusted the dark spots that resembled bugs of various sizes and shapes in the prepared food. Toilet "facilities" were ample—one merely used the side, or if fastidious, overboard via the back of the boat. Their audience for a bathroom break usually consisted of the myriads of Chinese in the immediate vicinity. As the boat pushed down the river, they settled in for the trip and managed to get some sleep during the day and considerable rest on the second night, due largely to exhaustion. The soldiers stacked outside their cabin were friendly, although they made a horrible racket at all hours of the night, waking them at ghastly hours. At 3:00 a.m. on the third night, they arrived at the end of the line and hired a small boat to take them to the next river steamer at Changteh.

As bad as the devastation in Changsha and Siangten was, Changteh (at the west end of T'ung T'ing Lake) impressed them the most as far as the devastation by bombing went. Here, as in Siangtan, the Japanese bombers had been extremely active over the summer. However, there was very little rebuilding that had taken place. Although they were there only overnight, every other building, it seemed, was in ruins. Like other cities on their route, a daytime curfew was in effect, and the natives, they were told, lived in mortal fear of the Japanese, as they concluded from the fearsome destruction all around them.[33]

They caught their next boat out of Changteh at 5:00 a.m. and made the seven-hour trip to Taoyuan in nice, clean accommodations. Taoyuan, just beyond Changteh and the last city before their arrival in Yuanling, had its share of bombardments, but it did not seem so bad off as the three cities just visited.[34] Here they went to the Presbyterian mission run by Miss Murial Boone, an American born in Shanghai, who took wonderful care of them. Murial was well known and well liked in that area. Staying overnight, they stocked up on American-style food and boiled water while she helped arrange a boat that would take them the 6½-odd miles to the bus leaving for Yuanling. That boat trip proved to be entirely pleasant, since it was a junk that they had all to themselves. The two crew members poled, steered, rowed, towed, and managed the sails while they lay around inside after spreading out their sleeping bags. Miss Boone prepared a lunch for them, which they polished off with gusto during the seven-hour trip.

Their junk landed in a shoreline of mud, where they were met by Curtis, a Chinese man, who was the star English student of Yali. He was sometimes referred to as the "prize package" for his unusual command of the language. Curtis had been waiting for them for five days. He was sent by their colleagues to guide them through the perils of the last lap of their journey, some 280 *li* (93 miles) to Yuanling.[35] He met them as they disembarked from the sampan into a sea of mud after an arduous three-day stretch of water travel from Changsha. He was anxious to oblige them and impress them at that first meeting. He was proud of his command of the English language, and although Fulton spoke Chinese fairly well, Curtis insisted that he speak in English when they wanted something, and he would translate for them to the person concerned. He talked happily and conversed with the three travelers on their way to a village where they were to get the bus to Yuanling, some four miles distant—not an insignificant distance in a drizzling rain with mud underfoot and a terrain that included a number of rice paddies. Upon arrival, they were put up in a nice, quiet hotel, where bugs and rats existed only in nightmares. They enjoyed an excellent Chinese dinner with all the trimmings, and their only objection was that their room seemed to be in the main passageway into the interior of the hotel. People, chiefly women, walked through at all hours and were, as usual, not particular where they spit. The Chinese they met had a peculiar habit of spitting on the floor whenever they got the urge, which was hard for the clean-cut Bachelors to get used to. They were grateful their bus would depart the following day.

Chinese Bus Ride

The next morning was uneventful, and they caught the bus at 12:50 p.m., with all scrambling to scarf down their lunch—since it departed ten minutes earlier than scheduled. The body of the bus was a fairly new Chevrolet, with a wooden body of ancient vintage. It was run on rice wine, which was almost pure alcohol and much cheaper than gasoline. There were no aisles, since all available room was taken up by seats. The seats were so close together that it became impossible for Paul and Art to get their knees in, and difficult to sit sideways since it was built for smaller passengers. Not all of the passengers were human, since there was some livestock, chiefly poultry, but they were not as objectionable as the constant spitters, all of whom seemed to occupy the center seats and insisted on spitting out the windows rather than on the floor, in complete disregard of another passenger sitting between them and the window. There was also a nauseated soldier on the back row who spent most of his time with his head out the window, making rather sickening noises.

Despite the internal distractions on the bus, the country scenery was superb, and the four men concentrated on it as much as possible between the multitude of stops, each accompanied by a demand for tickets. The long dirt road was muddy at times but quite smooth and wide enough for one and a quarter cars. The bus wound up and down the mountains in numerous hairpin turns, which would have been a thrilling ride even in fair weather. It rained steadily during this last leg of the journey, so the road had become harrowingly slippery. They arrived at Yuanling at 6:16 p.m. and took a ferry across the river, which brought them within walking distance of the Yali campus, a little over a mile away. A note left at the bus station informed them that Dwight Rugh and two fellow Bachelors, Don McCabe and Bob Clarke, had left for an appointment and would not return until 9:00 p.m. They walked to Yali, arriving at 7:00 p.m. on September 11, 1941. It had taken two months and four days for Paul to make the 12,000-mile journey from Camden, New Jersey. There was no one available to greet them at the end of this long and arduous trip. So Curtis, the student who had initially met them on their last leg, continued to guide them until he delivered them safely to their quarters. There were no male coolies about, so women carried their heavy bags from the bus station across the river, through the town, and up the hill, which they later dubbed "Yali Shan." They found it shocking at the time but soon became used to seeing women do backbreaking work in China. Most of their luggage was still left behind them at the river, since there was not room for all of it on the final bus ride. The rest was expected to arrive in three or four days.

Yuanling

Before the Japanese advance toward Changsha a few years before, Yuanling was a small village of a few thousand people located on the fork of the Yu and the Yuan Rivers. With the evacuation of Changsha at the time of the great fire on November 12, 1938, it swelled gradually to its current size.[36] The inhabitants were mainly Changsha refugees, living temporarily in Yuanling's comparative safety. The Yuanling campus comprised the Yali Middle School, which included the junior school and senior schools; the Hsiang-Ya nursing school; and the affiliated Hsiang-Ya branch hospital and Hsiang-Ya isolation hospital. The Yali school had an enrollment of 450 boys.[37] Dwight Rugh, as director, was the representative of Yale-in-China. Ying Kai-shih and C. C. Lao were the school's dean and principal, respectively.[38] Hsiang-Ya Hospital in Yuanling was fully staffed by its own Chinese nurses and doctors. There were eighty beds in this hospital, and two daily clinics receiving at least six hundred visits weekly. The overworked staff were also managing the instruction for the one hundred girls at the Yali School of Nursing on the campus. These institutions were the centerpieces of the Yale-in-China mission in Yuanling.

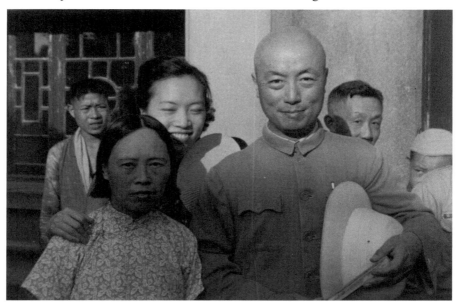

C. C. Lao with his family. He served as principal of the Yali Middle School in the 1930s and 1940s.
Yale-China Association Records, RU 232, Manuscripts and Archives, Yale University Library

Yuanling was a well-chosen location, better in many respects than Changsha, though lacking a large port. It was an inconspicuous town in a rural setting and was deemed to be of little military interest to the Japanese.[39]

Before the war, it was an old-style provincial town of perhaps 25,000 people.[40] Now it was a bustling little city of from 75,000 to 100,000 inhabitants, and, at times, the population had been even higher. A large percentage of the population in Yuanling were refugees, mostly from Changsha, with many from Shanghai and other coastal cities. In addition to the Yali school, the Hsiang-Ya branch hospital, the Fu-Siang girls school, and some others had moved to Yuanling in the past three years. Even so, it was considered relatively safe, although it had experienced hostile Japanese flyovers and the dropping of propaganda leaflets since April 21, 1939. Yuanling was somewhat distant from the population centers of Hunan and was void of wealth, ease of transportation, cultural excitement, and grand public buildings. The country was hilly, and the hills were inevitably filled with graves, just as the valleys and most of the hillsides were filled with tiered rice paddies. The hills were full of small game, and one often passed a hunter bringing in a pheasant or two or even a wildcat. The people were relatively prosperous, and their night-soiled farms were productive. There were no cars in Yuanling. Transportation within the town was by bicycle, foot, or rickshaw. Getting there was by bus or from boat. The rivers were clear (near to the headwaters of the Yuan River) and the fish were plentiful.

As Paul and Art walked through Yuanling for the first time, they were impressed by the electric lights all over the city. Yuanling had one of the best electric power stations anywhere in China. Much of the equipment was moved up the river from Hankow just before the invasion of the city by the Japanese. Paul remarked that "Yali is the best lighted city in the [Hunan] province, perhaps in all of China."[41] The lights were brighter than any he had seen since leaving Hong Kong. As they entered the school compound and walked up the steps, they saw a lighted room with a number of students. Curtis shouted, "Here are your new teachers!," and the boys gathered at the windows and saluted them with "Welcome!" They were soon greeted on all sides by the enthusiastic cries of "Welcome" from the beaming Chinese students. That hospitable cry made the three of them feel that all the torture of travel the past week was worth it. Paul reflected, "I felt the warmth in those voices, and my heart warmed within me for the first time since I had entered the Orient. Had the other Americans greeted us at the bus, perhaps this auxiliary greeting would have passed out of the channel of memory, but instead it burns warm and clear as one of the most compensatory moments of my life."[42]

After finishing the outdoor climb of about 120 steps, they arrived at the Bachelors' quarters, atop one of the highest spots on the Yali campus. They shared the quarters with Bob Clarke and Don McCabe, two Yali English teachers who had arrived in 1939 and 1940, respectively. For five young men there was only one small study— which was to contain all of their desks. There was a small dining room (the Bachelors' Mess), scarcely giving the assigned servant any room to serve them, with a hall connecting the two rooms. Nearby was a small stove and a screened-in porch with three single double-decker rope beds, flanked by their bureaus and wash basins. The porch became their hangout in good weather, despite that it had no chairs worthy of the name and was too narrow to permit any passage back and forth when someone was sitting. There was a small kitchen, which was a section of the porch partitioned off with rice paper and supported by a fragile wooden frame. To assist them, they had a cook and two servant boys, both of whom slept in a hovel below the house, in whose narrow confines they slept when the mosquitoes weren't active. Their section of the house was partitioned by a common wall, and adjacent to the apartment occupied by Dwight Rugh, the director of the school; Winifred, his wife; and their eight-year-old daughter, Betty Jean. The floor below was occupied by a woman missionary. Although the quarters were cramped, among the most-pleasant surprises was the outstanding cuisine.

The cook, Tou Shi-fu, lived with his wife and children in a three-room cottage near the house. He was a man of medium build, with a shaved head, oval face, and direct eyes. He started out each day in a starched white apron that became increasingly wilted and stained as the day progressed. He was an honest and sometimes uncomfortably upright man with uncompromising principles. He was an outstanding cook. His previous employers had been Danish missionaries who left Yuanling before Dwight Rugh and his family arrived. From them he learned to make pastries and cookies of outstanding quality.[43] He planned the menus, bought the food, and took charge of the entire culinary side of the needs both of the Bachelors and the Rughs.

For breakfast, Tou Shi-fu often made pancakes and waffles served with water buffalo butter and *bien-tan* syrup. He had whole-wheat cereal that he ground on a grindstone on the back porch from roasted kernels of wheat, out of which he made a beverage like Postum as a substitute for coffee. His orange marmalade was superb and his jams were made from kumquats, pears, or peaches. His peanut butter, made from roasted peanuts repeatedly put through a meat grinder and tinged with sesame oil, was rich and nutty—the perfect complement for toast with kumquat jam. He owned a gadget for making sausages, spending hours stuffing the translucent casings with ground pork and spices. He also made bacon and smoked the sausages and bacon in the smoke room under the back porch. Jim Elliott later referred to Tou Shi-fu as "the best cook in Hunan."[44]

In the top of their house was an attic space, where their "sanitary convenience" was kept—their toilet took the form of a bucket that was emptied twice daily by an *amah*, who frequently carried her small child on her back during these excursions. Given the lack of sanitation in the area, complications arose when the inhabitants of the house were hit with diarrhea ("Yangtze Rapids" as it was called in Chungking), a not-infrequent occurrence. Despite the efforts of their cook, there was often something in the food that did not agree with them. This situation was alleviated later in the year, when a second bucket was installed in the attic for emergencies. As they surveyed their new surroundings and unpacked the bags that arrived with them, they settled into their strange new quarters. At 9:00 p.m., their Yali colleagues returned and welcomed them, and they were soon resting in their double-decker rope mattress beds, which they found quite comfortable. Paul "slept like a top" that first night and felt in fine shape on the following day. Classes had already begun on September 5. Except for a short speech they would give their students the following morning, they were not expected to teach until the twenty-second. This gave them ten days to relax, get acclimated, and study the teaching techniques of their colleagues. This included the direct method of teaching English.

For the beginning classes, the teachers started with these four objects: a box, a book, a pen, and a pencil. They would hold the box up and say, "This is a box. Is it a book? No, this is a book. Is it a pen? No, this is a pen." Then they began to hold things up themselves and say, "What is it?" Then, the chorus of boys would answer, "It is a book" or "It is a box."[45] Starting with these words, they built a vocabulary of nouns and began stringing them together. The teachers also had some textbooks made of cheap paper. It wasn't very good material. The students came into the classes and heard these foreigners talking in a way in which they could not understand, so they were just waiting for the teachers to speak Chinese. However, because Chinese was not spoken by the teachers (at least, not at first), the students were forced to speak their first English by what was called the direct method.[46]

Paul passed these first few days reading, preparing an essay for the *Yali Weekly*, and observing his fellow teachers. He sat in on one of Bob Clarke's classes to gain a few pointers before inhaling the chalk dust himself.[47] Bob strode about the room calling on different boys, then returned to the board to illustrate a point or to copy a sample sentence on the board, explaining then why it was right or wrong. The class was attentive to a man, and Paul was later to find that was quite an achievement in itself. He wrote home frequently to his mother, not just about his new teaching position but also to describe his new surroundings. "I'll start this letter out here on the porch, where it is still nice on mild days. When I look up from the typewriter, I see the valley before me, with houses on this side of the river and hills on the other. The water is now clear blue in color, and it is quite a sight when seen through the fading green of the trees, about which numerous eagles float lazily. On Sunday I took a long walk with Art among those hills and visited a temple at the top of one of them which is now used as a soldier's encampment. There are many beautiful temples within easy walking distance. Temples which are centuries old, and which with their high, slender towers, give the commanding view of the surrounding countryside."[48] It was a blessed change of scenery compared to his journey into the interior of China.

Jim Elliott Departs Changsha

When Jim Elliott recovered sufficiently from his bout of malaria and Bob Smith collected enough information on Yali operations to complete his report on Changsha, they were ready to head for Yuanling. Smith would continue his inspection there. Elliott was to report for his teaching assignment. Marjorie Tooker accompanied them to Yuanling for two good reasons. First, she had not yet seen the nursing school in Yuanling and felt it necessary to visit the facility and staff. Second, because neither Smith nor Elliott spoke Chinese, Marjorie could act as a guide-interpreter for them while they acted as an escort for her. She was reluctant to leave Maude Pettis alone in the nursing office, since they had handled so many emergencies together in recent weeks, but Maude convinced her that she had a good grasp on things.[49]

It was a memorable trip. They left the Yali compound by rickshaw late at night on September 17, through the city to the river, arriving at the docks. There they found their boat, went aboard, and made ready for the night. In the darkness they could not tell much about their boat, but in the morning they found it was sort of a barge towed by a small steam launch. Both the launch and the barge were terribly crowded. When they boarded, the man in charge had to move about a dozen squatters who had taken over the space they reserved. They had expected to get a cabin for three but were put in a room with twelve bunks, and for two days and two nights they lived in uncomfortable proximity with nine other passengers who had paid the $9.00 Chinese fare, and also at least a dozen squatters on the floor. Less prosperous, the squatters had only passage tickets and were supposed to sleep on the roof, but it rained most of the two days and they all came down and crowded into the cabins. Aside from paid passengers and squatters, there was a third category of coinhabitants—the insects, bugs, cockroaches, and mosquitoes. They were there in droves, of all varieties, shapes, descriptions, sizes, and color. Elliott surmised their experience: "Poor Bob suffered terribly. They must have spotted him as the most tasty morsel in the place and attacked en masse for each morning he awoke with literally dozens of bites, his face all puffed out, his face swollen, great welts on his hands, and one eye completely closed. Marjorie was bothered a little but not very seriously; I had no trouble at all, felt not a single bite."[50] They were on the boat for two full days, from midnight Tuesday until about 6:00 p.m. Thursday. They passed the time by reading, playing cards, and observing their fellow passengers. Jim taught Marjorie and Bob how to play pinochle, and they had several interesting games. After dark they told stories to pass the time.

Fortunately, Marjorie brought a large basket of food with her that lasted them all day Wednesday and most of Thursday. As a result, they bought only one meal from the boat people. Jim was skeptical of the food. "After seeing them cook the rice in filthy, muddy river water, I had no great craving for their food, but Marjorie assured us the cooking would annihilate any disease germs lurking about. The natives, of course, thought us a great curiosity, and watched our eating, card playing, typing, indeed anything that we did—with avid interest. It's a toss-up who was most interested—we in them, or they in us."[51]

Their journey took the same path as the group that preceded them, with an overnight stop at the Presbyterian mission in Changteh, where they were met by Reverend Bannon, served an American meal, and given a bed for the night. Murial Boone, who ran a branch Presbyterian mission in Taoyuan, happened to be there and arranged a cabin and their passage on an otherwise crowded river launch that took them the remaining thirty to forty miles to Tauyuan. She hosted them overnight at her home in Taoyuan before they departed the next morning for another sampan trip on the Yuan River for about seventeen miles.

It was pouring rain. They crowded into the small center-covered section of the boat about 9:15 a.m., and despite the incessant rain, they had an enjoyable trip and were twice entertained by a pair of singers, one male and one female, whom Jim found to be "very interesting." They arrived at their destination before 2:00 p.m., thanks to a steady tailwind. Upon landing, the rain was still coming down, and they had misgivings as they saw their baggage being taken from the boat and placed in the slimy mud on the riverbank. Their coolie carriers would've left it out to soak in the rain while they were getting it ready, had they not insisted that they get it up the hill under some kind of shelter. Jim, Bob, and Marjorie pitched in and carried their baggage up to a sort of a shop-restaurant. There they rested for the three-mile walk ahead of them to the bus station. Bob and Jim had rubber boots, but Marjorie's white shoes were unprotected. She cast about in vain for a solution, partially remedied by purchasing a pair of straw sandals and fastening them on under her shoes. They strapped on their luggage as best they could and put some oilskin-wrapped pieces on top. Bob and Jim each donned a coolie straw hat, in an attempt to shelter themselves from the downpour. Elliott remembered, "All the pent up fury of heaven seemed to be unleashed during that 3-mile walk, and by the time we reached the inn at Ch'an Chia where the bus station is located, we were literally soaked to the skin."[52] It was a memorable bonding experience for the three of them. Upon arriving at the inn, they changed clothes, and Marjorie walked down to the station, about 100 yards distant, only to learn that their bus had departed at noon. There would be no bus until the following day, so they made themselves comfortable at the inn, which was actually a farmhouse with a tile roof and dirt floor, where pigs and chickens wandered at will from room to room. Marjorie was able to secure passage the next morning on an extra bus that had been placed in service.

Like all Chinese buses, it was small and tough, short on springs and upholstery, and long on passengers. The three of them were jammed into three rear seats that were, in Jim's opinion, "the smallest on the bus." He was so cramped that he could not stand it for more than fifteen minutes at a time; he had to get up and half stand, then half sit, just to restore blood circulation to his aching limbs. The rear part of that Chinese bus took up about a quarter of the total floor space, was partitioned off, and was reserved for baggage. Their seats were smack up against the partitions, so they had no room to stretch out. They were packed in so tight, they found themselves holding a neighbor's pig one minute and were requested to dangle a baby at the window for bathroom purposes the next.[53] They made good time, covering the final eighty-five miles or so in about four and a half hours, arriving across the river from Yuanling on September 21, fifteen days after the other Bachelors departed Changsha.

About 100 yards after leaving the final bus, they were met by Dwight Rugh, Bob Clarke, and Paul Springer. They helped the new arrivals get their baggage down to the river, where Dwight had a sampan waiting to ferry them across the water and thence to Yuanling's main street, past the West Gate, and finally to the evangelical mission compound upon which the Yali campus was situated. It had taken Jim Elliott two and a half months to reach his final destination.[54] Ravaged by malaria in Changsha, he continued to take quinine treatments for another five and a half weeks after arriving in Yuanling. Tired as he was, his spirits were high. The 120 steps from the street up to the Bachelors' quarters did not faze him in the least. It did not seem like much of a worry after the 12,000-mile journey that he had just completed. He had been looking forward to this day for a year and a half, since he first signed up for the program in 1940. He was a Yali Bachelor at last!

The five Bachelors were grateful to have a radio in their quarters from which they could get news from Manila, Hong Kong, Shanghai, and San Francisco. They heard a static-laden rebroadcast of President Roosevelt's speech on the war on Japanese subs in American waters and awaited a live news broadcast in the evening, which came with a clearer transmission. Mail would come in and out by clipper plane, with as much as a month between arrivals. Paul sent his birthday wishes to his sister Eleanore by letter, along with a little ivory brooch for her that Bob Smith would take with him on his next trip to the US. Bob was planning to leave in early December, so that he could be home in time for Christmas. Unfortunately, the brooch was lost with the rest of Bob's "treasures" that he was bringing in from China during his trip home.[55] They were all packed in a camphor wood chest that he brought for his wife. The chest got as far as Manila with Bob but for some reason was not put on board the ship he caught home to the US mainland. It was just one more small casualty of the war.

Paul Springer, Don McCabe, and Jim Elliott (*in coolie straw hat*), Yuanling, 1941. *Springer Family collection*

Chapter 5
THE WAR DRAWS CLOSER

The Japanese had been pushing a great military offensive toward Changsha in the fall of 1941, with large-scale troop movements and dive-bomb attacks on the North Gate section near the Yali campus. Jim Elliott and Bob Smith were still in Changsha after Springer, Hopkins, and Fulton left for Yuanling. Elliott's bout with malaria had worsened, and a rest and continued quinine treatment at Hsiang-Ya Hospital were needed for his recovery. Smith took some time to survey the damage to the Yali campus at Changsha and assess the operating status of the hospital. He also attended a meeting of the Changsha International Relief Committee, at the Presbyterian compound. Unknown to them at the time, this delay of several days put Smith, Elliott, and Marjorie Tooker at great risk, and they got out of Changsha just in time for the last leg of their journey.

The invasion was carried out by more than 120,000 Japanese troops, which included the support of naval and air forces. The Japanese entered Changsha on September 27, 1941, when they reached the North Gate of the city. This was a major military offensive to capture the city, since it was a strategic point on the Hankow-Canton Railroad. The objective was to capture Changsha, thereby cutting China in two. The Battle of Changsha was Japan's second attempt at taking the city, the capital of Hunan Province.[1] The Chinese defensive forces conducted a massive response to repel the Japanese and prevent the burning of the city. This resulted in heavy street fighting. The Chinese troops had been ordered to resist the Japs to the last man. The fate of the entire city hung in the balance. This struggle for control of Changsha became one of the most decisive battles of this stage of the war. The fighting began outside the city's Northeast Gate, before Japanese troops began spilling into the streets of the city.[2]

As Brank Fulton returned to Changsha on his way out of China, he found himself caught in the maelstrom of the war. *Yale-China Association Records, RU 232, Manuscripts and Archives, Yale University Library*

Eyewitness to Bombing

Brank Fulton's return through the area was an eye-opening experience to the ev-er-present dangers of the war. About ten days after Smith, Elliott, and Marjorie Tooker left Changsha, Fulton headed in the opposite direction, traveling from Yuanling through Changsha and Shiukwan to Hong Kong, where he ran head on into the maelstrom of the war. From Yuanling, Fulton traveled through Taoyuan, where he stopped at the home of Muriel Boone.[3] Quite by chance, Fulton met up with Elliott, Smith, and Tooker, who were overnighting there before the last leg of their journey to Yuanling. Fulton reported to his friends that Springer and Hopkins and all of their baggage had arrived at Yali intact. It was welcome news and a great relief to the weary travelers, who had seen evidence of heavy bombing en route to Taoyuan. Muriel Boone shared with the group that one bomb had hit practically in her front yard when the area was being attacked by air. She crouched behind her front gate during an air attack when a bomb whistled through the air and hit the ground directly in front of her compound, much too close for comfort. The impact was so close, in fact, that the concussion from the explosion blew the gate off its hinges and knocked her over backward. The gate somehow protected her, and she emerged from the explosion stunned but unharmed. She showed them the hole in the yard shortly after her guests arrived. In response to this terrifying incident, Murial constructed a makeshift bomb shelter in her backyard, mostly of heavy bamboo. It looked like a pint-size Indian tepee but was much sturdier. Fulton and the others shared their experiences over supper at Miss Boone's home, and all spent the night before departing their separate ways in the morning.

Fulton was on his way out of Taoyuan in the last week of September when he found himself in the midst of a Japanese bombing raid. Fortunately, he lived to tell about it. His graphic account of the savage bombing was published by the *South China Morning Post* in Hong Kong two months later: "We passed a minefield several miles below Changsha, on the Hsiang River, between three and four a.m., on the morning of September 25 on the way back from Yuanling. The military launch was the first through, then the nine junks that it was towing—each full of freshly collected rice from Hunan's bumper crop were collected at a time through the danger zone; and afterwards we reassembled and pushed up to Changsha, arriving just as the eastern sky began to lighten up."[4] It was about 6:00 a.m. when Fulton reached the Yale-in-China campus in Changsha, and a half hour later the bombers came, six in a straight line—with no warning save the sound of the motors; the air raid alarm in the northern part of the city was not activated, with the man on duty possibly asleep or away. The bombers circled to get their bearings, and one after the other went into power dives, with engines roaring in a terrifying manner. That day was perhaps the heaviest Japanese air attack the city ever received.

Fulton was confident the Japs would leave the Yali campus alone because it was American property. He stood out on the lawn during the raid, watching and taking pictures. It was an unjustified confidence, since he was to learn a few hours later that the same planes bombed the Standard Oil and Asiatic Petroleum installations; both

Dr. Win Pettus (*center*) with surgical staff, Hsiang-Ya Hospital, Changsha. *Yale-China Association Records, RU 232, Manuscripts and Archives, Yale University Library*

were far out of the city and were clearly marked as American and British properties. When the first raid was over, he went out on a bike to see what places had been hit, guided by a huge column of smoke coming from the site of the Ming Teh Middle School. The school's fine new buildings, erected just before the war, were in a mass of flames after the bombers made their mark.

Japanese spies undoubtedly had done their filthy work, since the school buildings had been recently used as a military headquarters, housing over a hundred soldiers and a large quantity of rice. Other places nearby were also destroyed, but Ming Teh had been the primary target in that area. After helping to put the wounded in transit bound for the Hsiang-Ya (Hunan-Yale) hospital, Fulton hurried up to the hospital campus to see what he could do to help.

Hsiang-Ya Hospital under Siege

When Fulton arrived on the hospital grounds, he found Dr. Win Pettus, the senior American Yale Mission representative in Changsha, outside and chronicled his observations as follows:

> Win's attitude throughout the whole episode was just what anyone who knew him would have expected—a combination of almost boyish interest in the new experience, apparent absence of personal fear, and a sense of family and community and professional responsibility. Having made his wife and child [a] guest and other household members as safe as possible in the compound air-shelter, he himself stood outside during the first attack taking pictures—only ducking inside the shelter when one plane seemed to be diving directly at him. And then, as soon as this first raid was over, he headed for the hospital to assist Dr. Y. T. Hsiao and others to take care of the victims that were brought in throughout the day. As a lay assistant, I watched him perform thirteen operations before three o'clock, when we all insisted on his stopping long enough to get a bite to eat and take a short rest.
>
> There was a calm efficiency about the whole performance that made a lasting impression on all who were present. Once, during one of the repeated attacks, a bomb landed so close that the whole hospital seemed to shake with the explosion, and the sound seemed to come from the direction of the Pettus home. However, as he was right in the midst of a very delicate operation involving the removal of a shell fragment from a raid victim's head, the young doctor just paused long enough to catch my eye and say quietly, "Will you please go and see if that hit my house?" and then he carried on with his job.[5]

The bomb that Pettus asked about missed his house, but the "shell went through an unimportant building on the Yali campus, injuring two people." Their hospital messenger was shot trying to get a cable through to America—three bullets through his chest. He reached the China Inland Mission Hospital just as he collapsed. Pettus later reported, "Now he is OK."[6] Fulton found that Dr. Pettus had a rare combination of persuasiveness and drive for which he was already well known. On the day of the Changsha bombing, Fulton assisted Dr. Pettus by bathing patients prior to surgery. After about ten seconds of humorous but persuasive argument, Pettus convinced Fulton to donate some of his blood—just the amount of blood (of the correct type) that he needed for one of the patients. Fulton went from washing patients to donating

Surgery in Hsiang-Ya Hospital, taken from balcony overlooking operating room. *Yale-China Association Records, RU 232, Manuscripts and Archives, Yale University Library*

blood within minutes. The bombers revisited the area several times as Fulton and Pettus worked through the rest of the day and into the night to repair the human carnage from the Japanese attack.

The bombing raid had all been rather exciting to Fulton, until the sight of horribly torn and twisted bodies brought home to him the stark tragedy of the whole beastly mess. A leg blown off, a foot in shreds, great gaping shrapnel wounds, intestines bursting out—injuries indiscriminately suffered by men, women, and little children. Fulton wrote, "I'll never forget the expression of terror and unspeakable grief on the face of one man who brought in his little four or five year old boy, covered with wounds. The mother (pregnant) had picked up the little chap from his bed at the sound of the planes and ran into the street, only to meet sudden death, together with a young nephew. If they had stayed in the house, all would have been well. But who can tell where the infernal things will hit? And then, either as a bitter joke, or more likely as an indication of the utterly abnormal functioning of the Japanese military mind, the planes having first dropped their deadly bombs then showered the city with pamphlets urging friendship between the Japanese and Chinese people and opposition to the bloodthirsty policies of Chiang Kai-shek, Churchill and Roosevelt."[7]

Hell Unleashed on Shiukwan

But if Changsha on September 25 was a kind of purgatory, Shiukwan on the twenty-eighth became hell itself. There had been no serious bombings in Shiukwan since January. Although there was an alarm on Saturday, no planes appeared, so people were not expecting anything serious to happen. Fulton spent Saturday night with some American friends in their house, located on the top of a hill across the river from the main part of the city. This place was regarded as so safe that the people living there and in the adjoining mission houses had not bothered to prepare more than a couple of small trenches in their front yards as a makeshift bomb shelter.

The Japanese planes started coming a little before seven on Sunday morning, the first batch of the sixty-eight that visited the city on that fateful day. It was obvious from the first that they were chiefly targeting the railroad station near the bottom of the hill, still far enough away that one thought it hardly necessary to get into the trenches. Fulton sat under a clump of trees and watched the repeated dives, the flash of sunlight on the descending bombs, and the ensuing geysers of smoke and dirt. The diving continued until the antiaircraft gunners persuaded the pilots to keep safer altitudes—safer, that is, for the Japs, but not for the Americans and Chinese on the ground. About 2:30 p.m., they suddenly saw high above a group of twenty-seven planes in regular formation flying in a path that would take them directly over the hill where they were watching the action. Fulton shouted for everybody to crouch down; a few people were looking up at the skies from outside the trenches and quickly changed posture to hugging the ground closely, where they waited breathlessly. Fulton recalled that a little Chinese boy next to him said, just as the planes were immediately overhead, "Well, if they drop any bombs now they won't hit us; we're safe." He scarcely had time to reply, "Yes, if they haven't dropped them already," when he heard the terrifying whistle of a bomb falling, seemingly right on top of them. In the next moment there was a terrific rush of air and a deafening explosion, followed by a wave of dirt and metal. Fortunately, the debris dispersed over their heads, accompanied by a strong smell of gunpowder. Then another and another and another bomb hit, each a little farther away, each still uncomfortably near.

When they picked themselves up, they discovered a great crater directly between them and the house—just twenty-three paces from where they had been lying. The doors and windows of the nearest house, in which most of them had been, were all blown in, and the floors were covered with broken glass. Then Fulton began to find the broken bodies. Some were still alive, and almost all of them were badly wounded. Others were beyond further suffering. A seven-year-old Chinese boy, adopted by an American lady who lived just below his friend's apartment, would no longer be able to play with his slingshot that was still clutched tightly in his cold little hand. Farther away, in a field, a crater was surrounded on four sides by the horribly mangled bodies of two men, a woman, and a little child whose bloody innards were strewn all over the ground. Nearby were the remains of another woman who had literally been blown into the embankment near which she had been crouching for protection. Her two little boys were crying bitterly, and the father was holding a badly wounded baby. Fulton learned later that the infant's arm had to be amputated at the mission hospital, where the doctors operated far into the night.

Refugees Seek Shelter

The bombings in and around the Yali campus in Changsha, Shiukwan, and the surrounding cities were a stark reminder of the "New Order in East Asia" that the Japanese attempted to impose on their neighbors. By September 26, 80 percent of the doctors and nurses at the hospital had left for the South, rather than expose themselves to a Japanese invasion. They had only two doctors and three nurses left, and a dentist and a bacteriologist offered to help. An operating-room coolie gave anesthesia and delivered a baby. A nearby woman missionary found a job for herself washing blood and dirt off patients waiting for operations. Fulton washed several patients and

Hsiang-Ya Hospital. View from rear, ca. 1940s. *Courtesy of David Elder*

donated blood again before he departed. The Changsha International Relief Committee arranged for three refugee camps to be opened if the fighting entered the city. One camp was to be located on now-deserted Yali Senior School campus. The missionaries were looking over the buildings late in the afternoon, planning where they might put the refugees when the gateman came rushing into the compound with the news: "The Japanese are here!"

Petrified men, women, and children came running from all directions. Forming a mob, they tried to jam their way into the hospital. They had seen the soldiers and were rushing for the only safe place they knew—American property. They were ushered across the street to the abandoned senior school just before the next small group of Japanese soldiers arrived. Later, additional soldiers marched by in full force, with long lines of infantry, artillery, and cavalry. Whenever the wave of soldiers stopped coming for a short time, a group of refugees, arms loaded with baskets, bedding, and babies, ran up to the mission gate and passed through into the school. By dark, over 8,000 homeless and desperate civilians had entered. The foreigners who reminded the Japanese that they were on American property were treated roughly, after which the Japanese soldiers left the way they had come. The news of the establishment of a refugee camp on the abandoned Yali campus in Changsha spread over the countryside like wildfire. Men, women, and children, as well as pigs, chickens, and cows, swarmed to the gates. Many women, afraid of being molested and raped if captured, had blackened their faces and rubbed manure on their clothes to make themselves disgustingly revolting. Dr. Pettus described the melee: "By the third day there were 8,000 refugees in the camp. Every inch of floor space in all the buildings was occupied; many of the doorways were blocked by people lying on the floor. Every tree sheltered a group. One little dugout scooped out of a bank the size of the space under my dining room table was occupied by a woman and her three children. The kitchens worked all day long to supply each refugee one bowl of rice, usually served in the recipient's lap and eaten with the fingers. We were forced to close the gates first to men, allowing women and children in, later to all new-comers. A large crowd camped outside the gate begging to be let in. Several Japanese soldiers passed by and searched their belongings for money and other lootable objects. A number of men were beaten over the head with rifle butts. Some were commandeered to carry loot for the soldiers. Of these, a few never returned and were never seen again by their families."[8]

Looting in Changsha

During a lull in the fighting, Pettus and two other mission representatives hunted up the Japanese army headquarters and called on the general in charge to arrange for the protection of foreign mission property.[9] The general agreed to send inspectors around to the various mission compounds to ascertain that they contained no soldiers or military supplies. If none were found, he would issue a notice forbidding the Japanese troops from entering the property. Foreign property would be respected, he promised.

When Pettus returned to the hospital, he was informed that a hospital cart carrying 500 pounds of rice had been commandeered along with four of their men who were pulling it. The missionary escorting the cart had been threatened with violence if he attempted to follow the soldiers who made off with it. However, one of the cart pullers escaped, returned, and told Pettus where they had gone. Pettus tracked them down and found the officer in charge. He described the exchange with the officer and the aftermath of their encounter:

> When we pointed out that he was violating American property, he offered to pay something for the rice but our provisions were not for sale. After two hours of arguing in sign language and bad Chinese, I found an interpreter to write the following in Chinese characters which the officer could read: "Your commanding officer promised me this morning that American property would be respected. If you refused to return the rice I shall have to take the matter up with him." The officer's next move was typically Japanese. He opened one of the bags, examined the rice, made some disparaging remarks about it, asked if all the rest were of the same poor quality and told us to take it away—the rice was too poor for the Japanese army. All faces were saved and everyone was happy. What was more important, we had established a precedent against the looting of American property.
>
> That night at two o'clock we were awakened by the roar of a cannon followed by machine gunning and rifle shots. I went out to the gate-house to see where the fighting was. Just then, the shooting started a few yards away. The guerillas (*sic*) were attacking right on our street, hardly a quarter-mile from Japanese headquarters. Shortly before dawn the firing ceased and the next day no Chinese soldiers were to be seen. The same thing happened every night for three nights.
>
> The looting of the city was now in full swing. Every shop, even the ones whose entrances had been bricked up, were broken into. Japanese soldiers wandered in groups of two or three from house to house, and street to street looking first for money, then for small valuable articles. Objects too big to

Japanese military officers direct the systematic looting of property in Changsha, September 1941. *Yale-China Association Records, RU 232, Manuscripts and Archives, Yale University Library*

Japanese machine gun unit on a pill box at the North Station, Changsha. Photo by Dr. Win Pettus on September 28, 1941. *Yale-China Association Records, RU 232, Manuscripts and Archives, Yale University Library*

carry were generally smashed. One old man had a bayonet wound through his head because the five soldiers who searched his house were angered by finding nothing worth taking. About half of the men gave similar histories. One was forced to carry a load for the soldiers; when his strength gave out they left him with three bayonet wounds—one through the chest resulted in pneumonia; one through the spine left him paralyzed on one side of his body; another gave him a deep abscess of the flank. Another man arrived holding his head with his hands because all the muscles in the back of his neck had been severed by an attempted decapitation with an officer's heavy sword. Six or seven others reached the hospital in the same condition.[10]

Hunan Province on Edge

To those in Yuanling, they could only wait through the unknown events for the fate of the city to swing one way or another. Although Yuanling was also in Hunan Province, it was a safe distance (about 200 miles) from the Yali campus at Changsha. Upon learning of the news of the battle, Springer made the observation that "even if Changsha fell, a Chinese counter offensive would make it difficult for the Japs to hold their positions for long."[11] In Changsha, Pettus took a walk about 300 yards from Hsiang-Ya Hospital. He came across a machine gun nest manned by group of Japanese soldiers. At first, he was afraid they would confiscate his camera. Instead, they were pleased to be photographed and proudly posed for him. Three days later they were driven out by the Chinese.

A report reached Yuanling on October 1, 1941, indicating that the Chinese army, some 300,000 strong, had dispatched troops to cut off the Japanese forces, thus preventing them from getting reinforcements and supplies. The Japanese army, now running low on ammunition and food, began to withdraw from Changsha. In the Chinching area, northeast of Changsha, Japanese casualties were particularly severe, since their line of retreat had been blocked.[12] Japanese columns fleeing northward were being cut up and subjected to annihilating attacks. Dispatches from the front placed the Japanese casualties on the north Hunan front at 79,500 men, of which 33,600 were killed according to the Chungking *Ta Kung Pao*. When the Chinese reoccupied the city, it was noted that the main body of Japanese troops had left with all the rice they could carry. Afterward, the Chinese troops declined to chase the bulk of the retreating invaders.[13]

The Chinese army expelled any foreigners who had been sympathetic to the enemy, some of whom were waiving Japanese flags, including a group of German and Italian citizens. Miraculously, the former Yali campus was largely undamaged by bombs during the brief occupation. A shell had struck the servants' quarters in the back of the Bachelor house, wounding one of the servants. Luckily, it was a spent shell. There were about 8,000 refugees on the former Yali campus at Changsha following the battle, many needing medical treatment.

Dr. Pettus showed some of the records of Hsiang-Ya Hospital to the United Press correspondents. Prior to the entry of the Japanese soldiers, the surgical cases were mostly from bomb wounds and amputations. After the occupation, the cases were primarily bayonet wounds, sword slashes, attempted decapitations, severed arms, and cases of rape. His account of the occupation was repeated without his consent over the Shanghai radio, and his name was used, giving Pettus a reason to evacuate if the enemy returned, since his name might be remembered for reprisal. One missionary said he saw six Chinese soldiers, with their hands tied behind their backs, shot in the back of their heads. Dr. Pettus and his wife, Maude, averaged six major operations and 150 minor treatments daily during the occupation. The missionaries became responsible for feeding the thousands of civilian refugees who sheltered in the camp. The missionaries clashed with the Japanese when they draped American flags over the containers in which their rice was stored. The Japanese had backed down from seizing the rice but virtually denuded the countryside of other food supplies. Fulton noted that Chinese opposition to Japanese aggression was strong and the morale of the people was high. According to British, American, and Norwegian residents in Changsha, there was street fighting on the nights of September 29 and 30, after which the Japanese left Changsha as suddenly as they had come.[14] Early on the morning of October 2, the Chinese troops reoccupied the city. What a relief! The commitment of the Yale-in-China staff to their various missions was steely and absolute and would continue stronger than ever.

Chapter 6

BLACKBOARDS AND BOMB SHELTERS

Teaching in Wartime China

By September 24, with Jim among them once again, Paul, Don, Art, and Bob Clarke settled into their daily teaching routine on the Yali campus. The Yali campus was located on the north bank of the Yuan River, just downstream from where the Yuan and the Yu (North) Rivers come together.[1] The west end of the town was just a few paces east of the gatehouse for the Evangelical Mission of Yuanling.[2] This was known as the West Gate. The edge of the Yali campus was on the north side of the street and continued up the mountain. It was a good-sized compound, housing about 200 students in the senior school, twenty faculty members (some with large families), and some clerks.[3]

The junior school was not on the compound. It was 2½ miles away, on the bank of the Yu River, where there were about 250 boys in grades comparable to those in junior high schools in the US. The Bachelors hiked there to teach English classes five days a week, rain or shine. The path to the junior school was a scenic walk along the river, except for the part of the path that wound through a dirty little town, Peh Tien To, about two-thirds of the way to the school.[4] The "commuting" teachers were issued permits, in the form of armbands with Chinese characters written thereon, to move about the city and to and from the school during the *chin-pao*s and otherwise prohibited times. These were also issued to the students, the school's dean and its principal, and a few other staff members by the local magistrate. Jim Elliott wrote, "I've never had to use mine really (although I always carry it with me and wear it during *chin-pao*s), but some of the boys have been accosted by soldiers during *chin-pao*s and have been a bit inconvenienced by the fact that they left theirs home that day."[5]

The junior school boys (ages thirteen to fifteen) were equivalent to junior high school students in America. The school had a classification system for student grade levels, further identified by the semester in which they were being taught. For example,

Yuanling Air Defense Command, armband pass, 1942. Issued to Paul Springer for travel across the Yuanling campus during periods of air raid alarms. *Springer Family collection*

the term "1-1 class" referred to seventh grade—first semester. The "1-2 class" referred to seventh grade—second semester. Likewise, the "2-1 class" referred to eighth grade—first semester. The "3-1 class" referred to ninth grade—first semester. The senior school (ages sixteen to eighteen) classification continued in the same manner. The "4-1 and 4-2 classes" referred to tenth grade, first and second semesters; "5-1 and 5-2 classes" referred to eleventh grade, first and second semesters; and "6-1 and 6-2 classes" were the equivalent of high school seniors in America. These terms were used repeatedly in the writings of Paul, Art, Jim, and Bob Smith.

Each course was a one-semester affair with a final examination in January or June. Besides the final exam, each class had two monthly exams that counted heavily toward the final mark. The classes were divided evenly among the teachers, with one exception. Bob Clarke, already there two years and staying a third year at the request of the trustees, had the two ninth-grade middle-school graduating classes. Don McCabe had three classes: two seventh grade and one tenth grade. Art Hopkins taught the eighth-grade and eleventh-grade classes, Paul Springer also had an eighth-grade and an eleventh-grade class, and Jim Elliott had a ninth-grade and twelfth-grade class. Winifred Rugh, who studied at the Yale Music School and played both the piano and violin, helped with music instruction in the senior school and taught the tenth-grade second-semester class. Winifred's husband, Dwight, was in charge of religious education in the senior school. He was a graduate of the University of California and earned his PhD at Yale in 1936, when he was about forty. He was the acting representative of Yale-in-China.

Paul Springer, Art Hopkins, Don McCabe, Bob Clarke, and Jim Elliott, Yuanling, 1941.
Yale-China Association Records, RU 232, Manuscripts and Archives, Yale University Library

The daily teaching routine and the weekly schedules were highly structured for the teachers, keeping them busy seven days a week. The senior school was housed in a one-acre walled compound on a steep hillside, with a gatehouse on the lower side. The kitchen and dining room were adjacent. The building had six classrooms, each with simple furnishings for about twenty students, a small table for the teacher, and benches and writing surfaces (a makeshift desk) for the students. Classes were held at the junior school five days a week (Monday through Friday).[6] Paul, Bob, and Don taught 7:30 a.m. classes, so they were up around 6:15 and off on their 2½-mile trek by about 7:00. Their departure was the signal for Art and Jim to get up. They usually managed to shave and grab some breakfast before their 7:30 classes began at the senior school. Art and Jim were finished for the morning after their class was over at 8:30. Jim began practicing his violin during this downtime until about 9:15, when Paul and Bob returned from the junior school. Don arrived later because he taught two classes at 7:30 and 8:30. The four of them (Paul, Art, Jim, and Bob) were around for the next hour and spent time marking papers or doing odd jobs that did not require too much concentration. At 10:30, Bob and Don taught a class at the senior school. Since Paul usually helped, things were pretty quiet in the Bachelors' quarters during that hour. By 11:30, everyone had returned, and it wasn't too long before their cook appeared and said *"Ko I ch'k fan"* or "You can eat." The ensuing stampede to the dining room usually left one or two of the less nimble Bachelors trampled underfoot!

Afternoons

They were usually through with lunch by 12:15 p.m., if not before. One hour remained before Art and Jim took off for the junior school, and they spent that time preparing for the ninth-grade class, studying Chinese, and taking care of things that needed attention. By 1:15 p.m., Art and Jim were off, sometimes stopping by the dean's office for the English bulletin board to drop off copies of any newscast postings Art had made. They were usually at the junior school by 1:55 and ready for their two o'clock classes. The class was over at 2:50, and they stayed until 3:00 p.m. to answer questions and to visit with the boys. Each Monday, Wednesday, and Friday, they stopped off at Tao Shi Pin, the athletic field a quarter of a mile from the school on the way back to Yuanling, to help out with youth sports. Paul and Bob spent their afternoon teaching. Paul had a 1:00 class two days a week, while Bob had a special class every afternoon as well as conference reading, Chinese lessons, and letter writing.

After dinner came two crazy hours when the Bachelors' mess was no less than bedlam. There were always at least two Chinese lessons going on at this time, sometimes three. Somebody was usually pecking away on a typewriter while another was conducting a student conference. Students knew their teachers were likely to be in their quarters after dinner, so they had constant interruptions. Things quieted down after 9:00 p.m., when the students had to retire. The teachers often had a bridge game for about an hour, which was the most downtime they had all day. By 10:00 p.m., they started going to bed, with Paul almost always first and Art soon afterward, if not at the same time—with Bob being the real nighthawk of the bunch, staying up until all hours of the night.

The senior school had Saturday classes, so they did not have Saturdays free. Art and Jim were usually through by 8:30 a.m. The other three could sleep in, since they had no morning classes. Saturdays were also busy with Chinese lessons, but by 1:00 p.m., they were all free. They usually headed to the East Gate to play baseball, basketball, football, or volleyball. Afterward, they went to the YMCA for a shower or back to the East Gate or to wherever a dinner party was for that particular night. After dinner, they played cards or other party games. Sometimes they just sat around and talked. The five teachers became very close to each other in their new surroundings.

Sunday was observed by all the Christian schools in town. It was usually a quiet and restful day. However, Paul got up early, since his eleventh-grade English-speaking

Bob Clarke with student, Bachelor's Quarters, Yuanling. *Yale-China Association Records, RU 232, Manuscripts and Archives, Yale University Library*

club met at 7:00 a.m. The club met twice a week, the other meeting being at 6:00 p.m. each Wednesday. Because of this, Paul missed out on the Wednesday dinner conversation and the congenial banter. None of the other Bachelors had regular engagements on Sunday, except Don, who was usually visiting his girlfriends, picnicking with them, swimming, or whatever came up. The rest of the teachers spent their day reading, writing letters, or handing out stamps to the steady stream of boys who visited. Several of the Chinese boys became interested in stamp collecting. The teachers were happy to provide them with samples of the American postage affixed to their letters from home. Paul was disappointed that the only letter he had received during his first month was from George Small, now back at his post at the US embassy in Chungking.

Settling In

By November 1941, Art Hopkins recalled, "Things are coming along very well now, however, and the interest, attitude, and spirit of the students make the teaching a most pleasant and inspiring occupation. The matter of discipline, which is so often an irksome problem in American schools, is not a problem here, as the students are eager to learn. They are very proud and sensitive, and early in my teaching days I was considerably embarrassed when one of my 2-1 youngsters, after doing very poorly on the dictation, refused to hand in his paper, and calmly ate it right in front of my eyes."[7] The Bachelors found that the students had a keen sense of humor. The new teachers were often tempted to believe that Art was quite a wit, since the students liked nothing better than a good joke. Some of their compositions were most humorous, but often that wasn't intentional on their part. A couple of prized sayings that appeared in Art's eleventh-grade classes were good examples: Reggie Chang wrote, "I am like flowers very much," and Noah Chin came through with this one: "Most students are stand in awe of their teacher," whereas Bruno Huang said, "Many students awe their teachers very much." Understandably, the students grew fond of their American teachers. Paul's nickname was "Mr. Big Nose" (in Chinese). The students probably did not think Paul understood his nickname, but he did![8] The teaching conditions during the war were anything but humorous. The staff at Yali tried to provide a nurturing environment for their students, but this grew increasingly difficult as the war with the Japanese became all consuming.

Daily *Chin-paos*

Paul described the academic environment in the context of the Japanese threat to his mother: "We are now in the midst of the fall air raid season and have alarms daily. The alarms mean simply that there are enemy planes in the province. There have been no bombs dropped since I've been here, and only an occasional scouting plane visible. Two days ago there was an alarm, and shortly thereafter fifteen planes flew over, throwing the town into a panic. It was learned later that they were Chinese (military) planes—the first I've ever heard of."[9] The urgent alarm, which sounded perhaps five minutes before the planes flew over the city, was a warning. "When the planes actually come over you are not allowed to move. So far I have missed two classes on account of *jin-bows* [*sic*] (as in *bow-wow*) and taught one class outdoors in front of the dugout."[10] These dugouts served as bomb shelters. Jim Elliott described them:

> Yali has its own dugouts—and very good ones too. They are hewn out of solid rock and are far below the surface of the hill. They would certainly stand anything—even a direct hit—that the Japanese have been using in the way of bombs. Of course, one of the super bombs of the European type might bring disaster, but far from the inferior Japanese missiles. I'm sure anyone protected by a Yali bomb shelter has nothing to fear. The only danger lies at the entrance of the dugouts. If a bomb should land right at the entrance, those nearby would certainly suffer. Those in the interior of the shelters would probably be all right and even though the entrance was blocked, they could get out by one of the other entrances. Both of Yali's two dugouts have three entrances. The Junior School dugout is a bit of a walk, perhaps a quarter of a mile away, perhaps even a third of a mile. At both the senior and Junior School school dugouts there is a crude thatched roof shelter, erected for the purpose of holding classes therein. It makes a picturesque site.[11]

At Yuanling, all of the Yali school classes were now being taught in front of dugouts. Yuanling was bombed frequently in 1938 and 1939, with the attacks often coming at midday, when the students were in class.[12] The current threat of a bombing was a real one. Blackboards were set up for the lessons, and the students sat on the ground in front of them. Although a workable arrangement, it was not as complete or thorough as needed for classroom work. To be an English teacher at the Yali Middle School was a rather rare position. The school was Chinese speaking, run by Chinese, staffed by Chinese, and attended exclusively by Chinese students. There was a faculty of forty-one, all but five of whom were Chinese. The five Bachelors taught English. Other courses in math, science, chemistry, and the study of Chinese texts were taught by Chinese staff, with English being taught as a second language.

The demand for English-speaking professionals was driven in large part because China had built up a westernized educational system of colleges, universities, medical schools, and engineering schools by the late 1930s.[13] These institutions had developed faster than its scholars had been able to produce textbooks in Chinese, resulting in the use of any available texts on the subject matter, most of which happened to be written in English. For these reasons, the English classes at Yali were at the forefront of an educational shift in China. Sports and physical fitness became part of their regular after-school routine. By 1942, Yali had the largest enrollment in its history, with a total of 482 students.[14] A typical English class consisted of fifteen to twenty students, an ideal size for the type of instruction, which involved a lot of student participation with a heavy emphasis on the mechanics and ease of a practical use of the language.[15] Speaking received as much emphasis as reading, writing, grammar,

Four groups of students at Yali Middle School, Yuanling. The steps on the hillside led to dugouts used as air raid shelters. *Yale-China Association Records, RU 232, Manuscripts and Archives, Yale University Library*

and spelling combined. The school's first overall goal was to enhance the ability to communicate in English. The three English classes each met five times a week, each explaining grammatical points in English and not relying on Chinese in any way in the classroom. This was not easy work for the students under any circumstance. It was difficult for first-year students after only one semester with an instructor to help dissolve their frustrations with the new language by answering questions in English, rather than in their native Chinese. The exposure of the students to the dangers and political aspects of the war was also fraught with tension. The students' ties to each other in the classroom and with their teachers became stronger with adversity, in the sense both of their social and academic standings.

To many students, the years in Yuanling were as much of an adventure as an academic challenge. They had enough to eat and a strong Christian community to care for them. This support was critical for their well-being, since they were cut off from their families, particularly after Changsha had initially fallen to the Japanese. Tragically, most had no idea where their parents were or what their fate may have been.[16]

Surprisingly, student life under wartime conditions was somewhat normal. The students loved sports, particularly volleyball, soccer, and basketball. Jim and Art stayed at the junior school in the afternoon, spending most of their time teaching the boys the intricacies of American touch football. The boys were extremely skillful at soccer and basketball. Despite their cloth shoes, they could run rings around any American boys they had seen play the game. Paul remarked that "my 5-2 class took the faculty (including me) over the hurdles in volleyball with ease the other day. Today there's to be a touch football game, but I shall be taking my 2-2 class for a swim. The boys are very courteous and respectful, and very desirous to learn. It is a great pleasure and satisfaction to teach them."[17] The swimming hole was in the Yuan River, which flowed past the playing field. In dry seasons it was beautifully clear. Although the current was sometimes swift, the bottom was shallow. On one occasion that fall, the Bachelors took as many as fifty boys swimming, to everyone's great delight.[18]

At one of his classes, Paul spoke to the students about his trip from New Jersey to China and about student life in America. The students were then asked to write a composition on "Our new teachers." Feeling like they knew Springer the best, several of the compositions described his teaching methods and descriptions as "He spoke funnily," "I think he is a humorous man," "He has a few mustaches in his face" (yes, he had grown one), "He is a tall, thin man," "He is a tall, strong man," "He is over six feet tall" (their American teachers were much taller, on average, than their Chinese counterparts), and "He talks in a light, clear voice." Paul felt that they said so many complimentary things, "which made my head a trifle too large for my hat. I hope their opinion of me won't sag too much—I always was one to make better first impressions than I deserved."[19]

The Bachelors found the fall weather to be pleasant. It was usually misty and cool early in the morning. The fog rolled back like a scroll about 8:00 a.m., followed by a beautiful, warm day. The hilltop quarters offered a great view of the surrounding mountains. They slowly became used to the lack of plumbing in the old oaken bucket as a lavatory. Jim wrote, "While I agree wholeheartedly and can't deny that the sound of a flush toilet would come like music to my ears, one gets along somehow."[20] The combined office, library, and living room resembled a struggling, but bustling, small-town newspaper editorial office. Their busy evenings had an oriental touch when two of them were taking their daily Chinese lessons, two others were going over papers, and the other one was trying to crawl out of the room without knocking over two people at the same time. It was all part of the game, and certainly no one ever got lonely for company—except for female company.

This change in lifestyle gave them some pause for reflection. "I personally get a great kick out of living like this. Things I cherished and thought quite essential in America have faded into strange unimportance out here," wrote Jim Elliott. "At home, one movie a week was considered a minimum for a sane, happy existence. Out here I shall perhaps see one a year—when I get to some metropolis like Kunming or Chungking—but strangely, I do not miss the flicks. I've always preferred a good book to a good movie, but in the States many factors contributed to my neglecting my reading and concentrating on the movies. Here, there is not that temptation and one looks forward with eager anticipation to a few hours of leisure in which to dig into a good book. Not since the carefree days of my early years have I done so much reading since I left last July." There were very few radios in town, one of which was next door in the Rughs' apartment. Radios were essential to keep abreast of news from America, although there was little of interest that fall. They were a luxury in Yuanling, and few and far between. Jim commented, "Only the filthy rich foreigners and the most wealthy of the Chinese have them."[21] This was during the period when avid radio fans delighted in various kinds of programs—including soap operas such as *Ma Perkins*, *Little Orphan Annie*, and the like. The broadcast of jazz and classical music were Jim's favorites. "Here, oddly enough, I don't seem to miss them," he wrote. The other obvious difference in Yuanling was an absence of cars. The Bachelors had not seen any kind of motor vehicle since they got off the rickety, old, truck-like bus that brought them part of the way to Yuanling. Although there were numerous cars and trucks on the Burma Road and in cities such as Kunming, Kweilin, and

Chungking, they noticed a strange absence of vehicles in the interior of China. "When we want to go somewhere we walk—there are not even rickshas [*sic*] in Yuanling . . . so we walk. We have our daily five-mile round trip to the Junior School and, in addition, our twice or thrice weekly jaunt to the East Gate—well over a mile each way. And, strange as it may seem, we don't mind it at all," wrote Jim.[22]

Even with the superb culinary skills of their own dedicated cook, Tou Shi-fu, one thing that the new American teachers missed was milk and dairy products. These foods were conspicuously absent from the Chinese diet.[23] There was a seemingly universal Chinese dislike of cheese. Although the shortage of dairy products in Chinese cooking may have been due to the lack of refrigeration, it was thought that many Chinese had difficulty with the digestion of milk. All the Bachelors took quickly to Chinese food, although it was served to them only once a day, at noon.[24] Tou Shi-fu prepared American meals for the Rugh family and the group of five American teachers both at breakfast and dinner. Although their cook was diligent in the food's preparation, another widespread dining problem in Yuanling and other parts of China was due in large part to China's unique system of fertilization, often called "night soil."

"Night soil" was a contemporaneous term for human excrement collected from cesspools, septic tanks, pit latrines, and buckets for use as a fertilizer. It was removed from the collection point, usually at night, by coolies employed to collect and transport it for use in farms and gardens. Because the night soil was usually untreated, pathogens could easily be transferred both to humans and food, creating an invisible and unhealthy sanitation problem. Jim Elliott described their paranoia: "Never, to our knowledge, do we drink one drop of unboiled water, never do we eat fresh vegetables that have not been cooked (and when traveling, we insist on them being served piping hot), never do we eat fresh fruit without first peeling off the skin. All live in fear of the dread dysentery which seems always sooner or later—to catch up with all foreigners living in China. All this is due mostly to China's unique system of fertilization, too well known to be more than mentioned here."[25] Despite these hardships, the Bachelors, especially Jim, found this simple life in Yuanling to be uniquely different but quite enjoyable.

Off-Key

There were about forty Americans in Yuanling. Most of them were connected with the reformed church and the Catholic Church. Paul described them as "a pretty nice bunch." One night after supper, they decided to have a party of sorts—another sing fest. The other Bachelors, having built him up as a singer, prodded Springer into a solo on "Swing Low, Sweet Chariot." He complied but in a quavering voice, off-key, and on the wrong notes. There was a dead silence when he finished, and he tiptoed shamefully away, thinking for a moment that his glory days of the Yale Glee Club may have been left back home. Paul's days were busy teaching classes and studying Chinese, interspersed with visits from students and stamp collectors, along with sports activities and the supervision of various clubs. He liked the work and felt like he was born to be a teacher. As he wrote to friends back home, "We are respected and revered by our students, who bow when we approach, and who besiege us with requests to participate in their sports and who, best of all, are really desirous of learning English."[26]

Wartime Essays

Being an English major at Yale, Springer endeavored to teach his young students the importance of composition. Less than a month into his tenure at Yali, he asked the boys to write about their recent experiences. The following two student essays, discovered over seven decades later among his personal papers, deliver a powerful message about the two students' day-to-day life in war-torn China. These are reproduced verbatim, as they were found, with the spelling errors detracting little from the emotional message of their compositions.

TWO ESSAYS WRITTEN BY CHINESE STUDENTS AT YALE-IN-CHINA

6th Oct. 1941 Bruno Huang Sin Fang

My Boyhoods's Friend

Five years ago I was studying in primary school. I had a good friend who sat beside me, had the same age as I. He was a wise and saucy boy, always tricked of the boys but his losson was very good he often get high marks. So their classmates called him the Litter Monkey. Since the war began, I have come Hunan and we separated. Never knew where he was.

Last winter when I was walking on the street, suddenly a stranger cried out my name, his body was tall and strong and dressed on military clothes. I was perplexed for a moment at last I remember that he was my old friend Litter Monkey. I holed his hands, cried with joy and asked "How you come here." He answered calmly and sadly that his home had been burned by Japanese soldiers. Father and mother had both been killed and he had captured like an animal. One night he has struggled away from the ties and fled in Chinese fortifications. No longer he had joined in army and he had transposed here was the army. When he finished his talk he wept out. I comported him. At last he said "Tomorrow I'll leave here to resist Japanese. I hope I'll see you again. Good bye."

This summer I received a letter from one of this company. It said that he had been captured by Japanese. For his disobey he had been killed cruelly. My heart almost broke while I got this bad message. I railed Japan. I respected his loyalty. Now I help the God will bless him in heaven.[27]

5th Oct. 1941 Morris Leo

A Splendid Sight

In the 23th early morning, We were driven to the dugout by the alarm, But not long we were released. As we just went back to our schoolrooms. Suddenly the Hong! Hong! Hong! sounds were sounding. Run! Run! We run as fast as our legs would take us. When we reached the dugout just in time the planes were hovering above our heads. You may imagine how terrible we were. But only for a while our terrors and urgencies disappeared.

We were told that they were Chinese plans. [*sic*] CHINESE PLANS!! OH! What the attractive words they should be. We were all attracted rushing out of the dugout and looking at them with a happy stair. Being taken by happyness and comfort we looked at each other with a joyful smile. The feeling in our hearts wer not easily described, and I can hardly mention them out with my pen also. They were quite splendid suiting our eyes greatly. Gladness courage filled among our talkings.

I know, as everybody knew that the bombing is a very crule action. But when we use it in a right way (to bomb the man who breaks the law of the world) I think it will not be crule. Perhaps someone would agree with that for that sort of bombing was just an instruction teaching the Japanese. "We are not unable to bomb you, but only for the conscience of all human beings and the law of the world." –END[28]

Springer wrote his friend and faculty advisor, Stuart H. Clement, at Yale about his experiences thus far in China: "The journey out here was thrilling, and the time (since Sept. 11) has been packed with school work and reading of the greatest interest. I am convinced that the two years of my life spent here will be most profitable. I do not regret having missed the glee club trip to South America in order that I might receive this job. I am indebted to you for your guidance and cooperation. Here I feel far removed from the cares of the western world. The Yali English department is doing a significant thing here at Yuanling, and I feel that I am helping. How much more useful we can be here to humanity than we could possibly be serving our terms in the draft!

The physical development may not be as great, but certainly the mental and spiritual development is far greater. Our students are devoted to their learning and many of them seem to realize their importance to China in her hour of need."[29]

The American teachers were also learning, since their study of Chinese was improving with each passing day. Jim remarked that he got a big kick out of studying this fascinating old language. "That's the only word to describe it—fascinating," wrote Jim.[30] "It never fails to intrigue the serious tourists, journalists, and adventurer. All books on China at least mention it; almost all praise it, perhaps not unreservedly, but praise it nevertheless. The characters are so wonderfully interesting that I'm learning to write them as well as read and speak them. That makes my task doubly hard but it's worth the effort to me." Each of the three Bachelors spent about two hours a day in this way, and their study was followed by an hour with their teacher. Their *hsien sheng* (teacher) was a 6-1 student, very intelligent, and well read, with impeccable manners. Jim noted that he came from an excellent family. Little by little, the three new American teachers learned to say the simple things, to the point that they could get along quite well with the servants and the shopkeepers. By late October, Paul in particular could say almost everything that was necessary for day-to-day life and had even learned to write a few sentences. However, it would be a long time before they would be anywhere near fluent in the tongue, and they were careful not to get any false hopes up about being able to carry on a conversation in the rapid-fire Chinese language.[31]

Living in rural China took a toll on the health of three of the teachers. Art had a bad cold for some time, and trouble with a tooth from which he had lost the filling. He had also grown a mustache, which did not live up to his expectations. Jim had recurring attacks of illness, lasting about a day or two, ever since his bout with malaria in Changsha. Don McCabe suffered with an unknown ailment that he thought was trachoma (a bacterial infection affecting the eyes, most common in areas associated with poverty and a lack of proper hygiene). He also had a rather bad ankle sprain from playing basketball. Fortunately, Paul and Bob Clarke remained in tip-top shape. They found it to be great hiking weather and planned to go camping on a free weekend.

Chinese Names

Living in China was nothing short of a culture shock for the Bachelors. Among the peculiarities they learned before they arrived was the importance of Chinese names. One of the first Chinese they met on board SS *President Harrison* was Mark Shouming Wu, a thirty-four-year-old man who had studied agriculture for the past two years at Cornell.[32] He was familiar with Yali and knew some of the people there, and they

Bob Clarke at his desk, Bachelor's Quarters, Yuanling. *Yale-China Association Records, RU 232, Manuscripts and Archives, Yale University Library*

soon struck up a friendship with him. Wu took it upon himself to endow the new Yali men (Bob, Art, Paul, and Jim) with Chinese names, since the Chinese make much more of their names than most other cultures. The first name (read backward) is always the family name, which every Chinese bears; the second and third names are the given name. Bob Smith was Shih Ming Teh (Brilliant Virtue), Art was Ho Yu Teh (Friendly Virtue), Paul was Hsai Pau Teh (Preserver of Virtue), and Jim was An Li Teh (Upholder or Champion of Virtue). The *teh* ("virtue"), common to all their names, made them brothers in a sense.[33] While on board *President Harrison*, the Chinese on board looked upon these names with favor and gave them their stamp of approval. Bob Clarke and Don McCabe had already adopted their Chinese names in Yuanling. After a few months in close quarters, Springer offered several observations about his fellow Bachelors, complete with their adopted Chinese names.[34]

Bob Clarke (Co Hsien Sin) was by far Paul's favorite Bachelor. He was the only one of the group older than Paul (Bob was twenty-five at the time) and "had more brains, more common sense, and a better sense of humor than the others."[35] He had been in Yuanling for two years when Paul arrived, and was serving one final year at the request of the association. He was the head of the English Department. He was a thinker and a doer. He thought before he spoke, and he spoke slowly but ably and clearly. Bob sat back and sized everyone else up. He was well versed in English and in literature and fiction. He enjoyed life anywhere and got a big kick out of people in general and their idiosyncrasies. Paul felt like he and Bob understood each other pretty well. "Co" was tall and slightly stooped—he had been a wrestler in college, and a good one. He had dark hair and a smile that made one feel that he was laughing at him (this was unfortunate) and that he held others' views in contempt. Paul liked that smile, perhaps because he felt he understood it, while others found it annoying and often humiliating. The smile was unescapable: those who might not have noticed it were drawn to it by his habit of pulling his lower lip while he pondered over a question.[36]

The second in command in the Bachelor ranks was Don McCabe, whose name in Chinese (Ma) meant "horse." This name was a source of constant amusement to the student body, since "Ma" was small framed. He was the butt of the others' jokes, but he took it in good spirit. He had a way with women that made him feel unbeatable. After a year in Yuanling, Ma was showing signs of wear. He was fed up with some of his students and was annoyed with living in China in general. He was the ladies' man of the group and was out two or three nights a week visiting one of his two girlfriends (one Chinese and one American) at the other end of the town. He was a sentimentalist through and through and at his best when squiring a woman or two about. He showered his girlfriends with presents on their birthdays and on Christmas. He had five or six gifts for each on his last Christmas in China. He spoke with a series of set expressions thoroughly peppering his conversations, among them "I claim," "It's a killer," "Guess what," and "Oh, boy."[37] If you remarked that it was a cold day, his response would be "It ain't hot."[38] If you asked, "Was she pretty?" he'd answer, "She ain't ugly."[39] "Don was a very likable chap nonetheless, and if you showed respect for him and listen to his views (which you could always guess in advance) he was immediately your lifelong friend and the protector of your good name."[40] The Bachelors were blessed to call him one of their own.

Art Hopkins (Ho Yu Teh) was the dope of the bunch (at least in Paul's eyes) and was often the butt of their jokes. Paul described him as "a loveable dope" and added, "He seems to think, for example, that a Chinese person could understand his English if he talks slowly enough, even though the Chinese has no knowledge of English. You should hear him trying to make our cook understand something! Also he has a number of peculiar conceptions and queer expressions about which we are always kidding him. His English leaves much to be desired, and he unconsciously uses idioms in his classroom which completely mystify his pupils. His examinations were mostly laughable and had to be almost completely re-written."[41] "Ho" also had definite political views, which the other Bachelors suspected were stereotyped to agree with those of his family. He was an ardent "Willkieite" and would boost the name of Wendell Willkie (the defeated Republican candidate in the 1940 presidential election) and defame Franklin Roosevelt as soon as politics entered the conversation. He was a great admirer of the Chinese army and spoke incessantly of their great heroism and holding off the Japs for so long with a minimum of equipment. Otherwise, Art was good humored and could take frequent ribbings from the others—until it reached a certain point, at which his temper snapped![42]

Jim Elliott (An Li Teh) was a silent, sometimes sullen type, but he had a good brain. He was first and foremost an individualist. He had signed up to teach at Yale-in-China for his own self-improvement while helping others. He wanted to work with foreigners, Chinese boys and men, getting to know their points of view, their language, and their mores.[43] Paul later recalled, "He had a supreme confidence in his own judgment and was apt to regard as fools those who opposed him. Nor was his contempt veiled. He is also hard to please at the meal table. He made no attempt to get along with the rest of us, and if we took issue with him he would sometimes sulk for days. He was a poor sport . . . as we were made aware during the sea voyage to the Orient." At Yuanling he was disliked by the Chinese faculty, a dislike that became intensified after a "friendly" game of volley ball." Paul added, "An had many things to commend him, nonetheless." He was a student, a scholar, and a prolific writer. He studied hard and amassed a great deal of information. He was, however, rather a "collector of information," to use Co's (Bob's) designation, rather than an original thinker. "If left alone, I suppose he would have been quite endurable, but ours was a small community, and the demands on each individual in our close quarters were great," recalled Paul.

Paul Springer (Tse) rounded out the group. He had been branded as the house wit and tried hard to live up to his reputation. They often had a great deal of fun at the noon and evening meals with their banter. "Tse" tried to look at their cramped quarters objectively and got a laugh out of the idiosyncrasies of the individuals, which cropped up over and over again. Laughing was sometimes difficult, as he found himself squabbling over small matters, just like the rest of them. He was a nagger of note and often heckled Art or Don to the point where they became flushed with anger toward him. He played the best game of bridge by far and often became annoyed with his partner's playing (usually Jim). At one point, Paul refused to play anymore and had to be coaxed back into the game by Bob, who pointed out that because he was angry with one player he shouldn't deprive the other two of the pleasure of playing.[44] He admired Bob and enjoyed talking with him, though he sometimes felt incompetent when it came to carrying on a discussion. Paul would invariably make some statement that Bob easily refuted—then asked him to support it with facts—facts that Paul did not have. Paul became good friends with Don, and they used to take walks together and discuss their love affairs, and what they would do when they got back to the States.[45] According to Jim, "Paul is the efficiency expert: he goes around turning off lights and closing doors all the time."[46] Paul was tapped to work as Dwight Rugh's assistant in the Yali Treasury Department and do most of the bookkeeping for him. His work experience at the bank in Philadelphia was undoubtedly a factor for his obtaining this responsibility.

Social Life

Despite their youthful heckling and sometimes clashing personalities, the five Bachelors remained lifelong friends. In the fall of 1941, they were invited to the social event of the season; a Halloween party at the Plitt's Reform Church on October 31.[47] Such socials were taken seriously in Yuanling, so the young teachers worked up a skit to be ludicrous yet steeped in the Yale traditions. They proudly marched in singing the Yale fight song, "Bulldog," and sat down in a line as spectators at a Yale football game.[48] Then they went shouting around as is usually done at a football game, standing up occasionally to sing a song or to yell, "Fire." They crossed and uncrossed their legs at regular intervals, which was quite ridiculous, then scrambled over one another looking for the correct seats, while one of them was acting as the radio commentator, giving play-by-play descriptions of the activity on the field, while another got up and hawked, "Peanuts! Peanuts!" The revelers at the party were cajoled into singing "Ho la di hoo la da," then they sang ditties about several of the guests to the tune of "Daniel in the Lion's Den," with Don on harmonica and the others singing in a quartet; Paul was wearing a bright-yellow raincoat and hat to match. It was great fun and a welcome respite from their daily teaching routines.

On Saturdays, the Bachelors usually played a softball game or some volleyball. They often had afternoon tea at the East Gate. The Yale men, especially Paul, were voracious readers yet could not resist the temptation to burst into song at the slightest provocation. Paul sang a bass solo before a Chinese audience one evening in November 1941. Being the only bass singer in town, he considered himself impressive. His love of music was something he always enjoyed sharing. Writing letters home about their experiences in this far-off land became an integral part of their daily routine. Receiving letters from home with an update on current events was treasured, since it was difficult to get any kind of world news in Yuanling, much less the all-important football scores from home. Their radio broadcasts were frequently jammed. The Germans had put a large station on the same wavelength as the Treasure Island station out of San Francisco. The Japanese were drowning out the broadcasts from Shanghai, Manila, and Hong Kong. Often the broadcasts were full of static or incomplete when they were able to pick up a rebroadcast of President Roosevelt's speeches. From their perspective, the news seemed to be merely rabble-rousing propaganda from the Axis powers. Paul wrote his father, "I wish the US would take some time out to put Japan in her place."[49]

Top line: "Kill Rats as You Kill the Enemy." These posters illustrate how the Yali Junior School and Senior School branches endeavored to protect the community. The Chinese characters in the lower left-hand corner of the poster, which the rat is sniffing, translate as "Ya Li Middle School Drawn by." *Yale-China Association Records, RU 232, Manuscripts and Archives, Yale University Library*

Kills the Rats as You Kill the Enemy

The Bachelors sometimes had difficulty sleeping as winter approached, in large part due to a lack of adequate heat in their quarters. Paul explained why in a letter to his mother: "In back of me is my double-decker bed, where you may imagine me with my head toward you. I used to lie the other way, but the noise of the rats in the kitchen woke me during the night, and also the huge spiders, the size of a man's outstretched hand, sometimes walk up and down the walls. The last night I slept that way I awoke to find one just above my head. They're probably harmless, and I believe are now gone for the winter."[50] Although the spiders may have been harmless, the rats that frequented the kitchen area of Yuanling soon became a much more pressing health problem than any of them could have imagined.

The Japanese military had recently developed chemical and biological weapons for use against their enemies in China. The US and Great Britain sent chemical experts to Chungking to investigate the Japanese deployment of poison gases.[51] The inadequacy of the Japanese chemical-manufacturing industry and the expensive process of its manufacture precluded its use on a large scale. For this reason, the Allies thought any attack would be concentrated against the most-important targets, such as Chungking, where authorities were already taking measures to improve their defenses against a poison gas attack. In addition to this threat, a crude form of biological warfare had been developed by the Japanese under the supervision of Lt. Gen. Shiro Ishee and was an immediate danger.[52] One of Ishee's units focused its attention on the bubonic plague. The plan involved spreading the plague throughout China by using infected rats. An American missionary reported seeing Japanese planes dropping odd-looking bombs that spread what looked like wheat over the city of Ningbo. The plague erupted just days later among the people.[53] Chinese officials tried to combat the plague with isolating, quarantining, and burning the most-infected parts of the city; still, over five hundred people died as a result of the nefarious attack of the biological agents spread by Ishee's forces. There had been only a few cases of plague in Yuanling, but in Changteh, 150 miles downriver, the Japanese had dropped wheat with infected fleas. A raging epidemic was stopped from spreading beyond the city by the superhuman efforts of the mission hospital personnel working with the unprepared and underfunded health authorities.[54] Art Hopkins reported this on a widely circulated memo on the back of the poster bearing an image of a dagger pierced into a rat wearing a Japanese flag, with a dramatic warning about the danger. "The Japs have been dropping rat food from airplanes and the food causes the fleas on the rats to transmit the bubonic plague to any human so unfortunate as to be bitten."[55] Something as simple as a bite from an infected flea could have devastating consequences for the recipient.

The Red Cross examined the wheat and rice grains and the paper and cotton wadding that had been dropped in the Japanese bombs, and found them impregnated with the bacilli of the bubonic plague. Therefore these posters had appeared all over Yuanling, and the caption over the rat said in Chinese: "Kill rats as you kill the enemy."[56] In addition to killing the rats, every family on the street was required to bring two rats a month per person to the Department of Health. If they failed to do so, they were fined $2.00 and their salt allowance was stopped. Some unscrupulous people began a business to breed rats and sell them for $0.50 each, therefore avoiding the fine, but this was soon discouraged by a jail term. A plague serum soon became available, bringing some peace of mind to those in the affected areas. However, there were twenty more verified cases of plague in Changteh in the following year, with many more suspected. Travelers passing through the area told "gruesome tales" of the plague victims.[57]

These warning posters were one small example that revealed the part that Yali was playing in Yuanling during the war. The students formed a Red Cross first-aid unit for helping victims of bombings, and during the summer and winter vacation they

After departing Yuanling, Robert Ashton Smith's reporting mission continued in southwestern China to the Hua Chung College. He is seen here typing in Miller's courtyard, Hsichow, Yunnan, 1941. *Yale-China Association Records, RU 232, Manuscripts and Archives, Yale University Library*

became teachers and worked with rural adult education projects. Hopkins wrote a letter to Yale-in-China describing these incidents of biological warfare and the students' reaction to combat the situation. His letter was reprinted in the *Philadelphia Inquirer* two years later, in December 1943.[58]

The Perils of Travel

By early December 1941, Bob Smith was traveling back home but was stuck in Hong Kong. He found no boats sailing for the US, and the city was declared in a state of emergency, with the usual blackouts. He hoped to get a boat to Manila and home from there. Brank Fulton, who narrowly escaped the bombings in Changsha and Shikuwan, was also on his way back to pursue graduate studies at Yale. Paul read the account of Fulton's ordeal in the *South China Morning Post* and found it quite thrilling, but very gory.[59] He wrote about the incident to his mother: "It will make you fearful and increase your dislike for the Japs."[60] He also reflected: "Brank was a good companion on the way in. If we had arrived a few weeks later, we should all have been in the thick of it."[61]

Hopkins, Springer, and Elliott were to have six weeks off from teaching in early 1942 and were planning a trip to Chungking. They felt it would be safe by then, since those months were always cloudy and rainy and therefore less likely for them to be bombed.[62] On December 2, 1941, they had the first *chin-pao* in weeks, but it was only two scouting planes. As usual, they were safely at the dugout before the planes arrived. They were well aware of the latest attacks by the Japanese, dispensing poison gas and diseased germs by dropping infected rice from airplanes for rats to eat. The nearest infected-rice bombing took place a couple of hundred miles from them. As for a poison gas attack, they thought it impractical against a small town like Yuanling. Springer offered his observation: "The Japs can't afford it at this stage of the game unless it is really to do great damage. If there should be one here, which everyone doubts, I think our house on the hills will be well above the blanket of gas, which hugs the ground in low places. I don't think Yuanling has anything further to fear from the Japs, as whatever they do now must be desperate, and directed against a big objective."[63] Five days after Springer typed these words to his mother, the Japanese directed their military forces to a full-scale aerial assault at the US naval base in Pearl Harbor, Hawaii, on December 7, 1941.

Chapter 7

"HEY JIM, WE'RE AT WAR TODAY"

News of the Japanese Attack

The Yale-in-China Association Board of Trustees were in the midst of a regularly scheduled meeting in Dwight Hall, on the Yale campus, Sunday afternoon, December 7, 1941, when a news broadcast came over the radio announcing the Japanese attack on American military facilities in Pearl Harbor, Hawaii, and Manila, Philippines.[1] The news was shocking. The trustees struggled to absorb it as they tried to assess the implications of the attack on their decades-long program in China. At the time, the association's work was in Hua Chung College (in Hsichow), the Yali Union Middle School and Hsiang-Ya School of Nursing (in Yuanling), Hsiang-Ya Medical College (in Kweiyang), and Hsiang-Ya Hospital (in Changsha). The entry of the US into a full-scale war with Japan could place their teachers, doctors, nurses, and staff in great danger, since they were no longer representing a neutral country in the ongoing war against Japanese aggression.

Dr. Anson Stokes, the former president of the association, rose and said, "This means that the work of the association will be more needed now than ever."[2] Other board members stated that they should immediately let the friends of Yale-in-China know of their determination to carry on their work in China. All were in agreement that the humanitarian, educational, and missionary work of the association should continue now, more than ever. The trustees passed a resolution on December 7, 1941, that was sent to all members of the association and their families, "The medical and educational work of Yale-in-China, scattered through free China, is of such great help to that country in its time of tribulation that we must approve of the effects the Trustees put forth to continue it and even add to its usefulness where possible. I would urge Yale men everywhere to continue the support they have given, and to increase it if they can. In this way we shall render service to China and accordingly our own interests and ideals."

The news reached the Bachelors in Yuanling on the morning of December 8. Don McCabe had been accustomed to getting the news report from Shanghai via a radio broadcast every morning at 7:00. The announcer, Elroy Healy (a personal friend of the Rughs), sounded excited and started off with "Due to the state of war existing between Japan and the U.S.A., I shall have to confine my reports to proclamations and edicts."[3] He then said that Japanese soldiers had taken over the Shanghai International Settlement for its "protection," and all foreigners were advised to stay at home and keep off the streets. All banks were closed. He concluded, "That's all this morning until I can find out how much they are going to allow me to say. This is sad news. But we must carry on."[4] Jim Elliott was sleeping. Don walked past his bed and said quite nonchalantly, "Hey Jim, we're at war today."[5] In his groggy condition so early in the morning, he thought he heard, "Jim, it's warm today."[6] The news did not sink in. Jim rolled back in bed for a catnap before he got up thinking that today he wouldn't have to bundle up against the cold for his 7:30 class at the senior school. The announcer never made it back on the air. The Shanghai station broadcast only Japanese propaganda and music after that initial announcement. The rest of that day and over the following days, the Bachelors spent their spare time crowding around the radio—eagerly listening to reports from Manila, Hong Kong, London, San Francisco, Australia, Chungking, and Tokyo. The students looked at their teachers with great interest—agog to hear the latest news flashes. The boys were unable to conceal broad grins over the fact that at long last, China had some powerful allies. Rumors ran rife in the streets that five hundred American planes had bombed Tokyo and that most of the American fleet had been sunk in Pearl Harbor. The students eagerly asked if they would have *chin-paos* in Japan now. In their compositions, they wrote that America had some failings, but the Asiatic aggressor would now be defeated—as they joyfully counted up the number of countries that had declared war on Japan. The adults in Yuanling were more reserved in their celebration. The Bachelors heard none of the salvos of firecracker celebrations, such as those that greeted the news of the Chinese victory in Changsha two months before. A Chinese news reporter from Chungking summed up the reaction: "The Chinese reaction was first one of horror and amazement at such a dastardly, treacherous act, and then one of relief that the democracies were finally united against a common aggressor."[7] The Bachelors kept a bulletin board of American press opinions of the attack that came in over a San Francisco radio station. Typical comments included "We have been struck by a world serpent with its head in Germany and its tail in Japan," and "Japan has declared war while under a flag of truce."[8] The clearest radio broadcasts in Yuanling were all in Japanese.

Propaganda

The Bachelors got fed up with hearing the fallacious and naive propaganda of what they called the "Nipponese."[9] Their noxious lies (often uttered by sweet-voiced girls speaking beautiful English) implied that the brave Imperial Forces of Japan had destroyed the US Navy and Air Force in Hawaii, that the American people were paralyzed by fear, and that American "Jewry" in conjunction with "International Jewry" was the cause of the war, since their goal was to thwart Japan's wish for establishing a coprosperity sphere in East Asia.[10] Upon remarking on the Japanese aggression, one of the elderly Chinese teachers told Jim Elliott that his people had felt much the same way almost ten years ago, when Manchuria was suddenly invaded by the Japanese.

When the Bachelors left America in July 1941, there was very little feeling against Japan. All public attention seemed fixed on the European phase of the conflict. They remembered that at the Yale-in-China annual meeting and other talks about Yale-in-China affairs, people were constantly deploring the apathy of the American people with regard to the Far East. All talk of war had centered on Germany and, at that time, on the invasion of Soviet Russia, which began on June 22, 1941. Jim Elliott remarked that a "war with Japan was not the remotest of possibilities in our minds, but we certainly did not expect anything so sudden, so quickly. Evidently, our gallant defenders of Hawaii didn't either. From what we can gather, they must have been taken completely by surprise. I most earnestly hope it isn't so, but the vaunted US military, particularly the Navy, seems to have been caught napping. Of course, in a way, it is not surprising. I don't suppose that many laymen suspected anything like what happened. Certainly we out here didn't. But, on the other hand, I had always supposed that the military, like the Boy Scouts, were supposed to '*hsu shih fen chen bei*,' i.e., always be prepared!"[11]

Art Hopkins called the attack on Pearl Harbor a "wickedly cowardly act," often referring to it as both "despicable and cowardly."[12] Paul thought that Art had been blindsided by the difficulties of the Japanese occupation of the industrialized parts of China. Art felt that they were willing to let China fall, but were not going to over-exert themselves here while they planned an all-out offensive against the interests of the US and Great Britain. The Bachelors' fears about the Japanese claims of total victory in Hawaii were confirmed when they were at the East Gate Ladies House for a dinner party on December 13. There they were told that "the whole US Fleet" was lying at anchor in Honolulu Harbor, so close together "that you could walk from one to the other."[13] The source was a letter from a friend of one of their dinner companions living in Honolulu, which was received in Yuanling only a week before. It was total war between the US and Japan.

On the same morning as the attack on Pearl Harbor, Japanese forces launched waves of bombing attacks on Hong Kong and the British stronghold of Singapore. Hong Kong was a British Crown colony. Singapore, too, was a British Crown colony and home to the largest British military base in Southeast Asia. It was the key to defense planning for British imperial interests in Southeast Asia and the Southwest Pacific. Churchill sent two of the Royal Navy's battleships to Singapore as a symbolic deterrent to Japanese aggression in Indochina. Instead, they became nothing more than targets. Both HMS *Prince of Wales*, a fast modern warship, and HMS *Repulse*, a powerful battle cruiser, were sunk by Japanese airplanes in the Gulf of Siam. Approximately 1,250 sailors went down on the two ships. An equal number were saved by their destroyer escorts. Churchill later reflected, "The efficiency of the Japanese at air warfare was at the time greatly underestimated by ourselves and by the Americans."[14]

The Japanese also attacked British and US warships at Shanghai without declaring war. This took place on the same day as Pearl Harbor, although it was December 8 in Shanghai because it was on the other side of the International Date Line. Japanese troops occupied Shanghai's International Settlement and took control of all the newspaper and radio stations, including the station whose final broadcast reached Yuanling. Britain declared war on Japan only nine hours before the United States did, in part due to the surprise Japanese attacks in Hong Kong, Singapore, and Malaya, and in part due to Prime Minister Winston Churchill's pledge to FDR to declare war "within the hour" of any Japanese attack on the United States.

Teamwork

Although communication was somewhat primitive between New Haven and Yuanling, there was extraordinary cooperation between the Yali staff. On December 23, Art Hopkins received a telegram from New Haven addressed to Dwight Rugh. It was marked "urgent." Upon opening it, Hopkins knew that Rugh was away attending a teachers' meeting in a small town named Wusu. Realizing its contents related to some critical equipment, he decided to get the message to Rugh immediately. Hopkins volunteered to take the telegram to Wusu, miles up the river and accessible only by boat or on foot. He set out on foot and picked up a student at the junior school who could show him the way. They followed the clear, sparkling river, which flowed through the steep hills. Every now and then they would pass through a tiny hamlet of a few houses or a single country farmhouse, most of them appearing hundreds of years old. Curiously, beside every house was a coffin, as if it was awaiting its owner. Their path wound through flooded rice patties to the little town of Wusu, built on the confluence of two

Dwight Rugh, Yale-in-China director. He lived on site with his wife, Winifred, and their daughter, Betty Jean. He was a capable administrator and had good relationships with students, teachers, and administrators. *Yale-China Association Records, RU 232, Manuscripts and Archives, Yale University Library*

rivers, just above some fast rapids. There were steep hills all around the town. Built on a rocky ledge, about 200 yards above the stream, was a perfect little Taoist temple with a beautiful red roof, so perfectly blended into the stone that Hopkins barely noticed it at first glance. He admired the work of the old stone temple builders, since they had a keen eye for placing the temples. They looked like they belonged in their location as an integral part of the countryside. They made the ten-mile walk in about two and a half hours. They delivered the telegram, then stayed for dinner in a private home in the town, afterward rowing downstream back to Yuanling in a small boat.[15]

Christmas in Yuanling

The Bachelors taught their classes as usual on Christmas Eve. Paul cajoled the cook into making "a mammoth batch of peanut brittle" with which Art and Don made Christmas baskets for the other foreigners in town.[16] At about four o'clock on Christmas morning, the Bachelors were awakened by "about the sweetest music I have ever heard," recalled Art.[17] They stumbled over to the window and could see a long line of "angels" dressed in white robes, with gold crowns and carrying long flares, singing Christmas carols. The "angels" were Yali Junior School students and included some girls from one of the other mission schools in town. The boys wished their teachers a Merry Christmas, and then all attended a service in the chapel just as dawn broke. The Bachelors enjoyed a Christmas breakfast with the Rughs, then watched the family open presents around the tree. The joyful eyes of eight-year-old Betty Jean Rugh brought smiles to them all. It was great fun to watch her open up the presents, some of which were brought from New Haven for her. At first, Art and Jim thought it an imposition for people to ask them to bring goods into China. Now they realized how much even a small package from home was greatly appreciated. The Bachelors got "a nice set of drinking glasses, some delicious pickles, two very attractive candlesticks, and a mess of horrible jam as group presents."[18] The Rughs gave the teachers some little leather notebooks along with some American candy and chewing gum, and each received a gift of shoe polish from their dog, Molly. She was a black cocker spaniel with floppy ears, liquid brown eyes, a pink tongue, and a stubby tail.[19] She took turns sniffing the guests, licking Betty Jean on her ears, then wiggling out of her hold before scurrying around exploring the room. The dog brought an intimate feeling of being with family on that special day.

Betty Jean Rugh.
Courtesy of David Elder

The Bachelors spent the remainder of Christmas morning delivering their special baskets in the community. They barely finished their rounds when it started to rain. During the afternoon they entertained a half dozen of their students who came to call. They went into a room and listened to the radio for an hour or so, then returned to the living room in their quarters and found twenty more students who gathered to sing some Chinese songs. The boys were very fond of Western music and put many tunes into Chinese words, singing them to the original score. After teaching classes the next day, Hopkins received a telegram from Philadelphia. Upon opening it, he found the message from his parents: "Greeting our thoughts are with you love—Arthur H. Hopkins."[20] Their first Christmas in China was as complete as it could have been.

Bob Smith arrived back in the US on December 25—the news of his safe arrival was a joyful Christmas message for his family and friends of the association in New Haven. He was asked by the Board of Trustees to spend some time in the San Francisco area, where he was to "call on our Yale-in-China friends out there." Smith spent ten days there, meeting with friends, building moral support, and soliciting financial contributions for the program before returning home to New Haven.[21]

There were friends, parents, and loved ones of the Yale-in-China staff who would suddenly find themselves in somewhat of a news vacuum, since letters that routinely traveled via clipper plane had to be rerouted due to the Pacific routes being soon engulfed in war. The association endeavored to keep the families of Yale-in-China informed of current developments, even to the point of sending a letter that news had been received from Yuanling with the words "ENTIRE STAFF FINE."[22] Messages were cabled back and forth between New Haven and Dwight Rugh in Yuanling and Dr. Win Pettus in Changsha. There were reports of another Japanese military offensive on Hunan, targeting Changsha. Dr. Pettus, his wife, Maude, and Marjorie Tooker were urged to evacuate to Yuanling, since the trustees felt it probable that Yuanling would remain unoccupied, even though Changsha might be taken.

Chinese junks such as these were used to evacuate hospital staff and civilians on the Hsiang River, where they were out of harm's way during the Japanese invasion. *Yale-China Association Records, RU 232, Manuscripts and Archives, Yale University Library*

Evacuation of Changsha

Meanwhile, in Yuanling, the middle-school classes were in full swing, each of the five Bachelors staying extremely busy. Toward the end of December they heard disquieting rumors about the Japanese massing troops and preparing for another attack on Changsha.[23] Dwight Rugh telegraphed a message to Hsiang-Ya Hospital for the staff to pack all the equipment of the hospital and put it on the river for transport as soon as possible. With the recent bombing of Pearl Harbor, Americans in China had lost their advantage of neutrality. The ability of the Yale-in-China staff to plan an evacuation in advance of another invasion by the Japanese suddenly became necessary. Before the Japanese troops approached the city in December, Dr. Win Pettus implemented their well-laid plans for the evacuation of the staff, patients, and all movable material.[24] As Japanese troops prepared to recapture Changsha, the hospital staff knew that this time their facility would not be spared, and readied themselves to evacuate, discharging patients and packing anything that could be moved into boats on the Hsiang River.[25] "Dr. Hsiao and I were planning to stay behind in Changsha to protect the property from being looted by thugs," wrote Pettus. "We could then follow in my little sailboat when the city was about to fall. On the 29th of December we could hear the firing very distinctly and the situation was too critical either to go north or to wait any longer, so in the afternoon we set sail and started south."[26] Changsha's remaining population had also taken to the river as a means of escape. "It was a sight I shall never forget," Pettus wrote. "We were racing with several thousand junks, all evacuating from Changsha or Siangtan. The blue river was filled with full sails of all sizes, some of them nearly a hundred feet high."[27] It was a race against time to get the hospital staff to safety from the impending assault.

The third battle for control of Changsha in December 1941 became the overwhelming factor in Hunan Province at this time. It was the first major offensive in China by the imperial Japanese forces following their attack on Pearl Harbor. Changsha was a key transportation link through Hunan. The offensive was intended to prevent Chinese forces from reinforcing the British troops, which were then currently engaged against the Japanese in Hong Kong. When Hong Kong fell on Christmas Day 1941, the Japanese decided to continue the offensive against Changsha in order to maximize the blow against the Chinese government. Changsha was evacuated of civilians, which included the Yali staff, leaving only about 160 individuals who wished to stay to help the defense of the city. Their resistance was supported by a significant number of British-supplied mortars and two batteries of French-supplied field guns and anti-tank guns. Eight new US-supplied tanks were deployed within the city itself. Chinese forces under Gen. Hsueh Yueh conducted a spirited defense and repulsed a Japanese attack.[28] On New Year's Eve, the Japanese troops stormed the southern defenses of the city but failed to make any gains. Then they made an attempt to breach the southern and then eastern areas but encountered fierce resistance. More than 2,000 Japanese were killed in this initial attack. In the meantime, the northern part of the city, where the Yali campus was located, was heavily bombarded. Although the Japanese cut through the first line of defense, they were unable to breach the second line of defense near the city center, in part because of the heavy artillery supplied to the defending forces by China's allies. On New Year's Day 1942, a Chinese counterattack surprised the Japanese, inflicting high casualties on them. At about the same time, the Chinese army units that had retreated to the mountains during the Japanese advance swept down and crushed the Japanese supply lines with the aid of local guerrillas.

Hsiang-Ya Hospital and most of the campus were set on fire, doing great damage to the facilities. As the besieged Japanese forces were retreating from the city, Dr. Win Pettus hastened back to Changsha. He rode through the bombed-out city on a bicycle to assess the damage and consider his options to reopen the hospital. Springer wrote about Pettus, "That guy is indomitable. He waited until the last possible minute, and returns as the Japs retreat. Before the US was in [the war], he's defied the Japs on the ground on a couple of occasions and got away with it. They are really after

Victorious Chinese soldiers file past the burned-out shell of Hsiang-Ya Hospital after the Battle of Changsha, in January 1942. The doors were opened to patients again within a month. *Yale-China Association Records, RU 232, Manuscripts and Archives, Yale University Library*

him now."[29] Dr. Pettus had developed a reputation for pushing his luck against great odds in order to keep the Yale medical mission open and operating in Changsha.

Since the communications were practically nil, it was impossible to accurately evaluate any damage reports from Changsha. Pettus decided to return to Changsha in order to gauge the situation.[30] On January 5, he rode a bicycle to Siangtan and was fortunate enough to get a ride on a military boat to Changsha the next day. He and another American missionary were the first foreigners allowed into the city following the battle. It was a place of sheer desolation, and impossible to get food. Pettus wrote, "When we reached Hsiang-Ya [the hospital] late in the p.m. I had the shock of my life. Usually the hospital building is a landmark for a mile or two in every direction. But as we got near it, somehow I couldn't quite figure out where it was. Finally I saw a partially burnt building which looked suspiciously like it, but I actually turned away and went back to look three times before I definitely identified it."[31] As it turned out, the hospital walls were not badly damaged, though the interior was gutted and the striking Chinese roof was gone. "One part of the hospital was still burning when we arrived. We helped the five servants who were there to get it under control. Stores of rice and coal, however, burned for days afterwards. The most serious loss (in equipment) was the X-ray machine. It was too large, heavy and easily damaged if transported. The Japanese tried to destroy the motor and burn the dynamo of the hospital power plant, but they had evacuated some of the parts with them. Five days after the engineers got back they had running water again and the electricity was restored shortly thereafter."[32]

Word of the Chinese victory at Changsha was sent to Siangtan by special courier. The Hsiang-Ya "fleet" of junks started back to Changsha on January 10, 1942. Dr. Hsiao, Maude Pettus, and several others reached Changsha on January 12. The rest of the fleet arrived the next day. Marjorie Tooker, two doctors, two other nurses, and seven attendants remained at the Presbyterian hospital in Siangtan. They took over two wards and cared for a large number of heavily wounded soldiers. Dr. Pettus, two other doctors, and three nurses started work on January 13 at the Catholic hospital, Changsha, which had previously closed for four months because of a lack of professional staff.[33] In this way, the professional staff was able to carry on their medical work in various ways until Hsiang-Ya Hospital could be sufficiently patched up to receive patients.

Yuanling Is Isolated

Cables and telegrams were now the only communications coming into Yuanling. The stateside mail was conspicuous by its absence, since no post–December 7 mail had been seen anywhere in China. Certainly none of the forty or so Americans in Yuanling had any letter postmarked after that fateful Sunday. No more news came from Shanghai, Hong Kong, or Manila, and very little from Chungking; and that news was usually several days old when received. Kept away from the violence by his isolation in Yuanling, Paul wrote to his mother that "I hope you haven't worried unduly, because as I have said before, I am in the safest place in the world, especially since the US became actively involved. There is little news here, you must have loads of it, and I hope to be getting it all one of these days. If the Army wants me perhaps I'll be going with them. I'd go just as soon, rather than miss it all and come back a slacker, though I was considered heroic—or foolhardy, by some when I left."[34]

Despite the turmoil going on in the rest of China, Yuanling may not have been the safest place in the world, but it certainly had its quiet and serene moments, somewhat of an oasis in war-torn China. The Yali Youth Group, composed of middle and senior-school students, staff, and the ever-present Bachelors, presented a New Year's concert at 6:30 p.m. on January 1, 1942.[35] Invitations to the show, held in the Life Everlasting Hall, were printed in Chinese and English. It seemed that almost everyone at Yali had a part in the event. In the first act, the Yali Choir Group was accompanied by Dr. Rugh on viola, his wife, Winifred, on violin, and Ms. Bayless on organ. There were student solos and an evangelical choir. Don McCabe played a trumpet instrumental on "The Church's One Foundation" and "I Would Be True." As if a metaphor for the ailing Chinese audience, Springer sang a rendition of "Nobody Knows the Trouble I've Seen" as a bass soloist. It was as fitting a song as any for the times. Paul also sang in a mixed quartet with Dwight, Winifred, and Betty Jean Rugh, singing "Angels We Have Heard on High," keeping their faith front and center in their mission and keeping themselves well grounded through their faith in God.

Although largely isolated over the holidays, news came in early January that there was to be an air route opening from Yuanling to America, via Chungking, Lashio (in Burma), Lagos (in Nigeria), and then to the Americas. This would allow for their mail to get through. Postage for a 5-gram letter was now $9.70 Mex (over $0.50 US). The cost of living, even in this supposedly low-priced area, was now skyrocketing at an alarming rate. Rice, the economic barometer in all parts of China, which constitutes the staple in the diet, had more than tripled in price from September 1941 through January 1942.

The Americans in Yuanling found prices about twice as high as they were in Chungking, Chengtu, and other larger cities. Paul, Art, and Jim found that the Chinese people were "plenty piqued" about the way the Americans and British were "letting" the Japanese take everything.[36] The Chinese seemed to have a childlike confidence in the power and the ability of the United States and fully expected the US to bring Japan to her knees in a couple of months at most. The question they were asked most often was "When are you going to bomb Tokyo?"[37] Not surprisingly, the lack of news seemed to eliminate distractions for the Bachelors in their teaching assignments. They gave their final examinations on January 14 and 15. Consequently, they spent the next two days correcting papers, entering marks, and having final discussions with their students as they wound down the semester.

They were planning their next adventure—a winter vacation and sightseeing trip to Chungking. They had six weeks before the second school term began. Jim Elliott wrote, "About that time, Springer, Hopkins, and Elliott pull out of Yuanling, God and the Chinese Government permitting, and head west, young man, head west. We're planning to visit Chungking and Chengtu, 'way off thar in Szechuan,' and shall undoubtedly go by way of Kweiyang, capital of Kweichow Province, and site of Yale-in-China's Medical College. . . . There seems to be a lot of red tape one has to go through just to move around in this country. We went downtown the other day and had our pictures taken—they tell us we will need plenty of them."[38] Given the maze of roadblocks and military checkpoints in war-torn China, they were issued identification certificates by Yale-in-China, written in Chinese and bearing their

Paul Springer's Yali ID certificate, issued January 13, 1942. *Springer Family collection*

photographs. The photo ID was one of several important-looking papers that the Bachelors carried with them. Each had a school pass, a military pass, a hospital certificate, and a letter of introduction, along with their all-important passport and calling cards.

Their concerns about freedom of movement were alleviated somewhat, now that the interests of China and the US were closely aligned against their mutual enemy—Japan. Jim Elliott was optimistic about the turn in the American diplomatic relationship with China: "We figure they should have no less than a brass band out waiting to greet us in Chungking."[39]

117

Chapter 8

VACATION ON THE BURMA ROAD

On the Road Again

After four months in Yuanling, Springer, Hopkins, and Elliott were ready to explore Hunan Province during the school's six-week winter recess. By Friday night, January 16, they were packed and ready to go, faced only with the challenge of securing tickets from the bus station master. Obtaining a bus ticket, usually the only way of travel available, was somewhat of an art in itself.[1] One had to apply days in advance for permission just to buy a ticket. Then you were given a registration number. Even so, you could purchase the ticket only if you were lucky enough to be at the bus station when your registration number was called.

The Bachelors got up early on Saturday, at 4:00 a.m. They loaded Li Si Fu, their coolie, with the luggage and traipsed over via a boat to the bus station across the river, about a mile away. Bob Clarke and Don McCabe accompanied them to the station. Bob pulled a few strings with the bus operator and secured their tickets about three hours later. They jammed themselves into the Kweiyang-bound bus to begin their great adventure. Their first day was one of the most interesting. It was the first day since their arrival in Yuanling that any of them had been more than three miles outside the relatively isolated city.

They had several encounters with the provisional constabularies (policemen), who checked their passports and travel documents repeatedly before they could proceed. Jim Elliott described the process: "The *hsien ping* would stop us, immediately spot the three *wei-gue jan* (foreigners) and call for things and stuff to look over. At one place, Chihchiang, they detained the bus about three quarters of an hour while they copied down pages of information gleaned from our various documents."[2] The first day of travel was marked by a bandit scare. About 4:30 in the afternoon they rolled into a little town, stopped, and heard people murmuring about "*tu fei, tu fei*" (bandits, bandits). They didn't know the word at the time and were at a loss to explain why the bus stopped and failed to proceed any further. Soon they began to get the gist of it. The men of the village were appearing on all sides, each bearing firearms of some sort, and were followed by a small detachment of blue-uniformed soldiers who came marching down the street on the double. The cries of "*tu fei, tu fei*" continued, accompanied by gestures toward the surrounding countryside. After a while, the soldiers and gun-toting men marched off down the road. Given their stumbling Chinese-language skills, the Bachelors concluded that the way was probably "all clear." They were by no means certain of this, and the driver had some doubts of his own. Every few kilometers the driver stopped to ask pedestrians, "*Yu tu fei, mei yu?*" (literally, "Any bandits?"). Although the replies were negative, there was an air of tension in the bus throughout the last twenty-seven kilometers, which the driver wasted no time in covering.

The first leg (about one-third) of their journey to Kweiyang was safely behind them. Upon arrival in Hwanghsien, they discovered they might have to stay in town for a few days in order for the people awaiting bus transportation ahead of them to be cleared. They had reservations to leave Kweiyang for Chungking on January 22 or 23, but they could not remember which day it was. On the following morning they talked with the bus station master in their rudimentary Chinese to explain their situation. They got their point across and were handed the registrations slips that afternoon to buy their bus tickets the next morning. The three Bachelors were elated not only for their good fortune in securing their ticket permits, but also for having made themselves understood in Chinese. The three of them felt that that day, Hwanghsien was most memorable for their conversational efforts "in this crazy-old language."[3]

The next morning they were introduced to two drivers in the Chinese army. Although they could not speak a word of English, they were glad to spend most of the day with their new American friends. During a walking trip into the main part of the town, a couple of miles away, their escorts warned the Bachelors not to buy anything. They were made to understand that if they were seen flashing any money, word of three wealthy Americans in town would spread to the ever-present bandits, and they might find themselves confronted by the business end of a gun on their return trip to the inn near the bus station. The three amused themselves sightseeing, practicing their Chinese on their new friends, and playing cards for part of the afternoon.

Cowboy Driver

The next morning's travel began at daybreak, and although they received the bus tickets, they were unable to take all their baggage with them. This meant that they

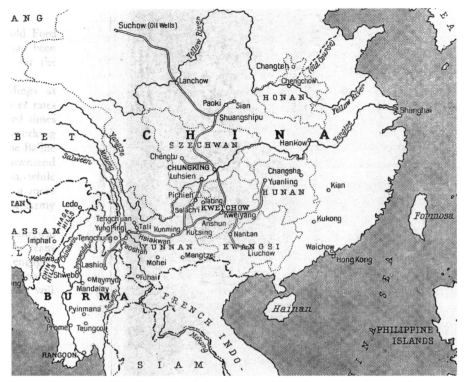

Map of China, ca. 1941, by Tengla Davis. Beginning at right is the road leading west from Yuanling, through Kweiyang, then north to Chungking. From Kweiyang, the Burma Road continues southwest through Yunnan Province to Lashio, Burma. *FAU collection*

would have to do without their bedding until the baggage arrived in Kweiyang, which was not a pleasant prospect. The day's journey was uneventful except for meeting an English-speaking Chinese man in the restaurant where they had lunch. They were fortunate enough to stay in a Chinese travel service inn, which was the best they had seen in China. That night, they each rolled up in their *peiwos*, the big, quilted blankets found on almost every bed in China.

On the following morning they lost the driver from the first two days. They were stunned with his replacement. The Bachelors tagged the new driver as a "cowboy" from the first. Jim Elliott described their trip:

> That morning, we were all sitting in the bus, ready to go, but fully expecting to wait another half hour or so—the customary thing in China, when this fellow in a leather coat came whipping out of the inn and into the driver seat. With one fast motion he shut the door, turned on the ignition, stepped

on the starter, took the brake off, and roared out of the inn yard. From that moment we sat on the edge of our seats, for this fellow was no respecter of machines or persons. What he did to that bus was a crime, and I know the wear and tear on my nerves was more in those two days of riding with him than is usually suffered in a year of ordinary driving. His favorite sport was going down those terrific, twisting hills with the motor cut, one foot on the clutch, the other on the break, jamming the latter to the floor board every time there came one of those interminable hairpin turns.

We hadn't appreciated how good our first driver was until we experienced this cowboy. Along about 10 o'clock, the bus began to have trouble—small wonder. On our second day out, the bus was continually stopping to buy some rice wine which they used to replenish the brake fluid which was leaking out. Well, on this day, everything seemed to go wrong at once. For a while, we had to stop every few minutes to add water. Then we ran out of gas. So, at 10:30 we were stopped along the side of the road, out in the mountains in the middle of nowhere.[4]

Rather than sit around waiting for something to happen, Paul, Art, and Jim decided to start hiking. They were still 122 kilometers out from Kweiyang, but anything seemed better than sitting on the side of the road, so off they went. A couple of kilometers down the road, they came to a village, where the driver looked in vain for help. When the Bachelors told him they were going on, he gave them a note to carry to the next town, six more kilometers ahead. Hot, tired, and frustrated, they arrived about an hour later, delivered the note at the bus station, and had what Elliott described as "a terrible meal."[5]

An hour or so after they finished eating, their bus came limping in. They were told they could start their trip again only after it had been fixed. However, the repair job took longer than anticipated, and an hour later they were told they had to stay overnight. They were not pleased in the least to get the news, but there seemed to be no other options. They inquired to see if it was possible to get a ride into Kweiyang on a truck or something, but everybody told them, "*Mei yu fa tze*" ("No way out")—to stay here. The evening was saved by a chance meeting with an English-speaking Chinese man, formerly from Shanghai and now living in Kweiyang, who worked for a transportation company. He helped locate the best inn in town, played cards with them, and invited the three Americans to have dinner with him. It was a wonderful meal. They ate in a remarkably clean and agreeable restaurant run by some ex-Shanghai people. The Bachelors began to realize that the interior of China was largely populated by refugees from the coastal cities who had fled the military threat from the Japanese. Jim Elliott described their dinner experience: "It's called a '*huo kuo*' (sounds like "hogo"), and consists of all sorts of meats and vegetables cooked in an odd-shaped contraption which is placed right in the center of the table before you. Charcoal is placed in the center, and the food is cooked in a sort of circular trough around the fire. In this trough you put all sorts of meats, vegetables, soups, sauces, spices—it makes a wonderful mixture. To top off the meal, we had some excellent wine, generously given [to] us by a truck driver sitting at the next table—the wine probably brought by him all the way from Burma and literally worth its weight in gold. Our opinion of the Chinese people was certainly very high that night."[6]

Their bus was repaired by morning, and the remaining 115 kilometers into Kwieyang was made without mishap, although the driver did not mend his ways in the slightest. He continued to roar down the mountain roads and jammed on the brakes in each hairpin turn. This, they learned later, was typical of many bus drivers in China and was done as a gas-saving measure. The driver was given only so much money for gas for each day's run. Anything he saved, he kept for himself and sold the excess for a tremendous price. The bus drivers of China managed to make some extra money for themselves on the spread between their allotment of gas and whatever was left over.

Kweichow (now Guizhou) Province was a wild, mountainous, sparsely settled area with a smaller population than any province in China. Its capital, Kweiyang (now Guiyang), had swollen to many times its former size by the westward migration between 1940 and 1942. In the spring of 1942, the population was around 200,000–250,000. At first sight, it seemed quite a city, nestled among mountains and laid out more or less symmetrically. The Bachelors' first appraisal of it was a generous one. The wide, comparatively clean streets, the well-lighted shops, the wealth of plate glass found in the shop windows, and an abundance of merchandise left a favorable impression, especially after leaving some of the war-torn areas of China behind them. The Bachelors felt they were now out of the backwoods and back to civilization again.

Once in Kweiyang, they headed for Hsiang-Ya Medical College, a good little walk outside the city. They located the home of Dr. H. C. Chang, the president of the college, and called on him. They had lunch at his house and were shown to a room in the teacher's dormitory, which was put at their disposal for the duration of their stay. They were given a tour of the college by Dr. Chang. They found it interesting, It was their first glimpse of a college operating under wartime conditions in the interior of China. They were amazed at what had been done with the school since it relocated from Changsha over three years ago. In Changsha, the college had the best of everything—buildings, equipment, books, and teachers. The school still had a good deal of equipment, many books, and excellent teachers, but the college was still using temporary buildings from more than three years ago (not intended to be used more than two years). The administrators were working with the knowledge that on any given day, they might have to stop working at a minute's notice and rush to a dugout to seek safety from another bombing raid. The college was also faced with financial difficulties, which at that time seemed impossible to solve. But after seeing the work that they were doing and the conditions under which they had to operate, the Yali men were impressed with the school's accomplishments. Their four-day trip to Kweiyang and their personalized tour of the medical college was a memorable experience for them. As word of their enthusiasm for the work being done at the college spread, it resulted in an unexpected employment offer.

That afternoon, after buying bus tickets from Kweiyang to Chungking, they ran into one of the Chinese friends whom they spent the day with in Hwanghsien. They all decided to meet up later at the offices of the International Relief Committee (IRC). Jim and Art arrived first, with Paul arriving later. There they met Bill Mitchell, in charge of the Kweiyang IRC office (the central office for all IRC work in China); John "Check" Hlavacek, a former English teacher, in charge of transport for the IRC; Al Ravenholt, an American adventurer, spending a year as a volunteer driver for the IRC; and several others, many of them members of the Friends Ambulance Unit (FAU).

Friends Ambulance Unit

The FAU was a volunteer ambulance service founded by members of the British Religious Society of Friends. It operated from 1914 to 1919, 1939 to 1946, and 1946 to 1959 in twenty-five different countries. The Sino-Japanese War led to deteriorating conditions in China, and in 1941 an agreement was reached for the FAU to deploy forty volunteers to deliver medical aid throughout China (dubbed the "China Convoy"). The first priority of the FAU was the delivery of medical supplies where they were needed most. The FAU's role was expanded to provide a range of medical treatments, preventive measures, and training of Chinese medical personnel. The FAU operations in China were international, employing personnel from Britain (the largest national group), China, United States, Canada, New Zealand, and elsewhere. Around two hundred foreigners took part in this operation, which was chiefly concerned with transporting Red Cross supplies into and throughout China. It was dangerous work. Eight men died during their service in the FAU in China, and others had their health permanently damaged.[7]

After talking about various subjects, Hlavacek suggested that since they were short on drivers, why couldn't the Yale boys drive some trucks up to Chengtu (now Chengdu)

Kweiyang Hostel
Building used by the
FAU. A chance
meeting led to an
unexpected job offer
for the Bachelors.
FAU collection

and back for them? The remark was made half in fun, but soon everyone was seriously considering it, especially the three Bachelors. That night, after sitting in on a committee meeting at the FAU office, Paul, Art, and Jim went over to their house (most of the staff lived in one house together), had dinner with the FAU group, and then came to an agreement about driving the trucks.[8] They decided to drive for them, the FAU furnishing a mechanic and an English-speaking Chinese man to assist with business and also taking care of their expenses on the road. They would have two one-week stopovers, both in Chengtu and in Chungking.

Faced with the possibility of being at the mercy of another crazy bus driver, they decided in unison to control their own destiny, while further advancing the Yali humanitarian mission in China. Paul, Art, and Jim accepted the job and, in no time, had their Chinese driver's licenses in hand and were ready to hit the Burma Road, the sole remaining route through the region.[9]

Jim Elliott offered the following observations about the spontaneity of the job offer:

> The fact that we were total strangers didn't seem to bother the I.R.C. men
> a bit. That they willingly entrusted their invaluable trucks and priceless
> drugs to us is, I think, a tribute to the reputation of Yale-in-China, and, to
> a lesser extent, an indication of the bond which exists between all foreigners
> in China (especially the English-speaking ones). Other aspects of the
> situation seemed quite amazing at the time too. First, they suggested our
> driving before even asking us whether or not we can drive, but Check
> [Hlavacek] then made the answer that, after he had made it, did seem rather
> obvious: "Did you ever see an American who couldn't drive?" None of us

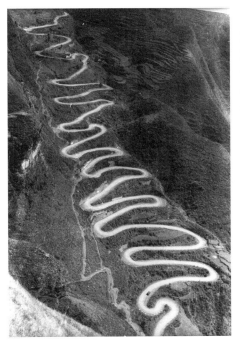

The Twenty-Four Bends are located on the northeast extension of the Burma Road in China's Yunnan Province. *FAU collection*

had ever driven trucks, though, nor had we ever driven a car with the wheel on the right side of the cab, the shift on the left-hand side of the wheel, etc., nor had we ever driven English-fashion on the left-hand side of the road. We had our doubts, but when we started out on the morning of our fourth day in Kweiyang, we still had not driven the trucks more than a few kilometers.[10]

The road from Kweiyang (where the FAU had its transport base) to Chungking was a particularly treacherous one, with a series of mountainous cliffs, sharp turns, and poor roads. They drove two 2½-ton trucks filled with tons of medical supplies, which were taken to Red Cross facilities in the city of Chengtu via Chungking and returning through Chungking back to Kweiyang.[11] Throughout the trip, there were three of them to drive in two trucks, so they alternated at the wheel. One of them drove all day, while the other two each drove a half day. They were five of them all together, including an English-speaking Chinese man named George Cheng, whom none of them liked very much, and a mechanic named Lu, a boy of perhaps eighteen, whom they nicknamed "Hsiao" or "Little Lu."

The first leg of the trip was from Kweiyang to Chungking, about 485 kilometers, which took two days and was considered good time. After stopping for an hour or so after lunch, they were put up in a respectable China service hotel that first night. This ended up being the best lodging they were to stay in anywhere on the road, with separate rooms, white-coated attendants, and good food. The second day's driving was one mountain after another, twisting up the side of one and then turning down the other side. During the first part of the trip, they had been in relatively flat country with small hills. During the last three-quarters of an hour of this leg, they did some mountain climbing in the truck and encountered a steep set of hills and curves.

Jim Elliott recalled the excitement and beauty:

Coming down the side of one monster, we counted one hundred and seventy-two (172) hairpin turns! And when I say hairpin, that's exactly what I mean—the horseshoe type of turn, but to say "horseshoe" is to give a slightly inaccurate impression. "Hairpin" is the much more emphatic and accurate adjective. Nothing of great importance or interest occurred on the Kweiyang–Chungking leg of our journey. The most memorable thing to me was the gorgeous scenery all the way. That part of China is the most beautiful of any I've seen today. It is mountainous, yet densely populated, and cultivated to an extent one would think impossible. Those terraced hillsides, with so many shades of green, are beyond description.[12]

The road dropped down off the mountains onto the hot and fertile plains of Szechuan Province, finally reaching the FAU's Chungking garage depot on the south bank, 4½ kilometers short of the Yangtze River. They made such good time that upon their arrival at the control station, about forty kilometers outside Chungking, they were reprimanded by an IRC official for excessive speed! They had no other mishaps along the way, except for running out of gas one day. They had carried all of their gasoline with them in drums, because a gas station was something no one ever saw in the interior of China. They had not seen one since they had left Hong Kong. When gas was needed, they just stopped, siphoned some gas from one of the drums into the truck's gas tank, and drove on. One of the emergency brakes went on the blink, and one horn would not work properly since it was blowing most of the time, but those were minor disorders. As they navigated the congested city traffic in Chungking, their most memorable incident was almost running down an old Chinese woman. Jim recalled, "She apparently was totally deaf, because we had been blowing the horn for some time behind her, but just as we reached her, she stepped out in front

The FAU Transport Depot, Chungking, on the south bank of the Yangtze. *FAU collection*

of the truck. Had we been going more than 5 miles an hour, there would now probably be one less old Chinese woman to wrack the nerves of truck drivers. As it was, we managed to stop in our tracks."[13]

They arrived in Chungking about 7:00 p.m. on Monday, January 26, ten days after leaving Yuanling. After finding a hotel for George and Lu and parking the truck, Paul, Art, and Jim headed for the American embassy. Paul had telephoned ahead to the embassy in an attempt to get in touch with George Small but found out that he was living in a house with no telephone. They walked over to a house where other staff members lived. After a twenty-minute walk, they arrived, hot and tired. Mr. MacDonald, the second secretary at the embassy, received them and introduced them to other members of the American military mission. They were treated like royalty, even though they had arrived in the middle of the dinner hour. They were given drinks and recent magazines and offered a wonderful meal, which they gladly accepted, complete with a lemon meringue pie.

After dinner, the Bachelors were given directions to George Small's house. MacDonald warned them that it was an hour's walk, all of which was uphill. They thought he was kidding, or certainly exaggerating. They were given the use of a servant to guide them up to George's house. They walked and walked, but, worse than that, they climbed. On and on, up and up. Every house they saw they thought must be the last one, and every time they walked past it. What made the climb worse was that they were all dressed for the winter, with heavy sweaters, extra pants, heavy coats, and travel bags containing their belongings. Finally, after an hour, they arrived! That night, the three Bachelors stayed in the house that Small and his roommate lived in on top of the "First Range," which, like the American embassy, was across the Yangtze River from Chungking. They were offered the luxury of a bathtub, something they had not seen since they left Changsha four months earlier. The house was perched 1,200 feet above the river.

During their return trip through Chungking, Paul described with fascination how his friend George was able to traverse the steep, stiff climb going to and from work every day to the American embassy offices:

> George is carried up in a chair daily after work, but he walks down in the morning. I have ridden up in a chair twice now, and it is really thrilling. The chair is supported by bamboo poles and is carried by two chair coolies, who rest a cross piece from the bamboo poles on their shoulders. They climbed steadily and tirelessly with their human burden for almost an hour, and for this we pay them $18 Mex, less than $.50 a piece [in]

gold. I have walked that stretch a couple of times, and must admit that it almost completely ragged me, and that after I stopped to rest several times, and took twice as long as the coolies. Just imagine them doing that feat in the heat of mid-summer!—and barefooted too. One of my most thrilling experiences in China yet was taking that ride by moonlight one night. The precipice veers off to one side most of the time, and the path is very narrow and slim in places. When we had our luggage brought up the other night on our return from Chengtu, one of George's bags slipped out from under its rope and clattered down the rocky chasm to our left, landing in the water at the bottom. One of the coolies climbed down and got it and we found it to still be in good condition. Fortunate for George, that it was a plenty tough suitcase![14]

On this first leg of the trip they stayed in Chungking for only one day. That day was mostly spent taking care of Red Cross business. Two of them had to drive the trucks across the river into the city proper, since they were on the south bank of the Yangtze River. They tossed a coin to see who got to go into town, and, as usual, Paul won the toss and stayed behind at George's house. Jim and Art went down the mountain and over to the hotel where they left George Cheng and Lu (the mechanic). To get across the river, they had to retrace their steps for about ten kilometers, then turn and approach the river farther up, where a ferry was located. There was a military checkpoint at the turn, where they encountered a bit of difficulty. Jim had been sick while they were in Kweiyang and had not gotten a Chinese driver's license; only Paul and Art had them. So they had only one licensed driver for two trucks. Not good. Somehow the authorities let them on, but not until they had been delayed for quite

Paul Springer being transported in a coolie chair uphill to George Small's house in Chungking. *Springer Family collection*

some time. They were ferried across the Yangtze River and drove into Chungking. They headed to the Canadian Mission Hospital, where George Cheng and Lu unloaded them. Jim and Art tried to get in touch with George Small at the embassy, but to no avail, since the telephones were not working.

In the meantime, Paul had his own business to attend to. Before he departed Yuanling, Dwight Rugh gave him a letter empowering him to act with full authority for Yale-in-China while in Chungking. Paul supervised some funds that arrived in Chungking from America, sending some to Yuanling and drawing some for Jim, Art, and himself. Since Paul had instructions to buy some testaments, bibles, textbooks, and songbooks for Yali, he made arrangements at one of the Canadian missions to secure those for the school.

On their way back from the Canadian Mission Hospital that afternoon, Jim and Art walked down to a pedestrian ferry, where they ran into George Small, coming back from some business in the city. Once at the embassy, they waited for Paul to arrive. When he returned, they went up to George's house. George had a chair carried by coolies who brought him up to his house. Art and Paul also hired a chair that night. Jim, thinking that he was not so tired, walked up. They spent the evening chatting, drinking, and playing bridge. Jim remarked that "George and his housemate, Boies Hart, third secretary at the embassy, live like kings up there on their own mountain. The house is a Standard Oil 'bungalow' but looked like a mansion to our provincial eyes. They have the whole mammoth place to themselves and must occasionally get lost wandering around its great wide open spaces. The four of us all slept there with no difficulty at all. They complain about their food, but it seemed fit for a king. They

Crossing the Yangtze River to Chungking via Ferry. *FAU collection*

Pulling away from the FAU transport depot, Chungking. *FAU collection*

Shanties on bamboo stilts, Chungking. *FAU collection*

griped about the inconvenience of life in Chungking, but they had the best of liquors, whiskeys, and gins, etc. and were smoking tobacco straight from London.[15] They dubbed their mountainside villa "The Lair." All we could say was "If you think this is bad, don't come to Yuanling."[16]

Their two-truck FAU convoy left the Chungking transport depot, along the south bank of the Kialing River, the next morning. George Small rode with them. He wanted to go to Chengtu to have an aching tooth extracted, as well as to get out of town for a little vacation. They headed northwest toward Chengtu.[17] They traversed down the 4½ kilometers of dusty roads that fell steeply down to the Yangtze River, arriving alongside the Kweichow highway. Across the wide expanse of the river, the city of Chungking unfolded, still enclosed in the ancient walls built around the center. The city stood high above the river, a cliff of several hundred feet to which clung a menagerie of small homes—shanties on bamboo stilts. These homes were elevated for flood protection from the Yangtze River, which rises dramatically in the spring. Beyond them were the more permanent buildings of the city, including the foreign embassies. The trip from Chungking to Chengtu was about 400 kilometers, a bit shorter than the journey from Kweiyang to Chungking. Although slightly shorter and less mountainous, it was no less of an adventure.

Military Checkpoint

They had gone no more than forty kilometers when an unexpected delay began to unfold. It was about noon when they came down onto the plains after crossing the mountains outside Chungking. Since they saw a small city ahead, they decided to stop for lunch. Jim Elliott was driving, with Paul and George Small riding with him. Art, Lu, and George Cheng were in the other truck. At the edge of town, they saw a military control station. A green-uniformed soldier was waving a red flag for them to stop. They stopped. Jim described what happened next:

> He said something in Chinese which we didn't understand and motioned with his flag. I thought he was telling us to drive over to the side of the road and wait, but Paul insisted that he was waving us on, so on we went—about 100 yards into town where we stopped at a restaurant and ate lunch. During lunch, soldiers appeared, talked to us in Chinese, which we did not understand, went away, and came back again. Finally, we gathered they wanted us to go back to the control station, so back we went. There, George Cheng was all excited. It seems the soldier had waved us to the side of the road—not ahead—and now we were accused of running roughshod over

the Chinese military, foreign devils that we were. George (Cheng) and Paul had words, George being rather nasty about it all. He and Lu had been riding in the rear truck with our driving and had been told about our driving on. That, of course called for an explanation, and when we (Paul and I) went in to talk with the officer in charge of the control station, everything was easily ironed out. The officer could speak English and was very courteous to us. The soldier who had flagged us was called in to verify our story that we had stopped and did so. The upshot of the whole thing was that we just lost a couple of hours while everything was being settled, and that we had a bad reputation with FAU who got a wrong impression from the muddle headed, high-strung George Cheng. He never did get it straight, I guess. When we got to Chengtu, it was all over the foreign community that we were irresponsible Yale boys, had been speeding through Chinese control stations without stopping, flouting the authority of the Chinese military, and other wild stories of that nature. The same stories preceded us back to Chungking and Kweiyang, all because we didn't understand a rapid-fire sentence in Chinese.[18]

Fortunately, there were no serious repercussions as a result of this. All the IRC officials and most of the FAU men understood as soon as Paul, Art, and Jim explained their side of the story. The FAU agreed with their opinion of George Cheng. Afterward, while they were standing around at the control station, one of the Chinese officers noticed

Horse-drawn carts were often encountered on the road trip to Chengtu. *FAU collection*

that Jim was carrying a camera. There was a military regulation in place making it against the law to take pictures anywhere along the road, so they wanted to confiscate his camera and keep it until he could get a permit from Chungking. However, Jim objected and was reluctant to give it up. An arrangement was made for his camera to be sealed in a box at the checkpoint. On the way back, they returned it to him with the seal unbroken. It was quite an exciting, although exasperating, experience.

Road Hazards

The Chinese roads were often full of pedestrians and vehicles drawn or pushed by men. Cars and trucks were few and far between. The pedestrian traffic added to the many difficulties of driving in China. Between Chungking and Chengtu, the Yale men passed innumerable two-wheeled (mostly rubber-tired) carts, including big ones, drawn and pushed by teams of men and boys. Elliott described them: "What they all carried, I don't know, but whatever it was, there surely was a lot of it for we passed hundreds of them. The carts themselves were strange looking affairs with wheels in the center, loaded high with bales and boxes. Besides the carts and ordinary pedestrians, there were, of course, the omnipresent *t'lao fu* (coolie carriers) with their loads swinging from either end of a carrying pole across their shoulders."[19]

Chengtu

After driving the rest of the day, they reached another military control station in the next town of Neichiang, only to find out that the officers had left for the day, and they were not allowed to pass through. They turned into the town, finally found a hotel, and put up for the night. It was the worst inn they had experienced during the trip, and all of them had to sleep in one room with a dirt floor and on beds that were the crudest they had yet experienced in China. They were up early the next morning, did a bit of shopping (mostly for Chinese curio and sugarcane), and reached the city of Chengtu around dusk. In Chengtu, they headed for the YMCA but found no rooms available. This turned out to be a blessing, for they went to the West China Union Hospital and then the IRC depot in Chengtu, where they were to unload their supplies. While there, they got in touch with Dr. Milford, director of the hospital, and he arranged sleeping quarters for all of them. Jim and George Small slept in a room at the hospital, while Art and Paul went to a house next door, where a Canadian couple named Cunningham lived. George Cheng also had a room at the hospital, and Hsiao Lu drove one of the trucks to his home in Chengtu.

Not long afterward, the Yale boys realized their mechanic had been stealing from them. Jim noticed while he was unpacking that he was missing fountain pens, a mechanical pencil, and a flashlight. Not high-dollar items, but they could be sold in

West China Union University, Chengtu. The campus added a new medical wing building, shown here, in 1943. The FAU hostel, with attic windows, is at right. *FAU collection*

China for considerable Chinese money. Lu had been the only person with access to the back of the truck, where their luggage was carried. The other Bachelors were curiously missing items as well, and it greatly tainted their opinion of Lu, who quickly denied any knowledge of the items.

Paul and Art stayed for six days with the Cunninghams, Canadian doctors and missionaries, who made them feel at home and took great care of them. Jim and George Small moved in with them after spending their first night at the hospital. From their base at the Cunninghams, the four Americans saw the sights of Chengtu and the surrounding areas, including the West China Union University campus, which they found to be magnificent. It was as large as any in the US. The city of Chengtu was the scene of their first good movie experience in Free China. They saw a couple of films there, finding the theaters nice, westernized, and comfortable. Also, the sound equipment was good, which was true in Chungking too.

There was a school of dentistry in Chengtu connected with one of the universities in Hua Hsi Pa (today's Hua Xi Ba), one of the few and undoubtedly the best in Free China. One of the chief concerns of the Yale boys was the health of their teeth. Everybody had advised them to go there if they needed any dental attention, so they decided to give it a try. All of them except Paul had some work done. George had a tooth yanked; Art and Jim had a couple of fillings, which were not nearly as bad an experience as they had been led to expect. The dental chair was out in the street, with no sanitation, and people casually walked by during the procedures. The dentist used a foot pedal drill on Jim as one of the student dentists hacked around on one of his teeth. Afterward, Jim noted that it was "not that bad." George Small reported a difficult experience. Jim recalled, "When they went after his tooth they took hammer and chisel and went to work on him like he was a block of stone to be sculptured. Art was there at the time and said that George did some considerable howling. George was a rather comical figure for several days thereafter, as it was a front tooth he had taken out. He let it be known that the situation at the time of the extraction was anything but comical though."[20]

Culture Shopping

While in Chengtu, they toured the campus of the West China Union University and met several Americans, including Dr. Graham, who specialized in ancient

Chinese history and archeology. Graham was the custodian of a large collection of Chinese artifacts at his home. The former French consul in Chengtu, Bechamps, had been a person of considerable means and collected many Chinese paintings, embroidery pieces, pottery, and other objects for many years. Following the fall of France to Nazi Germany in June 1940, this man was out of a job and left the city. For some reason, he found it necessary to dispose of his entire collection and placed it in the hands of Dr. Graham, a man with a good idea of the value of the various pieces. During a coffee one morning at Graham's house, they found out about Bechamps's collection. Art was the biggest buyer, but they all made several purchases that morning or on subsequent days since they were regular visitors to the home. Jim became enamored with embroidered pieces, large ones to be hung across walls, and small scrolls that came in pairs to be hung on either side of a doorway. Paul and Jim each got a Tibetan knife, supposedly quite old. Paul's specialty was carved prayer boxes and a tiny, intricately carved buddha. Jim bought a handsome, ceremonial, heavy robe with a wealth of embroidery work done in gold thread. Art, the biggest buyer, bought as much as he could carry. Dr. Graham assured them that these artifacts were being sold at "giveaway prices." Each man bought several hundred dollars' worth of carved ivory, wooden boxes, a Tibetan fur hat, and silver brooches as gifts, all of which were easily transported. They paid him in Chinese money (Mex.), and Dr. Graham assured them that if they could get the items back to America, they could sell them for the same price in American money. In other words, twenty times as much. In regard to Jim's ceremonial robe, Graham said, "It is not ordinary embroidery, but *K'e Ssu*, which is rare, and this is a fine sample. It should ultimately reach one of America's finest museums and be kept permanently there."[21]

The four young men found their immersion in Chinese culture fascinating during those five days in Chengtu. Their Yale calling cards were invaluable. They met numerous professors, businessmen, writers, and missionaries. Much of their time was spent reading, writing in their diaries, and sightseeing. Before they left town, Jim Elliott described one last shopping venture:

> Everybody but me bought "chops" in Chengtu, a little piece of stone or metal with your Chinese name carved thereon, used like a seal-ring (to identify yourself in letters or documents). Where we would sign our names, the Chinese take out their "chops," press them into clay-like red ink they carry in their "chop-boxes," and make their prints. I didn't get one in Chengtu because I've been hoping to get one made of Taoyuan

stone, reputedly the best obtainable anywhere in China. Taoyuan is a small city between here and Changteh. We passed through it on our way to Yuanling last fall, but at that time I knew nothing of "chops" and Taoyuan stones. The other boys all got metal ones, with carved animals on one end, their names on the other.[22]

On the return trip to Chungking, they came up with an idea to replace their depleted funds, having largely spent them on the Chinese artifacts. They unloaded the remainder of the Red Cross supplies in Chengtu, emptying the trucks. With room to spare, they advertised for passengers for the return trip. They had no trouble signing up nearly fifty passengers, mostly students from Hua Hsi Pa going home for winter vacation. This scheme was prompted in part because the Bachelors were aware of a wartime law in China that prohibited people from driving empty trucks, because gasoline was too precious to waste. This change of cargo caused a bit of trouble getting out of Chengtu. They were stopped at the control station just out of town, which they expected. However, what they did not expect was the heavy tax that was charged for paid passengers riding back to Chungking. It was the decision to take passengers for a fare that caused the trouble at the control station. The officers assessed them for about 20 percent of each passenger's fare, plus a tax on each truck—a total of about $2,000 (Mex.)! They were delayed a couple of hours before the matter was settled—time meant nothing to the Chinese! Jim commented, "Of course, George Cheng was buzzing around, mad as a wet hen."[23] They all agreed that without him along, despite their ignorance of the language, they would have gotten along faster and with less difficulty.

Return to Chungking

Due to their late start, they drove until late that night, not stopping until about 10:00 p.m. at the town of Neichiang. One of their passengers was a missionary woman, Miss Parsons, who arranged for them to sleep in a church that night. Jim Elliott noted, "This was quite unusual—the first and only time I've ever slept in a church, at night anyway—but infinitely more satisfactory than any inn we could have found. We simply put two benches together, unrolled our sleeping bags, and stretched out in them. Not exactly comfortable, but clean and safe. Everywhere in China you hear stories about people being robbed in inns while they are out, or even while they are sleeping!"[24] At least they felt safe for the night.

The second day of driving was uneventful, save for a broken spring in one of the trucks, arriving in Chungking at nightfall. It was a big city with well over a million people. It took the weary group of travelers almost two hours to travel from the outskirts of Chungking to the hospital at the city's center. Driving at night in China was always a challenge, and the traffic in the city was terrible. Complicating the transportation in this sprawling city was that many parts were inaccessible by motor. The only alternative was by rickshaw, which was very uncomfortable, but essential in traversing the hills of Chungking. In other parts of the city, such as the first range, where George Small had his abode—the only substitute for strenuous and difficult walking was to be carried up in a chair by coolies. These services had become expensive. The rickshaw coolie was formerly supposed to have been the poorest of the poor, but in Chungking they were rapidly climbing up the scale of economic welfare as they traversed the hills with passengers in tow. In addition to all the other transportation worries in Chungking, there was the Yangtze River between the main city and the south bank, where the American embassy was located. There was a steam ferry there where the wait was sometimes less than half an hour. The alternative to the ferry was a sampan, which was more dangerous, more expensive, and slower.

There were a few pleasant surprises in China's wartime capital. One of them was shopping, mostly for foreign items rather than for Chinese goods. Sought-after items were fountain pens, flashlights, and books. Another big surprise in Chungking was ice cream. One day while walking along one of the main streets, they saw a sign written in big English letters: "Ice Cream." At first they were skeptical of the quality, but after they consumed a couple of dishes each, it was needless to say—delicious! It was their first ice cream since leaving Hong Kong the previous August. For the remainder of their one-week stay in Chungking, they made daily trips to the Russky Café—the unlikely Russian shop for the coveted ice cream.

During their return visit to Chungking, Springer reported to Col. David Barrett, the embassy military attaché, to see what was expected of him now that America was at war with Japan. He was told that his services were not needed immediately, but that he could be used in a short time. Paul told him, "I should like to finish out the school year at Yali, but after that I might be free to join up."[25] It seemed to him that service was almost on an optional basis, but he felt that if the US Army needed him, he should enlist, rather than be seen as and feeling like a "slacker." He thought about his brothers, Joe and Victor, back at home and wrote to his mother asking for an update on their military status. He knew that his work in China would be civilian in nature even if he got in uniform, and thought that he might be offered a secretarial job in Chungking. However, he did not expect to accept one. For now, he liked the mission of delivering supplies for the Red Cross, and he told his mother, "I'd really like to drive down the Burma Road to Kunming, Lashio, and Rangoon just once."

He had yet to experience a bombing and repeated his former claim that "I am in the safest, most serene place in the world." He asked his mother in a letter, "Tell daddy that I'm trying to do my bit for my country, and that if I enlist out here I'll be an officer in no time."[26]

Springer's Interview

Sensing that Yali might be temporarily closed due to the war, Paul interviewed with the secretary of the American embassy, John Carter Vincent, while in Chungking.[27] Vincent was considered an "Old China Hand." Born in Seneca, Kansas, Vincent graduated from Mercer University in 1923 and was appointed as a foreign-service officer in the same year. He then served in Changsha, Hankow, Swatow, Peking, Mukden, Nanking, and Dairen before becoming secretary to the American embassy in Chungking in 1942. Springer told Vincent that he was on the lookout for other employment, and he would like to work at the embassy in the event that the Yali school was abruptly closed. Vincent liked the young man and told him that they would be in touch if their staffing needs changed.

After a week in Chungking, the Bachelors rendezvoused with Al Ravenholt, who was in town on IRC business. He accompanied them in the IRC trucks on the return to Kweiyang, in which they brought back a load of salt. The back leg of the journey was uneventful for the most part, except for the cold weather. It was in the middle of February 1942, and it was the coldest weather they had experienced in China. The morning after they left Chungking, the radiator of one of the trucks froze, and they experienced snow and ice on the roads. They found Kweiyang just as boring on the return trip as it was on the first visit. The boredom was such that one night they all went to bed at 5:30 since there was just nothing else to do. While they were in Kweiyang, they learned that Ed Gulick's library was there.[28] Gulick was a prior Yali Bachelor who arrived in Changsha in 1937 and assisted with the physical relocation of the Yali school to Yuanling in 1938. He returned to the US in 1939. Jim and Art promptly scurried around, located his book collection, and appropriated it for return to the school, where it would reside in the Bachelors' Mess in Yuanling.

From the moment they first agreed to drive for the IRC, the Bachelors had been planning a shipment of goods to Yuanling to coincide with the return trip. After five days in Kweiyang, they climbed aboard an FAU truck bound for Yuanling and headed on the road back. The return trip was much different from the outward journey. It had taken nearly five days to get to Kweiyang via a public bus, and they had been inconvenienced, scared, and worried about their luggage in the process. Returning under their own power took them less than three days. Two FAU men joined them:

Allen Hill (as a driver) and Frank Willsher (to inspect Yuanling's hospitals and others en route). Alan and Frank would also return the vehicles to the FAU once the Bachelors departed at Yuanling.

The night before they reached Yuanling, they stayed in Chihchiang, a quiet little city about 170 kilometers southwest of Yali. A newly constructed military airfield and facilities for a force of American aviators was being built there.[29] They had several things to unload from the trucks at Chihchiang, both for the China Inland Mission (CIM) and for the Catholic mission. They met Dr. Becker, head of the CIM station, and had dinner with him that night. Becker was a German and was having considerable trouble with the local authorities because he was suspected of being a spy. According to Becker's story, it was only through the intercession of Madame Chiang (the wife of Chiang Kai-shek) that he was allowed to remain in town. Even so, he was scarcely allowed outside his own compound and had to get special permission to supervise the transportation of the IRC supplies for his mission. He told the Bachelors the officials constantly accused him of having secret stores of munitions, a secret sending-and-receiving radio set, a secret hoard of money, and an automobile mysteriously hidden somewhere. Becker was not even allowed to preach in his own church!

Before they left, Paul, Art, and Jim went over to the Catholic mission for breakfast the next morning and marveled at the sugared fried cakes—the first they had eaten in China. After breakfast, Father Marcellus hitched a ride back to Yuanling with them, and they enjoyed his genial company during those last 170 kilometers back "home" to Yali.

They had embarked on an adventure together and ended up spending their entire midterm vacation driving across rural China and furthering the humanitarian mission of Yale-in-China in the process. The Bachelors enjoyed their time driving the trucks in service of the IRC. Paul sent a Western Union telegram on March 12, 1942, to his mother; sisters, Eleanor and Ruth; and brothers, Joe and Vic; and birthday wishes to his dad. It said; "HOWS EVERYBODY. IM SAFE N WELL [*sic*]. MAIL SCARCE THESE DAYS. VACATION DROVE IRC TRUCK BURMA ROAD = LOVE PAUL."[30]

Spring Semester

The Bachelors arrived in Yuanling during the last week in February and began teaching their respective classes within days. Their "winter vacation" had been quite an adventure. During their absence, the remaining staff, both Chinese and Americans, persevered with their missions despite overwhelming difficulties. In Changsha, parts of Hsiang-Ya Hospital and its premises were destroyed by Japanese soldiers before their rout of the city's suburbs in early January. It had now resumed somewhat normal operations with the help of the Chinese government. Win and Maude Pettus announced the birth of a daughter, Ann, who arrived on her father's birthday, February 25. She was born in the damaged Hsiang-Ya Hospital in Changsha.

While Art, Jim, Don, and Bob continued to teach at Yale-in-China during the spring, Paul's life took an unexpected detour as the war expanded in China. Art shared the story of how this came about in a letter to Bob Smith on May, 3, 1942: "Now there are only four of us here, as Paul Springer has left to work for the International Red Cross in Kweiyang, and the house seemed strangely empty without his presence. . . . Just two weeks ago we received an urgent request from the I.R.C. for two men to help drive vitally needed supplies and medicine up from Burma before the Japs got there. Dwight and the school authorities decided that at the most only one could be spared so we tossed a coin, and Paul was the winner. He left a week ago Saturday and we have heard from him twice."[31] While in Yuanling, Paul received a letter from his draft board, ordering him to report to the nearest US commandant for a physical exam. Needless to say, a trip back to New Jersey was not something that could be arranged at that point in time, so he just filed the letter.

With Paul gone, each of the Bachelors was assigned an extra class. Bob took the ninth-grade class, Jim took the eighth-grade class, and Don took the Hsiang-Ya classes (four a week taught in two sections). Art and Jim doubled up on Jim's senior arts class. The junior school students called on their teachers regularly to request stamps (some were collectors) or foreign pictures, or to pass the time of day. Art described their new students as "the cleanest looking and neatest group of students in town. Many of the little boys are particularly appealing, have beautiful manners, and are most enthusiastic and lively. Everything about us fascinates them, and after class the small ones come up and examine my clothes, watch, fountain pen, [and] the hair on my legs and arms, and ask countless questions."[32] To their teachers, these young students were very attractive, with their shaven heads, beautiful brown eyes, and good manners. Bob Clarke said that they were like "exotic little animals." The food they received seemed adequate in variety, since meat was served only once a week, but of course they had no milk, very little fruit, and rice three times a day. Usually these servings were coupled with dishes of cabbage or greens and some "tofu" or bean curd. The students were uncomplaining, and as Bob observed, "If they are undernourished, they didn't show it."[33]

Art was perceived as being too nice by at least one student, Bruno Huang Sin Fang, who wrote the essay "My Boyhood's Friend." Bruno also wrote a letter to Art about his academic experience in Yuanling. Some excerpts are below:

I cannot get any news here, but I think the war in Hunan is very serious. Many armies are camping. They are spreading in the country. Many roads here are annihilated. I think these armies will resisting [*sic*] invasion of our enemy after the crops. Now I study "Help Towards Correct English" and "A Dictionary of English Grammar and Composition" in two books. Many dubiousness of the English Grammar which I was often perplexed are answered by these two books. Last term our English course was very good. But I think our English course still needs the improvement. Last term we just learned useful words. This is not enough. I think we had better add a certain book to study. Because we can learn good sentences from the book. This is only my own suggestion. I do not know whether you agree with me. You have a defect for teaching. (Excuse me for my discourtesy). You seem very kind for teaching us. Of course this is your good character, but when you're teaching us you should not be so kind to us. I never saw your angry face in my class, and never heard any blaming word. Goodbye.[34]

This student was one of many who found the nurturing and patient American teaching methods to be in sharp contrast to the harsh, authoritarian styles they had experienced in Chinese schools before they began their studies at Yali with the Bachelors. The spring semester went quite well, considering they were short staffed with the absence of Paul. There were several factors for this. For one, the air raid alarms were much scarcer and less disruptive. Art reminisced about the semester:

Since March 1 we have had just 20 urgent alarms, and the release always comes at lunch time now, so that's not so bad. And you wouldn't recognize the dugout place now. The steps down have been rebuilt, and temporary, thatched-roofed shelters have been thrown up to protect us from the glaring sun. For a long time all of us had dreaded the necessity for going out to the shelter, as there [it] was always noisy, distracting, and uncomfortable, as the students were forced to sit on sharp stones in the broiling sun. I however, hit on a happy solution of this problem for the students. I told them that for every minute they did not work, or doze, or were distracted during a *ching-pao*, they were doing exactly what the Japs hoped they would do, as one of the main purposes of the raids was to disrupt all work, and terrorize the people. The boys really like the idea, and now work as hard as ever, despite the fact that they are sitting on a

141

sharp rock, and a group of yokels are standing around looking at the class, and they write compositions about the necessity of work during alarm.[35]

Due to the long winter vacation, classes were not over until later in the year, with final exams on June 24. Jim expected to leave early in June, since he had two graduating classes that finished at the end of May. Jim planned to go to work for the IRC in the summer, and Art expected to join him as soon as his classes were finished. Paul, Jim, and Art all planned to return to Yali for the beginning of the fall semester. Bob and Don still had plans to go home that summer, if possible, since their two-year tenure at Yale-in-China would be completed at the end of June. Paul would never see the Yali campus again.

Chapter 9
CHANGE OF OCCUPATION

First Assignment

The International Red Cross needed help moving medical supplies, and Springer had been tapped as an additional resource. Although he volunteered for the assignment (via the coin toss), the request for help came directly from the International Relief Committee (IRC) in Kweiyang. Dwight Rugh informed the Yale-in-China trustees in New Haven of this development via cable on April 25, 1942. The cable read: "APPROVE MEETING EMERGENCY REQUEST SPRINGER ASSIST INTER RED CROSS TRANSPORTATION BURMA CHINA ROUTE TILL FALL. DISCUSS WITH PARENTS. CABLE DECISION IMMEDIATELY."[1]

Rugh's cable took the form of a formal request. Springer's new assignment was already a fait accompli. Bob Smith wrote to Paul's mother a few days later and gave

Paul Springer, Chinese drivers license, issued for his FAU work on January 24, 1942. *Springer Family collection*

143

her a summation of his new assignment. Springer would continue under the jurisdiction of Yale-in-China, although he would for all practical purposes be an employee of the IRC. Their headquarters were in Kweiyang, in Kweichow Province. Because he was "loaned" by Yale-in-China to the IRC, this temporary change in occupation would not affect his standing with Yale-in-China. Springer was expected to return to work with Yale-in-China beginning with the fall term, so there was no prospect of sending him home to New Jersey. Dr. Rugh was Yale's representative in China and was responsible for official policy, so his approval of Springer's proposal to join the IRC was final. Springer continued to receive his regular salary (a teaching stipend) while doing work for the IRC. Yale-in-China had recently raised the monthly salary of the Bachelors by $7.00 per month (due to the rampant inflation in the region), making it retroactive to the beginning of the term in September 1941. Springer was included in the pay raise even though he was driving for the IRC. Smith tried to comfort Paul's mother in a letter by assuring her that her son would not go anywhere near Burma (now Myanmar), then a British colony in Southeast Asia bordered by Bangladesh, India, China, Laos, and Thailand. "I do not expect him to go that far west. Did you notice that he and the others spoke of trucking on the Burma Road in February? Actually they were not on the Burma Road but on the highway from Kweiyang via Chungking to Chengtu, which is several hundred miles from the official

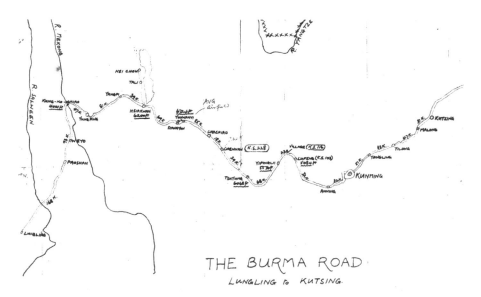

Drawing of the Burma Road as it enters China, running to Kunming and Kutsing. Sketch map by Bernard Llewellyn of the FAU. *Courtesy of Michael Llewellyn*

Burma Road running westward from Kunming."[2] Although well intentioned, Smith was mistaken in his assumptions that Springer's new job would not take him into the most-dangerous parts of the supply route.

The Burma Road ran from Burma through the mountains of western China to the city of Kunming. In response to the Japanese invasion of northern China in 1937, the Burma Road was urgently built as an essential supply route, an achievement of manual labor in much the same way that the Great Wall was. Over 100,000 Chinese workers built it after the Japanese occupied the coastal areas. Most of the road was one lane wide and crudely paved with rocks. After completion in 1938, it was the main thoroughfare through the region. Military supplies to support the fight against the Japanese were picked up from the port of Rangoon on the Andaman Sea, east of Bay of Bengal, then transported by train to the railhead at Lashio, in Burma, and finally by truck over the Burma Road to Kunming and beyond.[3] Between 1937 and 1939, the Japanese seized China's seaports. In 1940, they occupied Indochina and closed the railway between Hanoi and Kunming. It was this lifeline of supplies that enabled the Chinese to sustain their resistance against Japan.

Not only did Springer's new assignment take him down the Burma Road (going westward from Kunming), it also took him closer to the fighting on the front. The main purpose of the Japanese invasion of Burma in 1942 was to cut the Burma Road, which was the one remaining land supply route to China. Rugged, jungle-covered mountains split Burma into three roughly north–south valleys, with the Salween River in the east, the Sittang River in the center, and the Irrawaddy River in the west. This rough terrain made east–west travel very difficult.[4] Burma was defended by British and Indian forces, along with their Chinese allies, in a military campaign that stretched through the spring of 1942. By mid-March, the fighting was 100 miles north of Rangoon. Two British divisions struggled to contain the Japanese advance at Prone, in the Irrawaddy valley. About eighty miles east of them, an elite Chinese division held at Tuangoo, in the Sittang valley. The remainder of the Chinese army assigned to defend the region was hundreds of miles to the rear.

The Chinese wanted to marshal their forces for a decisive battle at Mandalay, but General Alexander sent a frantic plea for the Chinese to help his British troops at Yenangyaung. They were completely surrounded and were running short of water and supplies. The Chinese 38th Division, 66th Army, rushed to their aid. They attacked the Japanese on the morning of April 18. Over the next two days they bravely engaged the Japanese in bloody combat and pushed them back. Confusion gave the British enough time to escape. However, the diversion of Chinese troops allowed the Japanese to strike a mortal blow in the east. They veered across the country and broke through the lines along the Thai border, virtually destroying two divisions of the Chinese 6th Army and opening the road to Lashio. When the rout became apparent, Chinese tanks withdrew from the scene before ever meeting the enemy in battle. They were joined by a flood of British and Chinese soldiers fleeing the front lines. The town of Lashio was in flames when the tanks passed through on their way back to China. The scene along the Burma Road was chaos. If a vehicle turned off its engine, Chinese soldiers just pushed it off the road. Burmese partisans, eager to get rid of their British colonial masters, showed their scorn by setting fires and sabotaging buildings. They did not yet realize that they were about to be under a much more brutal administration of the Japanese.[5]

The FAU's Exit from Burma

The FAU teams were operating deep inside Burma. They set up a field hospital in Pyinmana, a town about 100 miles north of Rangoon. While there, the Chinese army was pouring down the road to confront the Japanese. They were commanded by General "Vinegar Joe" Stilwell, a US general with a staff of officers, based in Mandalay.

Rangoon was about to fall. When a request came into the FAU for ambulance support, two FAU drivers headed to the front with nothing except their three-ton Chevy trucks. They returned the next morning with a load of Chinese casualties, bullet holes in the trucks, and a flat tire. The FAU doctors and Burmese nurses got to work on the wounded in their makeshift operating room.

Unfortunately, when the Japanese cut off the Burma Road, this group of 114 officers, men, doctors, nurses, and drivers was stranded on the wrong end of the road. Their only way back to China was now in Japanese hands. The convoy consisted of a dozen trucks, several jeeps, and two Buick staff cars. On April 27, they crossed an old iron bridge over the Irrawady River, and then Stillwell's men blew it up to keep the Japanese from following them. The rough road wound its way northwest from Mandalay to the Burmese town of Shwebo, where they sheltered for the night in an abandoned church. The road deteriorated to little more than a zigzagging dirt trail. By May 5, they had covered 200 miles. At that point, the Buicks had long been abandoned, with the trucks and jeeps driving between the trees as far as they could. When the trucks were abandoned, the essential goods and food were transferred to the jeeps, which proceeded a few more miles until they reached a clearing where they could penetrate no farther.

At this point, the group struck out on foot to India—and safety. When they arrived at a riverbank, Stillwell commandeered a couple of dugout canoes from a local village and loaded them to the gunwales. The drone of aircraft engines sent the group scuttling for cover and readied their guns. When the plane made another pass, they noted

Chiang Kai-shek, Soong Mei-ling, and Gen. Joseph W. Stilwell. Stilwell served as the American military advisor to Chiang. His caustic and combative personality earned him the nickname "Vinegar Joe." *Joseph Warren Stilwell Papers, Box 108, Hoover Institution Archives*

it was a British twin-engine, long-range medium bomber, out of which came sacks and sacks of food that tumbled down from the sky. They had been discovered, although they were still a long way out from India. Their journey took them fourteen days, covering 200 miles by walking and rafting, and eventually climbing over 8,000 feet until they arrived at the city of Imphal in Assam, in British India.[6] It was one of the more notable and heroic retreats of the war.

Small Chinese Towns

Springer was lucky. The original purpose of his assignment was to rush supplies out of Lashio before the Japanese captured the city. When the Japanese invasion advanced in Burma in the spring of 1942, Lashio fell on April 29. The supplies were lost. Springer's mission was stopped forty miles from his starting point by a bridge washed out by several days of torrential rains.[7] Although he was on the Chinese end of the road, he could not go in either direction: Japanese troops were in the direction of Lashio, and a washed-out bridge was in the other. He found himself stuck in the small Chinese town of Chenki for eight days, with no instructions from his superiors. After spending a week in a town that is usually a five-minute stop for buses (and not important enough to be a military target), Springer felt that he was becoming an authority on small Chinese towns. His temporary residence was at the Village Hotel, which boasted a balcony overlooking the street. From here, he surveyed the minutia of village life and all of its phases, along with the people from beggars to merchants. Chenki lay in the fertile valley along the riverbank, where fish of all varieties were caught. The town had grown rapidly, due to the presence of easily mined coal and lime. The coal-mining section was filthy; the living conditions were unbelievably bad. The thatched-roofed mud shacks, constituting most of the housing, were not even rainproof. The shacks had no windows or lights, or sanitary facilities.

Springer described the monotony of his layover and his impressions of the town:

> Below the hotel balcony, which was a short distance west on the road from the coal mines, was a more prosperous looking strip. To my right was the bus station into which two buses streamed daily, one from each direction. . . . From dawn until after dark this section of the street is teeming with people—people who seem to wander about aimlessly as do Americans at an amusement park. To my left a group of small boys and girls play at jumping rope. . . . The rope jumping invites the surveillance of a passing coolie, and he stops and watches intently for a full 15 minutes, counting to himself the number of times each boy successfully jumps over the rope. He finally goes reluctantly away—to stop a few yards further on and watch a mechanic change a truck wheel. A mother comes out of the shop across the street and holds her small child in position while he has his regular bowel movement in the street. Even the fastidious foreigner is no longer shocked at this—he has seen it so many times already while on his way inland. The most interested spectators of this performance are the mother of the child and the local cleanup squad of monks.
>
> The coal cars, propelled by men, and each containing about one quarter ton, go roaring past on the single pair of narrow gauge rails from the mines to the dock. The men pursue their cars on the run and hop on for a long ride down the gentle grade. They enjoy it like children enjoy scooters. A group of soldiers bearing rice baskets go parading past double file, crying in unison, "*ee, er, san, shih*" (1, 2, 3, 4). Half are barefoot; all are clad in faded greenish yellow uniforms of varying shades! Behind them come two soldiers bearing a makeshift bamboo stretcher, on which rides a sick comrade.
>
> The foreigner dare not come down from his perch unless he wants to be all three rings of the circus, for he is immediately surrounded. Should he stop for a moment by a curious crowd from which voices question or call names, and hands feel his clothing or pull at him or his forearms [*sic*]. They laughed delightfully every time he speaks, and should he screw up his face a bit, the hilarity is literally thunderous. Mothers bring up their babies for all look at the *wei kuo jen*, and the babies cry or scream

with fright—for here is the Chinese counterpart of the bogeyman so dreaded by American children. The crowd soon becomes so uproarious that a policeman standing nearby has to request the foreigner to move or return to his quarters—and the latter is a fate worse than death after a week spent in such a place, with no immediate prospect of departing therefrom.[8]

Springer could hardly wait for the washed-out bridge to be repaired so that he could exit this wretched place and never come back.

Ambulance Unit

Upon arrival in Kunming on May 25, Springer wrote his mother: "I arrived here last night at 9:00 pm after a five-day trip from Kweiyang in a Ford truck which I drove. I'm a regular mechanic now—you should see me tighten up bolts, clean the carburetor, etc. Maybe I'll open a garage when I get back. There were two trucks in our convoy, and the other one, a Dodge, had no headlights. We had to run after dark twice, and

FAU trucks pass through Kunming, the starting point of Springer's transport mission on the Burma Road. *FAU collection*

had quite a time going over mountains with the Dodge following the Ford's tail-light. The average life of a truck in China is less than a year, and the Ford is two years old, the Dodge three."⁹

Truck maintenance was the major problem in sustaining the system, and the supply of spare parts and lubricating oil was the most critical element. Each convoy or individual truck was expected to be self-sufficient for any repairs or maintenance between bases. Drivers had to overhaul both vehicles every morning before starting, seldom if ever finding a tight bolt. It became second nature, drilled into all drivers on first trips, to examine all tires and springs at every stop and to check not only oil and water, but also engine mountings, fan belts, U bolts, and wheel bolts every day.¹⁰ Despite the labor, the opportunity for travel and excitement was a considerable morale booster for Springer.

The starting point was Kunming, which Springer described as "a beautiful city at 6,400 feet elevation with a perfect climate." He feared that the city was overdue for a bombing since the American Volunteer Group (AVG) was being redirected on to Chungking.¹¹ The AVG consisted of a group of volunteer air units organized by the US government to aid the Nationalist government of China against Japan in the war. This American force, the 1st AVG, was popularly known as the Flying Tigers. Under the command of Gen. Claire Lee Chennault, they experienced heavy combat in China. The pilots sported ferocious-looking nose art of tiger shark jaws on their Curtiss P-40 fighter planes. Springer wrote of the AVG: "I've met a number of them, and they're tough hombres—but they'll give you the shirts off their backs if you meet them halfway. I am indebted to them for several meals, lots of unprocurable canned goods and coffee. They actually have a 30–1 record over the Japs in planes shot down—they get $500 gold per plane. Unfortunately, their term is up this summer and most of them are flying back by ferry command—a way I could get out if necessary."¹²

Springer tried to be realistic with his mother about the realities of the war in China. He was no longer in the relative safety of Yuanling. There were constant Japanese attacks on the supply route he was driving, and his new assignment would take him dangerously close to the fighting. At the same time, he tried to reassure her that his safety was in the hands of God:

> The job is undoubtedly very dangerous, and I'll be in the midst of bombing, shelling and strafing. Naturally I'll take every precaution to keep my hide intact. I know that your prayers are with me, and I am comforted by that fact. If I return alive, and I fully expect to, I shall have profited greatly by the experience in the testing I have undergone. If I should die, it will

be in the pursuance of a very worthy cause, and my greatest regret would be that it brought unhappiness to my family. These are the times that try men's souls. Many mothers who have fewer sons than you do will lose them before this war is over. I don't think communications will be very good south of Kunming, so you may not hear from me for a long while. I'll write whenever there is the remotest chance of the letter getting through, and will cable immediately upon my return to Kunming, and safety in August.

Tonight I'm going to the AVG hostel here to meet a few more of the boys, as well as Lt. Col. McMoreland, who is the man to see about the Ferry Command. Planes come in daily from the US via India loaded with supplies for China, and they go back comparatively empty. Plane fare is $1,800. gold, but if a guy has no money and knows the right people, he can perhaps go free. My love to Ruth, Eleanor, Joe, Vic, and Daddy. I'll be thinking of you all often during the next few months, and know that you will be thinking of me. I hope that your brood will all be safely gathered again under your wing in the not-too-distant future. Meantime, fill the gap with prayers and meditation.[13]

FAU mobile surgical unit in Paoshan, southwest part of Yunnan Province. *FAU collection*

Springer's work for the FAU took him deep into the interior of China. He left Kunming in late May, as part of a surgical unit working for FAU, delivering supplies, medicine, and surgical equipment. On one delivery, his truck contained a crate that was assumed to be surgical instruments, but when it was inspected, it was found to be full of pajamas—a slight oversight somewhere, and he dismissed it as "a typical example of British muddling through."[14] After a long and difficult trip to Kweiyang, he found the situation in quite an uproar and learned that the FAU had sustained heavy casualties in Burma, losing twelve new Chevrolet trucks and twenty-two men between

Mandalay and Lashio when the latter fell to the Japanese.[15] Springer and Hopkins knew several of the missing British men in the unit, whom Hopkins described as "finest type of young Englishmen."[16] Springer found the FAU exciting work and took a gas mask and a tin helmet with him, just in case things got really hot. Hopkins later mused about the situation: "If it wasn't for the flip of a coin I should have been in his place."[17]

His next assignment was to work at the front as part of a twelve-man FAU surgical unit under the direction of Dr. Hank Lauderbaugh, an American who hailed from Englewood, New Jersey.[18] Paul described him as "a top-notcher" and was looking forward to the work. The other ten men included one American, three Chinese, and six British. Springer's main job was to drive up just behind the front near Paoshan at dusk to pick up wounded soldiers at a depot there, returning before dawn to the base hospital a few kilometers back.[19] On one of these journeys, he felt something hot ripping through his shirt, tearing across the skin of his chest and exiting out the window. Although the bullet put two holes in his shirt, it made for only a nasty flesh wound, leaving a small scar that stayed with him for life. Bleeding but otherwise unharmed, he shrugged it off and focused on the mission at hand. He knew that he had to keep his truck in shape and assist in any way that he could with the operations on the wounded soldiers. Springer's FAU convoy was the only medical transportation unit of the Allied powers on the Yunnan front during this bitter campaign fought by British and Chinese troops against the Japanese. All the others had fled.[20]

Shipments of supplies, including medical supplies, could no longer travel over the Burma Road after the route fell to the Japanese. The occupation forces completed their blockade of China. This included the cities of Tengchong and Longling in the westernmost part of Yunnan, although most of the population had taken refuge in the mountains north of the city. The local guerrillas and Chinese troops fought side by side against the well-trained and well-equipped invaders. Despite their best efforts, they were outnumbered and overwhelmed. The Chinese defenders were ultimately pushed back across the eastern bank of the Salween.[21]

Having advanced so quickly up the Burma Road, the Japanese had outpaced their supply lines and were desperate for food. They plundered rural villages of rice and grain. They took any chickens, cows, pigs, and other livestock they could find from local farmers. They tortured and killed any person suspected of being guerrillas or spies, and many others along with them. They were eager to exact revenge on their Chinese enemies, especially after enduring the stubborn guerrilla attacks that hampered their advance through the Shweli valley in Yunnan. Japanese soldiers often competed with each other to devise creative ways to kill the Chinese. Sometimes they would tie them to trees and practice bayoneting them until they bled to death.[22]

The Japanese occupation of southwestern China inflicted a horrific level of violence, rape, murder, and abuse on the local population.[23]

Aerial Lifeline: The Hump

Supplies now had to be flown in over "the Hump." This was what American pilots called the epic spur of the Himalayas that juts south into Burma, dividing China and India.[24] Future shipments for distribution by the FAU had to be flown into Kunming over the Himalayas from India, under British control. This created great difficulty for the FAU, who struggled to secure aircraft and an alliance with the US Army Air Corps to keep the supply lifeline open.

Shortly after his arrival in Kunming, Springer received a pile of mail. There were seven letters from his mother dated between January and April, as well as one from Julia Ravenel, his would-be fiancée in Charleston, South Carolina. Getting caught up on news from home was a pleasant diversion. Although food was abundant in Kunming, there were shortages in other parts of China. He noticed that with the sharp spike in inflation of food prices, Kunming had become somewhat of a speculator's paradise. There were "fearful" rises in the price of food and staples, ranging from bananas to cheese, ice cream, canned pineapple, canned tomato juice, fruit, cigarettes, and coffee.

Homesick

Traveling on the road so long had made Springer miss his girlfriend. He expressed this to his mother in a letter:

> Julia enclosed a picture of herself and her mother in the letter. I told her to send a copy to you if possible. She is #1 on the hit parade and I hope to marry her when I return. Her letter was a revelation to me after having given her up as a correspondent and potential wife. She now wears my picture in a locket and has said she is waiting for me, having found that I am the guy. I cabled her at once (instead of you) and encouraged her to keep writing. I also wrote the following day elaborating on my cable. You'll like her, I am sure mother. I hope she can get up to see you sometime soon. She sings beautifully and plays the piano. She is now in her last year at Charleston College. She is 20, so keep Joe at a distance. The Ravenel family is an old and honored one in Charleston. Julia's immediate family is not so wealthy as some, but she has an uncle who has a riding academy and a large estate, and others with large plantations, two of which I visited while there.[25]

Julia's letter also contained the sad news that two of Springer's friends whom he met on board SS *President Harrison*, Bob Fulton and Capt. Albert Rooks of the US Navy, were killed in the Battle of Java. Both served on USS *Houston*.

Remembering Rooks

USS *Houston* and an Australian cruiser, HMAS *Perth*, reached Tanjung Priok, Java, the main port of Batavia in the Dutch East Indies, on February 28, 1942, where they attempted to resupply but were met with fuel shortages and no available ammunition.[26] The two cruisers sailed to Sunda Straight, between Sumatra and Java, which the Allies believed was free of enemy vessels. When lookouts on *Perth* sighted a Japanese destroyer, she engaged it. However, as this happened, multiple Japanese warships appeared and surrounded the two Allied ships.

The two cruisers evaded the nine torpedoes launched by a Japanese destroyer named *Fubuki*. The cruisers then sank one transport and forced three others to beach but were blocked from passing through Sunda Strait by a destroyer squadron and had to contend with the heavy cruisers *Mogami* and *Mikuma* in proximity. At midnight, *Perth* attempted to force her way through the destroyers but was hit by four torpedoes in the space of a few minutes, then subjected to close-range gunfire until sinking about 12:25 a.m. on March 1, 1942. On board *Houston*, shells were in short supply in the forward turrets, so the crew manhandled shells from the disabled number turret to the forward turrets. *Houston* was struck by a torpedo shortly after midnight and began to lose headway. *Houston*'s gunners had scored hits on three different destroyers and sunk a minesweeper, but she was struck by three more torpedoes in quick succession! Captain Rooks was killed by a bursting shell at 12:30 a.m. As the ship came to a stop, Japanese destroyers moved in, machine-gunning the decks. Minutes later, *Houston* rolled over and sank. Of the 1,061 aboard, 368 survived, only to be captured by the Japanese and interned in prison camps. Bob Fulton and his wife had lived in Charleston. Springer fondly recalled his impression of Captain Rooks in a letter to his mother: "He was commanding officer and probably went down with the ship."[27]

When Burma fell to the Japanese in May 1942, many of the FAU volunteers in the Burma theater relocated to India or China. They regrouped and took on the distribution of medical supplies delivered via air transport over "the

As commanding officer of USS *Houston*, Capt. Albert H. Rooks was posthumously awarded the Medal of Honor for his extraordinary heroism in the battle of Java. *University of Houston Digital Library: USS* Houston *(CA-30) Photographs: Capt. Albert H. Rooks*

Hump." Meanwhile, back in Yuanling, both Bob Clarke and Don McCabe planned to return to America that summer, since their teaching contracts at Yali were near completion. There were several possible routes home. They originally planned to go to Chungking by bus, fly on a Chinese National Aviation Corp. (CNAC) plane to Calcutta, cross India by train, and then secure passage on a troop ship home. Springer wrote to them in Yuanling about another possibility. He noted, "Planes come in daily from the U.S. via India, loaded with supplies for China, and they go back comparatively empty."[28] He added, "It is sometimes possible for Americans to go all the way home free, from Kunming to Miami in eight days, with stops at Calcutta, Karachi, Bombay, Cairo, Gold Coast, Natal, Brazil, Trinidad, and Miami. What a trip!"[29] An estimated 80 percent of medical supplies distributed in China were through the work of the FAU. Clarke and McCabe departed for home from Chungking on the morning of June 30, via a plane bound for India.[30]

American Embassy

With the severing of the Burma Road and the demise of the FAU overland supply route, the FAU continued to deliver relief and medical supplies out of Kunming. Springer's services were no longer needed, since a number of fresh replacements had

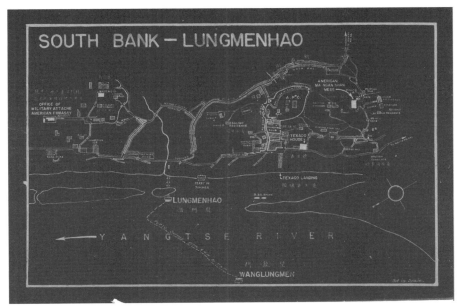

Drawing of the south bank, Chungking, showing the locations of the American Embassy, Office of the Military Attaché, Belgian Embassy, Chungking Club, ferry locations, and the British Consulate. *Springer Family collection*

arrived from India.[31] Springer had planned to return to Yali as soon as his job with the IRC was over. In the interim, he was offered a position as a cipher officer at the American embassy in Chungking. This was a result of his interview with John Carter Vincent earlier in the year. George Small, his friend and a member of the embassy staff, was in touch with Springer and informed the embassy of his address in Kunming. On June 8, Springer received a telegram as follows: "SIXTH EMBASSY HAS RECEIVED AUTHORIZATION FOR YOUR EMPLOYMENT PERIOD PLEASE TELEGRAPH IF YOU ACCEPT AND IF SO WHEN YOU CAN PROCEED CHUNGKING."[32]

Springer described his reaction: "My first intention was to wire that I regretted my inability to accept the offer. On second thought, however, as I very much wanted the job, and as I was no longer needed by the FAU due to a number of replacements freshly arrived from India, I wired 'Can leave here Wednesday (10th) work until September, uncertain about later. Please wire if satisfactory!' To this the answer came 'Arrangement Satisfactory,' and I left by IRC truck on the 10th, arriving at Chungking on the 15th, and starting work on the 16th."[33] It was a salary increase for Paul, $2,800 gold per annum, plus a small per diem allowance. He had legitimate concerns that the campus in Yuanling might close down due to the war, and he might not be able to get home to the US in a timely manner.

He accepted the job offer on a temporary basis, pending the approval of the Yale-in-China trustees. As it stood, his teaching contract was morally binding, although not legally. He did not want to abandon Yali and leave them shorthanded, but he felt that service at the American embassy at Chungking was of a higher calling to aid in the war effort. Chungking had not been bombed in over a year. Just in case, the embassy had the advantage of a substantial bomb shelter underneath feet of solid rock, as opposed to the FAU station in Kunming, which was without an adequate shelter from bombing raids.

The formal request for Springer's release from Yale-in-China came in a letter from the US ambassador to China, Clarence E. Gauss. Gauss had a long career in the US Foreign Service. He was posted in China as early as 1916 in Shanghai, Amoy, and Tsinan; served as US consul general in Mukden, Tsinan, Shanghain, and Tientsin; and then served in Paris in 1935. From 1940 to 1941 he served as the US minister to Australia before his appointment by President Roosevelt to China as the US entered the war with Japan. Gauss wrote, "Mr. Springer accepted the offer on a temporary basis, as he was reluctant to sever his connection with Yale in China without the approval of the trustees. There is a definite need for Mr. Springer in the code room here for the duration of the war, and it is extremely difficult to get new men out here at this time. Also, Mr. Springer has expressed a desire to become engaged in some sort of work more directly connected with the total war effort than is provided by a teaching post at Yali."[34] The trustees' response: "Mr. Springer's attitude of desiring release by the trustees of Yale-in-China Association before accepting regular appointment in the foreign service is most commendable, and I have authorized his appointment on a temporary basis in deference to his wishes."[35] The full board of trustees approved the request, and Springer formally entered the US State Department—his first position in what would be a stepping-stone to a career in the US intelligence service.

He had grown restless in Yuanling since the war broke out between the US and Japan. His new position was a form of war service, and he believed he was doing more for the war effort at the embassy than by teaching school in Yuanling. The increase in pay was no small consideration, since his new salary allowed him to pay off his college debt quickly. The debt was something that he had wanted to extinguish for some time and was unable to do so on his teaching stipend. His first day involved taking an oath and getting sworn into office, filling out forms and getting his picture taken a dozen times. He was issued a new passport and a government ID in Chinese with the name Tse, Paul (Mr. Paul L. Springer), identifying him as a secretary for the American embassy. He had been in China only about nine months, but this sudden change in occupation placed him at the epicenter of diplomatic and intelligence traffic that was received by and originated from the American embassy in Chungking.

Paul Springer with cigar, back porch of American Embassy, Chungking, 1943. George Small is second from left in white shirt. *Springer Family collection*

Code Work

Springer's first job was as a cipher officer, another name for a decoding clerk.[36] He found it interesting work, since there were several different codes and different systems to which the codes applied. He would both encode and decode messages coming into and out of the embassy. Some of the codes were used for the exchange of information concerning radio transmissions. This type of work involved understanding and knowing which codes to use in certain types of communications.

Encoding the transmissions of sensitive information from the ever-present eyes and ears of America's adversaries became complicated. Even the radio frequencies over which the messages were transmitted were encoded as five-digit groups and decoded on the other end by a one-time subtraction system from the decoding tables, without carrying the digit. Teletype codes took a different path. After the regular teletype connection was made, the transmitter asked the receiving end for identification. If this was given correctly, then transmission proceeded as follows: Each unique teletype code was a series of twenty-six four-letter words, with each word representing a letter of the alphabet, with another set of ten four-letter words representing numerals 1–9. These word lists varied by the sender. The receiving station decoded the words as they ranked alphabetically, and via a table they quickly spelled out the message, often abbreviated.[37] The messages to and from the American embassy in Chungking ranged from the mundane to highly classified military and diplomatic communications. Springer found the coding routine to be complicated at first but felt he was well on his way to mastering it.

The Lair

He settled into the job among familiar faces, since his first living quarters were on top of the mountain with his friends George Small and Boise Hart. The house was assigned to the embassy, consisting of six rooms in back for Small, Hart, Springer, and anyone else who arrived for embassy work needing a residence. Their flat took the entire second floor of the guesthouse on the mountain. It had a tennis court in the backyard. Like most young renters, Springer needed to buy his own household supplies on his own, including buying in on the food supply of canned goods that his roommates had available for the three of them. Paul noted, "I shan't economize on food, as two of the FAU boys died of typhus practically under my nose last week, due to skimping on food and the resultant run-down condition."[38] One of the men was John Briggs, who was assigned to supervise the building of a new depot. Only a few days after his death, another FSU member, Douglas Hardy, caught typhus fever and died.[39]

Communications improved, since mail came in and out via diplomatic pouch. His mother only needed to address the envelope to Department of State, Washington, DC, with his name, and American Embassy, Chungking. Then with the cost of affixing a five-cent stamp, he was able to receive regular updates from the family back home, in turn keeping his mother updated on his activities in Chungking.

By June 1942, Springer had settled into the routine of work in his new station. He was pleased to learn that he had a day off for the Dragon Boat Festival, a holiday, which fell on a Thursday. The code room was tedious work. He had so far learned three of the six or seven codes and had both encoded and decoded messages with the aid of books and charts. After decoding or encoding the message, he typed out the messages with the required number of copies. He began to get a good grasp of the intelligence capabilities of the US in China and felt that he was finally contributing to the cause.

Settling into Chungking

It was in Chungking that he came upon his first reading material dated after the attack on Pearl Harbor. These were the March and April editions of *Time* and *Fortune* magazines. He found the reporting intensely interesting after months of not knowing what the American people were doing and thinking in regard to the outbreak of the war. He was down to one roommate since Boise Hart had flown to India for a one-month vacation. Because Chungking was rated as an unhealthy post, embassy employees were granted sixty days of leave per year, which could be taken after working for six months. After three years, each staff member was entitled to home leave, which granted two months at home. The travel time was on top of that. During travel, each received a $7 per diem allowance. Office hours were 9:00 a.m. to 5:00 p.m., with two hours for lunch, and a half day on Saturday. The embassy had to be manned Saturday afternoon and even on Sunday, so his rotation came up about once every two weeks for one of those afternoons. His shift was usually spent reading a book. Occasionally, something urgent came through that had to be attended to. All in all, he felt that the employees were well treated.

Springer gave his mother the following description of his new quarters, along with its Chinese name, *Mei Foo Da Bon*:

It is on top of the so-called first range, 1233 feet above the Yangtze in an almost direct ascent, for which the cost by chair is now $30 one-way. We walk down in the morning, but it is usually too hot just now to walk up at night. The bungalow is semi-hidden in a grove of trees, whose shade, coupled with the breeze, make Mei Foo Da Bon the coolest and most desired place on the South Bank. Even the Ambassador wants it for his own. The last hundred yards or so of the walk is lined on both sides by our garden, cared for by the servants. We ate delicious corn from it tonight. . . . The other part of the house . . . includes a kitchen, rarely visited, dining room, living room, all, two large bedrooms with baths adjoining, as well as sections of the porch, and a mammoth screen porch extending the full length and half the width of the house. The most notable feature in the kitchen is the kerosene refrigerator, a Servel. It is just like a Frigidaire except that it runs on kerosene. It makes nifty ice cream, and add still more zest to those wonderful Chinese peaches, of which I eat several a day now—peeled, have no fear. We eat in the dining room only when we have guests. . . . The living room is quite large, has an extra-big fireplace (all the rooms have fireplaces), built-in bookcases, desk, sofa and four easy chairs, window seat (on which I am now sitting), radio, photograph, and various and sundry odds and ends. We eat dinner in here on a card table. Breakfast is eaten on the porch, from where we can look off down the hill on those rarely clear mornings (usually it is misty until about 10 am).[40]

Springer had come a long way from the oaken bucket that constituted the community toilet for his Bachelor's quarters at Yali. The bucket was what branded Yuanling as "shit-coolie town" in China. Their new house came with five servants, headed by a man named Liu, Shanghai bred, who was a model of efficiency—a veritable Jeeves. Liu supervised the handling of everything connected with the house, the laundry, their meals—right down to the shining of their shoes. The new residence was hereinafter labeled as "the lair." Most of Springer's belongings were still in Yuanling. He made arrangements for Bob Clarke to bring his suitcase full of his possessions on his way out of China when passing through Chungking.

Springer discovered the Chungking Club, which he and Small frequented for lunch. It was an exclusive club for foreign embassy personnel and their guests and offered bridge games, dances, movies, billiards, snooker, and table tennis.[41] There were a range of activities and plenty of English-speaking foreigners with whom to converse about the situation in China. Chungking was the nerve center for much of the military information in the area. In addition to the American embassy, the area around the club housed the offices of the American military attaché, the Belgian embassy, the British consulate, the British embassy, and several diplomatic and private residences.[42] There was a lot of intelligence gathering at the club as well. Visiting British pilots and military officers freely discussed their missions in restaurants and hotels—the club was no exception. For the most part they drank too much, which led the US to gather counterintelligence from them. Given the long record of British colonialism in China, their interests during this period of crisis were not necessarily aligned with those of the US government.[43]

Like those of many young men overseas during the war years, Springer's thoughts drifted home to a girl that he hoped to marry someday. Many of these World War II courtships occurred over great distances and through letters back and forth among sweethearts. His relationship with Julia Ravenel was no exception. He wrote to his mother and asked her to get in touch with Julia so that they could get acquainted:

> Have you heard from Julia anymore? I'm hoping that another letter from her will be forwarded to here in the near future. Could you do me a big favor and invite your probable future daughter-in-law to 2973 for a week or two this summer? She would have come for a short while last year, but I suddenly up and left. Don't go to any extra expense; just treat her like one of the family. You can use as much of the money I send in July for the purposes you need. It would be nice if there were a car available then, but that wouldn't be essential, with the present rubber shortage. You'll like her very much, as I have said before, and Eleanore and Vic can entertain her when Joe isn't around. Perhaps she could go bowling with Vic, and to church and riding with Eleanor. She is very fond of riding. I think she would be glad to sing a solo for you at the church too. I'm afraid I'll lose her while I'm so far away, and an acquaintance with my family might strengthen the tie which is now stretched out so thin. Please let me know by your next letter what you will about this. Of course she may be unable to accept, with her present war work, but she will certainly be pleased by the invitation. Never have I received better hospitality that I received from her family, even though I was a Yankee.[44]

Audrey Springer wrote to Julia, inviting her to visit Camden for part of the summer of 1942. By September 21, Julia wrote, "I've been out of town for about two weeks and returned about an hour ago. Unfortunately college starts tomorrow. I'll have to decline your invitation although I would like very much to know you and your family. It was very nice of you and I do appreciate it so much."[45] She was busy—citing her sorority's first rush party and that many of the girls returning to school had spent the summer volunteering on various USO jobs. She mentioned that Paul had sent her a birthday card, saying that he was well, but had not received a letter from him since July 23. She was frustrated that she had written him several times since then and found it difficult to stay in touch with him. Five days later, she wrote to Audrey again:

> Some very sudden developments have turned up, Mrs. Springer, which I should have informed you of three or four days ago. A boy with whom I have gone out for years came through Charleston on his way to Fort Custer, Michigan. He stayed with us a week and while he was here, we discovered that we were in love with each other and have become engaged. There are no plans for now as I would like to finish college and also—we would both rather know that this is the thing rather than go ahead and get married then discover that the high tension of the war caused our feelings which we considered love. There had been no feeling of any kind that this would happen until the time we were united just a very short time ago. After school ended, we both assumed that our friendship was a closed chapter when we should meet by accident except as far as corresponding was concerned. I guess none of us can judge his mind as to what he will do in certain circumstances until the time comes.

American Embassy, Chungking. George Small (*next to front bumper*), Jack Service (*next to front tire*), and Paul Springer (*in hat, behind car*). *Springer Family collection*

Mrs. Springer, I did enjoy knowing Paul so very much and value his friendship very much. He's a fine boy. I'm very sorry that things couldn't work out differently for him. It's very hard for me to write this letter to you, but I feel that it is only fair that you should know the conditions. I'll write to Paul immediately and tell him what had happened. I do hope sincerely that God keep all well and safe and bring him back to you soon. My friendship with Paul has been a highly treasured one. I do hope that it won't end with any bitterness. He deserves the very best of everything—I hope with all my heart that he will receive no different. Sincerely, Julia.[46]

When Springer received word of Julia's engagement that fall, he knew that he had been spurned. He did what any rational young man would do: he looked elsewhere for another girlfriend. In the meantime there was plenty of work to do. He was issued a picture ID as a secretary for the American embassy, which had a notation (in Chinese) that "All staff (police/military) must protect the holder of this certificate."[47] He stayed busy in the code room, took additional Chinese-language training, and carried a pocket manual of *Two Thousand Chinese Characters* with him as an easy reference.[48] The mail from home was slow in arriving at the embassy, possibly due to the State Department or delays in Karachi, the usual bottleneck.

A Christmas letter from his mother was delivered to Springer at the Christmas party by Sec. John Carter Vincent, who was dressed as Santa Claus.[49] He read it by the fireplace, facing the Christmas tree at the embassy. The tree decorations consisted of gold, red, and silver strips of paper with ping-pong balls wrapped in gold paper. He thought the tree was quite good considering the dearth of materials. They had goose for dinner, with plum pudding for dessert. The staff of fourteen sang Christmas carols. Despite all the festivities, Springer didn't get the same feelings of Christmas that he had back home.

Two days after Christmas, he accompanied Secretary Vincent to the Chinese-American Institute of Cultural Relations. Vincent was among the American diplomats who wanted to gather intelligence from and provide material to the Communist armies, then part of the Allied coalition in the war against Japan and ostensibly under Chiang's Kai-shek's command. He had been at Changsha at one time and almost accepted a Yali post there.[50] Springer felt privileged to work under Vincent. The official purpose of the trip was a special bridge session with Americans and Chinese in which photographs were taken to be radio-photoed to New York. Springer was told they were expected to appear in a New York newspaper. The photos were an attempt to show how well the Chinese and Americans get along together.

The consular staff became a tight-knit group, another of which was John "Jack" Service, the second secretary of the embassy. Service was born in 1909 in the city of Chengtu, in Szechuan Province.[51] By the age of eleven, Jack Service was extremely fluent in the local Chinese dialect. He had attended the Shanghai American School before moving to Berkeley, California, where he finished high school at the age of fifteen. After graduation from Oberlin College, with majors in art history and economics, Service took and passed the Foreign Service Exam in 1933. He was assigned to a clerkship position in the American consulate in Kunming. Two years later, Service was promoted to foreign service officer and was sent to Peking for language study. In 1938, he was assigned to the Shanghai consulate general under Clarence E. Gauss. When Gauss was promoted to ambassador, he brought Jack Service to Chungking with him. Service was already considered an "Old China Hand" at the age of thirty-three, when Springer first met him. He was tall and lanky with thick black hair. Service and Springer happened to share identical coat sizes. Springer wrote his mother, "I have another raincoat which I bought from Jack Service before he left on home leave, for which I am to pay him $15 US when he returns."[52] As his relationships with John Carter Vincent, Jack Service, and Ambassador Gauss grew, Springer was mentored in the seamless integration of diplomatic responsibilities and intelligence gathering.

War Rationing

All of the embassy staff were required to work forty-eight hours per week (commencing December 26) and received time and a half for all hours over forty. That gave Springer an extra $35 per month, which helped his budget considerably. Inflation was spinning out of control. Generalissimo Chiang Kai-shek issued a decree that prices were to be frozen on January 15 at the November 30 level for food, transportation, cotton, and various other commodities. It had not rained for most of the winter. An unprecedented drought brought on water rationing and a shortage of crops. Springer wrote, "Our tanks are so dry that our servant now brings in a teaspoon of water every morning for us to wash up with. Drinking water is served in eye-droppers. The Yangtze is so low that I'm planning to wade across when my feet get dirty enough." Although exaggerating, the drought's repercussions on food supplies had become serious. A shipment of groceries came into the embassy during the last days of 1942. It included salmon, Vienna sausage, oleo margarine, bacon, and jam but no milk. The staff still longed for some real milk. New Year's Eve brought an air raid alarm, the first Springer had experienced during the daylight since he had been in Chungking. The embassy staff carried all the confidential files, codes, etc. down to the dugout and stood around outside for an hour until the all-clear signal sounded. It was a beautiful, clear day, the best they had had that winter so far. With an increasing number of Japanese planes now at an enemy base fairly near to them, Springer feared that Chungking may be subjected to more bombings. He reassured his mother, "You may be sure there will be a good supply of solid rock over my head when the bombs fall (and I don't think they will). Chungking's warning system is about the best in the world, so there's nothing to worry about from that angle."[53]

Springer had heard from Dr. Phil Greene at Hsiang-Ya Hospital that one of the Yali Bachelors had been branded as a draft deserter in the US. Springer had every reason to believe that it was him.[54] This was of real concern, and he wanted to feel sure that the Selective Service was not stirring up trouble for him. He asked his mother to inquire about his status with the local draft board and find out if they wanted an official letter showing that he was now employed with the American embassy. Springer applied for his vacation leave and planned a trip to India in March 1943. "I'll need at least $400 gold at present prices, if I can get a free ride round-trip by Army plane," he wrote his mother. "What can I get you in India?"[55]

The news coming from Camden, New Jersey, was not good. He received a letter from a college roommate, Paul Graybell, informing him that two more of his class-mates had been killed, bringing the total to three he had heard of in recent weeks. All died in air crashes—one over Panama, one over Arkansas, and one in action in the Solomon Islands.[56] Springer knew them all, one very well. Bob Crockett had a wartime job making tank bearings. Graybell was with Hercules, a chemical-and-mu-nitions-manufacturing company known for its military-grade gunpowder. Both were expecting to fly for Uncle Sam in the near future. All the other college friends he had any news of were in the Army, Navy, or Air Force. The majority seemed to be pilots. He wrote a note to himself addressed to his mother: "Get back and join up, Springer, you slacker. I might at that. '43 will be the year if I do." Springer wrote her about the current status of the Yali campus:

> My old hunting ground around Yuanling is terribly bandit-ridden these days, so much so that the busses have stopped running. Several hundred bandits will swoop in and capture a whole town, then stop whatever vehicles enter it, robbing and sometimes killing all occupants. In one case, 600 or so heavily armed bandits held a village, and when my friend who bears the tale made his escape, 1,000 soldiers with a total of only 300 guns were out to retake it. Two of my FAU acquaintances were attacked by four or five bandits who hacked them up with knives. Both

will recover, fortunately, although one lost a couple of fingers and the other the use of his arm, which was the only thing which saved him from decapitation. Yuanling is so blocked up that the Yali Bachelors and Dr. Rugh, planning winter trips to Kweilin and Changsha respectively, were unable to go, as there was no transportation even if they should be foolhardy enough to venture forth. This condition has apparently been brought on by the near starvation of the people, due in the main to scanty rain and excessive taxation. This paragraph [is] just to give you the other side of that all too rosy picture painted in the US about China. Take what you read [from Yale] with a grain of salt. I could tell you lots more, but it would be censored.[57]

Communist Bandits

The problem of widespread banditry in China during this period was an unfortunate byproduct of the war. The Japanese were almost as unprepared for the responsibilities of occupation as the Nationalist government was for governing Free China in their retreat. This created power vacuums in areas not controlled by either force. Bandits were more common in rural China and shut down some of the traffic on many roads due to the threat of highway robbery. Kidnappings became common. Ransom demands were dealt with by the local community, since there was no authority left to which they could appeal. As the war went on, the authorities blurred the issue by using the term "bandit" to refer to groups ranging from criminal gangs simply out for theft and ransom to anti-Japanese partisans. Chiang Kai-shek had previously referred to the CCP as "Communist Bandits," in part because many of those who used the title "resistance fighters" were, in practice, "bandits" and accustomed to living off the exploitation of locals. In many cases they had little choice for their own survival.[58]

Chapter 10
CHANGES AT YALI

Summer Job with the Flying Tigers

The Yali Middle School, despite the presence of bandits in Hunan Province, was somewhat of an oasis of civility, education, and learning in 1942. The past year was one of great difficulty and hardships. The Yale-in-China reports, mailed to the alumni and parents, did not covey the true nature of just how dangerous conditions were on the ground. The Bachelor staff was depleted. Don McCabe and Bob Clarke had returned to the United States in the summer of 1942, and Springer had been commandeered by the State Department. Art Hopkins and Jim Elliott spent the summer of 1942 working with Gen. Claire Lee Chennault and the Flying Tigers.

General Chennault with a group of 14th Air Force pilots. *Claire Lee Chennault Papers, envelope B, Hoover Institution Archives*

During the summer, Hopkins was offered a senior staff position by General Chennault, the most senior commander of the US Army Air Force in China. Chennault had been in Changsha in the past and was familiar with Yali. During his initial interview with the general in July 1942, Hopkins was told by Chennault that there was work he could do for him during the summer, but that he must return to the school in the fall. Chennault told him, "It is essential to keep the schools going now. I am running a school myself, and have the utmost difficulty keeping teachers. They all wish to leave for something more active."[1] Hopkins noted that Chennault had been a school teacher in America and was still actively interested in education. By early September, Chennault changed his mind. He requested that Hopkins remain in his service for two extra months before returning to Yali.[2] The job that Chennault outlined for Hopkins was an interesting one: it involved traveling all over China by air, setting up post exchanges, libraries, and recreational facilities in all American army posts.[3] Hopkins liked the idea and felt strongly that he needed to be in uniform, as were all of his peers from back home. In view of the serious situation at the time, he felt that he could be of most help by remaining under Chennault's command.

As soon as Elliott received word that Hopkins's assignment might be extended and his would not be, he started making arrangements to get back to Yali. Up to that point, he had been counting on Hopkins to get them both a plane ride to Yuanling. Hopkins continually held this up as a possibility. Elliott went to one of the military missions and spoke with Colonel Alexander, the ranking air officer there at the time. He asked what the chances were of bumming a flight down to Hunan, Kweichow-Hengyang, or Chichchiang via a military plane. The colonel said frankly, "They were lousy."[4] They hadn't had a plane going that way for months. Elliott then asked Hopkins to see what he could do, given that he knew most of the ranking officers. Elliott had to sit tight and wait it out. Colonel Alexander told Elliott that he would let him know if they had any planes going that way, and indicated that if they did, he could catch a ride. In the meantime, Hopkins cabled his formal request to extend his leave from Yali for a couple more months to complete a specific assignment. The Yale-in-China trustees flatly refused.[5]

Yale-in-China had already lost Springer to the State Department and could not afford for their English Department to be devoid of teachers. Hopkins blamed himself for their denial, since he had not submitted any explanation because of the strict censorship, which forbade him to give his reasons in a letter or a cabled message. The decision of the trustees prompted a reply from Dwight Rugh, informing Hopkins and Elliott via telegraph that "it would be impossible" to release Hopkins and that they were to return immediately and be "provided with rapid transportation to the present town nearest to Yuanling." In response, one of the US Army Air Force pilots offered to drop Hopkins and Elliott over the middle school in parachutes. They politely, but firmly, refused the offer, thinking that the local guards might be nearsighted and that they would be subject to being shot if attempting to parachute down to the campus. As an alternative, Hopkins talked with some of the officers at the base, and they promised him that as soon as they had a plane going that way, he and Elliott could board as passengers. They also promised to land and drop them off at the most convenient point. They could not give any definite date or place because, said Hopkins, "They don't know themselves, and won't know until just before the plane goes."[6] They would have to be ready to leave on "five minutes notice."

This charade went on for several days, until Hopkins arrived to pick up his fellow Bachelor in a borrowed truck for a quick drive to the airfield. They were expecting a call from a pilot any time, but until now, nothing had happened. Upon arriving, they boarded a plane and covered the first 240 miles in the air, landing in an hour and forty minutes. The remaining 100 miles were traversed in a slow-moving, charcoal-burning truck.[7] By ingenious adaptation because of chronic fuel shortages in China, the gasoline engine used charcoal as an alternative fuel. Next to the front window, on the right-hand side, was a large metal cylinder with charcoal burning inside. A pipe from the cylinder fed the fumes to the engine. It wasn't very powerful, so when traveling uphill through hills of the mountains, sometimes the truck could go no faster than they could walk. Going downhill was a different story. They rapidly picked up speed on the downhill runs to make up for lost time, careening around corners with the horn blasting to declare their right-of-way, no matter what happened to be coming from the other direction. Every now and then, they were forced to stop and stuff more charcoal into the cylinder from a supply kept on the truck.[8] This made for a long, arduous trip back to Yali, which took one and a half days of hard travel. The two Bachelors arrived in Yuanling for their teaching duties on September 16, 1942, about one week late for their respective classes.

Hopkins later clarified his reasons for wanting to leave his teaching position in a letter to Robert Ashton "Bob" Smith:

> The situation then was very serious, the military outlook far from bright, inflation was apparently uncontrolled, and transportation in the interior was becoming more and more uncertain, inefficient and dangerous. . . . If I were to tell you the number of bombing planes which we have sent to China, you simply would not believe it. In my position, I had inside information on many subjects, and felt that, should China have negotiated

Art Hopkins and Jim Elliott made the last leg of their trip in a charcoal-burning truck similar to this one. *FAU collection*

for peace, I would have had a fighting chance to get out, which would have been preferable to internment or even worse being taken prisoner in Yuanling. Prices were soaring and the black market in Kunming was 50–1 for US money. Things were very unstable and discouraging. I had had previous military training—three years R.O.T.C. and the work I was doing was important. Among other things it was in the line of supply, recreational, and morale work. My time in China had been a value to me in my duties, as I knew some of the language and had some experience in dealing with the people.

My personal opinion is that the most important thing now is the winning of the war as quickly as possible, and that everyone needed to do this should be prepared to make all sacrifices. Ever since December 7th I have wondered if at Yali I was doing all I possibly could to help actively in the war effort, and felt that if the military should need my services, it was my duty to volunteer them immediately. Here in China I have been close up to the reality of the war for a year and a half, have seen innumerable ruins of viciously bombed undefended cities, heard first-hand accounts of Japanese atrocities and utter brutality, and have all too often felt the horrible impotence and extreme annoyance of sitting out numerous air raid alarms in the vicinity of the dugout. (You know what that's like, Bob.) I cannot be a conscientious objector to the savage aggression and utter ruthlessness of the Japanese, and perhaps it is with the idealism and enthusiasm of youth that I feel I should do my part in the most active way possible in this war effort. If the Japanese would win this war, institutions like Yale-in-China and Yali would cease to exist, and I am positive that the Japs have no comparable ones to establish.[9]

Skeleton Crew

Despite the hardships of war, the English Department, now under the leadership of Jim Elliott, was able to carry on, despite their depleted staff, with surprising efficiency. Dr. Rugh taught the graduating class. His wife, Winifred, had two senior classes, as

C. C. Lao teaches a class to junior school students, Yuanling, ca. 1940s. In the background is the entrance to a bomb shelter. *Yale-China Association Records, RU 232, Manuscripts and Archives, Yale University Library*

did Hopkins, while Elliott had the first-year senior class. In the junior school, they were forced to add two Chinese teachers, Ying Kai-shih and Peng Yilio.[10]

Hopkins's classes included one hour per week, where he taught dictation, pronunciation, and question-and-answer work. Elliott took on a mammoth load: a first-year, first-term class of eighty-seven students, divided into two divisions, as well as the junior school graduating class. Another innovation started in the junior school was having one of the Chinese teachers take each class for a one-hour-a-week session to explain the intricacies of English grammar in Chinese. The two American Bachelors thought this an excellent idea, since they had struggled with the grim limitations of trying to explain such things as transitive and intransitive verbs, as well as verb tenses, to boys in their classes. The teachers were handicapped by their students' limited vocabulary of a couple of hundred English words, which most of the boys had not yet perfected.

In the senior school, they continued a new system that had been inaugurated by Bob Clarke in the previous year, but had to modify many features of it due to the depleted staff. In the 5-1 and 6-1 classes, they returned to having a reader in class for several days a week. The boys were required to write in a diary, and while it made for a big pile of "sicty notebooks" (as in *sic*) to correct weekly, it was a definite help to the boys in writing clearer, everyday English. Each student was required to correct his own mistakes, writing the most-common ones on the blackboard and discussing them in class.[11] They also had speeches, conversations, and debates in class, with the boys acting as critics and judges. Hopkins and Elliott no longer had the time for personal conferences weekly with almost sixty boys. They told the students to see them during certain hours as needed. Outside reading work was designated as optional during this fall term.

The fall semester of 1942 contained a couple of teacher staff meetings. This brought forth some useful discussions. The old subject of the "Aims of the English Department" took up much of the first meeting. They made a list of mistakes most common in compositions (such as failure to start a sentence with a capital letter), with Elliott making an excellent list of suggestions for composition writing. These meetings were valuable in the interchange of ideas, and they planned to make them a regular affair.

The upside to the smaller teaching staff of only two Bachelors was that their living conditions greatly improved. "This year you would not recognize the Bachelor quarters, as we are living in roomy comfort which I think is easily comparable to Changsha accommodations. We have the same two servants—the Hsu brothers—that you met last fall, and they take wonderful care of us," Art Hopkins wrote to Bob Smith. "The lady who occupied the entire first floor has moved away, and Jim and I moved in there. We have a large sunny living room, in which our two big desks face each other, and are next to three enormous windows."[12] In back of the desk were two bookcases,

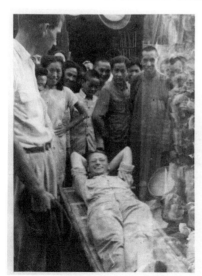

Art Hopkins on a cot, surrounded by students, ca. 1942. *Yale-China Association Records, RU 232, Manuscripts and Archives, Yale University Library*

one full of interesting books and the other half full of Chinese curios that Hopkins had collected from his travels. In the rest of the room were a couple of comfortable rocking chairs next to a tableful of magazines, a good reading lamp, a small table with a huge dictionary on it, another bookcase, and an old but excellent Victrola, with a fine collection of classical records. They actually had enough room to spread out and decorate. "On the walls I have hung some magnificent Chinese scrolls, one purchased in Chengtu during the winter vacation, and a beautiful one that one of my little students gave me last year," wrote Hopkins. In back of his desk was a large picture of Generalissimo Chiang Kai-shek in full dress uniform. Their lampshades were Chinese lanterns, and a large coolie's straw hat covered the little table light. In back of their office room was a large bedroom, with a tin bathtub. Wrapped around the house was a large porch. In addition to these quarters, they retained their old screened-in sleeping porch and a small sitting room upstairs. He added, "Dr. Rugh has moved into our old office, and that room where last year five men existed, now looks greatly crowded with one large desk, and a couple of bookcases in it. I don't know how we ever fit it in last year."[13]

Prayer Meeting

Their social life in Yuanling was quiet. The foreigners in Yuanling were divided about equally between Protestants and Catholics. The Protestants attended prayer meetings on Thursday evenings on a weekly basis. People took turns leading the gathering, including the Bachelors. Usually, the prayer meetings were led by a seasoned missionary who followed a predictable format. These were in the living room of one of the missionary homes at the other end of the city. It was followed by refreshments, cookies, cake, and the like. Their young neighbor, Betty Jean Rugh, recalled one prayer meeting that was particularly memorable, which was conducted by Hopkins, whom she affectionately referred to as "Uncle Art." On this Thursday afternoon, Hopkins and Elliott were blasting their music, playing some records, with the opening notes of Beethoven's Fifth Symphony reverberating through their common wall they shared with the Rughs.

"Hey, Art?" Jim called out, as if the music reminded him of something.

"You ready for prayer meeting tonight?

"What?" Hopkins yelled back. "Prayer meeting!" said Jim.

On the Rughs' side of the wall, Winifred gave her husband a worried look . . .

"What about it?" shouted Art. "It's tonight. Did you forget?" Jim reminded him.

The Beethoven music suddenly stopped playing. In the eerie silence, the Rughs heard Art ask Jim, "What time is it?" He answered, "It's almost five. What're you going to do?"

Art didn't reply.

"Oh dear," said Mrs. Rugh, trying to look serious.[14]

After supper, the Rughs started their walk through the main street to the designated home. As Hopkins and Elliott arrived, Betty Jean noted that Hopkins didn't have anything with him that looked like notes, papers, or a bible with which to lead the meeting. On the other hand, he didn't seem worried. After a few minutes of social time, everyone sat down and turned to Hopkins, who was leaning back in an armchair. Hopkins announced, "Tonight we will have a Quaker meeting." He explained that holding a Quaker meeting meant they would have an hour together of silent meditation and prayer. He added that during this time, anyone who felt moved to speak could do so. Betty Jean described the scene: "When the startled assemblage realized he had nothing to say, people tentatively started bowing their heads, as though not sure how far down they should go."[15] Her hopes for something interesting or edible vanished. Eyes twitched. Someone coughed. The hands on the wall clock barely moved for what seemed like an eternity. She recalled, "Of all the prayer meetings we attended, it was the most unforgettable and the most boring."[16]

Hopkins and Elliott had occasional bridge games and saw their foreign friends across town mostly on weekends. With the smaller household, the two of them had been able to have most of the Chinese teachers who spoke English over for a meal, and would've liked to have some of the students, but their finances didn't permit it. After returning to Yuanling, Hopkins was called upon to give several lectures on his summer experiences with the US Air Force. One talk was to the local YMCA, and the other was to the local girls schools. He recalled, "That was something, and I found myself stared at by almost 300 girls, but they seemed to enjoy the talk. That was the largest number of girls I have ever had to look at at once before in my life."[17] Fortunately, unlike the prayer meeting, he had prepared his remarks in advance.

On Thanksgiving Day, the foreigners celebrated over dinner across town, and every family brought their favorite dishes. It was quite successful and captured the real spirit of Thanksgiving. Occasionally, they stopped in to see the Catholic priests, who were as hospitable and affable as ever. Their bishop had returned from Hong Kong, where he was captured by the Japanese, and who was now a mere shadow of his former self, having gone from 220 to 140 pounds. He was now seriously ill and in the hospital at Yuanling as a result of mistreatment during his incarceration.[18]

Frustrations

During their winter break between semesters in December 1942, Elliott reached out to Bob Smith, voicing his frustrations in regard to staying on for another year at Yale-in-China once his commitment (and Art's) came to an end in July of the following year:

First of all, I know that Yali needs me next year—and as long as the war lasts. Dwight has emphasized this to me, but of course anyone could see it. With Bob, Paul, Don gone—and Art leaving next June (or possibly sooner), I am the only one of the full-time English teachers left. There is hope that Yali will be able to secure an English fellow named Peter Thompson, now with the FAU (Friends Ambulance Unit), but as yet he has not let us know his final word on the subject. Even were he to join us (probably this next term if he comes), the English staff would be undermanned and he would be rather inexperienced. I think I need not dwell longer on the need.

Secondly, I realize how deeply indebted I am to Yale-in-China. This experience is one I have enjoyed immensely and value beyond words. I am sincerely appreciative of the trust placed in me by the Yale-in-China Board of Trustees and of the opportunity for travel and education they have made possible. I only hope that my efforts here in Yali will reflect to some degree profound gratitude.[19]

Elliott's biggest consideration on whether or not to extend his stay at Yale-in-China was his local draft board. He asked Smith, "Can further deferment be secured for me? I can do nothing, of course, but leave that situation in your hands. As a conscientious objector, I can think of no place I could be of more use than right here in Yali."[20] Elliott had written his local draft board three weeks before, to emphasize this in his plea for further deferment. He made it clear in his selective service registration that he would accept noncombatant service. If his draft deferment was refused, he asked the trustees to facilitate matters so that he could join the American forces in China. He did not relish the prospect of an ocean voyage back to the US while the war in the Pacific was raging. With his knowledge of the Chinese language, he felt he could be of use to the American forces in China immediately, whereas if he made the long trip home, it would be months before he could be of any use to his country. Other considerations in regard to staying at Yali included his meager salary, the skyrocketing living expenses in China, and the possibility of a permanent position in the country.

Yali Staffing

Fortunately, the middle school was able to engage the services of the young Englishman, Peter Thompson, to assist the English Department that following spring. Thompson was in China and arrived at Yali on March 8, 1943. Before joining the FAU, Thompson was an artist by background. He studied for a year or so in the Cambridge School of Architecture. Despite Elliott's initial misgivings about how "some of his English traits don't fit in too well with our Americanisms," he proved to be a valuable asset and immediately began teaching three of the English classes.[21] Elliott and Thompson were assisted in teaching by Dwight and Winifred Rugh after Hopkins departed Yuanling following his two-year teaching contract in June 1943.[22] For a time, Thompson and Elliott had as many as 170 students in their respective classes. They were assisted by a recent Yali graduate, Philip Huang Ping-Lin, in doing administrative work, such as list checking, sorting papers, correcting papers, entering marks, and so forth. But

Jim Elliott and Art Hopkins, the "two fearful Bearded Bachelors," with boys of the 28th class, Yuanling, Christmas Day 1942. *Yale-China Association Records, RU 232, Manuscripts and Archives, Yale University Library*

suddenly they found themselves short staffed again when Philip developed an eye infection, for which he had to be hospitalized. It was difficult to get good help during the war.

A Challenging School Year

In the school year 1942–43, Yale-in-China met the challenges during this increasingly difficult environment by expanding the services it rendered to China through its various institutions. The middle school, the oldest, had the largest enrollment in its history, with a total of 482 students. The past year was one of great difficulties and hardships, caused by the war, the isolation of China, and rampant inflation. The impact of inflation bore down on the salaried staff, with the teachers suffering greatly in spite of subsidies. Salaries barely sufficed to buy food. An occasional shoe repair was a great luxury. New clothes were out of the picture for most. Some of the Chinese faculty with large families had been forced to leave and find better-paying employment. However, the great majority of teachers loyally remained with the school.

The students were taught by example to be socially minded and helpful during these difficult times. They established and ran schools for the underprivileged children of their neighborhoods. They took part in many other public-service activities, joining cleanup squads, air-raid rescue squads, firefighting, and the like. Yale songs were popular, in Chinese as well as in English. The boys shouted Yale cheers and delighted in athletics. Each boy's bed was decorated with a "Bulldog," the university's mascot.[23]

New Appointments

Two more Bachelors were appointed in the spring of 1943 for two-year service in China: Ross I. Dixon, Yale '42, and J. Kenneth Moreland, Yale '43.[24] Both were divinity students. Their appointment during wartime presented its own set of challenges. First they had to get permission from their draft boards as well as the US State Department. The draft board gave them the okay because the American military forces desperately needed Chinese who could understand English and, in turn, could speak so that their American counterparts could understand them. The recent Yali Middle School graduates had six years of learning English from American teachers using the direct method. They had to listen and understand English, and they had to respond so that their teachers could understand them. Several of them had already helped by coordinating the movement of Chinese ground troops with the American air forces. This improvement in Chinese communication was viewed as important to the war effort and was the primary reason that Dixon and Moreland were excused from the draft and permitted to go to China.[25]

Getting to China in the middle of the war presented its own set of challenges, since there was no passenger service across either ocean to Europe or Asia. The two newest Bachelors left New Haven early in July, took a train to New Orleans, then traveled by plane to Merida, Mexico. From there, they flew to Guatemala and then to Panama. While in Panama they learned that ships occasionally sailed from Buenos Aires to Cape Town, across the South Atlantic. After two weeks in Panama they found a flight to Colombia and then on to Lima, Peru. After leaving Peru they had to fly over the Andes Mountains in an unpressurized plane at about 25,000 feet. On that propeller plane they felt like they were going to throw up because of the tremendous difference in pressure. They spent much of their time sipping on a tube of oxygen to maintain consciousness. They finally landed in La Paz, Bolivia, after the long flight from Peru. Then they flew to Buenos Aires, where they waited for three weeks trying to locate a ship in which to cross the Atlantic Ocean. The port authorities would not tell them the embarkation schedule in advance, because from time to time the German submarines would sink those ships, although Argentina was officially neutral.

Loaded down with baggage and extra clothing, the two secured passage on *José Menendez*, a 4,000-ton passenger ship that bobbed across the South Atlantic in rough seas. While on the ship, they got to know another passenger, thoroughly anesthetized with Scotch whiskey, who told them this was his third time trying to get across, since

Ken Moreland and Ross Dixon, new Bachelors, arrived in Yuanling after a four-month journey across the world. *Yale-China Association Records, RU 232, Manuscripts and Archives, Yale University Library*

the other two ships were sunk by submarines. Ken Moreland recalled the conversation: "It was such a harrowing experience. The second time the ship was blown up, he had happened to go up on the deck; it was a little hot down below, and he was at one end of it and it was the other end that was blown up. He went into the water but was able to get a life preserver. Then the submarine came up near him and found out what language he spoke and they asked what ship did we just sink? He gave them the name of it and they plunged on down and went on, left him. They didn't have any room to take them in the sub, but another ship came along going back to Buenos Aires and picked him up."[26]

Moreland and Dixon stayed in Cape Town for about ten days before boarding a freighter around the Horn to Durban. They had a two-week delay in Durban until they were able to get passage on a British troop ship headed to India. It was in a convoy of troop ships surrounded by a fleet of destroyers protecting them. They did a zigzag course to avoid submarines across the Indian Ocean to Bombay. They had only a handful of civilian seats but welcomed the two Americans. That took three weeks. Once in India they stayed with missionaries, since they could not afford to stay in any kind of hotel. They traveled on crowded Indian trains through New Delhi, where they saw the Taj Mahal. They worked their way through Benares, where they watched people wade into the filthy sacred waters of the Ganges River, finally arriving in Calcutta, where they waited three weeks for a plane. There they were in the midst of the Bengali famine and a massive cholera epidemic. "People were just dying on the streets," Moreland recalled.[27] At long last, they secured a flight into China, crossing the Himalayas in a plane to Kunming.

Their ground transportation across China included walking, riverboats, hitching a ride with a British convoy of trucks to Chungking, and traversing across Kweichow and Hunan Provinces in a charcoal-burning bus. After staying in a series of horrible inns and dirty farmhouses along the last stretch, enduring nightly mosquito raids and travel through four continents, they crossed the Yuan River in a small ferry to Yuanling on November 3, 1943. Moreland and Dixon were a welcome sight to the short-handed staff at Yali, especially Dwight Rugh, who had assumed their teaching duties when they failed to arrive in early September as planned. The feeling was mutual. It had taken them four months and one week to travel the 25,000 miles from New Haven to Yuanling.

Because of his exemplary work, Peter Thompson was reengaged for the 1943–44 school year. Despite protests from his local draft board, Jim Elliott agreed to stay on another year until the summer of 1944, bringing the staff of Bachelors up to normal strength.

Robert Ashton "Bob" Smith, '38, executive secretary of the Yale-in-China Association, was given a leave of absence in July 1943 to accept a commission as an ensign in the US Navy. Brank Fulton, who survived the air raids at Changsha and Shiukwan as he made his way out of Yuanling in 1941, received his PhD from Yale and was appointed as their representative in China by the Board of Trustees, replacing Dwight Rugh, who now devoted himself to his special field of religious education. Fulton was entering his new position in China with great enthusiasm and farsighted plans for the reconstruction of the Yale-in-China program after the war. The process of rebuilding the program would be a difficult one.

Hunan-Yale Hospital

The Yale-in-China facilities in Changsha suffered immensely during the war. During the most recent Japanese retreat from Changsha, the Japs set fire to more than twenty of the Yale-in-China buildings. All of the former middle school and medical school buildings were completely destroyed, although the main hospital building was fire-proof.[28] Aside from the damage caused to a few doors and windows and two elevator shafts by fire, most of Hsiang-Ya (Hunan-Yale) hospital remained intact, despite being bombed, shelled, riddled with bullets, partially burned, looted, used as a fortress, and taken and retaken four times during two major engagements. Several of the Yale-in-China servants had been conscripted for Chinese military service, leaving the facility short staffed. Despite the hardships, the hospital continued to care for one hundred bed patients, as well as numerous outpatients every day. It continued to train doctors, medical students, and nursing students into 1944.

Dr. Pettus on Medical Leave

In addition to the dangerous wartime situation in wartime China, Dr. Win Pettus contracted schistosomiasis (also known as bilharzia), an acute and chronic disease caused by parasitic flatworms. People are infected when exposed to water contaminated by the parasites in tropical and subtropical areas, especially in poor communities without access to safe drinking water and adequate sanitation. The parasites are released from infected freshwater snails. Pettis and his family traveled to an over 4,000-foot-high mountain in West Hunan on a much-needed vacation to escape some of the Changsha summer heat.[29] His exposure undoubtedly occurred on July 1, 1942, when the boat in which he, his wife, and their daughters were traveling ran aground. "I put on my bathing trunks and got in the water, helping the boatmen pry the launch off the sandbar. I was in the water about two hours." remembered Pettus.[30]

At first, his symptoms were consistent with that of typhus, with a headache for five days followed by a fever. After a week of convalescence, the fever returned for about three and a half weeks, during which time he developed a severe, dry, hacking cough. In consultation with other doctors who were experienced observers of the ailment, he began a treatment lasting three months to rid his body of the disease. The treatment necessitated over two months in bed, during which time he immersed himself in the study of Chinese characters, devoting his afternoons to this until the following summer. By January 1943, Dr. Pettus had still not made a full recovery. He conceded this in a letter to Bob Smith: "From the point of view of health, I think it would also be wise to leave Changsha. I'm not pulling a full load now so far as work is concerned, but I could make real progress with the language. Last fall a couple of British Army doctors strongly urged me to return to America. I more or less laughed at the idea, but if this bally disease appears to progress any more, it might be considered. At present I do not favor it because of the expense, difficulty in getting passage, waste of time en route, and chance of not getting back."[31]

After conferring with Dwight Rugh and fellow physician Dr. Phil Greene, Pettus left Changsha with his wife and family. Two days later he arrived at the air base in Kunming. They returned to the US through Panama in 1943. After a brief stay in New York with stopovers in Washington, DC; Akron, Ohio; and St. Louis, Missouri, the family settled in Berkeley, California, for the next year. Pettus was a man of many talents. After his year of "sick leave," during which time he completely recovered, he put in six months of virtually full-time Chinese-language study, and another six months of further training in St. Louis in his field of medical specialization—chest surgery.[32] His time away from Changsha also allowed him to pursue another endeavor: learning to fly and securing a pilot's license. He would return to Chungking in January

1945 to resume his work, leaving his wife and daughters out of harm's way at home in Berkeley until the end of the war.

A Downed Pilot in Yuanling

Although Springer's letters back home were now subject to military censorship (with whole paragraphs sometimes cut out by scissors), Jim Elliott's were not. Elliott described the conditions at Yali in a letter dated June 16, 1943:

> Suffice it to say that so far Yuanling has had no great panic or fears of the necessity for evacuation, despite the recent evacuation of Changteh. Moreover there has not been an air raid since I've been here, and this year there have been very few *ching pao's.* The majority of the planes we see now are the welcome [American] P-40's, and not the dreaded Jap bombers and Zeros. We are on the direct route from one of the American bases to the Ichang area (a Japanese air base in the Hupeh Province, north of Hunan), and the American planes often fly over here. It's cheering to see how the people go out to look at them instead of frantically running for cover. I am still horrified at the tragic sight of men, women, and children scurrying for the dugouts and foxholes when an alarm does sound; the contrast when friendly planes go over is tremendous. Let us hope that America will never see these sights.[33]

Despite the serenity depicted to the parents by the Yale-in-China staff, the war was never far away from Yali. There was a terrible fire next to their home church in Yuanling, and the Bachelors, along with dozens of students in a bucket brigade, as well as local firefighters, spent hours pitching in to keep the fire contained. Despite their heroic efforts, they watched it spread in the other direction. When they began to throw water on it from the window of the house next door, the whole roof came crashing down on their heads, knocking them onto the floor and partially burying them in the wreckage of tiles, soot, and timber. Jim Elliott suffered a nasty cut, with a chunk of flesh dangling from the thick part of his hand at the base of his thumb. He hurried up to the house and cleaned out the wound and was advised by Dwight Rugh to go to the Abounding Grace Hospital in Yuanling for treatment. While he was waiting for the doctor, one of the nurses told him that an American pilot had been brought to the hospital just a few minutes ago. Elliott had heard about the wounded aviator, who had been shot down the day before. They said it was the same man. While waiting for his doctor, Elliott walked over to the aviator's room and introduced himself to Capt. Robert "Bob" Costello of the US Army Air Force. Elliott described him: "A young fellow of 23, very good-looking, blonde about 5'8" tall, about my build, he said he was not wounded badly—only minor cuts on the head and arms."[34] At that point the doctor came in and dressed Elliott's wound. The exhausted pilot promptly fell asleep. The doctor suggested Elliott might as well sleep in the same room with Costello, so he did. The next day, Elliott was with Captain Costello from the time he woke up until 9:30 that night, and heard him tell his story a dozen times.

Elliott described how the American pilot came to be in Yuanling:

> [On] Wednesday morning, 14 P-40's took off from a Hunan base and flew north to the area of activity around Ichang. Eight planes flew low to strafe Jap troops and material on the ground, while six, led by Captain Costello, flew above for protection against Zeros. The Zeros came, and a dog-fight ensued. One of them got on Bob's tail, and he dove to get away from it (the P-40s are faster than Zeros, but don't [have] their maneuverability). He picked up speed, pulled away, looped over and came back at the Zero, head on. The Zero pulled up, expecting the P-40 to dive again as the latter can't climb with a Zero ordinarily. However, Bob's plane was a late-model (P-40M) and is lighter than the usual P-40, and also has a super-charger that enables it to climb higher, so Bob went up with it, all six .50 caliber guns blazing. He hit the Jap and saw it (that is, the Zero) fall, pouring smoke. He didn't see it hit (not time for that!) so [he] can't count it a definite hit, but a "probable."[35]

However, the Jap Zero got a hit on Bob's plane in one of the few vulnerable spots, a fuel drainpipe, and immediately gasoline started pouring out of the plane and fumes came up into the cockpit, nearly knocking him out. Other Zeros, seeing this, hopped on his tail, determined to get him—six of them, so Bob streaked for home. His speed was too much for five of them and they peeled off, but one was determined not to let him get away, and stayed with him until Bob finally lost him in a cloud. All of this flying with an open throttle and leaking gas tank was fatal as far as the fuel consumption was concerned, and by the time Bob had gotten away from the last Zero, his gas was dangerously low. It was not long before he had only 10 or 15 gallons left, and he knew that he must land, since "to land with an absolutely empty tank is very dangerous," he told Elliott.[36]

Costello's plane came to the road between Yuanling and Changsha, and he saw that it had been torn up, so he figured the Japs were there or very near. He didn't dare make for the airfield at Changteh, since that was probably in Japanese hands. So he flew toward Yuanling until he came to the point where the road had not been torn up. There was a sandbar—two of them—in a river, and he decided to try to land there with his wheels down (in order to avoid a crash landing, which would wreck his plane). This proved to be his undoing, since the sandbar was not long enough. He had planned to land on one and hop to the other one, where he hoped his speed would not be too great to prevent him from pulling to a stop. However, a P-40 lands at more than 100 miles an hour, and the first sandbar turned out to be only 50–100 yards long, and when he came to the end of it, his wheels went over the embankment. This flipped his plane right over, and he landed on his back on the second sandbar. This naturally smashed up the plasti-glass canopy over the cockpit, as well as the rudder, and this caused the cuts on Costello's head and arms. His safety belt held him firmly enough to let him escape worse injuries. There he was, though, pinned in his plane, upside down, with gas fumes all around, and badly worried about fire breaking out.

Some bystanders in the area were afraid that he might be a Jap. They were cautious and wouldn't come to help him at first. He finally got out of his safety belt and, after fifteen or twenty minutes, managed to dig his way out through the sand. As soon as he crawled out, however, some fishermen seized him, knocked him down, and took his gun away from him. Weak as he was, and shaken up, he could do nothing to protect himself. He saw some soldiers coming toward him, and for a moment was worried whether they were Japanese. He soon saw they were Chinese, took out his identification card written in Chinese, and handed it to them, and they restored his gun to him. They then took him to the local magistrate, where his cuts were washed and sulfanilamide (which he had in his first-aid kit) was administered. Later, he was driven to another town, where there was a Catholic priest and two sisters; he stayed with them that day and proceeded to Yuanling on the following day (Thursday), arriving late that night.[37]

The next morning, Friday, before Elliott and Costello had gotten out of the hospital, there was a delegation of two men from the commanding general of the district, Gen. Sun Ssu-lin, to convey their greetings and welcome to the downed pilot. After breakfast, three of the city's leading citizens—the magistrate, the local Kuomintang party leader, and the head of the chamber of commerce—called on them. An assembly was held for Captain Costello with speeches and presentations, ending with Winifred Rugh directing the Yali Glee Club in a rendition of the first verse of "God Bless America" in English, followed by a rendition of "God Bless Jung Hua Ming Guo"—the Republic of China. Her daughter, Betty Jean, recalled the scene. "Actually, Captain Costello didn't look very dashing. He was a short, mild-mannered young man with a smooth, square face and honey-colored hair, who responded to all the adulation with quiet courtesy and few words."[38] Shortly after that celebration, Costello left Yuanling to rejoin his unit.

The drive to disrupt the Japanese airbase at Ichang had advanced thirty-two miles within less than a week. The drive was accomplished by joint American and Chinese air forces.[39] The Allied pilots had destroyed a minimum of twenty-eight Japanese planes, with two Allied planes lost, one of which was Capt. Bob Costello's. The air support, the most effective ever given to the Chinese armies, was carried out with strafing attacks to cut up the retreating Japanese. On a single avenue of Japanese retreat, the road back from Changyang, in Hubei Province, Chinese dispatches estimated that Allied planes killed more than 1,500 enemy troops struggling on the ground. A communiqué from headquarters of the 14th US Army Air Force told of ten powerful blows struck against enemy supply lines, troops, and communications on May 30 and 31, in the Lake Tungting–Yangtze area. This offensive became a turning point in the air war with Japan, as American-trained Chinese pilots became a significant factor against their common enemy.

Art Hopkins Leaves Yali

After administering final exams to the two graduating classes (both of which he taught), Hopkins was left with only two classes in June 1943. His two-year teaching commitment was almost complete. Dwight Rugh felt that the remaining classes could be wrapped up by Elliott and Thompson, so he released Hopkins from Yali a few days early and sent him to Hsiang-Ya Hospital in Changsha. Dr. Rugh was worried about a renewed military threat to Changsha and thought it wise to have another man in the city to look after Yali interests. Hopkins could also assist Marjorie Tooker, the nurse, in case the need for evacuation of the hospital rose again. Hopkins, on only three days' notice, got his affairs in order and his personal effects and numerous *ku tung* (curios) packed, and celebrated at as many farewell parties as could be arranged in two days.

On the scheduled date of departure, Hopkins found that there were no seats on the bus he had reserved, so this caused an unexpected delay. In the meantime, he found a seat on a Hunan Provincial Bank truck going to Hengyang, and early on June 2, he left. He was in Changsha less than a week after that. He wrote Elliott from Chihkiang that he just missed a ride on a US Army Air Force transport plane (C-47). It pulled in just as he was at the bus station. He could have gotten over to the field and on that plane but for the exasperating slowness of the Chinese officials looking over his passport and other credentials. He could have been in Hengyang in only an hour or so. He later found out that the plane was nearly empty, and he could have easily gone on with his baggage!

Ying Kai-shih, dean of the boy's school in Yuanling. *Yale-China Association Records, RU 232, Manuscripts and Archives, Yale University Library*

Gratuities from the Sky

Several weeks after Captain Costello left Yuanling, Betty Jean Rugh was playing on the swing next to their house when the air raid siren started to sound, then abruptly stopped. As soon as it stopped, she heard the planes. Their angry hum rapidly expanded to a deafening roar, and two American fighter planes streaked low over the town, circled out above the river and down to the other end of town, returned, zoomed down again, wagged their wings, screamed up into the sky, and disappeared into the haze toward the western mountains. The town was relived they were friendly aircraft. Everyone ran out to see what happened. Betty Jean soon learned that the planes dropped several large bundles onto the Catholic compound at the other end of the city. The packages represented Costello's show of gratitude.

Their contents were distributed to all the missions in town. These included K rations and other delicacies unavailable in Yuanling, such as cheese, powdered coffee and cocoa, tinned butter, and meat. Betty Jean's share of the bundle was a 1-by-3-inch block of US Army chocolate, which she described as "the most delicious chocolate ever created. . . . Its color was charcoal brown, and it was packed with such fulfilling flavor that one thin fragment scraped off by my incisors flooded my entire body with dark delight—barely sweet and not really bitter, just Chocolateness."[40] Having been in Hunan almost three years, the gift of chocolate that Costello dropped from the sky was a rare treat—and evoked fond memories of the downed pilot for the girl.

Hopkins sent word via letter for Elliott to join him in Changsha as soon as his final classes were over. Upon his arrival, Hopkins took over the management of the mission business while Marjorie Tooker embarked on a trip to Kweilin and Kunming to bring back medicines and drugs for Hsiang-Ya Hospital. The two Bachelors were expected to tag-team their watch over the hospital during the summer and report any suspicious activity back to Dr. Rugh during the extended absence of Dr. Pettus. Hopkins was expected to leave Changsha as soon as Elliott arrived to relieve him of duty. Once relieved, Hopkins proceeded to an Army post, where he took his physical exam in order to receive his commission in the US Army Air Force. He passed with flying colors. Elliott took care of most of the mission business in Changsha that summer. He assisted Miss Tooker when she returned to Changsha with her precious cargo of drugs three weeks later. She was infinitely grateful to the US Air Force personnel for getting her and her cargo safely home after stops in Lingling and Hengyang.[41]

Late in the summer of 1943, the spread of antiforeign feelings began to build in China. Several missions were being squeezed out of existence, not only by the hardships of the war but by harsh government regulations and taxes. Whether or not the Chinese wanted to take over these institutions as a matter of principle or for the money that they generated was not clear, although the emphasis seemed to be on the schools and hospitals rather than on churches. Yali was no exception.

Ying Kai-shih paid a visit to Elliott and Miss Tooker while in Changsha. With his eternal optimism, he represented the opposite school of thought. He looked toward an expansion of the educational system, the addition of more foreign staff, and a total reconstruction of their buildings after the war. A visit from Dr. H. C. Chang, superintendent of the medical school in Kwieyang, overlapped with Dean Ying's visit. The enthusiasm and excitement generated when these two leaders got together was something to behold. Dr. Chang's vision extended into the next fifty years, bringing all the schools back to Changsha and planning new buildings on the theory that any reconstruction must fit in with future progress. Just to bring the schools back to Changsha within the next year would entail a lot of building, since there were few empty buildings at the time. More-extensive plans would include research laboratories and gardens, dormitories and apartments, and more land to accommodate all this as well as basic classrooms.[42] But first, China had to repel the Japanese and win the war to reclaim the country. They could not do this without American help.

14th US Army Air Force

Longing to serve his country in the war effort, Hopkins joined the 14th US Army Air Force as a headquarters assistant to Gen. Claire Lee Chennault.[43] Hopkins was commissioned as a first lieutenant. This force continued to be referred to as the Flying Tigers. The Chinese-American Composite Wing (CACW) became a part of the 14th Army Air Force in July 1943.[44] The CACW consisted of Chinese aircraft and crews trained under a lend-lease program, with a combination of Chinese and USAAF officers serving as the wing's group, squadron, and flight leaders. Organized as two fighter groups of P-40s and one bomber group of B-25s, the CACW units began their first combat operations in the fall of 1943. The integration of the Chinese forces effectively gave General Chennault command and control over all tactical aviation operations within the Chinese theater.[45]

The force had been elevated to the status of a theater-level air force, although its mission remained essentially guerrilla in nature: to disrupt, harass, and confuse the movements of the Japanese, a numerically superior enemy. Their first priority was to destroy the Japanese supply boats and sampans on the Yangtze River in order to cut off valuable resources to their inland troops.

Air War over China

By this time, the improvements in pilot training and equipment in China became apparent. At first, many of the pilots were poorly trained, having been rushed through training and out of flying school with no flying time or experience with combat equipment. The situation had improved in the flight-training schools in the US as well as in the schools under Chennault's command in the rear areas of the China theater. Although the 14th Air Force was still hampered at times by inadequate fuel supplies, it became pretty evident by their improvement in pilot skills that the work was being done to win the war. The commanders, instructors, pilots, mechanics, ground observers, and combat liaison officers all worked together for the cause.

The small-scale air tactics by the 14th Air Force in China were particularly vicious in terms of inflicting damage on enemy supply lines. One of Hopkins's fellow officers in the 14th, Col. Bruce K. Holloway, described the "guerrilla" air tactics these units were engaged in during the fall of 1943. "With small-scale air tactics you have to make the most out of what you have. From July to October of this year, in addition to doing extensive damage to Jap installations, we have destroyed in one way or another about 90,000 tons of shipping and 175 enemy planes. We achieved this destruction with very little gas, ammunition, and bombs, with small comparative losses, and with a plane force totaling less than the number of Jap planes destroyed."[46]

The 14th Air Force took advantage of their interior position, with squadrons based at Kweilin, Lingling, and Hengyang. The Japanese bases were around them in a semicircle, from Ichang on around to Hankow and down around the coast to Canton and Hong Kong. The 14th used this position to their advantage. If the weather was bad in one direction, they would hit the enemy in the other direction. Frequently, they directed missions to the same place for two or three days until the Japs would expect a prolonged attack and reinforce the area with more aircraft. Then they would hit another place that was relatively undefended, or carry on counter air force operations against the reinforced objective. With a minimum of aircraft and equipment, they continued to inflict terror on the Jap positions, although they lacked the force to dislodge them. Colonel Holloway described the specific tactics that their units used against the Japanese supply lines in China during the fall of 1943.

On September 9, the 14th Air Force sent out a two-plane reconnaissance team from Kweilin around the Hankow–Kiukiang circuit. The mission shot up a couple of boats, setting one on fire. A second mission of four P-38s and two P-40s flew the same circuit and shot up two locomotives on the Shihhweiyao mine railroad and one locomotive camouflaged as a boxcar on the main line at Puchi. They also sank a boat, heavily damaged four more, and reported damaging a bridge at Puchi. At the same time, the Kweilin base sent a mission of twelve B-25s and thirteen P-40s to Canton. Four B-25s and two P-40s turned back. The rest of the squadron rained destruction on the building area of the White Cloud airdrome (a small enemy airfield), leveling several buildings and starting a big oil fire. Twenty to twenty-five Zeros intercepted them. One American bomber was shot up and lost an engine but succeeded in returning to base. Five Zeros were confirmed as destroyed, with four others noted as probable. At about 2:00 p.m., four P-38s were sent to the Whampoa docks at Canton, with two 500 lb. demolition bombs on each plane.[47] They dive-bombed the shop and building area of the dock, scoring direct hits with all the bombs. The pilots said that "they could see pieces of buildings flying in all directions." Just as they started their dive from about 7,000 feet, they saw a bunch of Zeros at about 13,000 feet, but they pushed on ahead and kept going. The Zeros never did catch them. After they pulled out of their dive, the American pilots saw a Japanese transport plane to their left, and two of them flew over and polished it off.

On the next day, the P-38s and P-40s carried their usual death and destruction to boats and military targets along the Yangtze. During the last two weeks they had heavily damaged twenty-five to thirty boats in the immediate area around Shihhweiyao, and Chinese guerrillas burned thirteen of these as they drifted helplessly. The Japanese were afraid of American airplanes in the daytime and of guerrilla activity at night. Besides the regular dive-bombing and strafing, nine B-25s left Kweilin at 10:30 a.m. and were joined by seven P-40s at Hengyang. The squadron proceeded to Hankow. They made a bombing run at the large Wuchow cotton-mill warehouse, but the bombs missed their targets. Another bombing run started some fires along the Hankow dock. Their mission was a success in spite of the poor bombing results, because they shot down nine confirmed Zeros and counted another four as probable. At 3:00 p.m. Colonel Holloway ordered six P-38s from Lingling to make another run on the Whampoa docks at Canton. Two of the P-38s provided cover while the others carried 1,000 lb. bombs. They made direct hits on the docks but found no boats in the vicinity. Just before the bombing approach, ten Zeros came in, so the top cover sucked them off to one side, shot one down and another probable, and dived away. Seventeen other Zeros attacked the four P-38s immediately after they completed their bombing approach. All they could do was run, and they had a hard time outrunning the Zeros, but all the P-38s succeeded in getting home and back to base.

These tactics were illustrative of what was accomplished against enemy positions with just a handful of airplanes. The biggest mission that was sent out up to that time was seven or eight bombers and eight to ten pursuit aircraft. The gunfire from the P-38s and P-40s was deadly, even if not immediately. Many of the boats that they destroyed were not bombed or destroyed directly in the water. Instead, the gunfire from the P-40s set the boats on fire and rendered them helpless and drifting ashore, where the Chinese guerrillas destroyed them.

General Chennault was convinced that the destruction of all Japanese shipping on the China coast was the key to breaking up of the Japanese Empire and the beginning of the end of the war.[48] The 14th Air Force had made substantial progress in cutting off Japanese supplies and supporting Chinese ground troops in the interior. The war was raging in China, and Lieutenant Hopkins was yearning to make his mark, as did so many young men of his generation.

Chapter 11
EMBASSY BUSINESS

Luncheon with Chou En-lai

The relative safety of Chungking to the rest of China offered the Americans an opportunity for interaction with high-level Chinese leaders on a regular basis.[1] Several US military officers and senior embassy staff attended a luncheon at the American Club on January 29, 1943, given by Chou En-lai, the Chinese Communist representative in Chungking. Chou was accompanied by Gen. Lin Paio, a high-ranking Communist army leader. Their American guests included several of Springer's colleagues: Col. David Barrett, Colonel DePass, Mr. Clubb, and Everett Drumright.

Col. David D. Barrett, the American Embassy Military Attaché. *David Dean Barrett papers, envelope A, Hoover Institution Archives*

Chou En-lai (*center*), as seen at an airstrip in Yenan in 1944. He possessed valuable intelligence on Japanese troop strength and courted the Americans for cooperation against the Japanese. *David Dean Barrett papers, envelope A, Hoover Institution Archives*

Chou outlined the deep internal political currents undermining the Chinese efforts to defend their homeland from the Japanese. The Communist military forces had received no military or financial support from the Nationalist Chinese government for the past three and a half years. There were still occasional military clashes between Communist and Nationalist government troops, chiefly in Kiangsi, Anhwei, and Hupeh Provinces.

Chou said that a Nationalist general, Wei Li-huang, "had been relieved of his command at Loyang, Honan, because he was too friendly with the Chinese communists and too active against the Japanese forces to suit the wishes of the Chinese high command at Chungking."[2] General Wei was now living in Chengtu. More pressing, Chou noted that China could be more active in the military struggle against the Japanese, especially in guerrilla warfare, if supplied with arms and ordinance. He believed the Japanese would try to crush all Chinese resistance, rather than expanding the war to Siberia, India, or Australia. Chou mentioned Yunnan Province as the most likely military objective of any new Japanese penetration. Although he noted that the cities of Changsha and Sian were possible military objectives, he seemed most concerned about the Japanese effort to strengthen their position to eliminate resistance in North China, where the Communist forces were based. In 1942, the Japanese had carried out a so-called Fifth Campaign with a view to eliminate Chinese resistance. Like the other campaigns, it had been a failure. The Chinese Communists remained in the area. During the campaign, Chou noted that the Japanese had looted central China of its food resources. He also expanded on internal intelligence available to him about a large Japanese troop division that had recently moved from North China to the South. These revelations from Chou were eye opening to the Americans. Drumright described Chou as "a very adroit fellow . . . who could get along with anybody if he wished to."[3] He was the public face of the Communist Party and was considered a "moderate" by some. Mao Tse-tung was at the opposite pole. He was a very radical type, who had no accommodation for anyone who wasn't a Communist and who wouldn't follow the party line. At the time, Mao's radical nature was largely unknown to the Americans. He played his political cards close to the vest while courting the Americans for help.

The relaxed setting in the exclusive Chungking Club allowed the Americans to become acquainted with Gen. Lin Piao, the Communist military leader, who accompanied Chou En-lai. Diminutive in appearance, Lin was thirty-five years old and a native of a village located not far from Hankow, Hupeh. In 1924, he was a student at Whampoa military academy in Canton under Generalissimo Chiang Kai-shek. He was wounded three times during Chiang's subsequent military campaign against the Communists. Lin directed the operations of the Chinese Communist forces during their most noted victory over the Japanese at Pinghsingkuan, in northern Shansi, in the fall of 1937.[4] He was already a battle-hardened veteran.[5]

General Lin stated that the Chinese Communists were faced with an acute shortage of ammunition (bullets, as he put it in Chinese) and medicines, neither of which was being supplied by the Chinese national government. He mentioned that the Chinese Communists had no supplies of copper, and their production of military equipment was limited to hand grenades and mines. He asserted that if the Chinese Communists were supplied with arms, ammunition, and medicines, they would go on the offensive and strike hard blows at the Japanese throughout northern China. The intelligence Lin offered was alarming. He declared, "The Japanese have withdrawn very few troops from North China since the start of the Pacific war. They now maintain eight or nine divisions in North China (not including Manchuria), of which about four are in Shansi. It is the definite policy of the Japanese to eliminate all Chinese resistance in the occupied areas, to drive all Chinese troops there from, to consolidate their political and economic position in these areas, to utilize the manpower and resources of these areas to assist them in gaining hegemony in all of East Asia."[6] General Lin went on to express his opinion that the Japanese would fail to attain these objectives. The Chinese people would never give their support to Japan, and the Japanese would fail in their endeavors to sweep Chinese resistance from the so-called occupied areas.

Lin was frustrated that his efforts failed to receive support from the national government. On two occasions since coming to Chungking, he had been received by his old teacher, Chiang Kai-shek. Chiang received him courteously, and they had discussed their Kuomintang-Communist relations. As a representative of the Chinese Communists, Lin requested that the blockade of the Communist area in northern Shensi be lifted and the Communist army supplied with needed funds, ammunition, and medicine. He went on to say that Chiang had expressed sympathy for their position, but no aid had been forthcoming. He said the Kuomintang also demanded that Communist forces be incorporated into the national armies, but Lin feared that this could not be accomplished as long as the national government and the Kuomintang failed to give the people of China democracy. The political divide between the two parties was a wide one. The divide between the Kuomintang and the Chinese peasants grew increasingly wider.

Corruption

The Nationalist government was notoriously corrupt. The black market and rampant inflation had resulted in disparity between the wealthy business and government segments and the ordinary people. The government controlled all vehicles. Even donkey carts had to have rubber tires in order to be licensed. Of course, the rubber tires were sold by the government. Gasoline was so expensive that only the military and the very wealthy could afford cars. Food costs in some places had tripled since the beginning of the year. Morale had suffered after years of bombing and depravation. Inefficiency and insubordination increased, inflation was destroying the economy and the health of the people, and the conscription of troops into the Chinese army interfered with food production and essential services.

The conscription system for soldiers in China initiated from Chungking. Each area was assigned a quota of conscripts to fill, depending on whenever they were needed. Draftees who could find the money (in the form of a bribe to the conscripting officer) went free. Those with no money, and often those needed most at home or on farms, were taken by force. They were sometimes chained together in gangs and were lucky if they ever saw their homes again. The death and desertion rate among conscripts was 44 percent according to some sources. Living conditions were dreadful. Army pay was delivered to the regimental commander to buy the soldiers' food. The less he bought, the more he could line his own pockets. As a result, disease was rampant, including vitamin deficiency, malaria, tuberculosis, dysentery, and venereal disease. The mission hospitals played a critical role in healthcare for both soldiers and civilians. The Chinese soldiers who sought treatment were usually dressed in shabby clothing and straw sandals or were admitted with diseases or untended wounds.[7]

Communist Liaison

In March 1943, John Davies Jr., a second secretary at the American embassy, had a follow-up conversation with Chou En-lai in Chungking. Davies explored the possibility of the US drawing on Communist intelligence regarding Japanese activities. Chou explained that in order to achieve an effective liaison, the Americans should have a small group of officers stationed in Communist-controlled territory. Although Chou's supply of information coming from North China was limited by poor communications, a steady flow of intelligence regarding the Japanese came through their command at Yenan and northern Shansi. Their intelligence was about enemy operations in North China, Manchuria, and the Yangtze valley. Chou reiterated his invitation for a small group of American officers to set up observers' posts in Shensi and Shansi. He pointed out that if the Americans planned to assist in driving the Japanese from North China, it was not too early to begin investigating sites for possible airfields in that area.

Out of the blue, Davies posed a blunt question to Chou. He said, "If we (the US) wished to extend lend-lease aid impartially to the Chinese Army, irrespective of political complexion and including those who seem most anxious to fight the common enemy, would we be able to do so?"[8] Chou shook his head, implying that the prejudices and suspicions of the Eighteenth Group Army (under Communist command) were too strong. Chou felt that in time, Chiang's attitude toward the Communists might change when he learned that the Japanese are much stronger than he now realized. "It is bad to overestimate the Japanese," Chou commented, adding, "It is quite as bad to underestimate them. The Generalissimo is guilty of the latter error. And when General Chiang discovers that the Japanese were not going to be easily rolled back into the sea, then he may feel that he will have to give more consideration to the Communists."[9] Chou was most concerned that the Japanese might attack Yunnan, in southwestern China, before the Chinese-American strength in the area was sufficient to defend it. If the Japanese occupied Yunnan, he observed, they will have gone a long way toward strangulating Free China.

Chou stressed that American help in supplying arms, logistical support, and medical supplies would be most welcomed, if permission from the Nationalist Chinese government could be obtained. In respect to the war against Japan, the situation in China was so fundamentally bad that no offensive military action could be taken against the Japanese either in North China or in inner Mongolia by either faction, until military cooperation was achieved.

As a result of these meetings, a memo went out to the US secretary of state on September 10, 1943, stating, "Because of the strategic importance of north China, it would be desirable for the United States to have American military observers in that area in order to obtain more complete overall information regarding the Japanese and to bring about needed military cooperation between the Kuomintang and the Communists, with the possible result of causing the Central Government forces to give attention to military matters rather than to political ones as was true at present." [10] The exploratory mission to visit the Communist stronghold was eventually given the green light.

Changes at the Embassy

Changes were coming to the American embassy in Chungking. Springer's office was moved across the Yangtze River, with more desks to follow as soon as quarters were provided for the staff. Chungking was swarming with hundreds of thousands of refugees from the coastal area. Springer thought the new location was more convenient for the staff as well as for embassy business. Now he had to cross the river and walk up the mountain in the dark every night. On some evenings, there were no lights on, to make it difficult for the Japanese bombers to locate. He sometimes did his work by candlelight. Even walking home uphill with a torch, it was difficult to see in the dark, as he realized one night when he ran into a pole. From his lair on the mountain he could retire to his den in the evening and forget about everything, if just for one night at a time.

Chungking recorded a rare snowfall early that winter, only the second time in about twenty years. It was a welcome change to the scenery. The snow melted almost immediately in the valley, but there were traces for a couple of days. The issue of draft notices came up again, which required some embassy staff members to fill out questionnaires regarding their status. Springer attached a letter from his local draft board, ordering him to report to Camden, New Jersey, at once, together with his answer.[11] The State Department implemented a policy stating that it could not, due to its manpower shortage, accept any employee resignations for the duration of the war. This policy was enforced by a refusal to pay anyone's travel expenses. The new policy prohibited him from reporting in person to the local draft board in Camden. His draft status was still pending, although his hands were tied by the embassy. In any event, he would not be headed home anytime soon.

New Quarters

By April 1, Springer moved from the house high on the hill and settled into new quarters at the home of a local couple, the Morosoffs.[12] He found his new abode more convenient and satisfactory in almost every respect. He had a bedroom with a small bedside table and chair. His clothes were kept in a closet down the hall. He had the run of the house and ate breakfast there. Sometimes Mrs. Morosoff sat and talked with him over coffee. She took good care of her guest. She thought he was too thin, and said that a big breakfast every morning would fatten him up a bit.

A new expense for Springer was Russian-language lessons, mandated by the State Department. His lessons began at 6:30 a.m. and continued until just before 8:00 a.m., when he dashed off to the embassy. The lessons were taken on Tuesday, Wednesday, and Friday mornings. After two weeks, he felt that he was speaking Russian almost like a native and pondered why the Russian language had been much neglected in American schools.[13] The US planned to open up a number of diplomatic posts in the hinterlands of China, including Kweilin, Chengtu, and Longxi in Ganzu Province.[14] In May 1943, Springer accompanied another diplomat to the Chinese city of Tihau (today's Urumqi), in Hsinchiang Province, near the Soviet border. Their mission was to deliver some embassy seals and establish a US representation in the area.[15] It was a long trip by plane to this remote area of China, to deepen the American presence near the present-day convergence of Kazakhstan, Russia, and Mongolia.

Springer kept in touch with his mother via letters, through which he received updates on the family. Audrey sometimes wrote about his brother's girlfriends and enclosed pictures. Having been away from Yale-in-China for over a year, Springer had settled into his new job at the State Department. One day he decided to give his mother an update on his social life:

I have a girl-friend here in Chungking. She is Mary Louise Lee, an American girl from Indiana, age 28 (on April 21), and married to a Chinese, from whom she is separated. They have a son, but in China the son goes to the father. I met her at a party at Ching Shiu Ch'i several months ago, and have been taking her to dinner in town about once a week since then. She is a nice girl—not the type you always feared I would bring home, but the type I usually did bring home. We like each other very much, and get along excellently. It is not inconceivable that I may marry her after the war and when I have gotten settled into a job I will be content to keep for life. I'll send you a picture of her as soon as I can get one. Your first question may well be, as mine was, how could such a girl marry a Chinese? However she could, it was a mistake—made when she was 20 and freshly disillusioned about another affair. You are probably shocked, as I once would be, at such an idea, but times and my outlook have changed. Be assured again that I won't rush into the thing blindly, and that no change in the status quo is imminent. I just wanted to acquaint you with someone which is assuming increasing importance of my life, so you won't be suddenly jolted in case anything comes of it.[16]

Bandits

In the last week of May 1943, Springer took an eleven-day trip to Kunming, five days of which were in a US Navy truck with a group of Seabees (construction battalion). This trip was no vacation and was not without incident.

Springer's group was attacked by bandits at about 1:00 a.m. while camped out one day's drive, south of Kweiyang. Four of them were sleeping under a tarpaulin supported by bamboo poles at the back of the truck. At the zero hour, head-sized rocks, capable of crushing skulls, were thrown at their tent, several hitting the canvas, and one striking a Navy lieutenant in the hip. They scrambled from the tent, and the five Navy guys got their guns in hand. When they saw a light flashing a minute later, two

Infantry training unit, Kunming. Colonel Barrett, *fourth from left*, stands next to Brig. Gen. Thomas Arms and Nationalist soldiers, 1943. *David Dean Barrett papers, envelope E, Hoover Institution Archives*

of them fired at it, and it was immediately extinguished. They stood watch—awake the rest of the night, but there was no other event, beyond a light signaling at ten-minute intervals down the road. It was an eerie affair, since it happened on a pitch-dark night with a slight drizzle of rain, in a mountainous spot forty kilometers from the nearest town of Annan. Springer surmised, "My understanding is that the bandits wanted us to flee, leaving our truck and supplies behind, or to flee with the truck, in which event the road would be blocked around the next bend (from whence came the other light signal). If we hadn't shown ourselves to be armed, the bandits would undoubtedly have closed in with knives sooner or later. They could have come from all four sides simultaneously. If they had chosen rather to close in first with knives, they could've wreaked havoc while we slept, and P.L.B. would have awakened, if at all, with a slit throat."[17]

After their arrival, Springer roomed at an Army hostel just outside Kunming. While there, he visited with Col. David Barrett, the former embassy military attaché, now working with an infantry-training center near Kunming. Colonel Barrett told Springer that he was almost certain he could offer him a commission as a first lieutenant under him, although his duties would be mostly clerical in nature. He jumped at the chance to serve his country in uniform and readily agreed to Barrett's offer, pending the approval of his release from the State Department. An officer's commission would give him a change of scenery, an increase in pay, and a chance to rest his eyes from the meticulous detail of hours upon hours of code work.

Colonel Barrett

Col. David D. Barrett became an important liaison with the Chinese military. At a young age, he made the military his career and learned of an Army program to train officers in foreign languages. Barrett arrived in Peking in 1924 and assumed the post of assistant military attaché for language study.[18] He mastered the dialect through five hours of practice with Mandarin teachers each day, followed by two hours of personal study. Barrett also made trips to the countryside to practice conversation with rural Chinese.[19]

Barrett's early military career was spent almost entirely in China. By 1931, he was permanently assigned to Tientsin as a regimental intelligence staff officer. Barrett's tour of duty in Tientsin ended in 1934. Two years later, he was assigned as an assistant military attaché to the American legation in Peking. When the legation fled the approach of the Japanese to Hankow, Barrett often drove out to the front line to observe the fighting between the Chinese and Japanese forces. By 1938, Hankow fell and the Nationalists again retreated, this time to Chungking. The armies in China varied greatly in modernity, ideology, and combat effectiveness. They acted in an ever-shifting kaleidoscopic theater of factional politics, personal relationships, and local ties. For a foreign observer, such as a military attaché, any success required a thorough command of the Chinese language, a long and intelligent immersion in the affairs of the country, and a capacity to unlearn many conventional US military attitudes.[20] Colonel Barrett was as well suited for the job as anyone.

Barrett assumed the post of chief attaché in 1942 and was attached to the embassy, so he was removed from much of the military planning and operations executed by the US, whose presence was constantly growing in the region. Barrett remained in that position through the summer of 1943, when he requested a transfer out of the embassy detail. He was assigned to assist in forming and training a Chinese field army in Kunming and Kweilin, where they schooled Nationalist Chinese troops with weapons and tactics. Early in his Army career, Barrett was appalled by what he had witnessed of the Chinese military apparatus. He now concluded, "The Chinese soldier is excellent material, wasted and betrayed by stupid leadership."[21] It was a conviction also shared by General Stillwell.

Working under Pressure

Wary of another dangerous truck ride, Springer managed to secure a flight back to Chungking by Army plane, but he felt it flew uncomfortably close to the mountains, which would have taken them five days to drive over. He was relieved when the plane climbed over the worst of them and started its gradual descent to Chungking. The truck that Springer was to have come back on wrecked about fifty miles out of Kunming, and a passenger was killed. It could have been him.

It was during his trip to Kunming that the remaining embassy offices were moved, with the American embassy relocated to the city side of the river. The offer for his officer's commission from Colonel Barrett was confirmed by letter, although the rank was changed from first to second lieutenant, with "excellent prospects of promotion to 1st Lieut. in six months" added as an enticement.[22] Springer pursued the opportunity, taking and passing his Army physical on the morning of June 22 and hoping to give his resignation notice to the State Department effective September 1. There were several reasons for this, the biggest of which was to "share the Army experience that my generation is largely going through," he wrote.[23] Another was that he continued to receive notices from his Local Draft Board No. 12, in Camden, New Jersey, demanding that he present himself for enlistment in the US military. He did not want to feel "on the outside" after the war was over, as well as while it was going on.[24] Furthermore, the climate in Chungking was horrible and had gradually sapped his energy and undermined his health. His eyes had been under continual strain from the months of repetitious code work.

The State Department had no interest in losing an employee; it was extremely difficult for them to get a substitute for Springer. The department delayed answering

Vice Consul Paul Springer in Chungking, overlooking the Yangtze River. *Springer Family collection*

the Army's telegram, requesting that Springer be allowed to join for military service.[25] They postponed answering the local draft board inquiry for a full year. They had more-pressing matters to attend to, and valid reasons for keeping him on board. According to his superiors, "Springer has become an expert in coding and decoding the large volume of secret and confidential messages transmitted for the Department of State. These messages were often of great value and use to the military intelligence units of the Army and Navy at Chungking."[26] He was entrusted with work connected with safeguarding the department's secret codes, a responsibility assigned only to those of unquestioned reliability. His experience as a teacher in China under war conditions from 1941 to 1942, and his knowledge of French, German, and, particularly, Chinese, made his services in the Chungking post extremely useful in the successful prosecution of the Allied war effort.[27]

The embassy staff had been working under pressure for several weeks. Frustrated that he could not join the Army, Springer asked his supervisors for an appointment as a vice consul, a diplomatic post.[28] A US consul is an official representative of the government in the territory of another, acting to assist and protect the citizens of the US and facilitate trade and good relations between the two countries. A consul is distinguished from an ambassador, the latter representing one head of state to another. There can be only one ambassador from one country to another. There may be several consuls and vice consuls, one in each of the main cities, providing assistance with trade, visa, and passport issues to US citizens traveling or living abroad and to citizens of the host country traveling to or trading with the US. If no promotion was forthcoming, Springer asked to be released to the military at the earliest possible date.

Springer continued to stay in touch with his mother, writing in regard to his new love in China, reassuring her, "However, as I don't plan to do anything rash until after I have returned to the states, you need have no immediate fears. . . . I know already, though, that she wouldn't consider marrying me unless I was certain we could be happy together, come what might."[29] He began to have doubts about finding the right woman. In the meantime, George Small moved into the spare bedroom at the Morosoffs' house when the previous tenant moved out. It had been two years since he and Springer had sailed together from San Francisco to the Orient. They had become the best of friends and sometimes frequented the Chungking Club together.

Changes in China

The month of August saw several noteworthy events in Chungking. The death of Lin Sen on August 1, 1943, brought a month of mourning across China.[30] Lin Sen was the president of China and had been the chairman of the national government of the Republic of China since 1931. Though he had little influence on public policy, Lin was highly respected by the public as an honest elder statesman who was above politics. His lack of political ambition, corruption, and nepotism was an exceedingly rare trait. He lent dignity and stability to the office while other state institutions were in chaos. Flags flew at half-mast for a month. Floral wreaths were presented only on the official burial day. The central executive committee elected Gen. Chiang Kai-shek as president a few hours after Lin's death, transferring all of those powers to him. The Generalissimo, as he was referred to throughout China, had consolidated his power in the government.

Chungking experienced its first bombing raid since 1941. There was a formation of about twenty-seven Japanese bombers accompanied by Zeros that attacked the city. Springer saw the bombs drop from the planes, the smoke arising from where the bombs hit, but he did not hear the explosions. There was some antiaircraft fire and a couple of Chinese-piloted P-40s, who tried to intervene, but their efforts were futile in spite of a glowing account of their role in the following day's newspaper. The antiaircraft fire seemed to be far behind and below the bombers. The *chin-paos* were sounded in the capital at 9:30 a.m. and lasted for two hours.[31] The raid in August marked the late opening of Chungking's "bombing season," which in previous years usually started in early May. The air raid dugouts were quickly teeming with people. About a hundred bombs were dropped on Chungking that day, according to reports from the Army. The heat in the city became insufferable as the peak of summer arrived. In addition to civilian casualties, there was significant damage to the city's infrastructure from the bombing. There was no running water in the city for five days. There was no ice being made during that time either, which compounded the problem of refrigeration when the electrical power grid experienced intermittent failures. Springer had grown frustrated with the living conditions and had grown mentally weary of working in Chungking. He was about to get the break he had long looked forward to.

Crossing the "Hump"

Springer's request for vacation leave had been approved, and he departed for India on September 1, on a China National Aviation Corp. (CNAC) plane at 6:30 a.m.[32] It took off from the small island airport—the runway stretched from one end of the island to the other, with no room to spare.[33] It was a twelve-hour flight to Calcutta, with a thirty-minute stop at Kunming and another stop of about ten minutes at Dinjan. During the flight, except when he was permitted to go up front with the pilot, he was sitting in an aluminum "bucket seat." His seat became icy cold when the plane reached an altitude of 18,000 feet to fly over "the Hump," the name given to the Himalayas by China-to-India-bound travelers.

Flying men and supplies from Kunming, China, over the Himalayas to India and back was one of the most dangerous assignments for a pilot during World War II. The US lost nearly six hundred aircraft flying over the most forbidding terrain on the planet, in the world's worst weather, often flying inadequate airplanes with few navigation aids and inaccurate maps.[34] Airlifting supplies over the Hump was not the original plan for moving supplies into China. Once the Japanese troops cut the Burma Road, thereby severing the overland supply route from Lashio, an alternative had to be found to re-supply the Chinese to keep them in the war against Japan. The first military Hump flight was flown on April 8, 1942, only eighteen months before Springer's first trip to India. It was a torturous route over the mountains and jungles of northern Burma before ascending over the world's most forbidding mountain range—the Himalayas. On this day, Springer's CNAC flight landed in Calcutta without incident and on schedule.

Upon arrival, Springer was taken to the customs station by the British in a bus over a smooth road—his first smooth road in two years. He went through customs at the Great Eastern Hotel, where he naively asked a uniformed attendant, "Where is the Great Eastern Hotel?" The attendant replied, "This is the Great Eastern."[35] Springer was dumbfounded that the airport customs was in the largest and best hotel in Calcutta. He was unable to get a room there but managed to squeeze in at the Grand Calcutta Hotel, overrun with American soldiers. He thought the price exorbitant at seventeen rupees, or about $5 US, but after being in China, it seemed frightfully cheap to him.

Springer spent some time in Calcutta shopping, drinking milkshakes, and watching movies. It was his first taste of real milk in two years.[36] Upon arrival in Calcutta and changing some money, he described his experience in civilization once again: "I felt like Robinson Caruso [*sic*] dropped suddenly down in the middle of New York after 30 years on a desert isle. My 2,500 rupees melted away as I bought a tailor made suit, shirts, ties, in fact everything in the clothes line, all at high prices but of very good quality. I'm very proud of that brown worsted suit, made by the Generalissimo's own tailor." After seven days of shopping, eating, and meeting with Chungking friends, he bought a train ticket for a hill station in the Himalayas. He and a Scottish friend from Chungking stayed in Darjeeling at the home of Captain Duplock, the secretary of the Gymkhana Club. Springer became a temporary member. The private club was a blessing; he had a fine room with its own bath and drinkable tap water, his first since leaving the US.

Springer enjoyed the change in climate and scenery. He went horseback riding three times during his five-day stay. He trekked over the bridle paths overlooking the city, where magnificent scenery unfolded. From the Observatory Hill, he saw the snowcapped Kinchenjunga, the world's second-highest mountain, rising majestically above the clouds at dawn. He would see Mt. Everest from the plane on his return journey. It rained every day he was there (the monsoon ran through October), but his spirits were never dampened even though he was soaked to the skin on one occasion and thoroughly sprinkled on a couple of others. He took an all-day trip with two men to Kalimpong, by hiring a small car. They went straight down to the valley from their 7,500-foot elevation and then up the next hill. Large cars were forbidden to use the steep road. They had a difficult time getting back, since the radiator boiled over periodically climbing the hill, and the terrain was so rough on the car that the fans scraped the radiator. They got back in time for coffee with friends, and he enjoyed the best confections since he arrived in the Orient. The higher standard of living in Calcutta as compared to Chungking was a pleasant surprise.

After dinner at the Grand Calcutta, Springer met with some friends the following day in Darjeeling, where he committed a faux pas with the two women who accompanied them. He assumed that both were English. He became comfortable enough to ask one of them where she got her strange accent. She denied any strangeness, but he persisted, despite several digs in his shins by her male companions. They told him later that she was Anglo-Indian and ashamed of the fact, therefore pretending to be pure English. Springer was told that Anglo-Indians generally had a strange singsong speech, which was much more of a giveaway than their dark eyes. The woman was especially sensitive to Paul's "obstinate questionings" and got her guard up, telling him she had difficulty understanding him, which caused her, her girlfriend, and their two companions quite a bit of embarrassment.[37] It was an awkward lesson in social skills that he would not soon forget.

Captain Duplock refused to charge Springer for his quarters at the Gymkhana Club, insisting that he pay only for the meals. The next morning, Springer and some friends embarked on a sightseeing trip via a narrow-gauge mountain train. Its engine sported a beautiful green paint offset with the shining brass of its parts. The train climbed from scratch to 7,500 feet with the aid of several loops and four or five switches, where it backed down and then went up on a different track. To gain traction, sand was sprinkled on the tracks when the train's wheels started to skid, applied by a man who rode the cowcatcher. Each car had its own brake, which was applied by having a man stand on it when the downgrade was too steep. His first-class car, having ten leather easy chairs and large windows, furnished a great view of the mountain scenery. The return trip was made the same way, with the small train leaving at 1:00

p.m. and arriving in the town of Siliguri that evening. There was just enough time for dinner before boarding the sleeper train for Calcutta. On the ride back, Springer struck up a long conversation with a "Russian woman, Vera Suhrawardy, twice divorced, second time from [an] Indian politician."[38] They made plans to meet again the following night.

Arriving in Calcutta at noon on September 14, Springer again checked into the Grand Calcutta, where he shared a room with the US Army Air Force officers he had met in Darjeeling. Springer went out on the town that night with Al Ravenholt, a friend from his FAU days, for a show and dinner at the Holiday Inn. Afterward, they went to the 300 Club to see Vera, the woman he met on the train the night before. She lived on the second floor of the hotel, above the nightclub. They had drinks together and she read their palms. Springer described her as "an authoress, very good at character reading, as she read me like a book."[39] He returned the next night for dinner and dancing with her. They had become fast friends. Vera insisted that he inform her when he returned safely to Chungking, and they arranged a meeting two years hence in New York City.

Vera Suhrawardy

Springer never mentioned Vera in letters to his mother, yet he was smitten with her, a Russian actress of Polish descent. Born in 1902, she had been a member of the Moscow Art Theatre, had significant stage talent, and toured through several European capital cities. She caught the eye of a Russian, Eugene Ticenko, in Berlin. They fell in love, got married, and continued to tour and live together in several European cities. They had a son, Oleg. When her husband insisted on pursuing his medical career in the UK, the couple separated. Vera moved to Calcutta with Oleg at the invitation of a friend from the theater, Hassan Shahib Suhrawardy, in 1938. She lived in Calcutta with Oleg and found comfort and solace in the teachings of Islam. She cabled her husband, then living in Edinburgh, Scotland, requesting that he also accept the Islamic faith. Having been raised a Greek Orthodox, Tiscenko replied that his faith was unshakable, and refused.

In the meantime, Vera began a relationship with the younger brother of her friend. He was a rising star in Calcutta politics, Hussain Shaheed Suhrawardy. They fell in love and wanted to get married, but before they could tie the knot, Vera's marriage to Eugene Tiscenko presented a legal obstacle.[40] Vera converted to Islam on June 27, 1940, and changed her name to Begum Noor Jehan. She then applied to the High Court of Calcutta on August 5, 1940, for a suit declaring the dissolution of her marriage on the grounds of incompatibility, citing that her husband refused to convert to the Islamic faith. The court declared that her marriage was dissolved, although a subsequent appeal left the case unresolved. She married the younger Suhrawardy later in 1940, and they had one son together. The Vera Tiscenko case became a landmark case in Indian legal history.[41] It was used where conversion to Islam by Hindus, Jewish, and women of other faiths was at issue in matrimonial cases.

At the time Vera met Springer, in September 1943, she was not, in fact, twice divorced, as she had told him, but a married woman, and active in social and political affairs in Calcutta and instrumental in her husband's rise in Indian politics. Suhrawardy was elected as the chief minister of United Bengal in April 1946. Despite their great partnership in high-wire politics, her second marriage was not a happy one. The couple divorced in 1951 in London. Her second husband subsequently was elected as the prime minister of Pakistan, serving in 1956–57.[42]

Return to Chungking

Springer did not wish to foot another large plane bill to get back to Chungking, so the consulate arranged for him to go by Army plane as a diplomatic courier. He carried two sacks of mail, one for Kunming and one for Chungking. Al Ravenholt, still in Calcutta on FAU business, advised him to take a B-24 (C-87) out of Chabua over the Hump, since other planes were not as safe, especially the C-46s, which had been crashing right and left. Ravenholt's concerns were quite valid.

The Curtiss C-46 Commando was a new US Army Air Corps cargo plane that began service in the China–India air route in 1943. The Commando had been rushed into production. When the first ones arrived in India, they were accompanied by technical orders that listed more than fifty modifications that had to be made in the field before it could be safely flown. Operationally, it continued to be plagued with mechanical glitches. There were major problems with the control systems, including those designed to prevent the engine's carburetor from clogging with ice at high altitudes. Most unsettling were the many midair explosions reported. The mysterious fires and explosions on the C-46 Commandos as they flew the Hump route became the stuff of legend. They were unsettling, to say the least, to the flight crews scheduled to fly them. The Air Force reported at least thirty-one known instances of explosions or fires in midair involving the C-46, and assumed that the other planes that went missing had experienced a similar fate.[43]

After a missed alarm and an antismuggling baggage inspection at 4:30 a.m., Springer got a late start from the hotel. He caught a taxi, which broke down at the start of the road leading to the airfield. He then hitched a ride in a station wagon, which took him to the runway. He boarded the plane, only to find it was going to New Delhi and

Motor-driven ferry and sampans at the Yangtze ferry-boarding dock, south bank, Chungking. *FAU collection*

not Chabua. After much hollering of "Stop the car," or something equally foolish, he grabbed his luggage and scrambled off. He was rushed by jeep to the correct plane, which had been temporarily grounded pending installation of a navigational device. He described the rest of the morning: "I waited around for a while, getting hungrier and hungrier, and finally deciding to try to get a bite to eat. I went to the Army canteen near the field, where I learned that breakfast is not served until 7:30 a.m. By continuous heckling I managed to get some toast and jam on the table by 7:25, but just as I was reaching for my first piece of toast an Army truck came roaring out, and a guy shouted "Are you Springer?" I assured him I was, and he said, "Your plane is ready to go." "I grabbed that piece of toast and ran for the truck, and he gunned her over to the waiting plane, which I apologetically entered, and we took off at once."[44]

Springer wore a parachute over the Hump this time but was relieved not to have to use it. He wanted to get his new clothes back to Chungking, along with his ivory chess set and himself in one piece. They landed safely in Kunming, in spite of the bumps after crossing the Himalayas. The bumps were so violent they thoroughly scared even the Army men on board, since they had come out by boat. Springer delivered the mail and stayed in Kunming with a Mr. Smith and Theo Willis, crew members he served with on the FAU. He brought them some tobacco from India.

The Kunming air base was bombed on Monday morning by the Japanese. They felt the shocks at the Smiths' house when they were awakened by explosions and the rattling of the window panes. The motor pool was hit, destroying fifteen cars. A C-46 Commando plane was destroyed. A nearby Chinese village was also hit. Following the attack, the 14th Air Force claimed that sixteen bombers and four Zeros had been shot down, out of the twenty-seven bombers and eighteen Zeros spotted. One American P-40 was shot down, and a P-38 had its tail shot off but landed safely. In regard to the attacks, one of the base commanders wrote, "As I have pointed out, it's damn tough to run offensive support missions and attempt to defend the bases at the same time with the number of fighters I have. We have done it and we can continue to do it, but our losses will be proportionally higher."[45] Springer left Kunming by plane the next morning at 7:30, arriving in Chungking just two hours later with the other sack of mail. The only casualties of the trip to India were his pajamas, left in Darjeeling, and wet green paint on a recently cleaned raincoat.

Springer started back at the office the following day and began to work in the afternoons at a colleague's desk downstairs. His duties to date had been paraphrasing, writing letters describing or summarizing dispatches, and writing memos to field officers and letters to various people. He was told to begin doing visa work, which he hoped would lead to a vice consul commission. George Small was preparing to leave for Calcutta en route to his new assignment in Karachi on the following Saturday, leaving Springer as the only employee left in the former embassy building on the south bank of the Yangtze River. This left him with the following commuting options to the embassy: taking a bus, taking a Navy truck leaving at 7:45 a.m., or crossing the Yangtze on a motor-driven ferry. Even the ferry was not a good option when an early-morning fog settled in.

The Yangtze Fog

When the Yangtze River was fogged in, the motor-driven ferry boats did not make the crossing until the fog lifted, often after 10:00 a.m.—two to three hours after Springer's normal commuting time. The only alternative for a determined commuter was a sampan. These frail craft departed regularly as soon as they had a sufficient number of passengers, generally one less than enough to sink the boat. Crossing the Yangtze anytime by sampan was an undertaking fraught with danger. On a foggy day, with thirty-five passengers in a small, leaky boat, which at some points during the crossing was completely in the grip of the swirling current, passengers felt like they had little better than a fifty-fifty chance of avoiding a watery grave. Springer described one such morning trip:

It was not without misgivings, then, that I stepped into the waiting sampan which was rapidly filling up with Chinese men and women, two of whom carried small babies. I remember the last time I crossed, on a clear morning, in this fashion. There were only 18 in the boat that time, and we foreigners— for I had had some moral support that day, all felt that the boat was overloaded. Now I was alone, and we numbered 35 as the three boatmen shoved off with their crude oars and headed into the mist. There is a stretch of quiet water along the south bank of the river, due to a sheltering line of rocks up-stream. If the boat turned over here, a strong swimmer might get ashore, and anyone who could stay afloat for a short time and a fair chance of being picked up, for there were invariably numerous sampans within hailing distance. But to capsize in the current! I shuddered involuntarily at the macabre thought of it.[46]

As the boat pushed into the current, the fog closed in. Land was not visible on either side. The other sampans had dispersed, and any sign of them was obscured by the white wall of fog. In the boat were three oarsmen and thirty-two passengers, struggling sightless against one of the most treacherous bodies of water in the world, and with such puny weapons! If the helmsman had a poor sense of direction (and how easy it is to lose that in a fog), he was soon unable to tell, even by the current, which way he was heading, for there was nothing stationary to mark their location. Sometimes boats set out on the Yangtze in fog, just as they had done now, and disappeared without a trace. A bloated body might wash up here and there, to be stripped and buried or left to rot. Springer remembered the story of Mr. Evans, a Canadian, who had disappeared in this manner two years before. No trace of him or his fellow passengers on the ill-fated boat had ever been found. As Springer crossed the river, he mentally pictured what might have happened:

The party set out, saw the south bank rapidly fade, [and] looked in the other direction, steadfastly waiting for the rocky hills of the north shore to loom up before them. Fifteen minutes passed; [then] a half hour. The passengers grew fidgety, the more vociferous berating the boatmen for their slowness, and one or two suggesting that the course was not quite right. All thought of landing anywhere near where they had expected was soon given up, for they must by now have crossed the mouth of the Chialing, which meant that the smaller river would have to be re-crossed after they landed in order to get back to the peninsular Chungking proper.

This had sometimes occurred before, and the passengers were not unduly alarmed; only annoyed at the delay prospect of a long journey back. But when an hour had passed since the embarkation, and still no land was to be seen, even the most intrepid among them became uneasy, while the more timid souls were becoming panic stricken. The boatmen were feverishly paddling now in one direction, now in another, as they followed the advice of their passengers, and caught their panic.

Suddenly, out of the fog, there rushed up to them an ugly array of rocks, and almost immediately the boat was thrown against them with a rending crash, and passengers and splintered wood flew in all directions. Mr. Evans was catapulted into the water with the screams of his fellow passengers ringing in his ears. He was a strong swimmer, but even a Weissmuller might find himself at the mercy of this boiling cauldron. It was every man for himself, and Mr. Evans was forced to pummel a man in the stomach who had his neck in a stranglehold; to kick off someone who had grabbed his feet. Then he struck out for shore.

But unknown to himself, he was swimming now upstream, now downstream, now cross-current. He grew weaker and weaker, and though the fog was now beginning to lift, he was unable to make much progress toward the shore which now appeared, wraithlike, before him. He made a final Herculean effort, but suddenly a lurking whirlpool seized him like a giant hand. A gasp, a gurgle, and he was gone. The muddy Yangtze had taken its toll. The bubbling, mysterious waters raced on, as they had for centuries past, and would for eons to come.[47]

Springer was aroused from his nightmarish vision by seeing land gradually materialize before him, the sampan moving slowly forward and majestically out of the mist. He offered a silent prayer of thanks for having been saved once more from the fate of Mr. Evans, having once again made his daily crossing of the mighty Yangtze River.

American Allies in the Air

While in the US, the B-24 bomber crews were primarily trained for high-altitude, daylight precision bombing, but once in China their support missions changed dramatically. Upon their arrival, they were required to fly whatever kind of military mission was called for from day to day. It was not unusual for them to fly a long mission to Hong Kong, a 1,400-mile round trip from their base at Chengkung (near Kunming), where they would drop bombs on the docks from 20,000 feet.[48] The next

Gen. Claire Lee Chennault confers with a group of Chinese military officers. *David Dean Barrett papers, envelope E, Hoover Institution Archives*

day, they might be ordered to make a low-level bombing run on a bridge or railroad tunnel. Like their predecessors in the AVG, they provided air support for Chinese forces on the ground.

As the year went on, the combat effectiveness and bombardment operations of the 14th Air Force were compromised by fuel shortages. A significant amount of gasoline for the planes was "stolen" by Chinese army units for use in their trucks. At first, the amount had been so small that it could have been easily overlooked to prevent an unpleasant situation with the Chinese. However, beginning in July 1943, "it has reached a degree that can, in my estimation, no longer be ignored," reported Col. Casey Vincent to General Chennault.[49] "I had noted the tremendous expenditures the last few days and decided to investigate," said Vincent. "The findings are staggering. A check reveals that if all the airplanes we have and have had in commission had been flown continuously, the amount expended could not have been much larger."[50] One entry on an expenditure report for a plane showed it listed as being refueled eight times—with a total of over 700 gallons used! In fact, the plane flew a total of only four hours on that day. Vincent informed Chennault, "The same thing is happening at Lingling and Hengyang—i.e., we are being politely robbed!" Not wanting to be confrontational with his Chinese counterparts, Vincent realized that this situation could be political dynamite, and did not want to bring the matter out in the open without first informing Chennault. He suggested that Chennault have a personal conference with Gen. Chow Chi-jou, the director of aeronautical affairs for the Republic of China, to address the crippling effect the fuel thefts had on the 14th Air Force's support efforts.

Compounding their frustration was the steadily increasing number of enemy aircraft. Vincent was dumbfounded, reporting to Chennault, "I cannot understand where all the Jap fighters are coming from. We have destroyed for sure 59 Zeros in the last three days. I don't see how they can replace them, considering their recent losses in the SW Pacific."[51] Vincent also noted, "It was a large price to pay but I'm confident they will—they must—adopt a defensive policy in this area now for several weeks to come. They won't, as you know, send bombers without fighters, and I'm sure, further, that we have destroyed a number of their bombers on the ground. I think, as you suggested, that we should continue our offensive policy, commensurate with our supplies, and finish the job we have begun."[52]

A host of other military objectives for the 14th loomed during the fall. Headquarters received a communication directly from the Generalissimo in regard to destroying the Japanese supply lines, preferring that the 14th Air Force concentrate on destroying enemy factories from Ichang to Wuho, vessels and wharfs in the Yangtze and the Hsiang Rivers, and air bases during the months of November and December.[53] "Please take action and let us have a reply," said the order.[54] Despite their dwindling fuel supplies and being vastly outnumbered, Chennault knew that striking back to cut off Japanese resources would hit them where it hurt their supply lines the most. By the sixteenth of November, Col. Bruce Holloway reported on one such successful attack against these positions:

> We used some interesting tactics in a mission against the Shihhweiyao docks on the Yangtze River, where there was a mine installation and a loading dock from the mine. There were six locomotives on the short railroad of about twenty-five miles, and we ruined all of them. To get at the loading docks we had to cope with a lot of antiaircraft fire. The Japs had moved in one destroyer and two smaller gunboats to defend the place. We flew in a number of P-40s at 5,000 feet and had them milling all around. The Japs don't have a pattern of AA [antiaircraft fire] like the Germans, and the noise of the P-40s running at 3,000 rpm, and all the bullets, confused the Jap defense. While the P-40s were doing that, the P-38s came in dive-bombed right through the middle of them, and got to the factories; nobody got hit. That's the way to do it.[55]

By the end of 1943, it became apparent that the Japanese had been engaged in occupying defensible positions along the line of the Salween River. Steep canyon walls lined the swift and powerful river, one of the world's longest free-flowing rivers, which extended through China's Yunnan Province into Burma and Thailand. The Japanese were determined to secure this line against a Chinese assault, since this was also the key to the Allied attempts to reopen the Burma Road. On several occasions, low-level bombing runs and strafing missions were requested from the 14th Air Force by Chinese units. Unfortunately, the American pilots were handicapped by faulty and indefinite information as to the exact location of targets (due to the language barrier) received from the Chinese.[56] This made the accurate low-level bombing and strafing of targets much more challenging. Nevertheless, these units gave it their best shot, getting as close to the ground as possible while still being able to clear trees and other obstacles, at times as low as fifty feet above the ground. "Sometimes we'd go right down on the deck and strafe, to shoot up the Jap supply boats on the rivers or maybe a train if we caught one," recalled Sgt. Hobart Jones, a nose-gunner and engineer of a B-24, appropriately named "Tough Titti."[57]

The 14th Air Force's most pressing problem was that of resupply. Their B-24 bombing units had to fly three to five resupply trips over the Hump to British and American air bases in India to bring back additional fuel, bombs, ammunition, and other supplies. These flights were a three and a half hours each way. All this was needed to mount a single combat sortie against Japanese positions. The continual theft of gasoline for use in Chinese army trucks put a steady drain on their fuel supplies. Compounding this was a shortage of spare parts, which made it difficult for the unit to keep a lot of the B-24s in service.[58] During this same period, the Japanese forces in China were bulking up to mount an offensive aimed at opening a north–south corridor via railroad from Hankow, in central China, to Indochina, in the South. The Chinese forces would have their hands full defending their homeland from another assault, as would their American and British allies.

Chapter 12
CONSULS AND COMMUNISTS

SACO Agreement

The wartime capital of Chungking produced one of the rarest and most-unprecedented military alliances of the war during Springer's tenure: the Sino-American Cooperative Organization (SACO). This cemented the joint military and intelligence effort between the US and the Chinese Nationalist forces during World War II.[1] This agreement was expanded by a conference in Chungking on December 3–4, 1943.[2] It was jointly led by the US Navy commander, Capt. Milton E. Miles, and China's Gen. Tai Li, who was, at the time, the head of China's intelligence organization. General Tai's US intelligence counterpart was Gen. William Donovan, the head of the Office of Strategic Services (OSS), the military forerunner of the Central Intelligence Agency (CIA). The US Navy wanted to keep an eye on Japanese ship movements in and around the Chinese coastal cities during the war. This joint cooperation agreement allowed them to do that. This was the first and only time in US history that an American military unit had been completely integrated into a foreign military force placed under the command of a foreign leader.

Vice Consul

Springer's duties at the State Department began to change. He received his appointment as a US vice consul on November 8, 1943.[3] He would be part of a consular unit at Kunming that included two vice consuls and three alien clerks. His new position included duties in the citizenship and visa sections of the American embassy. It was essential for him to have a thorough understanding of the pertinent laws and regulations in the handing of passport and visa applications, and a working knowledge of Chinese. He had to carefully examine all evidence presented by applicants to establish American citizenship or obtain immigrant or nonimmigrant visas. This was to prevent enemy aliens or enemy alien sympathizers from entering the US for the purpose of

American Embassy, staff softball team. John Carter Vincent (*front row, second from left*) and Ambassador Gauss (*second row, third from left*). Paul Springer is to Gauss's left. *Springer Family collection*

engaging in subversive activities.[4] On the recreational side, Springer was a key player on the embassy softball team.

Springer described the work as "interesting and varied, and I feel both that I am learning something and doing something worthwhile. My social status has also risen perceptively."[5] In addition to hosting an air base, Kunming was the site of the British Liaison Office (BLO).[6] This was a counterintelligence office with Chinese informants and British officers operating locally. Its function was to detect enemy agents and keep a watch on suspicious persons in Free China. In addition to China, this British intelligence arm was operating in Burma, French Indochina, and Thailand.

The British Army Aid Group (BAAG) was the most important and successful other British intelligence agency in China.[7] This group was originally established to help in getting prisoners and essential Chinese personnel out of Hong Kong when it was taken over by the Japanese in December 1941. When the Japanese started their military drive on Kweilin, the BAAG pulled out and began working in Kweichow, before establishing their headquarters in Kunming shortly before Springer was appointed as vice consul.[8] This group was manned by about ten officers, most of whom had China and intelligence experience. The BAAG was highly respected by the Americans and Chinese alike for its expertise in evaluating counterintelligence matters. Critical information was shared by the British with their allies when appropriate. By the spring of 1944, Ambassador Gauss informed Secretary of State Cordell Hull that credible intelligence had been received that indicated "Japan is preparing for a new drive in Honan."[9] Chiang Kai-shek was shaken by the report and was convinced that a major Japanese assault was imminent. If it took place as feared, the huge gap in the strength of Chiang's ragged, underfed, and underequipped forces versus the Japanese would be exposed in battle. The Chinese troops on the ground could not hold out without American air support.

Anti-American Sentiment in Yuanling

One Saturday afternoon in early 1944, Betty Jean Rugh came inside her home after playing with friends, to find her mother and father sitting at the dining-room table. Their expressions were sullen, their eyes wide and glistening, as though they had tears in them. Her mother told her to sit down. Then she said, "Betty Jean, dearest." She paused. "Something very sad has happened." Betty Jean's mouth went dry. Her mom continued: "Molly suddenly got very sick. When Daddy found her, she was already gone." The girl was in stunned disbelief. She had just played with her that morning, right before lunch. "What do you mean—gone? Where did she go?" she asked. "Dearest. Molly got sick and she died," said her mother. Their family dog, the beloved black cocker spaniel with floppy ears and a bright-pink tongue, had been poisoned.[10]

Betty Jean said, "Poison? No! Who would poison Molly?" They had no answers. Her mother said, "She didn't suffer long." Dwight explained that it happened very fast. He said it looked like she had eaten poisoned meat. He had found her lying outside her box on the back porch. She had thrown up and stopped breathing. Rugh had just buried her in the hills behind the house before Betty Jean returned. He didn't tell his daughter until much later that her tongue was swollen and stained black. After that day, Yuanling no longer seemed like a friendly place to the Rughs. Something wicked was lurking in the background. When Molly died, the family started to mentally prepare themselves to leave Yuanling.[11]

There was an eerie yet growing anti-American sentiment in the community. Ken Moreland noticed this in some of the student essays in the English classes he taught. Several students wrote that many of the Americans who came to China during the war to help the national government in their fight against the Japanese looked down on the Chinese people. The English-speaking students in Yuanling sometimes overheard the soldiers' comments: that the Chinese were backward, that these people had been here all these years and didn't have decent roads and didn't have good restaurants, and that they judged the Chinese from the point of view of their own society and culture. Yet, the soldiers were shortsighted and missed what was so moving and beautiful about China. "My students told me in no uncertain terms that they deeply resented the soldiers who are arrogant. They said some of them are very, very friendly and all, but some of them are arrogant," said Moreland.[12]

It was not just the soldiers but some of the missionaries who came across as being arrogant. Several students opened up to Moreland and expressed their concerns about being treated differently by them. In their minds, they were saving these Chinese students who they viewed as lost if they didn't break through and convert them to Christianity. Moreland recalled, "The missionaries made these negative judgments about how they could be saved from eternal damnation if only they would believe and do what the missionaries want them to do."[13] This turned him off from some of the missionaries who were there to convert. Moreland, a degreed divinity student himself, could only listen and empathize with the students' position, knowing that listening was much more important to their development than lecturing. He noted that there were other kinds of missions—educational and agricultural missions that would help with different aspects of life for the Chinese. These were not necessarily evangelical. It was an important lesson in ethnocentrism for the young Bachelor.

During those final months, Betty Jean heard children's voices chanting on the path in front of their house. She went out on the screened-in porch to see what was happening. When she stepped on the porch, the chanting became louder. She didn't understand what they were saying, but suddenly realized they were chanting at her. After a quick glance, she stepped back from the screen just as Tou Shi-fu came out from around the house and shouted angrily at them. The kids scattered. Betty Jean was in disbelief that these children were calling her names, in front of her home, near where her friends lived. They did not appear to be street children. Had any of her friends been among them? She wasn't sure. Maybe her friends wanted to be there to taunt her but could not because their parents would be angry. She was too ashamed to talk about it to her parents or to try to find out what happened.

She went back to being with her friends whenever she could, pretending nothing had happened. She mentally pushed the incident back into a dark place with other memories that she decided not to dwell on. As the reality of leaving Yuanling and returning to the US came closer, a thought occurred to her. "When we go home," she said to her mother, "I won't be a foreigner anymore." "That's right," said her mother. "You won't."[14]

Dwindling Fuel Supplies

The 14th Air Force operations in the early months of 1944 were characterized by poor weather conditions and a noticeable lull in activity by Japanese ground forces. The force was augmented by P-38s of the 449th Fighter Squadron and a handful of P-51 fighters to replace the aging P-40s. When weather permitted, they continued to fly sweeps and fighter-bomber strikes on enemy positions. The B-25s simultaneously concentrated on sweeping Japanese boat traffic on the Yangtze River and the South China Sea. Chennault was somewhat pleased that the flying weather was bad, since this cut down on the number of enemy aircraft that his pilots had to deal with. This gave him some time to reflect on his ever-dwindling supply of gasoline.

Beneath his "tough-as-nails persona," Chennault was worried. "I had taken to feeling that I had more troubles than any other man in the world," he wrote to Colonel Vincent. "Although your problems and troubles do not lessen mine, I am aware that you are carrying your share of the load."[15] Chennault was greatly disturbed over the aviation fuel position. He was constantly engaged in a fight to get enough fuel to maintain their operations in China, but the odds against him were increasing daily. Chennault instructed his staff to emphasize the necessity for the utmost economy in the consumption of fuel. "Every airplane coming in for a landing approach should plan its approach so that no fuel will be wasted," he ordered.[16] Vincent, too, was well aware of the shortage of gasoline and the "dribble" coming across the Hump. "I cannot relish the dreary prospect of running short of gas in the middle of the summer and perhaps being forced to abandon the fields in this area." he wrote Chennault in March 1944.[17]

Japanese Offensive

By mid-April, the suspicions of Gauss and Chiang regarding the mobilization of Japanese troops proved devastatingly accurate. The Japanese offensive, a three-pronged attack involving a force of 500,000 men and 200 bombers, was mobilized on April 17, 1944. The actions prompted American staffing changes in the field. In May 1944, Art Hopkins was reassigned as a secret intelligence and combat liaison officer to the 14th US Air Force and OSS in Kunming, China.[18] His language skills and familiarity with the cities, towns, and geography of southwestern China were seen as critical for the new assignment. When the Japanese began their military offensive, they brought enough fuel for eight months and enough ammunition to last them two years.[19] One of their key objectives was to destroy the American air bases in central China and knock the Nationalist army out of the war for good. The Japanese invasion thrust into central China continued through the remainder of the year. This eventually pushed the Chinese lines another 200 miles inland from Chengchow to Indochina and caused the 14th Air Force to lose thirteen of its bases in eastern China.[20]

By June 1944, the Japanese began their long-expected drive through central China. They recaptured Changsha, and like before, Chinese soldiers burned much of the city before abandoning it to the advancing Japanese. The 14th Air Force was making plans to evacuate several forward bases, including "moving practically everything out of Suichwan" except for one combat squadron, the 449th. "I am not an alarmist. We will fight to the last ditch out here and evacuate only when absolutely necessary," said Col. Casey Vincent of the 14th Air Force.[21] His efforts were to keep their forces concentrated for effective operations and still allow for the dispersion of aircraft to other bases on short notice. But by now, their meager forces were spread too thin for any effective operations anywhere in the region.

Evacuation

In areas of Hunan Province, not yet occupied by the Japanese, Nationalist soldiers returned to banditry and raiding the countryside, including several villages near Yuanling. Jim Elliott was still at Yali. He had wrapped up teaching the spring semester with the new Bachelors, Ken Moreland and Ross Dixon.

Despite the chaos of the war gripping the areas surrounding the middle school, Elliott was firming up the teaching assignments for the fall session. Moreland had taken over as treasurer of the mission, so he had only two classes to teach next term. Elliott and Dixon were to have four classes each. They were hoping to get Mrs. Liang (the wife of a Hsiang-Ya dentist) to bolster the English Department teaching staff in the fall term.

Just in case the war took a turn for the worse, Elliott reported to New Haven: "With regard to evacuation, we have decided to send some of the most viable scientific equipment and library books to Tunjen, Kweichow Province by truck. We're going to send also some trunks belonging to people like the Greens, Tyngs, and Rughs. To cover the cost of sending them, we are going to take out some of the things and sell them here (clothes and such things as can be easily replaced). In case of total evacuation, we don't have to bother about them. We might not be able to get them out at all. In Changsha, everything was lost because all boats and means of transportation were commandeered by the military. We don't want to get caught in the same way here. In preparation for possible evacuation, we are hiring some boats right now as to have them when the emergency rises."[22]

The American embassy and British consulates urged women and children to leave China as soon as possible. The escape routes out of the country would soon be cut off. Tensions were increasing in the American community in Yuanling. Dwight Rugh's term as the Yale-in-China director had ended. His replacement, Dr. Brank Fulton, had not yet arrived. Rugh did not want to leave until Fulton arrived, since he wanted to update his replacement on several matters. But once Fulton arrived in China, his travel was delayed because of the shifting military conflict and the difficulty of getting transportation to the interior.[23] Fulton was stuck in Kunming on June 24. He wired a message to Rugh at Yali, but it did not arrive until three weeks later, on July 16. Rugh did not know when his replacement would arrive, and became desperate to get himself, his wife, and their daughter out of China.

The Rughs left Yuanling on July 3, 1943, about 5:00 a.m. They crossed the river to the "bus station," an open area with a bus parked in the middle of it. Their first destination was Zhijiang, a city about 100 miles away, where the nearest US air base was located. From there, they were to catch a plane for the first leg of their journey out of China. It was a difficult goodbye for eleven-year-old Betty Jean, saying *zai hui* ("goodbye") to her childhood girlfriends. They arrived in Zhijiang in the late afternoon and arrived by rickshaw at a mission compound in time for dinner. Their plan was to stay at the mission until they found a plane to Kweilin (now Guilin), then another plane to Kunming. Once in Kunming, their plan was to take a transport plane over the Hump to India.

A Night at the Movies

Over dinner, a pair of American soldiers asked the Rughs if they would like to see the weekly movie at the air base that evening. Not counting a British propaganda film about the Blitz, the family had not seen a real movie since they were in Hong Kong four years before. They were assured that they would be completely safe, since the Japanese never bombed after dark. After an exhilarating jeep ride that bounded along the high road between rice paddies, the sweltering hot air and the smell of gasoline had a somewhat calming effect on their nerves. It was dusk when they entered the air base and the jeep skidded to a stop at a large quonset hut.[24] There were several hundred American troops inside the makeshift theater. The Rughs' host guided them through the door at the back and escorted the family of three down the middle aisle toward the front. As they walked down the aisle, the noise became deafening, punctuated with whistles and catcalls! One of the soldiers explained their behavior to Winifred: "They haven't seen an American kid in three years," he said. "And she has braids."[25]

As soon as the lights went out and the film began, several soldiers came to their row in the makeshift theater to say hello, handing Betty Jean a candy bar and a pack of chewing gum. As the movie progressed, more candy bars and gum were passed down the aisle, adding to a growing pile on her lap. Some soldiers asked them to come over to their row, so Betty Jean and her mother moved over. Another asked where they came from and where they were going. Another told Betty Jean that his little sister back in Iowa had braids just like hers. They were pleasantly surprised to see American civilians way out here in this part of the world. It seemed so natural to have these conversations. Betty Jean was flattered to be told that she looked like someone's little sister.

In the midst of one of these conversations, the movie abruptly stopped in the middle of a scene. The lights went on and the building emptied as everyone quickly walked out the side and back doors. The Rughs' host said that Japanese planes had been reported heading toward them, but not to worry, since they never bombed at night. They also said they should go back to the city to get away from the air base, "just in case." One of their hosts said goodbye, and the other quickly ushered them out of the side door to the jeep, where he and Dwight helped Betty Jean and her mother into the back seats. Their host hopped into the driver's seat.

With Dwight sitting next to the driver, the jeep dashed back the way it had come, this time without the headlights on. The full moon was so bright they could see the road and the rice paddies on either side. The noise of the jeep engine and the wind was so loud that they had to shout to be heard. Suddenly, ahead on their left, the huge shape of an airplane appeared, flying low toward the road. Betty Jean caught a glimpse of its propellers on the front of its wings, which looked like round circles in the moonlight. Its landing lights were on, making parallel lines of brightness running ahead on the water of the rice paddies. As they sped down the road, the giant shadow flickered overhead, followed by the great roar of its engines. They never saw the first bomb drop, but all of a sudden their world exploded in sound and light.

Betty Jean found herself slogging through water in the rice paddy up to her waist, with her mother pulling her hand and screaming frantically, "Dwight!" Her father was still in the front seat of the jeep. The driver was holding her mother's hand. In the darkness, they could not see the planes but could hear the roar of their engines. Another shadow flickered overhead, and a bomb exploded on the other side of the road. A huge earache punched both sides of Betty Jean's head as they ran away, as she splashed through water up to her knees. Another shadow crossed overhead, and again the sky lit up with flashes of explosion and deafening pressure. The driver shoved both mother and daughter into a deep ditch running along the edge of a rice paddy. He and Dwight followed.

More shadows flickered past in the sky as Betty Jean heard the driver yell between explosions, "We'll be okay here." Suddenly the air was filled with loud chattering, as tracer bullets from antiaircraft fire flew up toward the shadows that swept overhead again and again. Betty Jean began to shake and clung to her mother. "Those are anti-aircraft guns, dear. They're not shooting at us," her mother said reassuringly and pulled her closer. Suddenly their world exploded again, as Japanese bombs blew up around them as they crouched in the water at the bottom of the ditch. Their arms were over their heads, and Dwight's arms were soon over their backs as he gripped his little family tightly between the lulls and spasms of explosions lasting about two hours.

Gradually, the ditch filled up with GIs who came running across the paddies, so that by the time the air raid was over, the ditch seemed crowded. Betty Jean was still shaky at the end, and numb, with a dull ache in both ears. All was quiet. They waited for some time, but the planes did not return. "Is everyone okay?" someone asked, and then the GIs disappeared into the night. When they got to the road, they found the jeep where they had left it. Their host looked it over, turned on the engine, and, after a few minutes, they all got in and drove to the mission. The Rughs thanked him for the unusual evening and for taking care of them on that awful night.

A Chinese soldier guards a line of American Curtiss P-40 fighter planes, painted with the tiger shark jaws of the "Flying Tigers." *National Archives*

When the Rughs got to their room, Winifred said to her husband, "Dwight. What were you doing, sitting in the jeep like that? You didn't pay any attention to us!" "I was watching the planes," he replied. Because their landing lights were on, he had thought they were American planes. "And then there were all those fireworks," he said. "Beautiful!" "Honestly, Dwight!" Winifred said, shaking her head in hopeless exasperation. "You could have been killed!" The experience drove home the dangers of the war, but Dwight seemed to shrug it off. The ditch where they had sought shelter during the raid was actually parallel and quite close to the runway. While bombs had landed all around in the neighboring rice paddies, little damage had been done to the runway itself. Only a few American planes had been hit. By afternoon, the bomb craters on the landing strip itself were filled in.

There was a plane leaving for Kweilin the next day, and they planned to take it. The sooner they got out of China, the better! The tide of the war had turned in the Pacific as American forces island-hopped their way toward Japan. The Japanese reacted by moving to attack American airfields throughout southern China. The air base at Zhijiang was put out of commission several days after they left.

The family flew from Zhijiang to Kweilin in a C-46, the troubled workhorse of the Army air forces. As the plane leveled off to land, a look out the window revealed the fantastic mountains of Kweilin. The gnarled fingers of stone reached up from a flat quilt of rice paddies so green that the color vibrated with the roar of the engines. Betty Jean described it: "A wisp of cloud floated between two unbelievably vertical mountains, just like the improbable landscape of a Song Dynasty painting, and the plane tipped sideways again, leaving the mountains for an airstrip."[26] Upon landing, the plane taxied up to a quonset hut, its metal roof shimmering in the sunshine. With their ears stopped up from the change in altitude, everything was eerily quiet as they walked down the steps into the sweltering heat bath that was the Chinese summer. They spent the night at a hostel among pine trees, and the next day they took off again in another C-46 for Kunming, in Yunnan, the southernmost province of China. From there, they would fly over the southern Himalayas to India. This aerial bridge over the Hump remained the sole connection of Free China to the outside world. The Allies had to keep the route open at all costs. Betty Jean remembered, "In Kunming, we saw rows of General Chennault's famous Flying Tigers lined up along the edge of the runway with shark's teeth painted savagely white on the side of each fuselage. Their job was to escort the incoming C-46s from the farthest point their fuel would allow and fight off the Japanese Zeros that attacked out of the sun like swarms of monstrous mosquitoes."[27]

Winifred, Betty Jean, and Dwight Rugh in New Haven in the winter of 1944–45, about six months after their departure from China. *Courtesy of David Elder*

The Rughs stayed for several days in Kunming, waiting for a plane to carry them over the hump to Calcutta. Some Yali graduates came to see them and took them out for dinner in the city. The American GIs that Betty Jean remembered presented a stark contrast from their dispirited counterparts in Chiang Kai-shek's army, who were sick and underfed. She remembered the GIs as "American boys in khaki, their smooth faces friendly and innocent of profound thought, Army caps pushed back on their heads, chewing gum while they casually went about their business with effortless expertise. Their manner said they could afford to be casual because they knew we would win in the end."[28]

Within ten days of their departure, the 14th Air Force's base at Kweilin was rendered unusable for combat operations because of the Japanese advance.[29] The Rughs landed safely in Calcutta a few days later. Their long sojourn in Nationalist China was over.[30]

Living the High Life

Springer stayed in touch with George Small after Small was transferred to the American consulate in Karachi, India (now Pakistan), in 1943. In one letter, which was forwarded through a diplomatic pouch, he gave George a heads-up on a development in regard to converting their local paychecks into US dollars. "I just decoded a telegram which says the Dept. has no alternative but to permit Foreign Service personnel to exchange pay checks at Kunming for US dollars, and to sell these for the best price obtainable, and that this is to go into effect immediately and to continue until the Chinese Govt does something in the way of reciprocal lend-leases. Poor Mr.

Gauss; this will about break his heart."[31] This was a significant development, since embassy employees could now convert their paychecks, denominated in yuan, at favorable exchange into US dollars via Kunming. With the rampant inflation in China, they were free to sell those dollars on the black market for the best price obtainable. This was a financial windfall for the embassy employees in the various posts in Free China. Previous to this, Paul lamented that he had to sell a couple of watches for extra cash, and that he "[has] been living on the proceeds plus the 7,500 I picked up in the last two poker games plus my regular winnings at bridge of a couple hundred each time I play."[32]

Springer described his recent nightlife experience in Chungking. "I had a rip-snortin' time at last week's North South [dance], where I sang my lungs out, and incidentally met a Chinese charmer named Miss An (Angelina) who seemed to be entertained by my singing and keen wit (brusk). Anyway, she will be present at my behest at the American Club dance this Sat., and has expressed a willingness to sell her soul, etc. for the pleasure of hearing my solid jive recordings. She lives on the South Bank, by jove."[33] He expressed frustration in his letter that he had recently taken on two roommates, which compromised his privacy for entertaining young ladies, "but still have my lair in the hills, to which [I] repair on occasion, such as last weekend. . . . The albums of records on the Embassy racks are now available to us guys, and tonight I am taking home Rhapsody in Blue. Maybe Miss Chen would like to hear that, huh? Dis [*sic*] high life here is practically killin' me. Really though, things are looking up, and this exchange deal makes everything so cosey [*sic*] I don't even remember any pain I may have suffered in Shit-coolie town."[34] Springer was trying to find solace in female company and make the most of the difficult situation in war-torn China.

Groomed for Service

Springer continued his work at an office in Chungking through the holidays, where he attended a Thanksgiving service at the embassy hosted by Ambassador Gauss. There were a number of tables of four at dinner that evening. Springer's name card was placed on the same table with the ambassador, the Norwegian ambassador's wife, and a cultural-relations expert.[35] This was followed by a reception at the Sino-American Institute of Cultural Relations for the embassy staff. He was being carefully evaluated by his superiors and groomed for another foreign-service assignment. Springer requested a transfer to a warmer post for winter, perhaps Latin America. He found the physical facilities at the embassy in Chungking less than optimal. In many ways he found China to be a backward country. He described one such incident in a letter, "A few days ago the infant daughter of our coolie and our Amah (female servant) died of small-pox. The bereaved parents declined Mrs. Morosoff's offer to pay the funeral expenses, as they desired to dispose of the corpse in their own way. They tossed it in the river, in the belief that the evil spirit which inflicted it would pass on down stream, and would not remain to plague the survivors."[36]

The State Department plans were to retain Springer in China, with a transfer to another station, which caused any "dreams of a transfer to Mexico or South America" to be short lived.[37] But for now, his integration into the Chinese culture made him a valued employee in Chungking and Kunming. His position as vice consul kept him well informed on intelligence matters, shipping, and interaction with business people, while acting as an intermediary among Chinese, US, and British interests operating in the area.

The Dixie Mission

Springer's colleagues in the American embassy, John Vincent and Jack Service, were among the old "China Hands" who sought to gather the intelligence from and provide material support to the Communist armies, which were then part of the Allied coalition in the war against Japan. Although the Chinese Communist Party's (CCP's) Eighth Route Army was ostensibly under the command of Chang Kai-shek, the Generalissimo

Gen. Chu Teh, Col. David Barrett, and Mao Tse-tung in Yenan. Behind Chu Teh is Jack Service. The officer at left with his hands behind his head is Col. Morris B. Depass, who took over the detachment after Barrett left in October 1944. *David Dean Barrett papers, envelope A, Hoover Institution Archives*

fiercely resisted any suggestion of formal contact between the US and the CCP.[38] It was only in June 1944, when Henry Wallace, the US vice president, paid a visit to Chungking, that Chiang Kai-shek agreed to a meeting between US diplomats and the CCP. Wallace was not impressed with the Nationalist Chinese government that the US had been supporting during the war. In a gloomy report to Roosevelt, Wallace noted that Chiang had surrounded himself with "reactionary figures" and "showed himself so prejudiced against the communists that there seemed little prospect of satisfactory or enduring settlement result of the negotiations now underway."[39] During the early years of the war, Jack Service wrote increasingly critically harsh reports on the Kuomintang and Chiang Kai-shek, whom he sometimes criticized as "fascist," "undemocratic," and "feudal."[40] Although the US intelligence on the Communists came from secondhand information, certain points about the CCP seemed clear. The Communists, having a major base near important Japanese military and industrial centers, possessed valuable intelligence on their mutual enemy.

In the spring of 1944, General Stilwell made one of his infrequent visits to Chungking. One of his objectives was to combine China's vast manpower resources with American training, weapons, and logistics for maximum advantage. This had not worked out well with the Nationalist forces because of inept commanders, internal political in-fighting, and corruption. On the other hand, it was thought that Communist troops, if properly supplied and armed, could be a formidable force to engage the Japanese if a bitter, bloody, and drawn-out campaign was needed to drive them from China.[41] He summoned Jack Service to discuss the Yenan mission. Stillwell's first question was "Who shall head it?"[42] "Colonel Barrett," Service suggested, was the only logical man for this delicate and important assignment.[43] Stillwell, of course, knew Barrett well; he agreed and the orders were issued.

Ray Ludden, Lt. Herb Hitch, Col. David Barrett, Chou En-lai, and Jack Service in Yenan, 1944. Photo by Phil Cheng. *David Dean Barrett papers, envelope A, Hoover Institution Archives*

On July, 22, 1944, a group of nine Americans, led by Jack Service and Col. David Barrett, landed on an airstrip in Yenan, in northern Shannsi (today's Shanxi), on the south-central part of the Loess Plateau.[44] They composed the US Army Observation Group. Service was there to undertake a political analysis on the CCP. Colonel Barrett was in charge of gathering military information on the Communist army. His goal was to assess their forces and work on building a cooperative military strategy. Their exploratory venture into Communist territory was known by the code name of "Dixie Mission." This was a tongue-in-cheek reference to Union missions behind Confederate lines during the American Civil War. The Americans were met by the Eighth Route Army honor guard. Heading their reception were Mao Tse-tung and Gen. Chu Teh. They were wearing new matching uniforms for the occasion.[45] Mao was the leader of the CCP, and General Chu commanded the Chinese Communist army's northern forces after the Communists formed an alliance with the Nationalists to resist the Japanese invasion of China in 1937. Chu retained command of all Communist military operations against the Japanese until the war's end in 1945. The group of nine Americans was supplemented by another ten men a month later to gain further insight into the CCP's military capabilities.

Jack Service was crucial to the Dixie Mission because of his knowledge of China and the Chinese language. He traveled extensively through the area, asking endless questions. This information was all new, since little was known about the reality of life in Yenan, the stronghold of the CCP forces in China. The first impressions of the group were positive, with a universal sense that they "had come into a different country and our meeting a different people."[46] The differences between the Communists in Yenan and the Nationalists in Chungking were striking. Service reported, "Mao

At the Communist development project in Nanyiwan, near Yunan, summer of 1944. Ray Ludden and Colonel Barrett are astounded at the sight of soldiers doing useful work. *David Dean Barrett papers, envelope A, Hoover Institution Archives*

and the other leaders are universally spoken of with respect . . . but these men are approachable and subservience toward them is completely lacking."[47] There were no signs of the bodyguards, the hierarchy, or the strong reek of corruption and official fiefdoms that were prevalent in the Nationalist government in Chungking. Service recalled, "The confidence that we ran into, the difference in the morale, esprit, this was something that hit us right away. The ways things got done. If you asked for things, yes, they said they'd do it, and it was done, promptly, in fact, efficiently. In Chungking, nothing was efficient. Nothing seemed to work and everything took a long time."[48] The Americans were impressed with the simplicity of life and clothing and the lack of beggars and desperate poverty. Service also reported a lack of censorship and a sense of freedom. "Morale is very high," he wrote.[49]

Barrett and his officers spent a great deal of time in the field with the Chinese Communist troops, either observing their training or accompanying them on missions. Barrett was the prototype of a US Army colonel, whose personality was adorned by a warm humanity and an overwhelmingly infectious humor. He described himself as a rock-ribbed Republican and a "black-hearted reactionary."[50] The Communists loved him. His round jokes in flawless and fluent Chinese destroyed much of their preconceived notions of calculating American imperialism. To his surprise, the Chinese commanders emphasized that they had to give the troops political training because the political consciousness of the peasants who made up the Chinese Communist armies was very low. So, therefore, political training was needed. Barrett countered, "I told them in the United States Army we look with disfavor on political training. We think we should devote the whole time to military training."[51] And they said, "That is not the case in our army, because we consider military training and political training as equally important, and one cannot be neglected for the other."[52] Barrett's reports on the Communists were honest, hard-headed military assessments. A soldier himself, he recognized the Communists as effective fighting men; sound allies against a common enemy. They felt his respect and they reciprocated it.

The Communist hosts provided their new allies not only with food and shelter but with reasonably up-to-date captured Japanese newspapers.[53] The Americans noticed some social changes that the Communists had fostered. They stressed peasant art forms, such as folk dancing, a product of Mao's demand in 1942 for art and culture to find more points of connection with the culture of the peasantry.[54] As a social diversion while in Yenan, and to add some variety in their diet, there was an occasional pheasant hunt. The Allied visitors, in true military fashion, went after the birds in flight with their carbines, while the Chinese, less sporting in the Americans' eyes, peppered them on the ground with 12-gauge shotguns. There were also Saturday night parties in a pear

The reviewing stand at Nanyiwan, near Yenan, summer of 1944. On right of stand, "China, America, Russia, England united arise!" Slogan on left of stand translates as "Wipe out fascism!" *David Dean Barrett papers, envelope A, Hoover Institution Archives*

orchard, where the Americans ate watermelon and danced to the folk music of local musicians with limited skill but unlimited spirit. Chou En-lai was somewhat light of foot. Mao Tse-tung danced in a sort of grizzly bear shuffle and was eager to take a turn around the dance floor with any young lady who asked him.

On a more substantive level, Service attempted to get a feel for the political leaders in the CCP. He described them as having a striking lack of individuality, but overall they gave the impression of youth and vigor as well as pragmatism. The test of everything, he suggested, "was whether or not the system works—in China."[55] If anything, he was impressed with the level of leadership and inclusion in Yenan, their embrace of the peasant population, and the guerrilla tactics, which had kept up a fierce resistance against Japanese troops in northern and central China.

In regard to their military leaders, Service wrote, "The morale of the Communist Army is likewise good. It has a democratic character and officers and enlisted ranks receive equal treatment. This condition is in sharp contrast to other parts of China. The three divisions of the 18th Group Army have been expanded to more than normal size. They are fairly well equipped with light arms but are short of supplies."[56] Barrett offered his own observations from conversations with Mao Tse-tung, Chou En-lai, Chu Teh, Peng Teh-huai, and other officials: "My strongest impression is that these

Yeh Chien-ying, Chief of Staff, Communist forces, delivers a talk after Col. David Barrett received the Legion of Merit award. Mao Tse-tung is on the right of the US officer with camera. October 5, 1944. *David Dean Barrett papers, envelope A, Hoover Institution Archives*

people are interested mainly in two things, fighting the Japanese and gaining the support of the people."[57]

In some ways, the Communists had a good understanding of US politics. They were astounded at Harry Truman's nomination as vice president in the American political campaign in the fall of 1944. Their American guests were equally dumbfounded by the choice of VP when they heard the news on a radio set. Service and Barrett were having dinner on the evening of the announcement with the Communist leaders at the Army headquarters in Yenan. Service sensed that Mao was impatient in getting the respective parties seated in their appropriate places. As soon as they were all sitting down, Mao came out with the big question: "Who is this Too-lu-mun? Who is Too-lu-mun" ("Who is this man Truman?").[58] After a round of laughter, most of the dinner was devoted to trying to explain how it was possible that someone completely unknown, or almost completely unknown, with no great record of war or political service, could suddenly be chosen as the US vice president.

Vice President Wallace had only recently returned to the US following his trip to China. Service and Barrett found their Chinese hosts worried that Wallace's visit to China had done him in, because it was during his visit that the Americans got permission to go to Yenan. The Communists were concerned about US attitudes toward China and the Soviets. They had difficulty comprehending the domestic political situation in the US. Service remembered, "Well, we didn't know too much about it either. So we were sort of helpless. It was an amusing incident."[59] Mao had been giving Chou a hard time for failing to understand why Truman was nominated, until they realized their American guests were just as confused as they were.[60] All of them had a good laugh over it.

In August 1944, Service wrote his assessment as to the theoretical standpoint of the CCP for his superiors in the State Department:

> Socialism, it can come only after considerable development of the Chinese economy and after it has passed through a stage of at least modified capitalism. Their communism does not mean the immediate overthrow of private capital—because there is still almost no capital in China. It does not mean the dictatorship of the proletariat—because there is as yet no proletariat. It does not mean the collectivization of farms—because the political education of the peasants has not yet overcome their primitive individualistic desire to till their own land. The Communist Party becomes a party seeking orderly democratic growth toward socialism—as it is being attained, for instance, in a country like England, rather than in a party for minting an immediate and violent revolution. It becomes a party which is not seeking an early monopoly of political power but pursuing what it considers the long-term interest of China.[61]

Barrett submitted his recommendations in a September 30, 1944, report from the US Army Observer Section, Yenan. He wrote, "To sum up, I am convinced that the Communist forces can be of immediate assistance to the Allied war effort in China, and that this assistance can save American lives, and speed up the ultimate victory. The amount of use which can be made of the communist forces will in general be in direct proportion to the assistance which we can give them in arms, equipment and training."[62] Barrett also pointed out in his reports to Stilwell that his sole aim was to enhance their combat capabilities against their common enemy, the Japanese. He also advocated a gradual supply of military aid and on a strictly quid pro quo basis, a condition that Stilwell had vainly sought to propose on similar aid to Nationalist troops.[63]

As for the practical aspects of the CCP's policy goals, Service was quick to point out what could happen with the implementation of Communist theory. His words were prophetic:

Their espousal of democracy appeals to the great majority of the people of China and is a good club for beating the Kuomintang. Their proclamations of liberal economic policies based on private property are also useful in appealing to foreign sympathy. They can afford to sit back and wait. If things continue as they are now going, time will bring the collapse of the Kuomintang, leaving the Communists the strongest force in China. They will then be free, immediately or gradually as circumstances seem to dictate, to revert to their program of Communism. Even the almost over adroitness of the Communists in the field of public relations and propaganda inclines one at times to be suspicious of them.[64]

The intelligence furnished from Yenan was the most accurate and the most revealing that the US had access to. Ambassador Gauss was getting regular copies of Service's reports. He passed them to Washington, noting, "Mr. Service inclines towards acceptance of his first explanation of Chinese Communist policy although he admits that elements in the second probably enter into its formulation."[65] Service developed a somewhat rosy view of the situation but found it possible for the Communist regime to be both repressive and genuinely popular among its own people at the same time. Service also underestimated the political and military advantage that the Communist army had gained by avoiding the massive air raids and the refugee flights that hampered the regime of Chang Kai-shek from the start of the war. He was also not privy to the intraparty discussions that made it clear that Mao would never entertain a genuine alliance with Washington, since his ideological alignments were toward Joseph Stalin.

However, the problem with arming the Communists with American weapons was clearly discernible to those holding power in Chungking. As the CCP increased their military might, they would expand the territory under control. Even without American aid, this is precisely what happened. As more and more Japanese troops were withdrawn from North China to bolster the defense of the Pacific islands, Communist troops began to fill the vacuum that was created, seizing Japanese weapons and ammunition in the process. Mao was planning a more radical, violent, and indigenous revolution for all of China when the war with Japan was over.

While Barrett and Service felt they were making headway in Yenan, there was an abrupt turn of events in Chungking. A frustrated and irascible General Stilwell lost his political war with Chiang Kai-shek. President Roosevelt acceded to Chiang's demand, and Stilwell was recalled on October 18, 1944. He was succeeded by Lt. Gen. Albert C. Wedemeyer. Ambassador Gauss, weary of being slighted and upstaged by special envoys, promptly submitted his resignation. Maj. Gen. Patrick J. Hurley, who came to

Colonel Barrett (*with field glasses*) and Yeh Chien-ying, Chief of Staff, Communist forces, in the summer of 1944. Barrett wrote on the back, "Yeh asked me to look through them to see if I could discern any signs of US support for the Chinese Communists. I told him I could not." *David Dean Barrett papers, envelope E, Hoover Institution Archives*

China as a presidential envoy to assist Stilwell but ended up undoing much of his work with the Dixie Mission, stayed on to become the new American ambassador.[66] When Barrett's recommendation was conveyed through the US military to the Nationalist government, Chiang Kai-shek vetoed any such proposal to arm the Communists with the blunt words "You cannot arm my enemies!"[67] Gen. Tai Li, Chiang's chief of intelligence, was committed to disrupting any further American cooperation with the Chinese Communists, and the command hierarchy of the SACO Agreement sealed the fate of any military aid forthcoming as a result of the Dixie Mission.

Living Conditions in Chungking

It was widely known throughout the State Department that Chungking was a hardship post. Due to the lack of sanitation, the almost daily bombing of Japanese planes, the scarcity of certain staple foods, the lack of medical facilities, and the grossly inadequate housing, it was impractical to employ women or older men at the American embassy in Chungking. In the code room, there was a large amount of night work to be done to ensure the quick decoding of incoming messages and a prompt dispatch of outgoing ones.[68] Among Springer's final assignments in China during 1944 was writing a formal report on the American embassy in Chungking.[69] This report gives some insight into the size, staffing, living conditions, local organizations and churches, recreation, taxes, local transportation, and travel details to and from the embassy from the United States during the war.

Travel from the US to Chungking was done only via air through India. The trip from India was made either by US Army or China National Aviation Corp. (CNAC) planes. The CNAC planes flew from Calcutta via Assam to Kunming. Army planes took off from other fields in India. Persons with heart afflictions were told to consult their doctors in advance of taking this high-altitude flight over the Himalayas, since oxygen equipment was recommended and not ordinarily carried on CNAC planes. Military planes were usually not heated, and when crossing the "Hump," travelers were encouraged to take an overcoat or blanket, even in the warmest months of the year. On Army planes, only a "bucket seat" was usually available, and an inflatable rubber seat cushion was desirable if it could be obtained.[70]

The embassy staff consisted of one ambassador, one counselor, one commercial attaché, one first secretary, five second secretaries, and two third secretaries. Their duties included administration, political reporting, cultural relations, translation, and law, with one serving as a consul and dispersing officer. Three vice consuls were on hand (including Springer), one of whom was a private secretary to the ambassador. Their staff included a file clerk, two typists, and three code clerks. The embassy deployed the second secretaries to man temporary offices as US consuls in Kweilin, Chengtu, Sian, Lanchow, and Tihwa. In addition to vice consuls assigned to temporary posts, there were local employees who served as legal translators, interpreters, writers, chauffeurs, telephone operators, messengers, gardeners, and other jobs.

The report described Chungking: "The city itself is for the most part dirty, crowded and ugly, and is filled with makeshift buildings and shacks as replacements to structures which have been bombed."[71] Health conditions were poor. Prevalent diseases among the locals included malaria, tuberculosis, dysentery, venereal diseases, cholera, typhoid fevers, ringworm of the scalp, trachoma, smallpox, and rickets. Although there were free native clinics, they were inadequate to meet the people's needs. Victims of these diseases were seen daily in the streets. Foreigners living in Chungking usually didn't contract the worst of these diseases. They did, however, contract malaria, dysentery, tuberculosis, and parasitic intestinal diseases, the last being the most common due to the lack of quality and manner of preparation of food. In general, the environment in Chungking was found to be detrimental to health. "Persons assigned to this post should have the following injections or vaccinations: anti-typhoid, cholera, smallpox, tetanus, yellow fever, typhus. These shots are designed to provide immunity from diseases encountered in route to Chunking as well as for protection during residence in China," the report said.[72]

There was a good supply of food available, although it was lacking in variety. Fruits and vegetables were obtained only in season, which resulted in a growing distaste for each item as the season progressed. No vegetable could be eaten raw, no matter how well cleansed, because human excrement was widely used as a fertilizer. Fruits were the most satisfactory, the best being pomelos, persimmons, and tangerines. Oranges were abundant in season, as was a tasteless variety of pear. Meat included chicken, beef, and goat. Fish was scarce and obtainable only at a high price. The food supply was augmented by US Army commissary supplies—the embassy was being supplied monthly with hard-to-get items such as coffee, powdered milk, cheese, butter, and jelly. American tobacco cigarettes were generally obtainable from the US Army, although good cigars were scarce. Although considered a hardship post, it was not the worst place one could be stationed during the war. Except, of course, if you needed a top-notch medical facility.

Hospital Nightmare

In his report, Springer described the despicable conditions of the Canadian Mission Hospital of Chungking, once touted as "perhaps the best non-military hospital of its kind in the area."[73] His opinion changed dramatically after closer contact with the hospital and the bad experience of Boris Morosoff and his wife, with whom he had been rooming with for almost a year. Mrs. Morosoff went to the hospital for a surgical procedure after consulting with friends and the insistence of her Canadian doctor. She arrived on Sunday, May 7, 1944, to "undergo an operation for gallstones."[74]

She was shown to her private, supposedly first-class room. A quick survey of the room was sufficient to show that it was not a satisfactory place for her to spend her next two or three weeks. The walls and floors were coated with sputum and blood. The bed linen was filthy. The air reeked with odors of sickness and death. Mrs. Morosoff had her own servant scrub the room from top to bottom; she tore off the bedding and replaced it with her own from home. She supplied her own water for washing and drinking purposes. The water supplied by the hospital was covered with a green scum and stank as though it had been standing for months in a stagnant pond. Before the operation, she found it necessary to bring in all sorts of things from home, which her husband collected on his daily trips back and forth—fifty minutes each way over rough terrain. Since no tables were provided, a table was brought to avoid the necessity of placing dishes on the floor. The hospital food was neither well prepared nor appropriate. According to Mrs. Morosoff, "One patient was given dry toast right after having his tonsils out." Her husband had her meals prepared at home and brought them in. None of the nurses were able to read the hospital thermometer used for taking patients' temperatures. Boris brought his own thermometer from home.

The lack of hospital staffing was appalling. Mr. Morosoff discovered this as he toured the halls while his wife was incapacitated. He found cases of smallpox and typhoid, which were not segregated from the patients with noncontagious ailments. He walked into one room where a foreign girl with typhoid appeared to be in a coma. There was no nurse in attendance; the door was wide open. He roamed through the maternity ward at will. On another occasion, he was searching for some Vaseline. Without interference he roamed through the entire hospital and opened the unlocked cabinets where the medical supplies and surgical instruments were kept. He found no Vaseline but was given some Chinese oil. He decided to administer an enema to his wife, no nurse being available for the purpose. Not certain that the required instruments were sterile, he personally boiled a pot of water and kept the instruments immersed therein for a sufficient time to destroy any germs.

The operation was a surgical success, although the doctor was embarrassed to find that the patient did not have gallstones. He had insisted that she had—but refused to call in another physician so that an independent diagnosis might be obtained. He removed her appendix, which, however, was in good condition. The chief pain experienced by Mrs. Morosoff during the operation (performed with a local anesthetic) was caused by a hot-water bottle that was inadvertently left lying on her leg during the operation. It was filled with boiling water and uncovered. She suffered a large and severe blister, which was later pierced and addressed by the doctor and later attended to by her husband, the doctor apparently assuming that his one treatment was sufficient.[75]

Springer wrote his mother about Mrs. Morosoff's experience, adding, "If I should get sick, never fear; I would have them ship me to India, where hospital facilities are up to western standards."[76] He learned from a recent letter that his brother Joe had gotten married, and extended his best wishes. "Congratulations to Joe. I wish I could be on hand to kiss the bride, but I'm afraid he would have to postpone the wedding for a year to make that possible."[77] Paul was still in Chungking, but he expected to go to Kweilin upon the arrival of his relief, whom he confirmed was already in India. The weather was nicer in Kweilin, a smaller post, and "I will be a big fish in a small pond," he wrote.[78] "Will be nearer to the front and subject to frequent bombings, but the caves in that city are world-renowned. No more hill climbing, and I understand that the quarters there are very nice, and adjacent to the office."[79]

Business at Home

Springer's college debt was now behind him, and he was able to save money, so much that he insisted on helping his parents buy a house. He sent his mother a check for $2,000 to help with the purchase. His first preference for her was to find a home in suburban Philadelphia. However, he felt that Collingswood, New Jersey, was a second choice and described it as a "tip-top residential district."[80] His family was asked to vacate the rented house at 2973 Congress Road, since it had been sold and the new owner had other plans for it.[81] A good buy turned up in Collingswood, and his check covered the down payment. He was allotting part of his salary to pay the installments on the loan. Someday the house would be his, although the arrangement was made to provide for his mother and sister, since his father was away on military duty at Camp Lee, Virginia, at the time. Springer's own living arrangements were up in the air. He was fully expecting to go to his assigned post in Kweilin, although the transfer experienced a number of administrative delays.

He received a letter from Bob Crockett, his Yale roommate, who informed him that two of his classmates, Howie Knight and Hovey Seymour, both were killed in training crashes. Only the night before, Paul experienced an air raid alarm in Chungking, the second this season, although no air raid followed. He wrote to a friend: "I wouldn't bother to get out of bed anymore until I heard the planes."[82] In the same letter he mentioned that a Yale club was formed in Chungking a couple of weeks ago. About ten guys showed up at the first meeting, including three Chinese, and they expected about a dozen the next time. There were several Yale alumni in the Army in China—Art Hopkins, Bob Clarke, Preston Schoyer—but they were rarely in town. "We'll snag them whenever they are."[83] Springer was not looking forward to spending another summer in Chungking, nor had he mentioned Mary Louise Lee, or any other girlfriend, in his letters home for the past six months. He received his wish for a transfer, although it would not be to the post in Kweilin. The State Department had other plans for him.

Chapter 13

SHIFTED TO CAIRO

By the summer of 1944, a turning point was reached on the European front. Allied forces were turning back the armies of Nazi Germany. The US State Department and the Office of Strategic Services (OSS) began making plans for the postwar period. It was anticipated that intelligence-gathering OSS operations in the Middle East would be completely altered during the postwar period.[1] It seemed inevitable that there would be no American military presence in the area to which an OSS base could be attached once the war ended. Previously, their operations were a partially military and civilian intelligence function. Because Cairo would undoubtedly be the major communications center in the Middle East in the postwar period, plans were made to establish an intelligence headquarters there. It would cover Greece and possibly Bulgaria, as well as Turkey, the Arab states, Iran, and Ethiopia. A subsidiary office was to be maintained in the capitals of each of the countries, providing an intimate direction of intelligence activities in their respective regions. It was imperative that the counterintelligence unit of the OSS be maintained in the Middle East for US security purposes, even after the withdrawal of the Germans from Greece.

OSS Operations Base

The nature of the intelligence operation would be changed to a completely civilian function after the war. It was therefore necessary to attach the OSS headquarters in Cairo to a civilian agency such as the American legation. The civilian cover for an OSS operative came in the guise of an attaché to the legation, with special duties. This gave the OSS agent a legitimate diplomatic cover, such as a vice consul, with responsibilities at the legation. This person had to be thoroughly familiar with the techniques of diplomatic procedure relative to travel documents and be able to establish friendly relations with consular and diplomatic officials of the various countries with representation in Egypt. He needed to have experience in the handling of business details, including the maintenance of financial records, classifying and filing

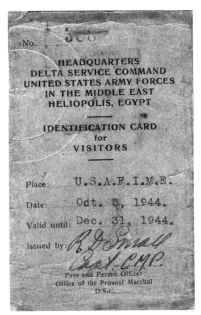

No. 300

**HEADQUARTERS
DELTA SERVICE COMMAND
UNITED STATES ARMY FORCES
IN THE MIDDLE EAST
HELIOPOLIS, EGYPT**

IDENTIFICATION CARD
for
VISITORS

Place: U.S.A.F.I.M.E.
Date: Oct. 5, 1944.
Valid until: Dec. 31, 1944.
Issued by: *R D Small*
Capt. CMP.
Pass and Permit Officer
Office of the Provost Marshal
D.S.C.

Headquarters, Delta Service Command, USAAF in the Middle East, Heliopolis, Egypt, cover of Springer's ID card. *Springer Family collection*

intelligence reports, and maintaining a registry, as well as performing routine secretarial functions. The job would also entail the use of two cipher clerks to handle the coding and decoding of messages, and the ability to paraphrase and type and be capable of doing finished work on intelligence reports. Finally, all personnel had to pass a thorough security screening and had to be trained in security practices.[2]

Although Springer was not yet twenty-seven years old, he already had a high-level security clearance with his two years of service in the State Department. He had a thorough knowledge both of State Department and OSS codes from his work as a cipher clerk, and his experience as vice consul provided him with a diplomatic cover. His disarming personality and professional manners put others in the highest circles of authority at ease. His orders came on July 8, 1944, from US secretary of state Cordell Hull. It stated in part that "Springer is assigned Vice Consul at Cairo, to proceed as soon as possible. This transfer not made at his request nor for his convenience."[3] Paul was one of the first officers to staff the new intelligence unit at the legation. The Cairo legation maintained cipher communications with Washington and all the Middle East advance military bases. Springer's legation duties included work in the code room, finance, supply, local security, servicing of field missions, securing of visas, and passports. Some travel was required. On July 12 he was granted a visa from the British consulate in Chungking for entry into Egypt.[4] Less than a week later, he departed from Chungking and arrived at his new post on August 1, 1944.[5]

The transfer to Cairo was a 180-degree shift for the young man. Once he arrived, Springer asked for a trunk containing his personal effects to be shipped to him from his parents' house.[6] He was issued a diplomatic ID card for frequent visits to the Delta Service Command Headquarters of the US Army Forces in the Middle East, at Heliopolis, Egypt.[7] He received an orientation and special training at the base. He enrolled in the American University at Cairo, where he took language classes and studied Egyptian colloquial Arabic.[8] He learned to understand nouns, verbs, phrases, and numbers and to tell time, as well as how to make conversation and small talk and ask directions in this ancient tongue. Shortly after his arrival in Cairo, Paul became reacquainted with Charles Bradford "Brad" Welles, Yale '24, his former Greek professor at Yale.[9]

Now known as Major Welles, this former academic was the head of the OSS Counter Intelligence Unit in Cairo and was running an OSS operation into Turkey. He was on leave from his full professorship of classics and ancient history at Yale for the duration of the war. One of Welles's counterparts in Ankara, Turkey, was Theodore Babbitt, formerly Yale's assistant dean of freshmen, now serving as an assistant military attaché.[10] Charles Vickers, who taught political science at Yale, was also in Ankara as a vice consul. Brad Welles and his counterpart, Stephen Penrose, the head of secret intelligence in Cairo, were easy to work for. Welles was a low-key, well-liked officer. At a time when relations with their British counterparts were sometimes strained, he was a particularly good liaison with the British. Penrose was in charge of espionage and counterintelligence.[11] He was preoccupied with getting his OSS operatives behind the lines in Greece, which, as the occupying Germans withdrew, was thrown deeper into a civil war.

Springer's first assignment in Cairo was in the code room, working with his former Yale professor, who exposed him to the inner workings of the complex diplomatic and intelligence community that enveloped their work. His four years of classical Greek studies were paying off, and his resurgent proficiency in the code room was noted by the American minister, S. Pickney Tuck. Tuck later reported that Paul "was far more competent to be in charge than the clerk actually in charge" of the code room.[12] Unfortunately, due to the other clerk's seniority, it was not possible for Tuck to place Springer in charge. There was an enormous volume of OSS code traffic coming through the legation, and Springer willingly accepted whatever work was assigned to him to help in the war effort, and completed it without complaint.[13]

In the summer and fall of 1944, US and British intelligence in Cairo supplied information to carry out several important functions. One objective was to buy strategic materials and metals needed by the Allies to keep the German military from getting it. This included chromium from Turkey. In August, when the Soviets reached the point where they could recapture eastern Europe through Romania, learning what the Allies could do to support the Russian drive in the East became critical. There was not much information coming from that area. It became clear when information was passed through that the tightest supply line for the German forces in the Balkans was in oil and oil resources. Among petroleum resources was a special type of lubricating oil that the Germans were in short supply of. It was coming from a Standard Oil processing plant in Romania, allied with Nazi Germany and in enemy hands. As a result of this intelligence, the Allies ran a bombing campaign against these resources in Romania, cutting off the supply and leaving a critical fuel and lubricant shortage for German and Romanian mechanized forces in the path of the Soviet advance. The targeted plant was a high priority and was eventually destroyed.[14]

The German and Romanian front lines collapsed within two days of the start of the Soviet armored offensive. Their initial breakthrough was twenty-five miles deep and destroyed the rear-area supply installations by the night of August 21. Romanian armored formations resisted the Soviet attack in many cases but were ill equipped to defend themselves effectively against a modern army due to a lack of modern antitank, artillery, and antiaircraft weapons. Two days later, the 13th German Panzer Division was no longer a coherent fighting force, and the German 6th Army was encircled to a depth of sixty-two miles. It was not coincidental that on this same evening, Romania's King Michael announced to the country via a radio broadcast that after four years of war, they were switching sides. Many of those Romanian troops facing off against the advancing Russians were ordered to turn their guns around and join the Soviet attack on their former German allies. The Soviet Red Army mobile group managed to cut off the retreat of the German formations into Hungary. Isolated pockets of German units tried to fight their way through, but only small remnants managed to escape the encirclement.[15] The Allied disruption of their military supply chains compounded their problems.

Other intelligence was passed to the US Navy via the code room. The combined British and American intelligence teams located enemy trade routes by sea, which, if disputed or closed, would particularly hurt the enemy. A third role of the group was to determine the state of political affairs in those countries that were soon to be occupied by Allied forces. Another was the status of their devastated economies when the Allies entered Greece. This was the central political point of the problem. The British had a strong role in Greece for a long time. The US had none. The British had a strong influence in Egypt in terms of intelligence collection. The US was just beginning. Joining the British in World War II was an immediate partnership in Cairo, soon labeled as the Combined Economic Warfare Agency–Middle East. It was one of the more obscure agencies of the war. The agency automatically received the whole flow of British reports both from the Middle East and the Balkans from British field agents.

Political Turmoil in Greece

The situation in Greece was exceptionally complex, as the British sought to retain Greece under their sphere of influence while the rest of the Balkans were presumed to be falling under the influence of the Soviets. The first signs of an internal civil war occurred from 1942 to 1944, during the German occupation. With the Greek government in exile, it was unable to influence the situation at home. This resulted in a highly polarized struggle between left- and right-wing ideologies that started in 1943. As a result, various resistance groups of differing political affiliations targeted the power vacuum resulting from the end of German occupation. The OSS had been advancing funds to informants and key political players in Greece for well over a year.[16] The first episode of large-scale civil violence took place in Athens on December 3, 1944, less than two months after the Germans had retreated from the area. After an order to disarm, leftists resigned from the government and called for resistance against the British-backed government. A riot erupted. Greek government soldiers, with British forces standing in the background, opened fire on the leftist National Liberation Front rally, killing twenty-eight demonstrators and injuring dozens. It was a bloodbath.

In the final months of the war, the Americans were looking to assist with food shortages, reestablishing basic services, and advising the military on the aspects and perceived problems of governance. The British feared, with good reason, that the OSS would prove hostile to their attempts to reimpose colonial rule after the war.[17] They were equally apprehensive about the footholds made by leftist groups who continued to push for control of Greece as an independent Communist state in the postwar period. Major Welles was an important asset in this drama, since there were few non-Greeks who could establish a working dialogue with operatives in Greece to advance American interests as well as he could. Undoubtedly, Springer finally appreciated his study of Greek under Welles, which he once described as the "most abominable subject" while at Yale.

In October 1944, Springer enjoyed a visit with colleagues to see the great pyramids of Egypt. His photo was taken by G. M. Georgoulas, who photographed the delegates from the Cairo Conference in 1921 at the Giza pyramids.[18] The photographer accompanied Springer and several legation members to these most famous of ancient sites.

"Official Business" in the Holy Land

Springer's new assignment in Cairo gave him an unexpected privilege over Christmas: a trip through the Holy Land. It was an unbelievable opportunity. With US government offices effectively shut down over the Christmas holiday, he and two American colleagues were determined to take the trip that they had only dreamed of. Securing the necessary visas for travel was relatively easy, since they were well versed on the subject of required documentation and well connected with the foreign embassies. Springer's passport exit stamp from Egypt stated that he was traveling on "Official

Paul Springer, *right*, with two colleagues atop a pyramid. Note the Sphinx in the background at right. Egypt, 1944. *Springer Family collection*

Paul Springer (*on camel at right*), Great Pyramids of Egypt, 1944. *Springer Family collection*

Business to Palestine, Syria, and Lebanon" and was signed off at the American legation. Whether or not it was official business may be subject to debate, since the party of three Americans and two Egyptians departed shortly before Christmas. The names of the other travel companions were never mentioned in the account of the journey. Perhaps it was a covert mission—with the men posing as tourists. With the possible exception of an overnight stay in Damascus, their trip appears to be a purely historical and spiritual vacation. In either event, an account of the trip survived among Springer's papers, which describe every detail worth mentioning along the way.[19]

The thought of being in the Holy Land at Christmas was the next-best thing to being home with loved ones. Paul wrote, "What a privilege! What a golden opportunity!"[20] So, like pilgrims, they started off, a party of five—three Americans and two Egyptians. Only three days of the Christmas weekend were available for the trip, so they departed from Cairo at 11:00 on Friday night, December 22.[21]

They drove through the night, crossing the Suez Canal at Ismailia on the ferry and passing over the Sinai Desert road to Beersheba. On either side of the road was a sea of sand with not a sign of life, except for an occasional desert rat, for miles and miles. They approached Beersheba about daybreak and then took the left road to Gaza, in Palestine, very near the Mediterranean coast. From Gaza, they drove along the coastal road to Tel Aviv, the new and modern Jewish city built beside the ancient city of Jaffa, and thence along the coast to Haifa and Acre. At this point, they turned away from the seacoast, winding their way through the mountains to Safad, Rosh Pina, and El Quneitira and on to Damascus. They arrived in Damascus about three o'clock in the afternoon, spent the evening and the next day until 4:00 p.m. there, and then returned to Jerusalem via Tiberias on the Sea of Galilee, Nazareth, Jennin, Bablus, and Ramallah.[22]

Much of the driving was done at night, yet they were able to see a good deal of the countryside during the day. It was beautiful. The drive from Beersheba to Gaza carried them through slight mountains with numerous curves, then on to the plain approaching Gaza and the sea. This was the season when rains are frequent throughout the Holy Land, and the fields along this road were green. The rain-laden grass sparkled in the rising sun. At times along the coastal road, they approached close enough to the sea that they could see the breakers crashing against the shore. There were great color contrasts—the blue sea, white breakers, a yellow beach, green fields, and the tawny-brown and grayish rocky mountains to their right. There were, along the highways, all the things peculiar to the Middle East—the camel caravans, the Bedouins and their lonely tents, the migrating Arabs on their donkeys, groves of ripe oranges, sections of shabby mud village huts, and mountain caves.

Their drive between Acre and Damascus was pleasing to the eyes. The roads wound up and down the mountains, at one point so they could look off in the distance to the

East Wall, Old City of Jerusalem. *Courtesy of Nancy Warrington Greenfield, from the collection of F. D. Warrington*

Sea of Galilee. Down the road, they were able to look to their left upon Lake Hula. After that, they had an unusual driving experience. They suspected they were having engine trouble, since the car could not gain more than 30 mph in high gear, even when going down a slight grade. They later discovered that it was not engine trouble at all, but that they were continually ascending, and though it appeared they were descending, they were actually going uphill. It rained most of the time along their way to Damascus.

They found that Damascus was not a particularly attractive city, yet it was interesting. It still bore evidence of ancient times—the cobblestone streets were narrow, and stone steps were worn until they were hardly steps. The ancient busy market still existed, and there were remnants of the ancient city wall. It was an astonishing step back into biblical times for the five young men.

They had reservations at the Orient Palace Hotel. Upon arrival, they rested for three or four hours from the strenuous trip. They got up and went out to dinner with some Syrian friends of their Egyptian companions and were generously welcomed. The Syrians said that the United States was their "second home," since they had so many of their people living there. They eagerly flocked around the visitors and engaged them in cheerful conversation—a mixture of French, Arabic, and English;

some of the Syrians spoke excellent English. They enjoyed a lovely dinner and then proceeded to one of the better cabarets in the city. They arrived just as the floor show was ending, but as a special favor to their party, the performance was repeated. The show consisted of oriental dancing and singing. The party broke up with *salaams* in Arabic and parting expressions of goodwill in English.

The next morning was Christmas Eve. When they awoke it was raining, but after they had breakfast, the rain slacked up and they were able to get out and tour around the city by car. They went to "Strait Street," which was a quarter of a mile long and contained the bazaar section of the city. The street was not very wide. It was covered with an arched roof like so many oriental streets. It was jammed with strange people coming to and from the market and in a great variety of costumes. As they made their way through the crowd, at a rate of about 5 miles per hour, their car occasionally rubbed against a donkey and nearly hit someone who paid little attention to their honking horn. At times, they had to stop completely because of donkey carts that were crosswise in the street. It was in Strait Street, at the home of Judas, that Paul, a blind man and an enemy of Christians, was healed by Ananias and became one of the greatest Christians of all time.

They stopped to see the Mosque of Omayyades, one of the main sacred spots of Muslims. Afterward, they went to the tomb of King Saladin, "the King of Kings," and later to an unnamed palace that just before the war "had been purchased for transfer to the Arab Museum in New York."[23] Parts of the palace had been shipped to New York—the rest was being made ready for shipment after the war. The caretaker of the palace provided them with Bedouin robes—also long swords—and they had their pictures taken in the courtyard of the Palace Museum. They bought a few things in a section of the palace that had been made into a shop. There were some fine handmade brocades, which Damascus was known for, and attractive pieces of inlaid mother-of-pearl. They went next to the ancient city wall at the end of Strait Street, then to the spot where St. Paul escaped from the city through a window in the wall. Time was slipping away for their planned trip to the Church of the Nativity, so they hurried back to the hotel.

It was from their hotel balcony that they were able to observe an unusual incident—at least in the eyes of the Americans. It just so happened that the Muslim pilgrimage to Mecca was returning to Damascus on that day. Thousands of people filled the streets in front of the railroad station, which could be viewed from their balcony, to greet the returning pilgrims. They went down from the hotel and to the station for a closer view of the congregation. Flags of Syria and other Muslim flags were waiving over the heads of the noisy crowd.[24] There was a group of about twelve men dressed in

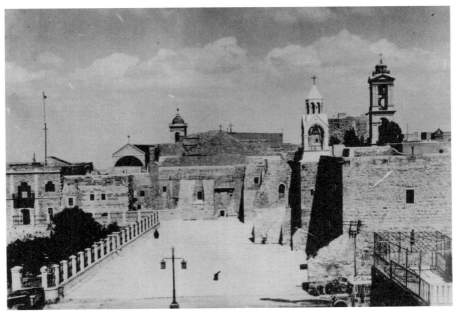

Church of the Nativity, Jerusalem. *Courtesy of Nancy Warrington Greenfield, from the collection of F. D. Warrington*

bold colors who were waving long swords in the air in tandem like some sort of ritual. At certain parts, they would clash their swords in the air, while others scraped them on the ground. It was a colorful ceremony, and one of Springer's colleagues took advantage of the scene with some fine shots with his color movie camera.

They left Damascus about 4:00 p.m. and came back by the route from which they came, almost to the town of Safad. Here, they turned off to the left in order to go down to the ancient city of Tiberius. It was getting late, it had begun to rain again, and there wasn't much they could see in Tiberius, Nazareth, or Nablus, through which they passed later, although they found a certain amount of joy and satisfaction just knowing that they had passed through these holy cities. Just before Tiberius, on the Sea of Galilee, they saw a fishing boat setting out from shore as they drove past it in the darkening hour. They remarked how much the scene reminded them of the Bible story of the fishermen and their nets.

After a long journey, their visit to the Church of the Nativity was upon them. It was a special place on a special night, the once-in-a-lifetime experience that Paul had dreamed about. Their visit was described as follows:

> We arrived in Jerusalem about 8:00 at night without reservations. We felt almost as Joseph and Mary must have felt when they entered the city on

that all-important night. Fortunately, however, we were able to contact the brother of one of our Egyptian companions, who is in charge of reconstructing certain Arab monuments in Jerusalem. He used his authority to put some of his subordinates out of their beds so that we would have a place to stay. The accommodations we had, consequently, were not the best, but comfortable enough and we were, and in our tired state, very grateful. After having some oriental food—Kabab, beans, cheese, and bread plus some Jaffa oranges, we proceeded to Bethlehem and to the Church of Nativity.

The road was absolutely jammed with cars and people going to the birthplace of The Christ, and it is reported that there were more pilgrims this year than there have been for at least 70 years. It took us some time to finally reach Bethlehem and after getting there, we had to work our way through a line in order to get to the manger. I guess I was one of the lucky ones because I was right in front of the manger when the bells started ringing at midnight. The place was so crowded that serious meditation was difficult. Nevertheless, it was a grand feeling. On coming out, the Star of the East seemed to shine brighter than I had ever seen it

Inside the Church of the Nativity, Jerusalem. *Courtesy of Nancy Warrington Greenfield, from the collection of F. D. Warrington*

shine before, and there was an extremely large circle around the moon which was almost full.

I could not help noticing what an effect the Church of Nativity had upon the visitors. People waited their turns in line, [and] there was no pushing and crowding; everyone spoke in a low voice and a strange sort of peace among men existed. This state contrasted sharply with the impatient situation along the highway just outside. We did not stay long in Bethlehem that night because of the tremendous crowd, and we were very tired.[25]

On Christmas morning, they walked the path Jesus took from the place of his judgment to the site of his crucifixion, known as "the Way of the Cross" or "Via Dolorosa," to the Dome of the Rock, also known as the Mosque of Omar. This is an Islamic shrine located on the Temple Mount in the Old City of Jerusalem. They surmised that the Mosque of Omar was probably the second-most-sacred spot for Muslims, the first being Mecca. The mosque was built over the stone on which Abraham is supposed to have offered his son, Isaac, as a sacrifice. It was also on the site of the ancient temple of King Solomon. The dull building was eight sided. The dome was supported by eight huge columns of stone, salvaged by the Muslims from

West Wall, Wailing Wall. Note the uniformed soldiers at left. *Courtesy of Nancy Warrington Greenfield, from the collection of F. D. Warrington*

the Roman ruins of Jerusalem. The stained-glass windows were beautiful, and each of a different design. Beneath the dome was the huge piece of rock of Mount Moriah, encased with steel. The floor space was decorated with attractive carpets that had been provided by Turkish sultans. Encased near the rock were two hairs from the beard of the prophet Mohammed.

They left the Dome of the Rock to pay a quick visit to the Mosque of el-Aksa, which their Egyptian host in Jerusalem was working on at the time. The day after their return to Cairo, they found a long article in the *Egyptian Gazette* about the reparations being made there. Upon leaving the grounds, they stopped for a few minutes for a look at the Jewish Wailing Wall. There were only two people before the wall at the time, but they were, in their customary manner, weaving back and forth as they offered their prayers. One was a man who, after his prayers and before he left, kissed the wall three times. The kisses resounded loudly to Springer's group some twenty yards away.

Next, they drove down to visit the Church of All Nations, built by the twelve leading Catholic nations, including the United States. This building was modern and beautifully done. Just before the altar was a white stone about ten feet across, marking the place where Jesus Christ made the decision to sacrifice his blood to save mankind. Each walked through the tiny gate enclosing the rock and touched it. One section of the church was contributed by the United States. It had the official United States seal inlaid in the roof. The church was right beside the Garden of the Gethsemane in Kedron valley. The garden was nicely kept at all times. Some of the olive trees they saw in the garden possibly existed at the time of Christ. Their girth was huge; new shoots come out from the base from time to time, and the life of the tree goes on and on.

They went back into the Old City again, through the Jaffa Gate, past King David's Tower, and down King David Street, which was the bazaar section, to the Church of the Holy Sepulcher. The church houses the tomb of Christ and is built on two sites— the Hill of Golgotha, or Calvary, and the garden tomb of St. Joseph of Arimathaea. One passes through a little green anteroom before going into the tomb. On top of the tomb are two stone slabs worn deep from the touch of pilgrims who have come to this, the holiest of holy places. A Greek priest stood in the corner of the enclosure by the tomb, and from him, visitors could take and light a candle to burn over the tomb. This they did. Another observation the travelers found most interesting: a Muslim guarded the entrance to the Church of the Holy Sepulcher and has since the time of King Saladin. They were told that this position had been handed down from father to son through the centuries.

Church of the Holy Sepulchre. Note the mass of Arabs in flowing robes on the roof.
Courtesy of Nancy Warrington Greenfield, from the collection of F. D. Warrington

Leaving the Church of the Holy Sepulcher, they drove out to the Mount of Olives, from which Christ ascended into heaven. Looking back across the valley of Kedron, again they could see the blocked-up Golden Gate centered in the long stretch of the ancient city wall. They wanted to stay longer, but it was 2:00 p.m. They went to the YMCA in Jerusalem, across the street from the modern King David Hotel, and had an American lunch. They found the YMCA building to be perhaps the nicest YMCA building in the world, complete to the last detail. From its tower they got an excellent bird's-eye view of all the biblical places surrounding the city. From this tower they could see the Dead Sea, which was several miles away and some 1,292 feet below sea level.

Shortly after leaving, some heavy cloud cover made the world dark. Their homeward journey was now just a matter of driving through the darkness of the long Christmas night through Bethlehem, Hebron, Beersheba, and thence to Cairo. Although they later conceded they should have allowed more time for the trip, they accomplished a great deal. They were dreadfully tired at the end of the journey, but all were happy and content from their shared experiences.[26]

Diplomatic Circles

Upon Springer's return, the Christmas celebrations continued in the diplomatic community, with a cocktail party on Saturday, December 30, hosted by the American minister to Egypt, S. Pickney Tuck. Tuck's father was a prominent jurist who served on Egypt's international courts for over twenty years.[27] Nicknamed "Kippy," the younger Tuck was educated in Switzerland and Germany, graduated from Dartmouth College in 1913, and became a career foreign-service officer. He served as vice consul in Alexandria, Egypt, as early as 1916 and remained in Egypt until 1921, when he was transferred to Vladivostok, Russia. In 1942, he was interim ambassador to France, where he condemned collaboration with Nazi Germany and publicly protested the deportation and internment of French Jews. Tuck served until the Nazis occupied

Vichy France, and he was briefly imprisoned at Lourdes. In 1944, he was named US minister to Egypt, later appointed as the first US ambassador to Egypt in 1946. Well known in Egypt from living there with his father, and fluent in Arabic, he was admired by his State Department peers for his ability to handle crisis situations, most notably when he later helped calm anti-American unrest in Egypt after the founding of Israel.

New Year's Eve brought Springer to a party hosted by Princess Chivekiar, the first wife of King Fouad, and Hussein Pasha, a senator in the upper house of the Egyptian Parliament.[28] The hostess, Princess Chivekiar, was not the mother of King Farouk, since he was born to King Fouad's second wife in 1920. Hussein Pasha had previously served as Egypt's minister of war and marine from December 1937 to April 1938. He also served in the royal court as chief aide-de-camp to Kings Fouad and Farouk. As chief aide-de-camp, he commanded King Farouk's Military Household (predecessor to the Republican Guard of Egypt), which included the royal guard and other elite military formations. Despite being educated at Eaton and Oxford, he was sometimes overheard railing against the British. Several American diplomats were on the invitation list for this exclusive party bringing in the New Year. While trying to engage the host in conversation, one of Springer's colleagues said, "Well, Pasha, you'll always be grateful to the British for driving the Germans out of here; they came pretty close to Cairo, didn't they?" To his amazement, the Egyptian replied, "We wouldn't have minded being occupied by the Germans. We'd have gotten on well with the Germans. We degenerate countries have to know how to play one power against the other."[29] It was widely known that Pasha was the king's mother's lover. The American diplomats were worried that the young king was not getting good advice from a man like that, although he was brilliant and well educated.

King Farouk

In the aftermath of the Egyptian Revolution of 1919, the United Kingdom ended its protectorate over Egypt and recognized it as a sovereign state on February 28, 1922. On March 15, 1922, King Fouad issued a decree changing his title from Sultan of Egypt to King of Egypt. In 1930, he attempted to strengthen the power of the monarchy by abrogating the 1923 Constitution and replacing it with a new constitution that limited the role of Parliament to an advisory status only. Prince Farouk of Egypt succeeded his father as king at the age of sixteen, when his father died in 1936. His sister Fawzia was Queen of Iran for a brief period. Upon his coronation, the young king made a public radio address to the nation, the first time a King of Egypt had ever spoken directly to his people.[30] His father, Fouad I, did not speak any Arabic and relied on representatives to make his wishes known to his subjects in their native language. The teenage monarch was enamored of the glamorous royal lifestyle. Although he already had thousands of acres of land, dozens of palaces, and hundreds of cars, the king never seemed satisfied with his wealth. He often traveled to Europe for grand shopping sprees.

During the hardships of World War II, criticism was leveled at Farouk for his lavish lifestyle. His decision to keep all the lights burning at his palace in Alexandria, during a time when the city was blacked out due to Italian bombing, was detested by the masses. He was urged by the British to rid his royal servant staff of Italians, some of whom were thought to be spies for the Axis powers. There was an unconfirmed story that Farouk told British ambassador Sir Miles Lampson (who had an Italian wife), "I'll get rid of my Italians, when you get rid of yours."[31]

As he grew older, King Farouk began pilfering objects and artifacts while on state visits abroad, including a ceremonial sword from the Shah of Iran and a priceless pocket watch from Winston Churchill. Common people were also often the victims of the kleptomaniac monarch, who developed a reputation as a highly skilled pickpocket. His well-known panache for thievery soon earned him the nickname "the Thief of Cairo." This excess would be one of the leading sparks that triggered the July 23, 1952, military coup by Gamal Abdel Nasser, who forced Farouk to abdicate and exiled him to Italy, where the former king lived until his death in 1965.

Top-Secret Telegram

One day in early 1945, an unusual telegram came into the American legation in Cairo. Springer delivered it to the US minister, Kippy Tuck.[32] Tuck dismissed him and summoned a senior aide, Cecil Lyon, into his office. "Look at this," said Tuck. He handed Lyon the telegram, which said, "This message to be decoded by the Minister himself."[33] Kippy said, "I haven't decoded a telegram in years; I don't know how to decode a telegram. Can you do it?"[34] After a quick study, the aide confessed that it was encrypted with something more complicated than what he had decoded before. He said, "I haven't done one either. I'm not sure I can."[35] "What will we do?" asked Tuck.[36] They decided to get the code clerk, or the chief code clerk, swear them to secrecy, and then have them decode it and not to tell anyone else in the code room anything. After delegating the task, the chief code clerk brought back the telegram, which said, "The President will be aboard the USS *Quincy* in the Great Bitter Lakes," after which it gave the dates and stated, "He would like to meet Emperor Haile Selassie, King Ibn Saud, and King Farouk. Please make all arrangements."[37]

Tuck and Lyon were astounded by the news. It was a difficult assignment, for which they had only about three weeks to prepare. At the time, they did not even know where Roosevelt was coming from, although they later learned he was on his way back from the Yalta Conference in Crimea. The US Secret Service secured an office in the American legation in Cairo and used it as a communication post to coordinate security arrangements for Roosevelt's visit.[38] The legation tapped several key men, including Vice Consul Springer, to arrange the transportation, logistics, and security for the respective visits by the leaders of Ethiopia, Saudi Arabia, and Egypt for the high-level meetings aboard USS *Quincy* with the US president. Two of them would come to Egypt to pay their official visits. One of them, King Farouk, was already there. Cooperation by the Egyptians was imperative. In the meantime, the American legation was a beehive of political activity under an enormous veil of secrecy. The security of President Roosevelt's visit to North Africa could not be compromised.

Chapter 14
THE AMERICANS STRIKE BACK

Intelligence Liaison

The 14th US Air Force developed a network of eight ground liaison units to interact with Chinese ground forces. Each unit consisted of an officer, an interpreter, and a signal operator. For security reasons, the interpreters were obtained from ex-employees of US firms or consulates, rather than from the regular pool of Chinese interpreters. Some were former Yali Middle School students. Each unit was developed as a team. Every attempt was made to assign only compatible personnel to serve together. Lt. Arthur Hopkins was assigned to one of these units. Five units were assigned to combat areas, and three spare units were kept back for relief rotation and in cases of illness. A training period of seven to ten days was needed to ensure a proper understanding by the officers and interpreters of the relevant importance of targets and coordinates on their assigned missions.[1]

Each unit was issued a jeep, cots, bedrolls, clothing, and condensed rations. Communications consisted of two sets of no. 10 sea rescue radio equipment, four spare batteries, and visual ground/air panel signals. One intelligence unit was kept in training during the rotational relief so as to continually improve the system of operation and give each unit the opportunity to make recommendations for more-effective work. This relief period was used to improve codes, transmission of information, and the use of photos to improve the air and ground actions against the Japanese. Each liaison was

Lieut. Arthur H. Hopkins, Jr., of Merion, Pa., with U. S.-Chinese insignia on his arm.

Lt. Arthur H. Hopkins Jr., from the *Philadelphia Inquirer*, December 12, 1943. *Springer Family collection*

required to evaluate and condense all reports from the ground in a clear and concise message to the 14th Air Force headquarters. Radio stations were set up throughout the area to keep headquarters personnel informed of movements of the enemy and the enemy planes. They correlated air support with ground forces so as to have the maximum effect in terms of results. This involved developing accurate target objectives to allow maximum damage to be inflicted on the enemy.[2] They also organized rescue operations for downed pilots and set up emergency-landing fields, supply depots, and refueling points for advance troops and intelligence agents.

Counteroffensive

It was during the all-out Japanese offensive in China during late 1944 that Lt. Art Hopkins made his mark on the Allied war effort with the 14th Air Force. He was assigned on the ground behind enemy lines in the East China theater. This 68th Wing unit operated as a frontal unit for this area, which extended from Shanghai to Indochina and included the shipping lanes in the South China Sea and Formosa Strait (now Taiwan Strait). Hopkins's mission was to gather and disseminate intelligence information from behind enemy lines in East China and maintain working relationships with the Chinese military headquarters in his area, as well as Chinese troops on the ground.[3]

Even with the loss of its valuable bases, the 14th Air Force was not deterred by the Japanese onslaught. It was resupplied with two new groups of Republic P-47 Thunderbolt fighter-bombers. These planes were armed with eight .50-caliber machine guns and could also be fitted with 5-inch rockets or a bombload of 2,500 pounds. These planes were supplemented with two more squadrons of B-25s in the spring and summer of 1944. The Mitchell B-25 was a twin-engine bomber that became standard equipment for the Allied air forces in World War II, perhaps the most versatile aircraft of the war.

The 14th began a series of intensive interdiction strikes along the newly established north–south Japanese corridor. This required Hopkins to operate under adverse conditions in occupied territory, maintaining constant communications with Air Corps fliers and reporting all targets to his headquarters, as well as keeping the USAAF bases informed of conditions in his area. Chief among the enemy targets were the railways—bridges, tunnels, locomotives, and railyards. Cutting off the Japanese advance by destroying their vital supply lines included the Yangtze River to Woosong and waters between Canton and Hong Kong. "I want them to devote the major portion, if not all, of their effort to the destruction of shipping in these areas rather than to distant sea searches," ordered Chennault.[4] Consequently, the B-24s of the 308th Bomb Group stepped up their attacks on Japanese shipping in the sea lanes and the rivers, which included laying mines as fighter units flew hundreds of sorties in support of the Chinese army all over the front.[5]

By New Year's Day 1945, the 14th Air Force's determined interdiction efforts during the enemy offensive had made major progress. The Japanese advance was permanently stalled, and counterattacking Chinese forces, supported by the 14th and Chinese pilots of the CACW, were starting to regain territory. Just as important, after a yearlong effort the Allies were able to recapture enough of Burma to reopen the overland supply routes from India. As a result of his actions in the field, Hopkins was awarded the Bronze Star for meritorious service during this period. His citation stated, in part, "His outstanding accomplishments in direct intelligence, tact and skill in managing highly difficult situations and his great devotion to duty in spite of imminent danger reflect great credit upon himself and the Armed Forces of the United States."[6]

By the end of the war, the 14th Air Force had more than 20,000 men and 1,000 planes in China. From the formation of the China Task Force in July 1942 to the end of the war, the 14th Air Force destroyed 2,135 Japanese aircraft, shooting down ten enemy planes for every American plane they lost. They continue to be known as the Flying Tigers.

Win Pettus Returns to China

Dr. Win Pettus returned to China in the first weeks of January 1945.[7] His first destination was Chungking, and the first two weeks on Chinese soil were full of logistical challenges and interesting events. On the day he arrived, he managed to find Dr. H. C. Chang (an old friend) just as he was taking a bus to Hsin Ch'aao to attend a feast given by the minister of health, Dr. P. Z. King. It was a great reintroduction to the

Dr. Winston Pettus, Yale-in-China medical mission. *Yale-China Association Records, RU 232, Manuscripts and Archives, Yale University Library*

medical community of China and the people there. He became reacquainted with the minister of health, the vice minister of health (who taught surgery for Hsiang-Ya when he was the head of the Kweiyang Central Hospital), a former professor of surgery at the Presbyterian United Methodist Church, and the heads of three different medical colleges. These connections proved invaluable as he began to operate, teach, and administer at several hospitals in Kweiyang and Chungking.

During the dinner, Pettus learned that there were some medical supplies (enough to last ten months) waiting in storage at a place near Chengtu. He decided to try to find a way of getting them to Chungking. The river waters were low due to a drought in the area, which made river transport difficult. When Pettus asked the US Army for a plane ride to Chengtu, giving them the reason, they offered to give him a ride both ways and volunteered to fly the items from there to Chungking. After waiting four days because of bad weather, Pettus finally caught a plane to Chengtu. Since he was unable to transfer the medical supplies by boat or truck, the use of an Army plane to transport the goods was a real blessing. Pettus looked up some old friends in Chengtu to spend the night with, but they were out in the early evening. When he went back again to inquire about a spare room, they were already asleep, so he spent the night in an Army hostel.

When he was eating breakfast in the mess hall the next morning, a soldier who looked familiar sat down beside him. The soldier did not recognize Pettus at first, but the doctor recognized him instantly as Bob Clarke, the former Yali Bachelor. Clarke had just come in from his base for a physical exam. He was on track for and preparing to receive an officer's commission. Only minutes later, Jim Elliott sat down beside him. Elliott was doing work for the Office of War Information (OWI) since leaving Yali in second half of 1944. The conversation started flowing among the three friends.

After three continuous years at the Yali Middle School, Elliott had strong convictions in favor of the return of Yali back to its old home campus in Changsha. He understood there had been much correspondence on the matter between Dwight Rugh and C. C. Lao (the principal) with the Yale-in-China trustees in America. Though Elliott felt that Rugh had already stated his opinion supporting the move back to Changsha, he felt compelled to verbally offer his support for it, as well as the support of fellow Bachelors Ken Moreland and Ross Dixon, to anyone who would listen. These men were wholeheartedly behind the same opinion that had been expressed by Dwight Rugh, C. C. Lao, Ying Kai-shih, and the entire Yali constituency. They, too, realized that once the war ended, Changsha was a far-superior campus. Elliott was concerned that the Yale-in-China office in New Haven failed to grasp the importance of the original Changsha campus as the preferred location for the Yali Middle School.

Pettus undoubtedly shared the same opinion, since he supported the move and planned to do whatever he could to help reestablish the Yali presence in Changsha after the war. Elliott had previously written to New Haven about this in 1944. "However, as you must know, the Yali Middle School is now an organization almost entirely Chinese," he wrote.[8] The mission's part had become increasingly smaller. "The school now revolves about and depends upon a small group of leaders Lao, Ying, Wang, Sheng, and Ho. Without one of them, the school could continue; if they all left, there would be no Yali."[9] These five leaders, who were in essence Yali, along with some alumni, attached a vast importance to the Changsha campus. These administrators were not living in Yuanling. They were merely existing until the time when they could get back to their old homes, where they could begin living again. Changsha was home to them in every sense of the word: the place of their former lives before the war and the location of their houses.[10]

Chungking Rotary Club and the Blood Bank

While working at the Chungking Military Hospital in March 1945, Pettus performed his first major chest surgery. The patient was a lieutenant who had been wounded in the fighting around Hankow in 1938. He had developed an empyema complication (an infection in the pleural space of the lungs) resulting in a nonexpansible lung. The patient needed a blood transfusion, so Pettus went in search of blood. He managed to pull together a group of about fifteen American and British friends, including some of the FAU staff and drivers, all of whom were willing to give blood. Fortunately, it was a common blood type. Although the patient survived, it was the most difficult thoraco-plasty Pettus had ever seen, since the patient's ribs were deformed by the six-year-old infection. The surgery required all the blood and saline that was collected and stored at the hospital, but that wasn't enough. Then a nurse and a doctor volunteered to give blood. After five transfusions, the surgery was over and the patient pulled through.

This incident was the catalyst that gave Pettus the opportunity he was looking for. He was now determined to establish a permanent blood bank in Chungking. Within two months, he received an offer for three refrigerators, as well as for their transportation from India to Kunming. He arranged for the American Red Cross to transfer them from Calcutta to Assam, then to the China Relief Unit in Kunming.

Dr. Pettus enlisted the help of the Chungking Rotary Club in the matter of getting blood donors.[11] The Rotary committee included four professional publicity men and one motion picture man. Pettus had expected to do most of the canvasing for blood donors himself. Instead, he found the Rotary men full of ideas—most of them excellent ones, which they were in a position to carry out. This included the publication and distribution of pamphlets, advertisement slides in motion picture theaters, filmstrips, and filming examples of the work of the blood bank. The Rotary Club scheduled one organization each week that welcomed a mobile team from the blood bank. They prepared promotional posters for the project. Pettus heard one of the Rotarians jokingly say that "within two or three months they will have so many donors for us that we will ask them to put out publicity against giving blood!"[12] The Rotary Club of Chungking also committed to financial support for the blood bank publicity campaign.

Ground travel in China was still slow, but sometimes unavoidable. Whenever Pettus traveled on Yali business, he flew, if possible.[13] His associates looked upon him as a sort of "glorified messenger," since he was faster than a telegram and much more wordy. He loved flying and now held a pilot's license. While he was on his health furlough in America in 1943–44, he had learned to fly and had become an accomplished pilot. He flew thousands of miles with airmen in China, making many friends among them. Always reaching for the next way to improve access to medicine, he was interested in getting a couple of surplus Stinson L-5s from the Army for use as air ambulances. The L-5, affectionately known as the "Flying Jeep," had been developed as a liaison aircraft for courier and communication work, artillery spotting, and casualty evacuation.[14] The fuselage of later models was redesigned so the aircraft could also be used as an air ambulance or for cargo work. With a wider and deeper rear fuselage section and a large rear door that folded downward, a heavy patient or 250 pounds of cargo could be quickly loaded aboard. During a layover at an airfield for three or four days, a mechanic gave Pettus a thorough course in checking on and learning what ways a Stinson L-5 plane might develop engine trouble.

By the summer of 1945, Pettus developed a plan to link all the mission hospitals in Hunan Province with the central Yale Hospital in the capital of Changsha. This is where patients with life-threatening issues or special cases were sent for treatment. The fact that seventeen small airfields were scattered all over the province, one of which adjoined Hsiang-Ya Hospital, made this plan a worthwhile pursuit. He wrote, "On my way here I saw a fleet of over twenty [Stinson L-5s]. They are becoming plentiful. I am feeling out the prospects of getting one or two to use for hospital ambulances after the war. These are fitted out with a stretcher. Yesterday by sheer luck I found myself talking to a pilot who flies one. He introduced me to his crowd and they showed me all the fine points of the plane. It's not too different from the plane I flew in St. Louis, but it is faster and much better fixed up. It would be ideal for my purpose."[15] With renewed enthusiasm for the Chinese language and his new medical and flying skills, he was as enthusiastic as ever about furthering the Yale-in-China medical mission.

Roosevelt's Visit to Egypt

Franklin Delano Roosevelt (FDR) boarded the heavy cruiser USS *Quincy* at Newport News, Virginia, for a transatlantic trip to the Mediterranean Sea.[16] It would be his first leg of a long journey to the Yalta Conference, to meet with Prime Minister Winston Churchill and Soviet premier Joseph Stalin to discuss Europe's postwar reorganization. During the journey, FDR's ship was accompanied by a light cruiser that brought up the rear. For protection, three destroyers steamed ahead, flanking the president's ship.

"When we got to the Straits of Gibraltar, they figured if the Germans were going to make their move, they would make it there because the straits are narrow," recalled Angelo Marinelli, a boatswain's mate stationed on the ship. "They blanketed our ship with three flights of fighter planes that crisscrossed the *Quincy* and protected us." Eventually the ship reached the island of Malta without any problems. When it arrived, the British ships in the harbor gave the president a twenty-one-gun salute. "Churchill and his daughter Sarah were at the dockside to meet Roosevelt and his daughter when they arrived. You couldn't see land or the buildings for the thousands of people who turned out to see Churchill. The people of Malta loved the prime minister," said Marinelli.[17]

From there, the two Allied leaders were whisked to the Soviet Union with their entourages by military plane for a weeklong conference from February 4 to 11, 1945. When the US Secret Service advance team arrived in Yalta, only three buildings were still standing. The retreating Germans had blown up everything of any size, and the only reason these buildings were spared was because they had been promised by Hitler to three of his generals.[18] The conference was convened in the Livadia Palace in Crimea. While Roosevelt was meeting in Yalta, USS *Quincy* sailed on through the Suez Canal. She dropped anchor in Great Bitter Lake, a large saltwater lake between the Suez Canal and the Red Sea. Although the sailors on *Quincy* didn't know it, the president would return aboard the ship a few days later for a series of meetings with the leaders of the oil-rich Middle East. The meetings were kept top secret, since only the ship's captain and a handful of officers on board knew their commander in chief would rejoin them.

President Roosevelt and Secretary of State Edward R. Stettinius wrapped up their conference at Yalta and proceeded by car to an airfield at Saki, USSR, on the morning of February 12, 1945.[19] It had been a grueling week, with six formal meetings and elaborate dinners with Winston Churchill, Joseph Stalin, and senior staff members from the three Allied powers, including Secretary Stettinius and Soviet foreign minister Vyacheslav Molotov. Their departure was given departing honors by the Soviet Guard and a military band as Roosevelt entered one of two US military planes at 11:40 a.m. for his final departure from the Soviet Union.

The planes took Roosevelt and his entourage to the US Army Air Force base located at Deversoir, Egypt, on the shores of Great Bitter Lake, seventeen miles south of Ismalia. Roosevelt was met by US minister S. Pickney Tuck and several foreign-service officers. One later recalled, "I was shocked by the President's appearance." He "looked frightful," with a sunken face, and appeared to be very ill.[20] Roosevelt and his party motored to the nearby Suez company boat landing, embarked in USS *Quincy*

King Farouk of Egypt and Franklin Roosevelt aboard USS *Quincy* in Great Bitter Lake, Egypt, February 13, 1945. *Franklin D. Roosevelt Presidential Library & Museum*

Emperor Haile Selassie of Ethiopia boards USS *Quincy* in the Great Bitter Lake, Egypt, with his staff to confer with President Roosevelt. He is escorted by Admiral Leahy. *Franklin D. Roosevelt Presidential Library & Museum*

tender boats, and transferred to USS *Quincy*, which was guarded by two Italian battleships. The president arrived on board at four o'clock in the afternoon. Upon his safe arrival, FDR dispatched a message to Joseph Stalin, thanking him for the USSR's hospitality during the Crimea Conference. He praised several officers, in particular, for their jobs well done and included many favorable comments he had received indicating the enormous success of the Crimea Conference.

The lavishly decorated deck of the destroyer USS *Murphy* during King Ibn Saud's trip to Egypt. February 14, 1945. *Franklin D. Roosevelt Presidential Library & Museum*

State Visits on USS *Quincy*

On February 13, King Farouk and his party arrived on board, escorted by Roosevelt's chief of staff, Adm. William D Leahy.[21] The the royal entourage was flown from Cairo to Deversoir in an Army Air Force plane and were met at the Suez company boat landing by Leahy.

The president was on deck to receive the king and his party. A USS *Quincy* crewman described his arrival: "Our entire crew was lined up along the railing in full dress uniform for hours while Roosevelt and the Middle Eastern heads of state were doing their thing on deck."[22] The two heads of state settled down to conversations shortly after Farouk's arrival on board. Roosevelt hosted a luncheon for the king in his quarters aboard the ship. Other guests were Minister Tuck, Harry L. Hopkins, Hussein Pasha, Adm. William D. Leahy, General Giles, and Mrs. John Boettiger. Their conversations continued after lunch. Roosevelt pointed out the purchase of large quantities of Egyptian cotton during the war by the US. He stressed hope for increased trade in other commodities with Egypt in the future, and the importance of a robust two-way trade agreement for the future of the two countries. Afterward, King Farouk and his party were taken on an inspection tour of the ship. Before leaving, Roosevelt presented him with a Douglas two-motored transport plane and an autographed copy of his (FDR's) inaugural address.[23]

At 5:30 p.m. that day, Haile Selassie, the emperor of Ethiopia, and his party arrived on board from Addis Ababa, Ethiopia. After the customary greetings, Roosevelt and the emperor sat down for a conversation about communications between the US and

Ethiopia. Ethiopia had recently gifted a land site and buildings in their country to the US for use as an American legation in the city of Addis Ababa. Roosevelt thanked him on behalf of the United States for the gift and told him he hoped the two countries would come to know each other better now that their communications had improved. Roosevelt liked him, and the feeling quickly became mutual. Following their meeting, Emperor Selassie and members of his diplomatic party were taken on an inspection tour of the ship, followed by a tea hosted by the president. Before leaving, Haile Selassie presented Roosevelt with a gold cigarette case and a gold-plated globe. The president gave the emperor four command and reconnaissance cars.[24] Tired from the long day, Roosevelt dined that evening with Capt. Elliot M. Senn and members of the ship's mess.

On the morning of February 14, USS *Murphy*, a destroyer, approached the port from the south. USS *Murphy* had been sent to Jidda, Saudi Arabia, a port on the Red Sea.[25] Its mission was to provide transportation for Saudi Arabian king Ibn Saud to Great Bitter Lake for a forthcoming conference with President Roosevelt. USS *Murphy* came alongside and moored to the port side of *Quincy*. The decks of the destroyer, usually bare, were covered with oriental rugs and gold-gilded chairs scattered around the decks. King Ibn Saud sat on one of these chairs, surrounded by his entourage of forty-eight as they approached USS *Quincy*.

The king came on board USS *Quincy*, limping badly, to call on President Roosevelt at 11:30 a.m. He was a huge man, well over seventy years of age and badly crippled. His vision was impaired by cataracts, but in his flowing black robes and red-and-black turban, with gold head ropes, he was an impressive foreign statesman. The two men exchanged greetings, after which they settled into their respective seats. The US minister to Saudi Arabia, Col. Bill Eddy, accompanied the king and acted as an interpreter. He knelt at the feet of Ibn Saud and Roosevelt as the president began their

King Ibn Saud and President Roosevelt confer aboard USS *Quincy*. The US president found the meeting difficult. *Franklin D. Roosevelt Presidential Library & Museum*

conversation. "As I flew over this vast desert I thought how marvelous it would be if we could irrigate it all and have it all green again as in biblical days." To which the king replied, "Yes, and if you send me any more God damned Jews, I'll murder them."[26] Roosevelt was stunned. Ibn Saud wasn't impressed at all by the power of USS *Quincy* as he came aboard. He took the military trappings in stride as he spoke his mind with the president. Shaking off the remark, Roosevelt tried to probe the king's willingness to allow displaced Jews from central Europe to settle in Palestine. When pressed, Ibn Saud replied, "What injury have the Arabs done to the Jews of Europe? It is the Christian Germans who stole their homes and lives. Let the Germans pay."[27] His solution to the resettlement of Jews was to let them have the choicest lands and homes in Germany. Their meeting did not get off to a good start. Shifting the conversation, they discussed a postwar alliance between the United States and Saudi Arabia. The Saudis recognized the need to find a new ally to replace the weakened Royal Navy of Great Britain, which had protected Saudi independence for decades. The Americans wanted to ensure a growing and reliable source of oil to fuel the postwar recovery of the world economy.[28]

Roosevelt hosted a luncheon for King Saud, Prince Abdullah, Prince Mohammed, Prince Mansour, Adm. William D. Leahy, Col. William A. Eddy, and Charles E. Bohlen. Kippy Tuck and General Guiles came on board to confer briefly with the president that afternoon, after which Roosevelt and King Saud continued their discussions. Although the two leaders never agreed on the Palestinian question, the US agreed to defend Saudi independence, and the Saudis agreed to be a reliable source of energy for the world. Ibn Saud gave Roosevelt two leather cases containing four complete Arabian wardrobes for himself, and two sets of Arabian harem attire for the first lady and their daughter. The president presented the king with a Douglas two-motor transport plane and his own wheelchair, which overjoyed Ibn Saud. The king's doctor was presented with a supply of penicillin. The king was greatly interested in the gift because of its success in treating venereal disease. That was a subject in which many of his entourage had a personal interest in.[29] Despite several misgivings on both sides, the agreement hammered out on USS *Quincy* remains largely in effect to this day.

King Saud had traveled more than 800 miles to meet President Roosevelt. It was the first time that he left his country. Although a cabin on USS *Murphy* was assigned to the king, awnings were rigged in tentlike style, and the king slept on the deck at night because he preferred to sleep outdoors. Some of the cultural observations by the crew of USS *Quincy* were eye opening. On one end of the destroyer, King Saud's slaves had a herd of his goats or sheep penned up. "They didn't eat anything but freshly killed meat. At 11:00 a.m. every day, a slave would take one of those animals and in two minutes he had it disemboweled. It was amazing how quickly he butchered it on the bow of the destroyer,"[30] said one of the crewman. "They put their tents up and their carpets down on the destroyer's deck. They built campfires on the deck of the destroyer. Every sailor aboard was carrying a fire extinguisher in case the fires in their tents got out of hand. They were lucky. They never did. Because we were representing the United States of America, you always had to be in full dress uniform when the president was on board. That meant you might be cleaning or sweeping on deck in your dress uniform."[31]

After the meetings wrapped up, a Suez Canal harbor pilot came on board USS *Quincy*. Before departing, Roosevelt turned to his ambassador to the UK, John "Gill" Winant, and said, "Gil, you ought to have been aboard yesterday; I had them all aboard." He said, "I've got one of them over there now on one of my destroyers."[32] It sounded impervious, but in his mind, they were his destroyers. He added, "I got nowhere with the big one [Ibn Saud]. I was a 100% failure with the big one. I rather liked the little one [Haile Selassie]."[33] When asked by reporters about King Saud's remarks regarding the resettlement of Jews, Roosevelt refused to even paraphrase it, only telling them "it was perfectly awful."[34] The ship embarked for Alexandria, Egypt, via the Suez Canal. USS *Quincy* passed through the antisubmarine net gate and into the Mediterranean for the long journey back to the United States, where Roosevelt died a few weeks later.

On February 20, 1945, a letter from the US minister to Egypt went out to Paul Springer:

Paul. L. Springer, Esquire American Legation, Cairo

Dear Mr. Springer, "I want to express to you my very sincere appreciation for the valuable cooperation which you gave in connection with the recent visits of President Roosevelt and the Secretary of State here. I am well aware that at considerable discomfort to yourself you have performed a very useful task during the past 10 days. I am grateful for the discretion you have displayed and I want you to know that you contributed not a little to these two important and successful visits."

Very sincerely yours,

S. Pickney Tuck

Following the presidential visit, business at the American legation returned to normal. During the last six months of his assignment in Cairo, Springer's duties embraced the entire range of consular work, including passports, visas, invoices, and routine reporting. Paul's previous legation experience in Chungking was paying off. Minister Tuck reported, "He has willingly assumed responsibility for a large amount of work and has shown himself to be conscientious, able and accurate. . . . He shows considerable initiative, is anxious to be helpful, and has displayed good judgement in handling consular problems. I have no hesitation in recommending his admission to the foreign service for which I think he is suited from the point of background, personality and ability."[35]

Springer continued his studies at the Egyptian American University during the spring. He studied Arabic and prepared for a written examination to enter the US Foreign Service. The school offered a fellowship group for Springer and other American students. These included excursions under the leadership of faculty and staff to historical sites in Cairo and surrounding areas.[36] There were informal social evenings in private homes, and supper dishes solicited by ladies of the program committee. Never wanting to miss a meal, Springer was glad to partake in a garden party, a backyard barbecue, a boat ride, or any number of social affairs that were offered.

He studied that spring and received a notice via a telegram on June 1, 1945, that he successfully passed the Foreign Service exam.[37] After three years in the State Department, Springer was eligible for home leave at the government's expense.[38] He left Cairo on June 4, 1945, and departed Egypt on June 10 through the Suez Canal.[39] After a nineteen-day trip across the Atlantic by boat, he arrived in the Port of Baltimore on June 30. His return to North America coincided with a thirty-day post assignment in the US consulate, housed on the second floor of the Canadian Bank of Commerce building on Front Street in Sarnia, Ontario.[40] Paul received the news of the Japanese surrender while he was stationed in this somewhat obscure American consulate in Canada.

The Japanese Surrender

On August 6, 1945, a US bomber named Enola Gay dropped an atomic bomb nicknamed "Little Boy" on the city of Hiroshima. The magnitude of the weapon and the destruction it caused, burning some 66,000 people to death, was still not enough to force the Japanese into surrender. President Truman promised a "rain of ruin from the air, the like of which has never been seen on this earth."[41] In the days following, the US Army Air Force dropped millions of printed propaganda leaflets revealing the nature of Hiroshima's destruction.[42] The leaflets predicted similar fates for more

Japanese cities in the absence of an acceptance of an unconditional surrender by the Japanese. By August 9, more than five million leaflets about the atomic bomb had been released over major Japanese cities as a warning that the bombings would continue unless Japan surrendered. Yet, the Japanese still refused to capitulate. On August 9, a second atomic bomb, "Fat Man," was to be dropped on Kokura, the site of one of Japan's largest munitions plants. When the navigator of the USAAF bomber "Bockscar" could not get a visual sighting of the target, the pilot directed the plane to a secondary target, the city of Nagasaki, killing another 40,000 people or more.

On August 14, at 10:50 a.m., Emperor Hirohito declared that it was time to "endure the unendurable and suffer the insufferable" in a prerecorded surrender statement to the Japanese people.[43]

Meanwhile, in Chungking, Generalissimo Chiang Kai-shek was meditating after his morning prayers and heard the recording of the Japanese broadcast over the radio. Within minutes, he headed to the radio station to make his own broadcast of victory at 10:00 a.m. "Our faith and justice through black and hopeless days and eight long years of struggle has today been rewarded," he declared.[44] On August 15, the Japanese government accepted the terms of the unconditional surrender of Japan. Chiang Kai-shek, the supreme commander of all Allied forces in China, then telegraphed instructions to Lt. Gen. Okamura Yasutsugu, the commander of Japanese forces in central China, to order the forces under his command to cease all military operations. General Okamura replied back, informing the Generalissimo of his acceptance and appointing his deputy chief of staff as his surrender envoy.[45]

The war of Japanese aggression against China, which escalated from a military skirmish in June 1937 near Peking into a horrific global conflict, had come to a sudden and abrupt ending. The war with Japan was fought for Chinese nationhood and sovereignty, a sort of continuance of the 1911 revolution, which had brought Sun Yat-sen to power.[46] World War II was finally over. China had paid a terrible price, with a loss estimated at fourteen million people. Chiang was looking for a reunification of the parties. After finishing his radio broadcast, he sent a cable to Mao Tse-tung, inviting him to come to Chungking for a dialogue. Mao replied that he would have Chou En-lai represent him in the talks, but Chiang insisted that Mao himself should make the journey. Mao stayed for six weeks in Chungking, and in their initial discussions, both sides made some show of compromise.

Both Chiang and Mao knew it was vital to maintain the appearance of a negotiated solution, but both were privately convinced that a civil war in China was inevitable.

Chapter 15

ON TO CHANGSHA!

Reclaiming the Yali Campus

In June 1944, the Japanese army had returned to Changsha and occupied the city until the end of the war.[1] With a formal Japanese surrender imminent, Dr. Winston Pettus was sent to Changsha in order to protect the Yale-in-China property during the turnover. He reached Changsha ahead of both the Chinese and American troops. "Getting in early is very important in order to protect property during the change-over and to occupy, if possible, before any buildings are commandeered," Dr. Pettus recalled. Getting there first was a challenge. Fortunately, he succeeded by securing a small plane and a pilot to reach the Yali campus in Changsha before the Chinese troops arrived.

The plane did not have dual controls, so it wasn't possible for Pettus to do any of the flying. Hence he became the navigator, setting the course, identifying landmarks, and keeping track of their location. The plane's gas tanks were inadequate for the round trip, so they carried aboard extra fuel in cans and were able to get additional gas at a field en route. The most difficult part of the flight was over the mountain range (5,000–6,000 feet) to Wenhwa, where the clouds were right down on the mountains, leaving very little room underneath. They were not equipped to fly on instruments over the clouds, so they kept just out of Japanese-held territory by flying north of Siangsiang and Shihtan, then west of Siangtan, then north to a point west of Changsha. From there, they followed the highway westward to Ningsiang, looking for a place to land. There were several places where they could have landed, but they were hampered by a strong crosswind, making an attempted landing too hazardous.

About three or four miles west of Changsha, Pettus and the pilot saw a large detachment of Chinese soldiers moving east. They dove down close to them and confirmed they were Chinese. With Chinese troops that close, it seemed unlikely there would be any Japanese on that side (west) of the Hsiang River. They were running low on fuel and needed to gas up, so they landed in a pasture on the riverbank a little south of Yoloshan. A few minutes after landing, some Chinese approached who said that they were guerrillas and that there were Japanese troops nearby at the base of Yoloshan. One asked Pettus in a confidential tone if he had brought any message from the Generalissimo. As they were preparing to transfer some gas from the cans into the fuel tanks, word came that some Japanese would be on the spot in a few minutes. Although not anxious to get captured, their belongings were already out of the plane and they were planning to stay. The pilot (a sergeant) asked Pettus what to do—remain on the ground, gas up, and talk with the chaps, or jump in, take off, and find a sandbar upriver to land on and refuel. Pettus asked, "You know the Japs better than I do. What do you think I'd better do?"[2]

Without thinking, Pettus pushed the pilot into the plane, threw the gas cans in behind him, and urged him to get going. Pettus recalled, "I was not afraid of anything they would do to him, but we are not supposed to be that close to the Japanese, there was a slight possibility of their holding the plane temporarily, and finally they might make me get in and fly back with him. So all in all it was better to get him and the plane out. He took off just as the Japanese were approaching the plane 3 or 4 yards away."[3]

Returning to Changsha

Dr. Winston Pettus hoped to get into Changsha within a few hours of the Japanese departure, and—if possible—before the Chinese troops occupied the city. No one knew when that would be. The day he arrived, September 4, 1945, was two days after the peace signing aboard USS *Missouri* in Tokyo Bay, but before a separate peace signing for the China theater of the war took place in Nanking.

Following that second formal surrender in Nanking on September 9, General Okamura, the Japanese commander, was handed a supplement to the Act of Surrender.[4] Japanese troops in China were ordered to surrender only to the forces under the command of Generalissimo Chiang Kai-shek. There were over a million Japanese troops still in China, and over half a million Japanese civilians. The China theater was divided into sixteen areas (including Formosa), and the commanders in those areas were empowered to receive the Japanese surrender and disarm Japanese troops. It was a slow but methodical process. Even after the formal surrender, the Japanese were asked to retain responsibility for maintaining public order in places such as Nanking, Shanghai, and Hong Kong. Much of the Japanese army remained in China for the better part of a year after the surrender. Most of its troops were fully armed and frequently remained in charge of rail zones, cities, and even many towns in northern China.[5] In Hunan Province,

Aerial view of Changsha, 1945. Note the bombed-out sections to the right of the road. Dr. Pettus was the first American to arrive on the scene to reclaim the Yali campus. *Yale-China Association Records, RU 232, Manuscripts and Archives, Yale University Library*

although the Japanese knew the war was over, they had not yet surrendered. This state of purgatory created a vexing situation for Pettus as he attempted to reclaim the Yali campus from the Japanese who still occupied it.

Upon his arrival in the area, Pettus was promptly captured by a Japanese officer who was riding a horse. The officer had arrived on the scene undetected, before the rest of the Japanese troops. Pettus was his sole American prisoner. Oddly enough, the officer who captured him was a medic—actually a veterinarian. At first, Pettus resented being captured by a veterinarian, until he recalled that in Changsha, he had once operated on a Chinese general's horse.

Once in Japanese custody, Pettus acted as though his capture was intentional, as if he had turned himself in. He thought it possible that he might get to stay on the Yali campus and be there when the Japanese were ordered to pull out. He told his captor he had returned to evaluate the condition of the buildings, make plans for reopening the hospital, and protect the Yale property during the changeover. All of this was true. Pettus requested a room on the Yali campus to stay in until the Japanese left, and asked for a couple of guards to take him across the river into the city to see the Japanese headquarters. His captor told him his orders prevented that, but that he would report his request for him. He added that he would not prevent Pettus from going by himself should he wish to take a chance. Pettus started to go, but his Chinese friends wisely pleaded with him not to risk it. Curiously, he had not been asked to show any papers of identification, and none of his baggage had been inspected. This was fortunate, since he was carrying large amounts of Chinese money in cash. His identity in Changsha was well known, and he was easily identified by the way people on the street greeted him by name.

On Thursday, September 6, Pettus saw the first Chinese soldiers entering Changsha. He took a picture of them crossing in from Yoloshan.[6] On Friday morning, he learned that the Japanese military police (MPs) had left Yoloshan during the night. There were still some Japanese troops around, but not many. He decided to cross over into the city and get as close to the Yali campus as possible. The armed Japanese soldiers just stood around and watched him come in. Pettus described the scene:

> The situation here now is absolutely cock-eyed. Both Chinese and Japanese soldiers (armed) are in the city. Some guard one street, some another; but neither one stops anyone except at entrances to military headquarters. Both have headquarters. South of Chung Shan Ma Lu is supposed to be Chinese and north of it is Japanese until tomorrow, but I can't see any difference between the two sections. There are thousands of Japs camped inside and outside the buildings in the North and East suburbs. These are in process of moving out. There is a single track railroad to Hankow but almost no locomotives. They use trucks, without tires, to push several small flat cars each. It takes three days to Hankow, 100 miles. Contrary to the treaty, Japs have been destroying property, both military and otherwise. They are also moving furniture and woodwork from houses they occupy, to burn or sell. Chinese civilians have been for months doing likewise so that many buildings are without any wood.[7]

The Yali Campus

Pettus found it possible to go right into the campus and walk around, even though the Japanese were still there. So much of the walls were gone that there were dozens of entrances. As he and a companion walked past their bungalow, there was a gunshot nearby, but nothing happened, so they kept going. Pettus noticed that a friend's house was largely torn apart since he last saw it. The rest of the residences looked good from the outside, although a few doors and windows were missing. Only a little furniture, including twenty-seven iron hospital beds, were left in the houses. Nearly all doors and windows of the hospital were gone, but most of the window frames remained. There were trucks all over the campus, with men camped inside and outside.

Pettus called on a Japanese officer, a captain in charge of the campus, to ask if he could inspect the interiors and start rebuilding the wall. The captain told him "not before they left," which would be about ten days or more, without an order from his headquarters.[8] Pettus could not have access to the campus because the Japanese had ordered him to stay out of the city. Another officer promised to stop removing Yale-in-China property, but the practice continued through the night. Preserving the facilities and rebuilding the hospital had become Pettus's highest calling.

Nearly all the missions in town had sent delegates asking Pettus to help protect their property from the Japanese, Chinese civilians, and the Chinese army. Pettus found a room in Mr. Tyng's house at the Episcopal mission. It was the closest he could get to Yali for the time being. As the only missionary or foreign civilian in town, he conferred with the (Chinese) chief of police and the (Chinese) garrison commander about putting protective notices on all mission properties, but he wasn't sure that that would do them any good.

The Americans Arrive

During the week ending September 17, 1945, the first American convoy arrived with ten vehicles. By the next day there were twenty-nine more. One was a large group attached to the Chinese 18th Army, headed by Colonel Lake. It took them five days to drive the 390 miles from Chihkiang. The road didn't go all the way through, and they had to build many of their own bridges as they came in.

Arriving with the convoy was a unique character whom Pettus called Colonel "Q." He was a full colonel and a West Point graduate. He was in command of another American group attached to the Chinese army, but there was nothing of military importance happening where they came from. So, Colonel Q decided to go to Changsha to pick up some souvenirs. Out of curiosity, he went along with several 18th Army officers to inspect the Yali campus. When he saw the Japanese living in American houses, and observed the destruction that had been wrought by the enemy, he was infuriated. Colonel Q assumed the prerogative of his rank, took command, ordered all the Japanese officers into one room, and started pushing them around and talking to them very roughly. Accompanying him was an American lieutenant who could speak Japanese. The lieutenant informed them that he represented the US government, that they had no business on American property, that they had acted disgracefully, and that they would leave the premises immediately. The Japanese replied that they could not leave without orders from their superiors and that he should deal with a higher-ranking officer. Finally, the lieutenant approached the commanding Japanese general, in turn, who put the matter in the hands of his chief of staff. The Japanese replied that the proper channel was with the Chinese commander, General Lu. Colonel Q stated that this was about American property and did not concern the Chinese. The Japanese general replied that General Lu was in command of all Allied troops in the area, which was true.

Pettus pulled Colonel Q aside and told him, "I had approached General Lu the day before about getting the Japs off the campus and that he had agreed to help."[9] The colonel then told the Japanese, "General Lu has been informed of this atrocious situation. He fully approves. There is no need to consult him further. You will follow out my orders in this matter. It is now twelve o'clock. By 2 p.m. all Japanese will be out of all American property in Changsha; they will clean up as they leave. All furniture will be left in place. I will make an inspection tour with you at 2 p.m. to see that this is carried out."[10] After these instructions, Pettus marked all American property on the city map, and the US Army officers agreed to see that it was done. Their inspection on the following day proved otherwise.

Pettus described the scene at Hsiang-Ya Hospital:

When we made the tour, the evacuation was not complete from the hospital. The hospital was one terrific mess. It had been used for transient troops, because it is so close to the North railway station. No one had ever bothered to clean up for months. It was filled with ashes, rags, feces, and filth. Fires had been built on the floors. It was simply unbelievable. Colonel Q hit the ceiling. He preached three or four sermons to the poor Japanese lieutenant (who spoke excellent English), called such indecency a crime against humanity which ranked among the savages any army guilty of it, etc., etc. He ordered that all Japs, including one lying dead on the floor, be removed immediately and that starting the next day, 200 Japanese soldiers be detailed to go there daily to clean up until some semblance of order was gained. They would come unarmed. Another 150 would clean up the Yali campus. It was a grand bluff, but the Japs fell for it, and Yale-in-China profited immeasurably. The work done by the Japanese on our property saved us several weeks of hard labor. For three days thereafter Colonel Q made personal inspection tours to supervise the clean-up. When I expressed our deep appreciation for his work, he said that he had gotten a bigger kick out of it than anything else he had done in China.[11]

Pettus observed: "He had the opportunity which most military men must dream of—the chance to dictate as a conqueror. He certainly had the Japs licking his boots—but very few other men could have accomplished it. So far as I was personally concerned, I was not quite sure what the attitude of the Japanese on the campus toward me was. It was perfectly obvious that I was giving the colonel the information on which he was acting, and that I was reporting what I had seen during the previous week. True, I had warned them two days before that the American Army was coming. But if they had been able to foresee what happened when Colonel Q went to work, some of them would have favored shooting me as a spy."[12]

Unofficial Billeting Officer

Two more large Army groups arrived days later. One was the Liaison Group, which was attached to the Chinese 18th Army, headed by Colonel Lake, and the other was the CCC Eastern Command, attached to the Chinese High Command, headed by General King. Both were initially quartered in buildings furnished by the Chinese near their headquarters, but neither commander was satisfied. Pettus lobbied Colonel Lake three times in twenty-four hours to take a look at the Yali campus, but he was not interested, thinking it was too far away. It was only when several of his officers urged him to take a closer look that he changed his mind. Pettus was no fool. What better way to protect the abandoned campus from Chinese squatters than to house American troops in the vacated buildings? Although General King had not yet arrived in Changsha, within an hour after Colonel Lake occupied the campus the general's representatives also wanted the place. Pettus took them over to the Presbyterian mission and offered them the use of it. Pettus justified this as follows: "My authority for dealing out other people's property in this manner was that the local Chinese church members had asked me to protect their property, and it was greatly to their advantage to have American troops in occupation. So it seems I have fallen into the job of unofficial billeting officer for US forces in Changsha."[13]

Japanese Surrender in Hunan

On the morning of October 14, 1945, the first big plane landed at Changsha, bringing Gen. Wang Yaowu (China) and General King (US) to receive the Japanese surrender of all troops in Hunan and start the process of disarming them. There was a big welcoming party, which included the Japanese generals, held at the airfield. The surrender date was pushed forward several days because General King said that he would not permit the Americans to remain in Changsha unless the Japanese had signed the surrender.

Pettus went to see Gen. Hu Lien, commander of the 18th Army, about protecting the Changsha Union Hospital buildings. During the discussions, General Hu invited Pettus to attend the surrender ceremony, provided that he could attend in some official capacity. Knowing that Pettus had a camera, General Hu appointed him as a press reporter and said that he could take pictures, representing the "Great American Public." Pettus, the only civilian in attendance, described the affair: "The ceremony itself was held in the Hunan University buildings at Yoloshan, at noon. It was very simple and dignified, with about thirty American and sixty Chinese officers attending. The room, which was not large, was nicely decorated with United Nations flags and pictures of the leaders. The Japanese generals and staff entered, listened to the terms of the surrender, signed the document, presented it to General Wang and were led out. They did not wear samurai swords. Their facial expressions were remarkable. They were solemn and dignified, but you could see that they were going through a terrific ordeal—surrendering to an army which had not beaten them."[14]

Rebuilding Yale-in-China

Brank Fulton, now the field director of Yale-in-China, and his party brought a CNC $2,000,000 cash infusion to restore the Changsha campus.[15] The cash was needed to hire contractors, pay workers, obtain food and supplies, and begin the rebuilding process. It was a start, but they needed much, much more to bring the hospital up to standard. The rebuilding of the Yali and Hsiang-Ya campus walls was costing nearly CNC $1,500,000. Because prices continued to rise, by getting the cash to Changsha quickly it was thought it would save millions of dollars in the long run.

After Pettus started repairs on the property, other members of the staff arrived to take over. Dr. H. C. Chang, the director of Yale's medical work, decided that Pettus's most valuable contribution at the time was touring the country, keeping the various Hsiang-Ya units in touch with each other, getting help for the Changsha reconstruction effort, and scavenging for as many medical supplies as possible. The scavenging of medical supplies became an exciting adventure as the American army posts were abandoned. "Medical supplies," Pettus wrote, "are divided into two categories, expendable and unexpendable. The former includes drugs, dressings, etc. and does not have to be accounted for. Rather than turn these back into the army storehouses, now that the war is over and everyone is going home, all the medical officers I have met prefer to see them used to help mission hospitals where they know they will meet an urgent need. Non-expendables, such as instruments, x-ray machines, etc., have to be accounted for and turned in. In playing this army game you have got to be on the spot at the exact time that a unit is closing up, and you have got to have your transportation to take it away. There is a terrible amount of stealing after and before people pull out."[16] Among other things, Pettus found six large Army tents that were given to him if he would pull them down and move them away. Yali had been thinking in terms of using tents for their students in Changsha, since the dormitories and class rooms had been completely destroyed.

Road Trip via Army Surplus

Transportation was the ever-present problem, so it was logical to try to obtain surplus Army vehicles. Pettus wrote: "We have been trying through various channels to secure several American Army vehicles to use permanently for the hospital. But there has been no way whereby this was possible. The US Army has been turning over its vehicles to the Chinese army. They don't have enough drivers to use them all. So today I went to the American major who was turning over vehicles and acted as his interpreter. After turning them over, he stated that our hospital needed a truck and an ambulance very much [and] that it would please him personally if the Chinese army would see fit to give us one of each. The request was, of course, unofficial, but it was the psychologically perfect time to make it since they were deeply obligated to him. So they gave us a "six-by" (truck) and an ambulance! And we won't have to beg for transportation any longer. For that matter, there won't be any after tomorrow that we can beg, because the last convoy will leave tomorrow morning."[17]

On one occasion while in Chihkiang, Pettus was asked by a China Combat Command officer to drive his jeep to Changsha, where the Eastern command headquarters were.

Ken Moreland in a recently acquired army surplus jeep. Moreland accompanied Pettus on a literal scavenger hunt to resupply Yale-in-China with surplus military supplies. *Yale-China Association Records, RU 232, Manuscripts and Archives, Yale University Library.*

The officer was leaving for the US and would not need it anymore. By mistake, it had been turned in, but the ordinance officer reissued it to Pettus for temporary use. In addition, they gave him a trailer so that he could take a substantial load of medical supplies to Changsha. On the way, Pettus took a side trip to Yuanling to discuss some important issues with Hsiang-Ya and Yali leaders. Among other things, he told them about the large Army tents that had been given to him, and he needed help taking them down and moving them away. It was good news. Ken Moreland went back to Chihkiang with him to get the tents and take them to Yuanling. Outside of a broken spring and two simultaneous flat tires, the trip was uneventful.

Upon returning to Chihkiang, they were told that the medical supply depot had set aside a "few things" for them. They were thrilled to learn that the "few things" included five or six tons of drugs and dressing material for the hospital! In addition, the US Army was selling slightly used equipment at salvage prices. This included sheets and wool blankets at very low prices. Fortunately, Pettus had a suitcase with a large amount of Chinese money in cash with him. He and Ken Moreland drove around to various Army units (there were more than ten units, spread out over about fifteen miles), picking up other material that was being discarded, including clothing, rations, and athletic equipment. Because the Army wanted to get rid of these items, they considered themselves doing them a favor and relieving them of the bother, knowing that the surplus materials would go to a good cause.[18] Once they loaded up the supplies, they transferred them to the newly acquired Army surplus truck.

Driving the newly donated 6 × 6 giant Army truck was a new experience for Pettus, having driven jeeps and trucks burning alcohol and other improvised fuels. The truck was a lifesaver for transporting medical goods back to the hospital in Changsha. Leaving Chihkiang one night with a heavy load, Pettus and Moreland decided to try their hand at truck driving. Neither of them had ever driven a "six-by," especially not on a 400-mile trip over a rotten road with no repair facilities along the way. This was not a bright prospect. If successful, they could deliver between $25 and $50 million (Mex) worth of equipment and supplies to further the Yali mission. It took them three days to make the 400-mile trip from the air base at Chihkiang to Changsha. The truck was powerful enough to pull 6½ tons of supplies both on truck and trailer over the high mountains along the route. On one mountain the curves were so sharp that they had to stop and back up to get a big truck around them. At a ferry crossing, they ran into an Army Air Force convoy en route to Hankow. Dr. Pettus was asked to treat a driver who had been slightly injured when his truck had been forced off the road by a reckless driver, a road hog. The truck had gone over a cliff, but he had jumped clear in time to save himself. By the end of the trip, the surgeon and the Bachelor had learned a lot about driving the "six-bys." They were so exhausted on the first night that they slept without budging for a full nine hours. Their host was his old friend, Colonel Q, whose generosity was unending. About to pack up and depart the next day, he took Pettus and Moreland into his storeroom of stateside food and stores and told them to take whatever they wanted. Already "loaded to the gills," they were still able to load up a few boxes of food. The road trip from Siangtan was terrific, with their truck passing through places where the road was destroyed (to prevent the Japanese advance) not having been filled in but merely rounded off, almost like a continuous rollercoaster ride through the countryside.

In one place, they were passing a group of Chinese troops who occupied most of the road, and turned the truck over. Fortunately, there was no damage. The soldiers helped them unload the trailer, turn it right side up, and reload their cargo. En route, they had four flat tires, which was not uncommon, considering the heavy loads they were carrying and the poor condition of the road. Fortunately they had four spare tires with them, so they did not have to patch any tires—just change them with a fresh one. Upon their arrival in Changsha, the supplies were unloaded and distributed accordingly. This was followed by a nice surprise. While they were gone, Jim Elliott of the Office of War Information had been in Changsha the preceding week and delivered an electric generator.[19] It was promptly hooked up by some Army electricians and provided electricity and proper lighting in all of the Yali residences, but not in the hospital. Progress was being made. The hospital power plant was being repaired, and they were expecting to have running water in the hospital within another week or two.

Red Tape

Ground travel was slow, although inevitable. Surplus trucks were one thing, but buying a surplus Army airplane was full of red tape. Pettus traveled to Chungking, expecting to find the L-5 deal completed, and being able to fly one of the planes back to Changsha. While there, he went out to the Peihsiyi airfield to see if the planes were still there.[20] He found that all the L-5s had been sent away, except the two that were set aside to be turned over to Yali. The base commander had orders to keep them until Pettus called for them after their purchase. The base commander wanted to complete the sale quickly to get the planes off his hands, and suggested that Pettus travel to Shanghai and track down the papers declaring the two small airplanes as surplus. The commander arranged for Pettus to get a ride on one of the 14th Air Force's planes the following day. Air travel to Shanghai carried a great premium, but he was allowed to go on a cargo plane since he was officially flying on Air Force business. Not sure where he would stay, Pettus ended up being quartered with the Air Force headquarters officers in Shanghai's newest skyscraper hotel—the Broadway Mansions.

The young doctor recalled the step into luxury: "After living in wartime free China, to be suddenly thrown into this place, with fast-moving elevators, private bath and shower, running hot and cold water, private phone, indirect lighting, etc., is quite a shock. During the dinner hour we are entertained by two grand pianos, playing superbly. It seems like a dream." It was a long process, but his military hosts were accommodating. The colonel who spearheaded the sale of the two planes to Yali acted as a courier, taking the papers from office to office and department to department. He walked them through the 14th Air Force, the Air Service Command, and the Army Air Force headquarters to the theater headquarters. At each place the papers had to be checked in and out by several people in the adjutant general's office before the proper person could even see them and start to act. Their efforts got the sale approved by three generals and quite a few colonels and stamped by innumerable clerks. Once approved, the papers were sent to Chungking by courier, where the base commander could turn them over for use by Hsiang-Ya Hospital. It took months of effort and numerous trips to secure the planes. Pettus recalled that the matter of their sale "would have died a natural death if I had not come to Shanghai, so I think it has been a worthwhile trip—as well as a nice vacation."[21]

The planes were put in perfect condition by the Army, and extra parts and fuel were generously thrown in with the purchase. Pettus was the driving force behind these acquisitions to equip Hsiang-Ya Hospital for their medical mission in southwestern China. Once the planes were handed over, he spent two weeks in training at the American Army Flying Headquarters in Chihkiang, learning how to take off and land in the L-5 and also a great deal about the technical aspects of the plane. Pettus continued to fly on Yali business and used the recently acquired planes to improve communications and transportation throughout the region. He loved flying and took to this newest passion in aviation to serve the Yale-in-China mission with enthusiasm and skill upon his return to China.

On November 18, 1945, Pettus was flying one of these planes from Chungking to his home in Changsha, crossing the most treacherous flying area in China—Kweichow Province. During the flight, he became lost in the heavy fog shrouding the high mountains. With no visibility, his plane crashed against a rigid mountain peak in an isolated section of the province. Pettus was found dead the next day in the twisted and wrecked plane by local peasants.

Herman L. Armstrong, an American pilot, received word of the crash on November 20 while at Laowhangpin, Kweichow.[22] Being the only representative of the US Army in the area, he accompanied the Chinese authorities to investigate. The airplane was a civilian Stinson L-5, now a twisted mass of metal. Inside the wreckage they found the remains of the pilot. His death was almost certainly instantaneous. Although no personal effects were found on the body, such as a watch or wallet, one of the Chinese peasants handed Armstrong a passport, confirming the dead pilot's identification as Dr. William Winston Pettus. On November 22, Armstrong telephoned the Chihkiang Army Air Base to inform them of the crash.[23]

On the same day, the telegraphed word arrived at Yali that a small plane had crashed somewhere in eastern Kweichow, with a question as to whether Pettus had ever reached Changsha. Brank Fulton recalled: "Our fears were of course aroused, but we still hoped for the best, as it seemed impossible that Win would not join us again. But two days later came the shattering announcement that he had definitely been killed in an accident and the plane which he was piloting—apparently the very bad flying weather was too much even for him."[24]

The announcement that Fulton was referring to was the following cablegram from Chungking, China, received in New Haven on November 23, 1945:

> Doctor Pettus killed in airplane accident at Huangping, Kweichow. Immediately sending man to the scene. Have wired Fulton. Please cable instructions regarding burial. Please inform family our condolence. H. C. Chang, Dean.[25]

Dr. K. S. Lou, one of Pettus's medical colleagues in Changsha, took it upon himself to retrieve his friend's body from the crash site. A Friends Ambulance Unit (FAU) truck helped him get there. Huangping was a small city, one day's drive from Kweiyang, the provincial capital. It was surrounded by high mountains and was known as a mountain city. Surprisingly, there was no fire, since the wrecked plane did not get burned at all. Some of his personal items were recovered near the crash site, including his passport and a long, unfinished letter to his wife. "We seemed to have found everything of his except the large sum of money he was taking back to Changsha, which was to be used for the reconstruction of our Medical College," recalled Dr. Lu.[26]

The tragic news of Win Pettus's untimely death was a shock to his colleagues, students, and friends in China and the United States. They knew how greatly they had counted on him and his continuing presence and cooperation. And they knew that their loss, far too great to be expressed in words, was absolutely irreparable, not only from the standpoint of personal relationships but from that of the work to which he had given himself so generously and effectively. Win Pettus's spirit of selflessness and unstinted sacrifice for the welfare of others will forever remain as an inspiration to the Hunan-Yale staff and students.[27] His body lies buried behind the Yali chapel near his beloved Hsiang-Ya Hospital in Changsha, China.

EPILOGUE

Following the end of the war and Japanese occupation, Yale-in-China began a massive rebuilding operation of the Changsha campus. Brank Fulton stepped in as a committed and capable administrator. Some of the buildings in Changsha were merely shells of their former structures, so the students had their classes crowded in offices and treatment rooms. Paper was pasted across the windows, and boards and boxes served as tables and chairs.[1]

For all their jubilation at the end of the war and their shared determination to move on, it was clear that the war had once again left China dangerously unstable. "Anyone who comes from present-day China without a vivid awareness of the desperately serious problems in every area of the nation's life would indeed be blind," Brank Fulton told the Yale-in-China trustees in a 1946 letter from Wuhan.[2] "We all know what they are—political strife extending to military combat, graft and corruption in high places, serious inflation and tragic famine, together with vast physical destruction and major population dislocation, as products of long years of war."[3]

Dwight Rugh, who had long been responsible for religious education at the Yali Middle School, returned to Changsha in 1945. He felt that his work was needed more than ever during this uncertain period. Students were eager to return to their studies regardless of the conditions. No sooner was the rebuilding process underway than the short-lived peace in central China was threatened by a full-scale civil war.

The Communists began to consolidate their power in northeastern China within months of the end of World War II. They first attempted to secure the whole region but clashed with some of the Nationalist troops being flown back into the region with American help. During the first six months of 1946, American attempts to achieve a political breakthrough were undermined by the escalation of fighting both by the Nationalist and Communist Chinese. By the summer of 1946, the Communists were firmly entrenched in the Northeast. Chiang Kai-shek continued to demand that the Communists give up their arms, believing that they were weak and unable to defend themselves, while the Communists insisted that the Nationalist troops must give up the advances they had made during the course of 1946.[4]

The actions of the Nationalists hardly reassured the Chinese people that their fate was in safe hands. Their economy was in a perilous situation at the end of the war with Japan, but not so much that it could not have recovered.[5] Yale-in-China was no exception. The rebuilding of the Changsha campus had already begun. By 1947, inflation, which had badly sapped the purchasing power of the people during the last years of the war, ran out of control. The Kuomintang lost much of the goodwill of the victory over Japan by its arbitrary and corrupt actions, regularly expropriating property and acting with arrogance within the territories it had reconquered. Although the Nationalists had made political progress in the immediate postwar period, much of it was in the international arena rather than with the Chinese population.

The civil war ground on in China during the remainder of 1947. The Communist military campaign in North China drove the Nationalists farther and farther back. Col. David Barrett described the People's Liberation Army (PLA) as "one of the toughest and most politically indoctrinated forces the world has ever seen.[6] While most major cities were under Nationalist control, as were the rail lines, much of the territory was now under Communist influence. It echoed the situation under Japan just a few years before. By November 1948, the CCP had consolidated power in the North, and their army was moving south. The US advised American citizens in China to consider leaving before transportation channels were disrupted. By Thanksgiving, several members of Yale-in-China's American staff left Changsha on a plane provided by the American consulate. Dwight Rugh chose to remain in China, as did Brank and Ann Fulton, Yale-in-China's representatives at Hua Chung College. Ying Kai-sheh was concerned that if the Communists should get control of China, "there might be no place for American or Christian work in the country."[7] His concerns were shared by many of the Chinese staff, who watched with alarm as the Communists grew in strength. Even so, the American staff in China remained cautiously optimistic about the future. Many of those who evacuated to Shanghai in November soon returned to Changsha to resume their work.[8]

During the first few months of 1949, tension gripped central China as the Communist and Nationalist armies regrouped on opposite sides of the Yangtze River. When the Nationalists refused to surrender in April, the Communist army launched an all-out military campaign to victory. The Nationalist rejection of the Communist proposals brought a rapid change to the political atmosphere, as well as new developments to Yali. A Changsha student association was formed, and all educational institutions were forced to join. The group dictated what shall and what shall not be done, teaching propaganda songs and dances that were full of slogans directed against the UN, America, Westerners, and imperialism. The Chinese staff at Yali unanimously agreed that the school administrators and teachers could do nothing to prevent it. They could only preach moderation.

Chinese administrators at Yali and Hsiang-Ya were under increasing pressure and struggled to negotiate the political forces buffeting their schools. The people in the vicinity of the Changsha campus still regarded Yali as a place of safety. Several teachers who lived outside the campus were moving their families inside. Many people were asking to come to the campus for shelter, which for practical reasons was refused. On August 26, C. C. Lao wrote a hasty letter to Yale-in-China's longtime secretary, Rachel Dowd. "This is probably my farewell letter to you. The Communists are approaching Changsha from the east, north, and also from the west. The only way open now is to the south by railway, but it is reported that they are going to cut off the railway at Hengyang. Also the airline is irregularly open. Those who can afford to have all left Changsha and the now remaining are mostly poor people," wrote Lao.[9]

On October 1, 1949, the People's Republic of China was declared, its capital once more in Peking. The changing relationship between American teachers and the Chinese students and colleagues was shaped by political forces beyond their control. As the new government consolidated power, major changes were introduced, beginning with a massive propaganda campaign, pursued in part through committees and study groups to teach the concepts of communism. Students were the primary target of this campaign, including all the Yali campuses. They were urged to participate in student unions and other political activities, which many remembered as a heady time for young people caught up in the spirit of the revolution.

With the entrance of the US into the Korean War in the summer of 1950, anti-American rhetoric, which had been stoked by continued American support for the Nationalist Chinese, rose to a fever pitch. The US was now considered an enemy of China, and most Americans were ordered to leave the country. All of the American staff were withdrawn, until only Dwight Rugh was left. He asked the Chinese government for permission to leave, but the request was denied.

Rugh was the last American staff member at Yale-in-China. In November 1950, his home was searched by soldiers, who discovered a collection of antiques as well as a short-wave radio that could potentially be used to transmit messages. He was placed under house arrest for six months and accused of trying to steal cultural treasures and of using the radio to spy for the Americans. Although he was granted permission to leave the country, the Communists determined that Rugh was to be publicly chastised and humiliated at a large gathering in the Yali gymnasium in 1951. This was the building for which he had recently secured funds from Yale-in-China to build, and he was seeing it for the first time. Faculty and students from the schools were invited to speak about how Rugh had "oppressed the Chinese people."[10]

There was a lot of anger in the room, since the anti-American sentiment was aroused by the US involvement in the Korean War. The most dramatic moment came when C. C. Lao took an ax to the Yali signboard, cutting it in two. The crowd roared its approval with a loud chorus of anti-American slogans. It was announced that the school was changing its name to "Liberation Middle School," meaning that the school had been liberated from American imperialist control.[11] Dr. Rugh was then led away to a train station, accompanied by two armed soldiers, with a suitcase in one hand and a furled umbrella of oiled paper and bamboo in the other.

The next few days were grim. When he arrived at Canton at two o'clock the next morning, he expected to be put on the first train to Hong Kong. Instead he was arrested and taken to a prison, where his suitcase was confiscated. He was put in a room that was so crowded with other men there was not enough room for all of them to lie down. Every now and then a guard would remove a prisoner. On the third day the guards came for him. They tied his hands behind his back and took him to the prison courtyard, where they pushed him to his knees and put a gun to his head. Seconds passed. He felt the presence of Jesus right next to him . . . he felt very peaceful and told himself, "Whatever happened, it would be all right."[12] The gun was quickly withdrawn and Rugh was jerked to his feet. The guards untied his hands, gave him a suitcase, and put him on a train for Hong Kong under the guard of two young soldiers carrying rifles.

It was a blazing-hot day. When they reached the border, there was a long line of people waiting in the sun to be processed through a gate to the British colony of Hong Kong. On China's side of the gate, an official was inspecting the papers and baggage of people going into Hong Kong. As Rugh got closer, he recognized the Chinese border guard as one of his former students. They knew each other well. The guard didn't give any sign of it, and neither did Rugh. He just looked at Rugh's passport and gave it back to him without changing his expression. Then he put Rugh's suitcase on a table and told him to open it. And there, sitting on the top of his clothes, was a two-way radio. It was a trap. Rugh thought to himself, "They must have put it there while I was in prison."[13] The guard just looked at it calmly, closed the lid, and handed him the suitcase. The guard didn't say anything, and neither did he. Rugh walked through the gate and into the safety of British-controlled Hong Kong.

Ken Moreland left China in 1946 and returned to New Haven, where he took up duties as the new executive secretary of Yale-in-China. He kept in touch with some of his favorite former students via letter, but once the Peoples Republic of China was established in 1949, he was asked by the students not to write anymore, since any letter they received from America would get them into trouble. This created a gap of twenty-five years in which he heard nothing from the students and learned nothing about them. It was not until a liberalization of the Communist Chinese party in the late 1970s by Deng Xiao-ping (following the death of Mao) that Moreland started hearing from his former students again.[14] Moreland later served as a professor and chair of the Department of Sociology and Anthropology at Randolph-Macon Women's College in Lynchburg, Virginia.[15]

Jim Elliott served in the Office of War Information until the end of the war. His experience in China grew into a lifelong attraction to Asia. He joined the US State Department in Washington and Japan until the US Information Agency (USIA) was created in 1953. Elliott served the USIA in Washington, DC, for eight years and overseas for twenty-two years in China, Japan, Indonesia, Malaysia, and Singapore. He spoke fluent Mandarin Chinese and Japanese. On one assignment, Elliott headed the Chinese branch of the *Voice of America* (VOA) radio program.[16] One of the most widely used forms of media at the onset of the Cold War was the radio. This began as an unbiased and balanced "Voice from America" as originally broadcast during World War II. In 1953, the program was authorized by Congress and was used to spread American propaganda behind the Iron Curtain and to "tell America's stories" to information-deprived listeners in Communist-controlled countries.[17] In retirement he became interested and active in Elderhostel, Inc., spending study weeks at educational institutions, primarily colleges and universities, in all parts of the US and a few countries overseas.[18]

Art Hopkins attended graduate school after the war and taught as an assistant instructor at the University of Pennsylvania from 1946 to 1947. His teaching experience at Yale-in-China and his military service with the 14th Air Force attracted him to a career in public service. He joined the US State Department as a foreign-service officer in 1947 and served in China (1949); Salonika, Greece (1949–51); Libya (1952–54); Washington, DC (1954–56); Zagreb, Yugoslavia (1956–59); Bonn and Marburg, Germany (1959–62); and Washington, DC, beginning in 1962.[19]

Paul Springer was reassigned to the American consulate in Singapore in October 1945. The consulate served as the base for an OSS intelligence-gathering operation in the Far East, focusing on the political climate in recently liberated countries. He was reacquainted with several Yale classmates at this post and drew upon their experiences. In 1949, at the suggestion of one of them, he interviewed with the newly formed Central Intelligence Agency (CIA). Springer was accepted. With his working knowledge of French, he was assigned as an intelligence officer in Saigon, French

Indochina in 1950 and was later promoted to CIA Chief of Station. Following three years in Vietnam during the French-Indochina war, he served in Washington, DC, returning to Asia at a CIA intelligence base on Saipan, where he supervised case officers and interrogated intelligence targets; he was successful in cultivating several as counterintelligence agents for placement in their home countries.

Springer was transferred to the Belgian Congo in 1957, providing intelligence on the turbulent internal political movements that culminated in the Congolese independence from Belgium in 1960. From 1963 to 1968, he served in senior CIA posts in South Africa and Rhodesia. During his career, he participated in the drafting of many mission directives for CIA stations abroad.[20] Some of Springer's diplomatic colleagues he worked with in China did not fare so well after the war.

Col. David D. Barrett served more than thirty-five years in the US Army, almost entirely in China. Barrett's critical role in the Dixie Mission cost him a promotion when US ambassador Patrick Hurley falsely accused him of undermining his mission to unite the Communists and Nationalists. Hurley naively thought that the political differences between the CCP and the Kuomintang were as ideologically reconcilable as those of Democrats and Republicans. Hurley withdrew a nomination to promote Barrett to the rank of brigadier general and had him removed to a small corner of the China theater for the rest of the war. After the war, Barrett was assigned as a military attaché to the Nationalist government after it had fled the mainland in 1949. This was his last post before retiring from the US Army. As a civilian, Barrett served as a professor at the University of Colorado. He was instrumental in establishing a modern Chinese-language course there and lectured on the modern history of China and occasionally in Shakespearean studies.

John Carter Vincent was among the Old China Hands who saw value in gathering intelligence from and providing arms to the Communist armies, then part of the Allied coalition in the war and ostensibly under Chiang Kai-shek's command. When Vincent and other China Hands, including John Service, accompanied Vice President Henry A. Wallace on a state visit to the Soviet Union and Chungking in June 1944, they helped persuade Chiang to grant permission for the Dixie Mission, which opened their contact with the Communist base areas.

During the 1950s, hundreds of government employees, entertainers, educators, and union activists were accused of being Communists by Senator Joseph McCarthy. Careers were ruined and reputations were smeared as people found themselves on black lists and the victims of unjust persecution. In 1951, Vincent was attacked by Senator McCarthy and accused of having been a member of the Communist Party. A committee investigated McCarthy's claims of Communist penetration of the federal government and military. The hearings revolved around McCarthy's charge that the fall of Chiang Kai-shek's Nationalist regime in China had been caused by the actions of alleged Soviet spies in the State Department. The hearings were extremely stormy and attracted much media attention. The committee investigating the McCarthy accusations later published a report denouncing McCarthy and his claims as a hoax.[21]

Vincent was attacked by a former Communist Party activist who stated in the summer of 1951 that Vincent had been a member of the Communist Party. The source admitted that he had no proof but claimed to have learned that from having overheard other party leaders, who were discussing the anti-Communist views of Ambassador Hurley. Similar accusations were made against all the China Hands because of their allegations of ineptitude and corruption of Chiang's regime. After having been cleared by security panels of any disloyalty, in December 1952 the Civil Service Loyalty Review Board found reasonable doubt on Vincent's loyalty by a margin of one vote. In 1953, Secretary John Foster Dulles requested Vincent's resignation. Dean Acheson, Truman's secretary of state, steadfastly defended Vincent and thought that the China Hands generally were being unfairly and demagogically maligned for political purposes. Acheson tried to intervene with Dulles to save Vincent's career. He was unsuccessful.

John S. Service was among the foreign-service officers in China whose careers were destroyed, interrupted, or curtailed in the early 1950s in the wake of the McCarthy hearings. McCarthy alleged that the State Department was filled with Communist sympathizers. Few accusations were ever proven, but scores of foreign-service officers and other civil servants were forced into early retirement, resigned under pressure, or saw their prospects for career advancement evaporate when their loyalty was questioned. Service was fired from the State Department in 1951 after a Civil Service Commission Loyalty Review Board said it had "reasonable doubt" about his loyalty. On six previous occasions the board had cleared him of charges that he was disloyal and a security risk.[22]

Jack Service and other members of the Dixie Mission correctly predicted that Chiang Kai-shek would fall because of the Kuomintang's corruption, incompetence, and brutality. However, this position ran afoul of McCarthy, who blamed Service and his colleagues for "losing China" because of their Communist sympathies. In 1950, McCarthy singled out Service as one of "the 205 known communists" in the State Department.[23] The US Senate grilled many of these longtime diplomats in a series of hearings, which became somewhat of a public circus. The witnesses interviewed for the hearing focused on Jack Service even included former ambassador Clarence Gauss. Jack Service was dismissed from the US Foreign Service on December 13, 1951.[24]

Gen. Claire Lee Chennault had a high opinion of Chiang Kai-shek and advocated international support for Asian anti-Communist movements. Returning to China, he purchased several surplus military aircraft and created the Civil Air Transport (later known as Air America). These aircraft facilitated aid to Nationalist China during the struggle against Chinese Communists in the late 1940s and were later used in supply missions to French forces in Indochina. The same force supplied the intelligence community and others during the Vietnam War.

Col. Bruce K. Holloway earned his status as a fighter ace, shooting down thirteen Japanese planes during the war. After graduating from the National War College in 1951, he progressed through a series of key assignments in the US Air Force. He was promoted to general and commander in chief of the US Strategic Air Command in 1968.

Maude Pettus returned to the US from Changsha with her two daughters and continued a long career in nursing. She never remarried. She returned to China to celebrate her one hundredth birthday in 2015, and again the following year as a guest of the Chinese government, to join the national celebrations of the seventieth anniversary of the end of World War II in Beijing.

Appendix A
SPELLING STANDARDIZATION

Hanyu Pinyin is the official system to transcribe Mandarin Chinese sounds into the Roman alphabet. It was invented in the 1950s and adopted as a standard in mainland China in 1958. Pinyin is used for several purposes, such as teaching Chinese, transcribing names and places into the Roman alphabet, and as an input method for typing Chinese characters.

An older system called Wade-Giles was used in the first half of the twentieth century, and it left its mark on the English language. The Bachelors, as did their American and British colleagues, used the then-current Wade-Giles spellings during their time in China. These earlier romanized spellings to refer to cities, towns, and provinces as they were written in their letters and reports, and direct quotes in dozens of examples. As a result I chose to standardize all of the romanized Chinese spellings in the text into the Wade-Giles format that was used during the time period of World War II and the five-year period afterward. The present-day "Pinyin" spellings are also shown here for the benefit of the modern reader.

WADE-GILES	PINYIN SPELLINGS	
Anhwei Province	Anhui Province	安徽省
Canton	Guangdong	广东省
Chahar Province	Chahaer Province	察哈爾省
Changsha	Changsha	長沙
Changteh	Changde	常德
Changyang	Changyang, Hubei Province	湖北省长阳
Chengtu	Chengdu	成都
Chengkung	Chenggong, Yunnan Province	云南省呈贡
Chenki	Chenxi, Hunan Province	湖南省辰溪

Chihchiang	Zhijiang	芷江
Chungking	Chongqing	重慶
Hengyang	Hengyang	衡阳
Hong Kong	Hong Kong	香港
Hopei Province	Hebei	河北省
Hupeh Province	Hubei Province	湖北省
Hsiang River	Xiangjiang	湘江
Hsiangtan (Siangtan)	Xiangtan	湘潭
Hwanghsien	Xinhuangxian (a.k.a. Huangxian),	
	Hunan Province	湖南省新晃县 (原名晃县)
Ichang	Yichang	宜昌
Kialing River	Jialing River	嘉陵江
Kiangsi Province	Jiangxi Province	江西省
Kowloon		九龍
Kweilin	Guilin	桂林
Kweiyang	Guiyang	貴陽
Kweichow Province	Guizhou Province	貴州省
Kunming	Kunming	昆明
Lanchow	Lanzhou	兰州
Laowhangpin (Kweichow)	Huangping, Guizhou Province	贵州省黄平
Lingling	Lingling, Hunan Province	湖南省零陵
Loyang	Luoyang	洛阳
Namyung	Nanxiong	南雄
Nanking	Nanjing	南京
Neichiang	Neijiang	內江
Ningsiang	Ningxiang, Hunan Province	湖南省宁乡
Peking	Beijing	北京
Pingsingkuan	Pingxingguan, Shanxi Province	山西省平型关
Shanghai	Shanghai	上海
Shansi	Shanxi	山西省
Shensi	Shanxi (a.k.a. Shaanxi)	陕西省
Shihhweiyao	Shihuiyao (Huangshi), Hubei Province	湖北省石灰窑, 现为黄石
Shiukwan	Shaoguan	韶關
Sian	Xian	西安
Siangsiang	Xiangxiang, Hunan Province	湖南省湘乡
Siangtan	Xiangtan, Hunan Province	湖南省湘潭
Suichwan	Suichuan, Sichuan Province	四川省遂川

Szechuan Province	Sichuan	四川
Tauyan County	Taoyuan	桃源
Tientsin	Tianjin	天津
Tihau	Dihua (now Wulumuqi), Xinjiang Province	迪化 (现新疆乌鲁木齐)
Tsinan	Jinan, Shandong Province	山东省济南
Tunjen	Tongren, Guizhou	贵州省铜仁
Wanping County	Fengtai District	豐台區宛平县
Whampoa	Huangpu, Guangzhou	广州市黄埔
Woosong	Wusong	上海吴淞口
Wuho	Wuhu, Anhui Province	安徽省芜湖
Wuchow	Wuzhou, Guangxi Province	广西省梧州
Yangtze River	Changjiang	長江 (揚子江)
Yenan	Yan'an	延安
Yoloshan	Yuelushan, Hunan Province	湖南长沙岳麓山
Yuanling County	Yuanling Xian	沅陵縣

Appendix B

YALI MIDDLE SCHOOL CLASS DESCRIPTIONS AND US EQUIVALENTS

The Yali Middle School boys (ages 13–15) are those who were called junior high school students in America. The 1-1 and 1-2 boys corresponded to 7-B and 7-A (7th grade) students; the 2-1 and 2-2 boys, to 8-B and 8-A (8th grade); and 3-1 and 3-2, to 9-B and 9-A (9th grade). The senior school (ages 16–18) took over from that point: 4-1 and 4-2 were 10th grade, first and second semester; 5-1 and 5-2 were 11th grade, first and second semester; and 6-1 and 6-2 were seniors.

The following table shows each Yali class as mentioned in writings by the Bachelors, along with their equivalent classes in a typical US school district:

Yali Class Description	US Equivalent	Semester
1-1	7th Grade	First
1-2	7th Grade	Second
2-1	8th Grade	First
2-2	8th Grade	Second
3-1	9th Grade	First
3-2	9th Grade	Second
4-1	10th Grade	First
4-2	10th Grade	Second
5-1	11th Grade	First
5-2	11th Grade	Second
6-1	12th Grade	First
6-2	12th Grade	Second

ENDNOTES

Prologue

1. Edward Gulick, *Teaching in Wartime China: A Photo-Memoir, 1937–1939* (Amherst: University of Massachusetts Press, 1995), 231–35.

Chapter 1

1. "Negro Troops Riot in Houston," *New York Times*, August 25, 1917.
2. Paul Springer to mother, New Haven, February 2, 1939.
3. Paul LeBaron Springer, "Three Tales of My Childhood" (no date), recounting three vignettes.
4. Paul Springer to Eleanor Springer, 171 Yale Station, October 1, 1937.
5. "Camden Youth Wins Scholarship at Yale," *Courier-Post* (Camden, NJ), September 2, 1937.
6. Paul Springer to mother, 171 Yale Station, September 27, 1937.
7. Yale Glee Club, Christmas Trip Program, 1940.
8. Paul Springer to Eleanor Springer, 171 Yale Station, October 4, 1937.
9. Paul Springer to Eleanor Springer, 171 Yale Station, October 4, 1937.
10. Paul Springer to mother, 171 Yale Station, January 1, 1938.
11. Ibid.
12. Paul Springer to mother, 171 Yale Station, February 28, 1938.
13. "The Freshman Boxing Season," in *The 1938 Yale Banner*, vol. 97 (New Haven, CT: Yale University).
14. Paul Springer to mother, 171 Yale Station, October 28, 1938.
15. Paul Springer to mother, 171 Yale Station, May 9, 1938.
16. Paul Springer to mother, 171 Yale Station, May 16, 1938.
17. Georgie Magargal to Audrey Springer, Beaver College, June 7, 1938.
18. Paul L. Springer, "Personal History Summary," 1969.
19. Paul Springer to mother, 1772 Yale Station, September 27, 1938.

20. Paul Springer to mother, 1772 Yale Station, October20, 1938.
21. Ibid.
22. Paul Springer to mother, 1772 Yale Station, October24, 1938.
23. Ibid.
24. Paul Springer to mother, 1772 Yale Station, November 20, 1938.
25. Paul Springer to mother, 1772 Yale Station, Feb. 12, 1939.
26. Paul Springer to mother, 1772 Yale Station, January 25, 1939.
27. Paul Springer to mother, Pelham, New York, November 30, 1939.
28. Paul Springer to mother, 1772 Yale Station, December 9, 1939.
29. Paul Springer to mother, New Haven, December 10, 1939.
30. Paul Springer to mother, New Haven, January 13, 1940.
31. Paul Springer to mother, New Haven, January 22, 1940.

Chapter 2

1. Xu, Zhao, "The Conflict That Changed China," *Weekend China Daily*, July 9, 2017.
2. Paul Springer to mother, New Haven, February 10, 1940.
3. Paul Springer to mother, Palm Beach, March 20, 1940.
4. Paul Springer to mother, New Haven, April 1, 1940.
5. Paul Springer to mother, New Haven, April 9, 1940.
6. Paul Springer to mother, New Haven, April 21, 1940.
7. Paul Springer to mother, New Haven, June 1, 1940.
8. Paul Springer to "Daddy," New Haven, October 8, 1940.
9. Paul Springer to mother, New Haven, October 17, 1940.
10. Paul Springer to mother, New Haven, October 17, 1940.
11. Paul Springer to mother, New Haven, October 30, 1940.
12. Paul Callan, "Charles Lindbergh:

Hitler's All-American Hero," September 25, 2010, http://www.express.co.uk/expressyour-self/201613/Charles-Lindbergh-Hitler-s-all-American-hero.

13. Paul Springer to mother, New Haven, October 30, 1940.

14. Yale Glee Club, Christmas Trip Program, 1940.

15. Marshall Bartholomew to Paul Springer, New Haven, April 5, 1941.

16. In some years, there were four Yale Bachelors accepted.

17. Paul Springer to Kenneth Latourette, Camden, New Jersey, YUL, March 20, 1941.

18. Gulick, *Teaching in Wartime China*, 2–3.

19. B. J. Elder, *The Oriole's Song: An American Girlhood in Wartime China* (Norwalk, CT: EastBridge, 2003), 180.

20. Nancy E. Chapman and Jessica C. Plumb, *The Yale-China Association: A Centennial History* (Hong Kong: Chinese University Press, Chinese University of Hong Kong, 2001), 16.

21. Ibid., 11–15.

22. Ibid., 25.

23. In China, middle school usually includes grades 7 to 12. The formal name was Yali Union Middle School. The College of Yale-in-China in Changsha was merged into the Science Department of Hua Chung University (College) in 1929.

24. Gulick, *Teaching in Wartime China*, 85–86.

25. Ibid., 90–91.

26. Ibid., 91.

27. K. S. Latourette to Paul Springer, New Haven, YUL, April 15, 1941.

28. Bob Smith to Paul Springer, New Haven, YUL, June 4, 1941.

29. Kenneth S. Latourette to Arthur Hopkins, New Haven, YUL, May 22, 1941.

30. Bob Smith to Paul Springer, New Haven, June 25, 1941.

31. Paul Springer to Robert Ashton Smith, New Haven, YUL, June 11, 1941.

32. Yale University, "Instructions for Members of the Graduating Classes at the Baccalaureate Service Graduation and Commencement, June 15, 17, and 18, 1941."

33. Bob Smith to Paul Springer, Yale-in-China Association, New Haven, May 27, 1941.

34. Bob Smith to Paul Springer, New Haven, YUL, June 10, 1941.

35. *A History of the Class of 1941*, Yale University, Arthur Haddon Hopkins Jr., 433–434.

36. *A History of the Class of 1940*, Yale University, James Ackerman Elliott, 361.

37. "Application of James Ackerman Elliott," Preliminary Information Blank for Short-Term Appointees, for the trustees of Yale-in China (YUL), March 1, 1940.

38. "Appointees to Yali Take China Posts," *Yali News*, September 22, 1941.

39. Paul Springer to Bob Smith, Camden, New Jersey, YUL, June 23, 1941.

40. Bob Smith to Paul Springer, New Haven, YUL, June 19, 1941.

41. Paul Springer to Bob Smith, Camden, New Jersey, YUL, June 26, 1941.

42. Robert Ashton Smith to Paul LeBaron Springer, June 25, 1941.

43. Rachel Dowd to Paul Springer, New Haven, YUL, July 1, 1941.

44. Bob Smith to Paul Springer, New Haven, June 30, 1941.

Chapter 3

1. James Elliott, letter #1, on board *President Harrison*, YUL, July 29, 1941.

2. Passport stamp, Paul LeBaron Springer, US passport issued July 10, 1941.

3. James Elliott, letter #1, on board *President Harrison*, YUL, July 29, 1941.

4. Guest list, SS *President Harrison*, sailing from Honolulu, July 30, 1941.

5. James Elliott, letter #1, on board *President Harrison*, YUL, July 29, 1941.

6. Ibid.

7. Ibid.

8. James Elliott, letter #2, on board *President Harrison*, YUL, August 5, 1941.

9. Paul Springer to mother, Honolulu, August 13, 1941.

10. James Elliott, letter #2, on board *President Harrison*, YUL, August 5, 1941.

11. James Elliott, letter #1, on board *President Harrison*, YUL, July 29, 1941.

12. Paul Springer, "Essay on Yuanling,"

February 11, 1943.

13. Paul Springer to mother, Kunming, June 4, 1942.

14. "Shanghai, a City of 3,500,000," *Chicago Sunday Tribune*, August 15, 1937.

15. Rana Mitter, *Forgotten Ally: China's World War II, 1937–1945* (Boston and New York: Houghton Mifflin Harcourt, 2013), 108.

16. Ibid., 167–68.

17. James A. Elliott, letter #3, Yali campus, Changsha, YUL, September 11, 1941, 1.

18. Ibid., 1.

19. Ibid., 3.

20. Ibid., 2.

21. Ibid.

22. Ibid.

23. Ibid., 4.

24. Ibid., 3.

25. Ibid., 4.

26. Ibid., 8.

27. Ibid., 5.

28. Ibid., 7.

29. Ibid.

30. Ibid.

Chapter 4

1. *Yale in China: Report of the Thirty-Seventh Year* (New Haven, CT: Yale University, 1942–1943).

2. R. A. Smith, letter #2, received in New Haven on October 13, 1941.

3. Paul Springer to mother, Changsha, September 4, 1941.

4. Gulick, *Teaching in Wartime China*, 10.

5. James A. Elliott, letter #7, Yale, YUL, November 9, 1941.

6. Paul Springer to mother, Changsha, September 4, 1941.

7. Ibid.

8. Ibid.

9. Ibid.

10. Ibid.

11. Paul Springer to Elmerdeen and Mac, Yuanling, October 1, 1941.

12. Paul Springer to mother, Changsha, September 4, 1941.

13. James A. Elliott, letter #3, Yuanling, YUL, September 11, 1941, 9.

14. Paul Springer to mother, Changsha, September 4, 1941.

15. James Elliott, letter #7, Yali, YUL, November 9, 1941. Jim Elliott described the decrepit, moth-eaten dogs that roamed the shell of a city as "warmed[-]up death."

16. Paul Springer to mother, Changsha, September 4, 1941.

17. Yale-in-China Association, "Biographical History of William Winston Pettus."

18. Edward H. Hume, *Dauntless Adventurer: The Story of Dr. Winston Pettus*, Xiangya Culture Inheritance (Wuhan, China: Wuhan University Press, 2016; originally published in 1952 [New Haven, CT: Yale University Press]), 3.

19. Hsiang-Ya Hospital was derived from the literary name of the province, "Hsiang," and the first syllable of the name of the Ya-Li mission, "Ya." This allowed everyone to recognize that "Hsiang-Ya" meant "Hunan-Yale," a real cooperation between the two (Hume, author of *Dauntless Adventurer*, 41).

20. Marjorie T. Whittlesey, *The Dragon Will Survive* (Ft. Lauderdale, FL: Ashley Books, 1991), 50.

21. James A. Elliott, letter #4, Changsha, YUL, October 5, 1941.

22. Whittlesey, *The Dragon Will Survive*, 50.

23. R. A. Smith, letter #2, received in New Haven on October 13, 1941.

24. Ibid., 5.

25. Paul Springer to mother, Yuanling, September 12, 1941.

26. There were several different spellings of *chin-pao* (Pinyin: jing bao, 警报) used in letters written by the Americans.

27. Maochun Yu, *OSS in China: Prelude to Cold War* (New Haven, CT: Yale University Press, 1996), 35–38.

28. James Elliott, letter #7, Yali, YUL, November 9, 1941.

29. Ibid.

30. Whittlesey, *The Dragon Will Survive*, 99–100.

31. Paul Springer to mother, Yuanling, September 12, 1941.

32. Ibid.

33. James Elliott, letter #7, Yali, YUL, November 9, 1941.

34. Ibid.

35. Paul Springer, "Essay on Yuanling," February 9, 1943.

36. Paul Springer, "Essay on Yuanling," February 4, 1943.

37. *Yali News Bulletin*, from Yale-In-China Association, New Haven, January 24, 1942.

38. Although he was usually known as C. C. Lao, the principal's Chinese name was Lao Chi-Chiang, 劳启祥.

39. Gulick, *Teaching in Wartime China*, 173.

40. James Elliott, letter from Yuanling, YUL, October 23, 1941.

41. Robert Ashton Smith to Dr. Arthur Hopkins, YUL, February 11, 1942.

42. Paul Springer, typed essay on "How to Write a Book," Chungking, February 3, 1943.

43. Elder, *The Oriole's Song*, 83–86.

44. James A. Elliott, letter #5, Yuanling, YUL, November 6, 1943.

45. Recorded interview with Kenneth Moreland, former Yali Bachelor, on February 20, 2002, 30.

46. Ibid., 30.

47. Paul Springer, "Essay on Yuanling," February 11, 1943.

48. Paul Springer to mother, December 2, 1941.

49. Whittlesey, *The Dragon Will Survive*, 101.

50. James A. Elliott, letter, #4, Changsha, YUL, October 5, 1941, 4.

51. Ibid.

52. Ibid.

53. Whittlesey, *The Dragon Will Survive*, 101–02.

54. James A. Elliott, letter #4, Changsha, YUL, October 5, 1941. 4.

55. Rachel Dowd to Mrs. J. A. Springer, New Haven, YUL, April 11, 1942.

Chapter 5

1. "Battle of Changsha," https://en.wikipedia.org/wiki/Battle_of_Changsha_(1941).

2. Robert Ashton Smith to "Trustees & Friends in America," October 1, 1941, 5.

3. Ibid.

4. "Savage Bombing, American Eyewitness in Changsha, Shiukwan," *South China Morning Post*, December 2, 1941.

5. Remarks by R. Brank Fulton at the Pettus memorial service, held in New Haven at Dwight Hall, YUL, June 23, 1946.

6. Win Pettus to "Dear Folks" (Yale-in-China), Changsha, Hunan, China, YUL, October 2, 1941.

7. "Savage Bombing, American Eyewitness in Changsha, Shiukwan," *South China Morning Post*, December 2, 1941.

8. Sarah Pettus, *A Life for China*, biographical sketch of William Winston Pettus (Berkeley, CA: China Council, n.d.).

9. Ibid.

10. Ibid.

11. Paul Springer, Yuanling, Hunan, to "Dear Mother and all," September 24, 1941.

12. "Hunan Fighting, Retreating Japanese Units Trapped, Changsha," *South China Morning Post*, October 4, 1941.

13. Paul Springer to "Mother and family," Yali, November 21, 1941.

14. "Atrocities Told, Stories by Changsha Missionaries," *South China Morning Post*, October 15, 1941.

Chapter 6

1. Gulick, *Teaching in Wartime China*, 174.

2. Ibid., 176.

3. James A. Elliott, letter #6, Yuanling, YUL, October 23, 1941.

4. Ibid. The town, Peh Tien To, is pronounced like "but in dough" (Pinyin: Bai Tian Tou, 白田头) according to Elliott.

5. James A. Elliott, letter #7, Yuanling, YUL, November 9, 1941.

6. Letter from James Elliott, Yali, YUL, November 15, 1941.

7. Arthur Hopkins to Dr. Arthur Hopkins, Yuanling, YUL, November 5, 1941.

8. As later told to Sarah Springer by her father, Paul, when reminiscing about Yale-in-China.

9. Paul Springer to mother, Yuanling, September 24, 1941.

10. Ibid. Springer's spelling of *chin-pao* (Pinyin: jing bao, 警报).

11. James A. Elliott, letter #7, Yuanling, YUL, November 9, 1941.

12. Chapman and Plumb, *The Yale-China Association*, 61.

13. Gulick, *Teaching in Wartime China*, 18.

14. *Yale-in-China: Report of the Thirty-Seventh Year*, 2.

15. Gulick, *Teaching in Wartime China*, 56–57.

16. Chapman and Plumb, *The Yale-China Association*, 61.

17. Paul Springer to "Mother and all," Yuanling, September 24, 1941.

18. Arthur Hopkins to Dr. Arthur Hopkins, Yuanling, YUL, November 5, 1941.

19. Paul Springer to "Dear Mother and all," Yuanling, September 24, 1941.

20. James Elliott, journal #9 from Yuanling, YUL, December 14, 1941.

21. Ibid.

22. Ibid.

23. Gulick, *Teaching in Wartime China*, 69–70.

24. Bob Smith to Dr. Arthur Hopkins, New Haven, YUL, February 11, 1942.

25. James Elliott, journal #9 from Yuanling, YUL, December 14, 1941.

26. Paul Springer to Elmerdeen and Mac, Yuanling, October 1, 1941.

27. Essay by Bruno Sin Fang, Yali Middle School, October 6, 1941 (Pinyin: Xin-fan Huang, 黄新范), who graduated in the summer of 1943. Please see p. 18 of 群英荟萃, published by Yali School, Changsha, China, in 2006.

28. Essay by Morris Lao, Yali Middle School, October 5, 1941. See p. 19 in the same book mentioned above; he might have been Huang's classmate 廖瑄.

29. Paul Springer to Stuart H. Clement, Yali Union Middle School, October 21, 1941.

30. James Elliott, journal #9 from Yuanling, YUL, December 14, 1941.

31. Ibid.

32. James Elliott, on board SS *President Harrison*, Honolulu, YUL, August 5, 1941.

33. The Pinyin spellings for three of these "Chinese names" are translated as follows by George Zhongze Li: Bob Smith, Shih Ming Teh (Brilliant Virtue); possibly, its Pinyin is Shi Ming De, 史明德. Paul Springer, Hsai Pau Teh (Preserver of Virtue); most possibly, its Pinyin is Xie Bao De, 谢保德. Jim Elliott, An Li Teh (Upholder or Champion of Virtue); Pinyin is An Li De, 安立德, with *teh* (virtue) translated in Pinyin as *de*, 德. There was no direct Pinyin spelling provided for Art Hopkins, "Ho," or Don McCabe, "Ma."

34. Paul Springer, "Essay on Life in Yuanling, China," February 2, 1943.

35. Ibid.

36. Paul Springer to mother, Yali, October 27, 1941.

37. Paul Springer, "Essay on Life in Yuanling, China," February 2, 1943.

38. Ibid.

39. Ibid.

40. Ibid.

41. Paul Springer to mother, Yuanling, October 27, 1941.

42. Paul Springer, "Essay on Life in Yuanling, China," February 2, 1943.

43. James Ackerman Elliott's Yale in China Application, Preliminary Information Blank for Short-Term Appointees, March 1, 1940.

44. Paul Springer, "Essay on Life in Yuanling, China," February 2, 1943.

45. Ibid.

46. James A. Elliott, letter #6, Bachelor's Mess, Yuanling, Hunan, China, October 23, 1941, 6–7.

47. Paul Springer to Rachel Dowd, Yali, YUL Collection, October 26, 1941.

48. Paul Springer to mother, Yali, October 26, 1941.

49. Paul Springer to "Daddy," Yali, November 5, 1941

50. Paul Springer to mother, Yuanling, Hunan, November 21, 1941.

51. "Allied Experts Study Gas War in China," *South China Morning Post*, December 7, 1941.

52. Sheldon H. Harris, *Factories of Death: Japanese Biological Warfare, 1932–1945*,

and *American Cover-Up*, rev. ed. (New York: Routledge, 2002), 33–34.

53. Ibid., 101–03.

54. Elder, *The Oriole's Song*, 79.

55. Article on Lt. Hopkins, *Philadelphia Inquirer*, December 12, 1943.

56. Ibid.

57. Whittlesey, *The Dragon Will Survive*, 124.

58. Article on Lt. Hopkins, *Philadelphia Inquirer*, December 12, 1943.

59. Paul Springer recalled Fulton's account as printed in the *South China Morning Post*.

60. Paul Springer to mother, December 2, 1942.

61. Ibid.

62. Ibid.

63. Ibid.

Chapter 7

1. Yale-in-China Association to Friends of the Yale-in-China Association, December 15, 1942.

2. Ibid.

3. James Elliott, journal #9 from Yuanling, YUL, December 25, 1941.

4. Ibid.

5. Ibid.

6. Ibid.

7. Ibid.

8. Ibid.

9. Arthur Hopkins to "Dear Friends," Yuanling, YUL, December 21, 1941.

10. Ibid.

11. James Elliott, journal #9, Yuanling, Hunan, YUL, December 14, 1941, 9. Pinyin: Xu Shi Fen Zhun Bei, 需十分准备.

12. Paul Springer, "Essay on Life in Yuanling, China," February 2, 1943.

13. James Elliott, journal #9, Yuanling, Hunan, YUL, December 14, 1941, 9.

14. Winston Groom, *The Allies: Roosevelt, Churchill, Stalin, and the Unlikely Alliance That Won World War II* (Washington, DC: National Geographic, 2018), 321–22.

15. Arthur Hopkins Jr. to "Dear Family," Yuanling, January 11, 1942.

16. Paul Springer to "Dear Family," Yuanling, January 6, 1942.

17. Arthur Hopkins Jr. to "Dear Family,"

Yuanling, January 11, 1942.

18. Ibid.

19. Elder, *The Oriole's Song*, 70.

20. Ibid.

21. Yale-in-China Association to Members of Board of Trustees, December 26, 1941.

22. Yale-in-China Association to "Families of our Yale-in-China Staff in Yuanling," December 30, 1941.

23. Arthur Hopkins Jr. to "Dear Family," Yuanling, January 11, 1942.

24. Robert Ashton Smith to Dr. Arthur Hopkins, YUL, February 23, 1942.

25. Chapman and Plumb, *The Yale-China Association*, 54–55.

26. Ibid.

27. Ibid.

28. John N. Hart, *The Making of an Army "Old China Hand": A Memoir of Colonel David D. Barnett* (Berkeley: Institute of East Asian Studies, University of California, 1985), 31.

29. Paul Springer to mother, Yuanling, January 6, 1942.

30. Report of the Effect of the Third Battle of Changsha (January 1942) on the Work and Property of Yale-in-China, March 27, 1942.

31. Pettus, *A Life for China*, 5.

32. Ibid., 5.

33. Report of the Effect of the Third Battle of Changsha (January 1942) on the Work and Property of Yale-in-China. March 27, 1942.

34. Paul Springer to mother, Yuanling, January 6, 1942.

35. "Yali Youth Group Presents Musical Concert," Yuanling, January 1, 1942.

36. James Elliott, journal #10, Yuanling, March 5, 1942.

37. Ibid.

38. James Elliott, journal, Yuanling, Hunan, YUL, December 14, 1941, 7.

39. Ibid.

Chapter 8

1. James Elliott, journal #10, March 5, 1942.

2. Ibid., 2. An alternate spelling of the town name was Chihkiang (now Zhijiang).

3. Ibid., 2.

4. Ibid., 3.

5. Ibid., 3.

6. Ibid., 4.

7. Andrew Hicks, ed. and comp., *Jack Jones, a True Friend to China: "The Lost Writings of a Heroic Nobody"* (Hong Kong: Earnshaw Books, 2015), xiv.

8. Ibid., 30. This was most likely at the Kweiyang hostel building, where many of the FAU men lodged while in town. To get to the FAU garage depot, they walked toward the rural setting of the garage, nestled beneath a range of curious hills.

9. Paul Springer to mother, Chungking, February 8, 1942.

10. James Elliott, letter#11, Yuanling, YUL, May 4, 1942.

11. *Yali News Bulletin*, New Haven, April 10, 1942.

12. James Elliott, letter #11, Yuanling, YUL, May 4, 1942, 3.

13. James Elliott, letter #11, Yuanling, YUL, May 4, 1942.

14. Paul Springer to "Dear Mother," American embassy, Chungking, February 8, 1942.

15. James Elliott, letter #11, Yuanling, YUL, May 4, 1942, 5.

16. Ibid.

17. Kialing River; Pinyin: Jia Ling Jiang, 嘉陵江.

18. James Elliott, letter #11, Yuanling, YUL, May 4, 1942, 6.

19. Ibid., 4.

20. James Elliott, letter #12, Yuanling, YUL, Late in May, 1942, 1.

21. Ibid. Jim Elliott's purchase of the robe what quite a find. *K'o-ssu* (Pinyin: *Ke Si*, 缂丝 or 刻丝) is a technique in Chinese silk tapestry, admired for its lightness and clarity of pattern. The name means "cut silk," a name that comes from the appearance of cut threads created by color in the pictorial designs typical of the style.

22. James Elliott, letter #12, Yuanling, YUL, late in May 1942, 2. *Author's note*: Paul's chop, which is still owned by his family, was carved from a marble-like stone, rather than metal.

23. James Elliott, letter #12, Yuanling, YUL, late in May 1942.

24. Ibid.

25. Paul Springer to mother, Chungking, February 8, 1942.

26. Ibid.

27. Paul Springer to Trustees of Yale-in-China, Chungking, YUL, June 30, 1942.

28. James Elliott, letter #12, Yuanling, YUL, late May 1942, 7.

29. Ibid., 5.

30. Paul Springer, Western Union telegram to his family, March 12, 1942.

31. Arthur Hopkins to Bob Smith, Yuanling, YUL, May 3, 1942.

32. Ibid.

33. Ibid.

34. Arthur Hopkins, memo from Yuanling, YUL, September 5, 1942.

35. Arthur Hopkins to "Dear family," Yuanling, YUL, May 30, 1942.

Chapter 9

1. Yale-in-China Association to Mrs. J. A. Springer, New Haven, Apr. 29, 1942.

2. Ibid.

3. Hicks, *Jack Jones, a True Friend to China*, xii.

4. Daniel Jackson, *Famine, Sword, and Fire: The Liberation of Southwest China in World War II* (Atglen, PA: Schiffer, 2015), 31.

5. Ibid., 34–35.

6. DevizesPeaceGroup, "Exit from Burma: A Conscientious Objector's Story," WW2 People's War (an online archive of wartime memories contributed by members of the public and gathered by the BBC), www.bbc.co.uk/history/ww2peopleswar/stories/71/a6913271.shtml.

7. Paul Springer, "Essay on Small Chinese Towns," May 15, 1942.

8. Ibid.

9. Paul Springer to "Dear Mother," Kunming, May 25, 1942.

10. W. A. Reynolds, "Operation and Maintenance of a Road Transport System in West China, 1942–46," *Journal of the Hong Kong Branch of the Royal Asiatic Society* 16 (1976): 135–61.

11. Paul Springer to "Dear Mother," Kunming, May 25, 1942.

12. Ibid. The Ferry Command's mission included the ferrying of multiengine Army aircraft and Lend-Lease aircraft from manufacturing facilities to overseas bases. In this case, Springer was referring to the air transport of troops from one area to another.

13. Ibid.

14. Paul Springer to mother, Kunming, Yunnan, June 4, 1942.

15. Letter from Arthur Hopkins, Yuanling, YUL, May 28, 1942.

16. Ibid.

17. Ibid.

18. Paul Springer to Bob Smith, Kunming, YUL, June 1, 1942. Paul's spelling; a.k.a. Henry Louderbough.

19. Paul Springer to "Dear Mother," Kunming, China, May 25, 1942. Springer's writing noted "probably *Pao shen* (?) (P pronounced B)." Pinyin: Paoshan, 保山, in Yunnan Province.

20. Ibid.

21. Daniel Jackson, *Famine, Sword, and Fire*, 43.

22. Ibid., 43.

23. Ibid., 44.

24. Ibid., 11.

25. Paul Springer to "Dear Mother," Kunming, China, June 4, 1942.

26. "Albert H. Rooks," https://en.wikipedia.org/wiki/Albert H. Rooks.

27. Paul Springer to "Dear Mother," Kunming, China, June 4, 1942.

28. Paul Springer to mother, Kunming, May 25, 1942.

29. Letter from Arthur Hopkins, Yuanling, YUL, May 28, 1942.

30. Paul Springer to Trustees of Yale-in-China, Chungking, YUL, June 30, 1942.

31. Ibid.

32. Paul Springer to mother, Chunking, June 16, 1942.

33. Ibid.

34. American embassy, Chungking to Yale-in-China Trustees, June 29, 1942.

35. The handwritten postscript releasing Paul on a temporary basis is written on the following: Letter from the American embassy, Chungking to Yale-in-China Trustees, June 29, 1942.

36. Paul Springer to mother, American embassy, Chungking, June 16, 1942.

37. OSS Archives, Record Group 226, box 114. Examples, explanations, and directions for codes and ciphers, ca. December 1943–June 1944.

38. Paul Springer to "Dear Mother," American embassy, Chungking, June 16, 1942.

39. Hicks, *Jack Jones, a True Friend to China*, 14–15.

40. Paul Springer to mother, American embassy, Chungking, June 21, 1942.

41. Chungking Club, Entertainment during December 1942 (typed memo).

42. Map of American embassy, Chungking, China, ca. 1944.

43. Memorandum on "British Intelligence Services in China," Headquarters, OSS Su Det. 202, APO 627, China, January 5, 1944, NARA.

44. Paul Springer to mother, American embassy, Chungking, June 21, 1942.

45. Julia Ravenel to Mrs. J. A. Springer, Charleston, September 21, 1942.

46. Julia Ravenel to Mrs. J. A. Springer, Charleston, September 25, 1942.

47. Ministry of Foreign Affairs, for Tse, Paul (Mr. Paul L. Springer), November 6, 1942. Translation by Patricia Holmes.

48. J. E. Moncrieff, *Two Thousand Chinese Characters* (Chengtu, China: J. E. Moncrieff, 1938).

49. Paul Springer to mother, American embassy, Chungking, December 30–31, 1942.

50. Paul Springer to Bob Smith, Chunking, September 23, 1942.

51. Biography of Service by Oberlin College via John Service Papers, www.oberlin.edu/archive/holdings/finding/RG30/SG119/biography.html.

52. Paul Springer to "Dear Mother," Chungking, December 30–31, 1942.

53. Ibid.

54. Paul Springer to Trustees of Yale-in-China, Chungking, YUL, June 30, 1942.

55. Paul Springer to mother, Chungking, January 22, 1943.

56. Paul Springer to "Dear Honor,"

Chungking, January 26, 1943.

57. Ibid. Paul's FAU acquaintances were Tom Thompson and Rob Chapman. Thompson's arm was almost severed. Information from an emailed letter in June 2019 from Andrew Hicks, author of *Jack Jones, a True Friend to China.*

58. Mitter, *Forgotten Ally*, 184–85.

Chapter 10

1. Arthur Hopkins to Bob Smith, Yali, Yuanling, December 12, 1942. In this letter, Art paraphrased in quotation marks the conversation Gen. Chennault had with him.

2. Hopkins noted that military censorship prohibited him from discussing the reasons in a December 12, 1942, letter to Bob Smith.

3. Jim Elliott to "Dear Mother, Dad and all," American Red Cross, China Relief Unit, Chungking, September 2, 1942.

4. Ibid.

5. Art Hopkins to Robert Ashton Smith, Yali, Yuanling, December 12, 1942.

6. Jim Elliott to "Mother, Dad and all," American Red Cross, China Relief Unit, Chungking, September 2, 1942.

7. Art Hopkins to "Dear family," letter #11, Yali, Saturday October 3, 1942. To avoid censorship, his letter declared, "I am afraid it is impossible to give details of my trip down here, but I did not come most of the way by truck or by boat, and about 240 miles of the distance were covered in an hour and forty minutes, so draw your own conclusions."

8. Elder, *The Oriole's Song*, 143. Dwight Rugh and his family traveled part of their way out of China in one of these trucks. The description of the truck was given by B. J. Rugh, then about eleven years old.

9. Art Hopkins to Robert Ashton Smith, Yali, Yuanling, December 12, 1942.

10. Hopkins's letter named the two Chinese teachers only as "Mr. Ying" and "Mr. Peng." George Zhongze Li consulted with the son of Ying, Kai-shih and concluded that "Mr. Peng" was Peng Yiluo, 彭义裸.

11. Art Hopkins to Robert Ashton Smith, Yali, Yuanling, December 12, 1942.

12. Art Hopkins to "Dear Family," letter

#11, Saturday October 3, 1942.

13. Ibid.

14. Elder, *The Oriole's Song*, 113–14.

15. Ibid.

16. Ibid.

17. Ibid.

18. Ibid.

19. Jim Elliott to R. A. Smith, Yuanling, Hunan, December 26, 1942.

20. Ibid.

21. Letter from James Elliott to Mr. Smith, Yuanling, April 3, 1943.

22. Ibid.

23. "Yali Middle School Flourishing," in *Yale in China: Report of the Thirty-Seventh Year.*

24. Ibid.

25. Transcript of a recorded interview with former Bachelor Kenneth Moreland on February 20, 2002. 30.

26. Ibid., 22–23.

27. Ibid., 25.

28. Win Pettus, per Maudie to Dr. Phil Greene, Hsiang-Ya Hospital (YUL), September 2, 1942.

29. Maudie, Win, and Ann [Pettus] to Bob, Miss Dowd, et al., Changsha, Hunan, YUL, October 28, 1942.

30. Win Pettus, per Maudie to Dr. Phil Greene, Hsiang-Ya Hospital (YUL), September 2, 1942.

31. Win Pettus to Robert Ashton Smith, Yale-in-China, Changsha (YUL), January 24, 1943.

32. Memorial service for Dr. William Winston Pettus, Changsha (YUL), December 9, 1945, "Remarks on Dr. Pettus's Life and Work by Various Friends and Colleagues."

33. Jim Elliott to Robert Ashton Smith, Yuanling, June 16, 1943, 7.

34. Ibid., 4–5.

35. Ibid.

36. Ibid.

37. Ibid.

38. Elder, *The Oriole's Song*, 135.

39. "Chinese Push Reaches Yangtze, Imperils Enemy Base at Ichang," *New York Times*, June 4, 1943.

40. Elder, *The Oriole's Song*, 135–36.

41. Whittlesey, *The Dragon Will Survive*, 150–52.

42. Ibid., 156–57.

43. Arthur H. Hopkins Jr., Veterans Records, National Personal Records Center, St. Louis, MO. Hopkins served as an assistant at HQ 14th Air Force from July 21, 1943, to May 7, 1944; as a combat liaison officer from May 8, 1944, to April 25, 1945; and as OSS intelligence officer from April 26, 1945, to September 28, 1945.

44. "Yali Middle School Flourishing," in *Yale in China: Report of the Thirty-Seventh Year.*

45. E. R. Johnson, "World War II: Fourteenth Air Force; Heir to the Flying Tigers," *Aviation History*, November 2005.

46. Interview with Col. Bruce K. Holloway, November 16, 1943. US Army Air Forces, 14th Air Force, 1943–1945, box 9, folder 7. Claire Lee Chennault Papers, Hoover Institution Archives, Stanford University.

47   Whampoa docks at Canton; Pinyin: Huangpu Gang, Guangzhou City, Guangdong Province, 黃埔港.

48. C. L. Chennault to Col. Clinton D. Vincent, January 24, 1944. Box 8, folder 48, 68th Composite Wing, 1943–1944. Claire Lee Chennault Papers, Hoover Institution Archives, Stanford University.

Chapter 11

1. Regarding Chou En-lai and Lin Piao; Pinyin: Zhou En-Lai, 周恩来, and Lin Biao, 林彪.

2. Everett F. Drumright, "Memorandum for the Ambassador, Subject: Call on Chou En-Lai, January 20, 1943." State Department Central Files, NARA, College Park, MD.

3. Transcript of a recorded interview with Ambassador Everett Drumright, diplomat and consular officer in China (1935–62). Interviewed on July 27, 1989, by Hank Zivetz (ADST).

4. Regarding the victory of the Japanese Pinghsingkuan; Pinyin: Pingxingguan, Shanxi Province, 平型关.

5. Everett F. Drumright, "Memorandum for the Ambassador, Subject: Discussion

with General Lin Piao, January 30, 1943."

6. Ibid.

7. Whittlesey, *The Dragon Will Survive*, 139.

8. John Davies, "Memorandum for General Stillwell, Conversation with Chou En-Lai, Chungking, March 16, 1943." State Department Central Files, NARA, College Park, MD.

9. Ibid.

10. George Atcheson Jr. to "The Honorable Secretary of State," "Views of General TENG Pao-Shan, Commander of Central Government's 22nd Army in Shensi, Regarding Kuomintang-Communist Relations. September 10, 1943." State Department Central Files, NARA, College Park, MD.

11. Paul Springer to "dear Mother," Chungking, February 18, 1943.

12. Paul Springer to "dear Mother," Chungking, April 7, 1943.

13. Paul Springer to "dear Mother," Chungking, April 23, 1943.

14. Transcript of a recorded interview with Ambassador Everett Drumright, diplomat and consular officer in China (1935–62). Interviewed on July 27, 1989, by Hank Zivetz (ADST).

15. Paul Springer to "dear Mother," Chungking, April 28, 1943. Pinyin: Dihua, Hsin Chiang Province.

16. Paul Springer to "Dear Mother," Chungking, May 18, 1943.

17. Paul Springer to "Dearest Mother," Chungking, June 8, 1943.

18. Hart, *The Making of an Army "Old China Hand,"* 3.

19. "David D. Barrett," https://en.wikipedia.org/wiki/David_D._Barrett.

20. Foreword by John S. Service, in Hart, *The Making of an Army "Old China Hand."*

21. Ibid., 32.

22. Paul Springer to Maj. Joseph A Springer, Chungking, June 22, 1943.

23. Ibid.

24. Ibid.

25. Paul Springer to "Dearest Mother," Chungking, July 21, 1943.

26. G. Howland Shaw, Chungking, to

Local Board No. 12, "Affidavit, Occupational Classification, Selective Service System, re: Paul LeBaron Springer. Feb. 17, 1944." State Department Records, Springer 123 file, NARA, College Park, MD.

27. Ibid.

28. Paul Springer, "August, Misc. Notes," August 23, 1943.

29. Paul Springer to "Dear Mother," Chungking, July 31, 1943.

30. Paul Springer, "August, Misc. Notes," August 23, 1943.

31. Ibid.

32. CNOC ticket certificate for passenger: Paul L. Springer.

33. Paul Springer to "Dear Mother," Chungking, October 1, 1943.

34. Dennis R. Okerstrom, *Dick Cole's War: Doolittle Raider, Hump Pilot, Air Commando* (Columbia: University of Missouri Press, 2015).

35. Paul Springer to "Dear Mother," American embassy, Chungking, October 1, 1943.

36. Paul Springer to Mrs. J. A. Springer, American embassy, Chungking, September 22, 1943.

37. Paul Springer to "Dear Mother," American embassy, Chungking, October 1, 1943.

38. Paul Springer, miscellaneous notes outlining his recent trip to India, September 22, 1943.

39. Ibid.

40. "Vera Alexandrovna Tiscenko Calder," www.wikipedia.org/wiki/ Vera_Alexandrovna_Tiscenko_Calder.

41. *Noor Jehan Begum v. Eugene Tiscenko*, December, 19, 1941. Equivalent citation: AIR 1942 Cal 325, https://indiankanoon.org/doc/358792/.

42. Dr. Arif Azad, "The Story of Vera Suhrawardy," TNA, News on Sunday, http://tns.thenews.com.pk/story-of-vera-suhrawardy/#.WsDkFkxFyUk.

43. Okerstrom, *Dick Cole's War*, 132–33.

44. Paul Springer to "Dear Mother," American embassy, Chungking, October 1, 1943.

45. Clinton D. Vincent, colonel, Air Corps, to Maj. Gen. C. L. Chennault, HQ 14th Air Force, August 25, 1943. Box 8, folder 48, 14th Air Force, 68th Composite Wing, 1943–1944. Claire Lee Chennault Papers, Hoover Institution, Stanford University.

46. Paul L. Springer, "Yangtze Fog," Chungking, October 30, 1943.

47. Ibid.

48. Regarding the base at Chengkung; Pinyin: Chenggong, now a district of Kunming, Yunnan Province, 呈贡.

49. Vincent to Chennault, 14th Air Force, Kunming, China, July 29, 1943. Box 8, folder 47, 14th Air Force, Chinese American Composite Wing, 1943–1945. Claire Lee Chennault Papers, Hoover Institution, Stanford University.

50. Ibid.

51. Ibid.

52. Ibid.

53. Wuhu, in Anhui Province, 芜湖.

54. Gen. C. J. Chow to General C. L. Chennault, US 14th Air Force, Kunming, October 4, 1943. Box 8, folder 47, 14th Air Force, Chinese American Composite Wing, 1943–1945. Claire Lee Chennault Papers, Hoover Institution, Stanford University.

55. Interview with Colonel Bruce K. Holloway, November 16, 1943, 3–4. Box 9, folder 7, US Army Air Forces, 14th Air Force, 1943–1945. Claire Lee Chennault Papers, Hoover Institution, Stanford University. Regarding the target area in Shihhweiyao (Pinyin: Shihuiyao, 石灰窑, in Hubei Province, a.k.a. Huangshi 黄石).

56. Raymond P. Luddon, American consul to secretary of state, Political Report for the Month of October, 1943, Kunming (Yunnanfu), China, November 10, 1943.

57. Johnson, "World War II: Fourteenth Air Force; Heir to the Flying Tigers."

58. Ibid.

Chapter 12

1. SACO: The Sino-American Cooperative Organization," DelsJourney, www.delsjourney.com/saco/saco.htm.

2. Minutes of a conference held as a result of instructions by general Tai Li and General

Donovan, Chunking, December 3–4, 1943. OSS Records, box 340, National Archives.

3. Department of State, "Oath of Office for Paul L. Springer," American embassy, Chungking, November 8, 1943.

4. G. Howland Shaw, Chungking, to Local Board No. 12, Affidavit: Occupational Classification, Selective Service System, re: Paul LeBaron Springer. February 17, 1944. State Department Personnel Records, 123 Springer, Paul L., NARA, College Park, MD.

5. Paul Springer to "Dear Mother," Chungking, November 8, 1943.

6. "Memorandum on British Intelligence Services in China," January 5, 1944, HQ, OSS SU Det. 202 China, British Liaison Office, US National Archives.

7. Ibid.

8. "Background information for X-2 activities in Kweilin," March 25, 1944. OSS Records, box 340, National Archives.

9. Mitter, *Forgotten Ally*, 316. Referencing foreign relations of the United States and China, March 23, 1944.

10. Elder, *The Oriole's Song*, 41–42.

11. Ibid.

12. Recorded interview with Kenneth Moreland, former Yali Bachelor, on February 20, 2002, 40–41.

13. Ibid., 41.

14. Elder, *The Oriole's Song*, 141–42.

15. Chennault to Vincent, APO 430, March 18, 1944. Box 8, folder 48, 14th Air Force, 68th Composite Wing, 1943–1945. Claire Lee Chennault Papers, Hoover Institution, Stanford University.

16. Ibid.

17. Vincent to Chennault, APO 430, March 30, 1944. Box 8, folder 48, 14th Air Force, 68th Composite Wing, 1943–1945. Claire Lee Chennault Papers, Hoover Institution, Stanford University.

18. Arthur H. Hopkins Jr., Veterans Records, National Personal Records Center, St. Louis, MO.

19. Mitter, *Forgotten Ally*, 319.

20. Johnson, "World War II: Fourteenth Air Force; Heir to the Flying Tigers."

21. Clinton D. Vincent, colonel, Air

Corps, to Maj. Gen. C. L. Chennault, HQ 14th Air Force, June 3, 1944. Box 8, folder 48, 14th Air Force, 68th Composite Wing, 1943–1944. Claire Lee Chennault Papers, Hoover Institution, Stanford University.

22. James A. Elliott to Dr. Kenneth Latourette, Yuanling, Hunan, July 17, 1944.

23. Elder, *The Oriole's Song*, 142.

24. A quonset hut was a lightweight, prefabricated structure that was made of corrugated steel and had a semicircular ceiling. They were common to military bases in World War II when a quick assembly was required.

25. Elder, *The Oriole's Song*, 142–45.

26. Ibid., 147.

27. Ibid., 148.

28. Ibid., 148.

29. C. L. Chennault to Brig. Gen. Clinton D. Vincent, June 14, 1944. Box 8, folder 48, 14th Air Force, 68th Composite Wing, 1943–1944. Claire Lee Chennault Papers, Hoover Institution, Stanford University.

30. Ibid., 144–49.

31. Paul Springer to George Small, Chungking, November 2, 1943. State Department Personnel Records, 123 Springer, Paul L., NARA, College Park, MD.

32. Ibid.

33. Ibid.

34. Ibid.

35. Paul Springer to "Dear Mother," Chungking, February 16, 1944.

36. Paul Springer to "Dear Mother," Chungking, February 21, 1944.

37. Paul Springer to "Dear Mother," Chungking, February 9, 1944.

38. The Eighth Route Army was officially known as the 18th Army Group of the National Revolutionary Army of the Republic of China. It was under the command of the Chinese Communist Party, and nominally within the structure of the Chinese military headed by the Nationalist government.

39. Mitter, *Forgotten Ally*, 327.

40. Senate Internal Security Committee, *The Amerasia Papers: A Clue to the Catastrophe of China*, January 26, 1970.

41. Hart, *The Making of an Army "Old China Hand,"* 53.

42. Ibid., foreword by John S. Service.

43. Ibid.

44. The Yenan CCP base was located in Shensi (Pinyin: Shanxi, 陝西). Shensi is located in the western part of Shannsi, per George Zhongze Li.

45. Mitter, *Forgotten Ally*, 327–30. "Chu Teh" accompanied Mao to the airfield. Mitter uses the Pinyin spelling "Zho De" in his epic work.

46. Ibid.

47. Ibid.

48. "The Civil War in China, Part II—the Dixie Mission and Losing China," Moments in US Diplomatic History, https://adst.org/2013/12/the-civil-war-in-china-part-ii-the-dixie-mission-and-losing-china/.

49. Mitter, *Forgotten Ally*, 329.

50. Hart, *The Making of an Army "Old China Hand,"* 43–44. The description of Barrett was given by Theodore H. White, who visited Yenan as a correspondent for *Time* and *Life* magazines.

51. Ibid., 41.

52. Ibid.

53. E. J. Kahn Jr., *The China Hands: America's Foreign Service Officers and What Befell Them* (New York: Penguin Books, 1975), 116–17.

54. Mitter, *Forgotten Ally*, 329.

55. Ibid.

56. John S. Service, memorandum, enclosure no. 1 to secretary of state, Washington, from Chungking, September 2, 1943. State Department Central Files, NARA, College Park, Maryland.

57. Hart, *The Making of an Army "Old China Hand,"* 41.

58. "Sorry Mao: It's Pronounced 'Truman,' not 'Too-Lu-Mun,'" https://adst.org/2013/11/mao-asks-who-is-this-too-lu-mun/.

59. Ibid.

60. Ibid.

61. Kahn, *The China Hands*, 118–19.

62. Hart, *The Making of an Army "Old China Hand,"* 42.

63. Ibid., 43.

64. Kahn, *The China Hands*, 118–19.

65. Ibid.

66. Hart, *The Making of an Army "Old China Hand,"* 45.

67. Ibid., 43.

68. G. Howland Shaw, Chungking, to Local Board No. 12, Affidavit: Occupational Classification, Selective Service System, re: Paul LeBaron Springer. February 17, 1944. State Department Personnel Records, 123 Springer, Paul L., NARA, College Park, MD.

69. Post report, American embassy, Chunking, China. Transmitted to the department with dispatch number 2321, March 17, 1944.

70. Ibid.

71. Ibid.

72. Ibid.

73. Ibid.

74. Paul L. Springer, "The Canadian Mission Hospital of Chungking." A typed account of his friend's experience at the hospital for removal of her gallstones.

75. Ibid.

76. Paul Springer to "Dear Mother," American embassy, May 10, 1944.

77. Paul Springer to "Dear Mother," Chungking, March 21, 1944.

78. Ibid.

79. Ibid.

80. Paul Springer to "Dear Mother," American embassy, May 31, 1944.

81. Paul Springer to Paul Graybeal, American embassy, May 31, 1944.

82. Ibid.

83. Ibid.

Chapter 13

1. Stephen Penrose, chief SI, memo on "Future Plans for Cairo Intelligence Headquarters," July 22, 1944. OSS Records, box 340, US National Archives. 7.

2. Ibid.

3. Cordell Hull, Department of State, to AMEMBASSY, CHUNGKING, telegram sent July 8, 1944. State Department Personnel Records, 123 Springer, Paul L., NARA, College Park, MD.

4. Special passport, US Department of State, for Paul LeBaron Springer.

5. Department of State to Mrs. Joseph A. Springer, Washington, July 24, 1944. This letter informed Mrs. Springer of a telegram dated July 21, 1944, in which her son, an American Foreign Service clerk, had been transferred from Chungking to Cairo, Egypt.

6. US Government Despatch Agency to Mrs. J. A. Springer, August 19, 1944.

7. Paul L. Springer, identification card for visitors, Delta Service Command, Heliopolis, Egypt.

8. Booklet on *Egyptian Colloquial Arabic*, complete except for missing title page with author information.

9. Paul L. Springer, speaker's notes to Yale Club of Austin, July 22, 1994.

10. Robin Winks, *Cloak and Gown: Scholars in America's Secret War* (London: Collins Harvill, 1987), 136–38.

11. Richard A. Helms, *A Look over My Shoulder: A Life in the Central Intelligencer Agency* (Novato, CA: Presidio, 2004), 67–68. In 1946, Penrose offered Richard Helms a senior intelligence post for Central Europe, covering Germany, Austria, Switzerland, Poland, Czechoslovakia, and Hungary. Helms served as director of the CIA from 1966 to 1973.

12. S. Pickney Tuck, American minister, American Foreign Service Annual Efficiency Report, Paul LeBaron Springer, Cairo, December 1, 1944. Unclassified US Department of State case no. F-2019-00051, doc. no. C06798601 8/19/2019.

13. Ibid.

14. Transcript of a recorded interview with Thomas W. Wilson, Combined Economic Warfare Agency, Cairo, (1942–1945). Interviewed by Charles Stuart Kennedy on October 30, 1996.

15. "Jassy–Kishinev Offensive (August 1944)," https://en.wikipedia.org/wiki/Jassy%E2%80%93Kishinev_Offensive.

16. Office of Strategic Services, Cairo, cable #555, Action: Special Funds to Panos Morphoposos, August 11, 1943. US National Archives.

17. Winks, *Cloak and Gown*, 505.

18. From a photo of Paul Springer marked "Georgoulas Pyramids, 28-10-44."

19. A five-page, self-described "book letter" to his family, discussing the trip to the Holy Land in 1944. It was written by one of Paul Springer's American colleagues, although their names are not known. Cairo, Egypt, December 27, 1944.

20. Paul Springer, American legation, Cairo, Egypt, December 27, 1944. Springer also wrote a shortened account of the trip to the Holy Land.

21. The date of their departure from Cairo was listed as Friday, December 23, although the 1944 calendar lists December 23 as a Saturday. The departure date may have been an uncorrected typo in the letter, since Springer's passport stamp indicated he entered Palestine on December 24, 1944, which is consistent with their arrival in Jerusalem on December 24, after a night in Damascus.

22. A five-page, self-described "book letter" to his family, discussing the trip to the Holy Land in 1944. It was written by one of Paul Springer's American colleagues, although their names are not known. Cairo, Egypt, December 27, 1944.

23. Ibid.

24. Ibid. The original text used the term "Moslem flags."

25. Ibid.

26. Ibid.

27. "S. Pickney Tuck," www.findagrave.com/cgi-bin/fg.cgi?page=gr&GRid=21084979.

28. Invitation to Paul L. Springer from "La Princess Chivekiar de Egypt et Tlhamy Hussain Pacha" for a reception on December 31, at 10:00 p.m.

29. Transcript of a recorded interview with Cecil B. Lyon, consular officer, Cairo (1944–46). Interviewed in 1988 by John Bovey. Lyon recalled the conversation with Hussain Pasha.

30. Matt Patay, "King Farouk," IMDb Mini Biography, www.imdb.com/name/nm1531603/bio.

31. Ibid.

32. S. Pickney Tuck, American minister,

American Foreign Service Annual
Efficiency Report, Paul LeBaron Springer,
Cairo, December 1, 1944. Unclassified US
Department of State case no. F-2019-00051,
doc. no. C06798601 8/19/2019. One of
Springer's duties was listed as "routing of
telegrams."

33. Transcript of a recorded interview with
Cecil B. Lyon, consular officer, Cairo
(1944–46). Interviewed in 1988 by John
Bovey.

34. Ibid.

35. Ibid.

36. Ibid.

37. Ibid.

38. Michael Reilly, *Reilly of the White
House: Behind the Scenes with FDR*, as told
to William J. Slocum (Chicago: Phocion,
2017; originally published in 1947 [New
York: Simon and Schuster]), 146.

Chapter 14

1. *Intelligence Liaison Activity with
Chinese Ground Forces*, draft, USAAF in
China, Fourteenth US Air Force, APO #627,
March 29, 1943. Claire Lee Chennault
Papers, Hoover Institution, Stanford
University.

2. Ibid.

3. Citation for the Bronze Star to First
Lieutenant Arthur H. Hopkins, 02 051 753,
of the Air Corps, Army of the United States.
OSS Personnel Records, NARA, College
Park, MD.

4. Chennault to Vincent, APO 430, June 5,
1944. Box 8, folder 48, 14th Air Force, 68th
Composite Wing, 1943–1945. Claire Lee
Chennault Papers, Hoover Institution,
Stanford University.

5. Johnson, "World War II: Fourteenth Air
Force; Heir to the Flying Tigers."

6. Citation for the Bronze Star to First
Lieutenant Arthur H. Hopkins, 02 051 753,
of the Air Corps, Army of the United States.
OSS Personnel Records, NARA, College
Park, MD.

7. W. W. Pettus to Dr. Rimlon, Yale-in-
China, and Maude Pettus, Berkeley, CA,
April 20, 1945.

8. James A. Elliott to Dr. Kenneth

Latourette, Yuanling, China, July 17, 1944.

9. Ibid. Their full names were Chi-Chiang
Lao (劳启祥), Kai-Shih Ying (应开识),
Kuang-Ting Wang (王光鼎), James Ken
Sheng (盛铿 [盛群铎]), and Jackson Ho (何
家声), as stated in an email message from
George Zhongze Li.

10. Ibid.

11. W. W. Pettus to Dr. C. K. Chu,
director, National Institute of Health.
Chungking, May 28, 1945.

12. Ibid.

13. Pettus, *A Life for China*.

14. "Stinson L-5 Sentinel," https://
en.wikipedia.org/wiki/Stinson_L-5_
Sentinel. Observation, artillery-spotting, and
liaison aircraft; 1,538 built, 79 transferred to
USN/USMC as OY-1.

15. Pettus, *A Life for China*, 16.

16. Don Moore, "He Took President
Roosevelt to Malta to Attend the Conference
at Yalta." *Charlotte Sun Newspaper*,
February 13, 2003.

17. Ibid.

18. Reilly, *Reilly of the White House*, 146.

19. *Franklin D. Roosevelt Day by Day*,
February 12, 1945; a project of the Pare
Lorenz Center at the FDR Presidential
Library.

20. Transcript of a recorded interview
with Cecil B. Lyon, consular officer, Cairo
(1944–46). Lyon recalled meeting Roosevelt
aboard USS *Quincy* and the concern that he
and others had about the President's health.

21. *Franklin D. Roosevelt Day by Day*,
February 13, 1945; a project of the Pare
Lorenz Center at the FDR Presidential
Library.

22. Moore, "He Took President Roosevelt
to Malta to Attend the Conference at Yalta."
The crewman was Boatswain's Mate Angelo
Marinelli.

23. *Franklin D. Roosevelt Day by Day*,
February 13, 1945.

24. Ibid.

25. *Franklin D. Roosevelt Day by Day*,
February 14, 1945; a project of the Pare
Lorenz Center at the FDR Presidential
Library.

26. Transcript of a recorded interview

with Cecil B. Lyon, consular officer, Cairo (1944–46). Lyon recalled the conversation with Col. Eddy, who served as Roosevelt's interpreter during the meeting.

27. Geoffrey C. Ward and Ken Burns, *The Roosevelts: An Intimate History* (New York: Alfred A. Knopf, 2014), 445.

28. "Saudi Arabian Guests, February 12–14, 1945, aboard the USS *Quincy*." David L. Byrd papers, East Carolina Manuscript Collection: military records, repository, special collections, reference.

29. Reilly, *Reilly of the White House*, 156–57. Reilly, Roosevelt's chief of security for the Presidential Secret Service detail, recalled the intimate trappings of the Saudi Arabian king.

30. Moore, "He Took President Roosevelt to Malta to Attend the Conference at Yalta." The crewman was Boatswain's Mate Angelo Marinelli.

31. Ibid.

32. Transcript of a recorded interview with Cecil B. Lyon, consular officer, Cairo (1944–46). Lyon recalled the conversation with John G. Winant, then serving as the US ambassador to the UK, who was in Cairo after the meetings.

33. Ibid.

34. Groom, *The Allies*, 409–10.

35. Unclassified US Department of State case no. F-2019-00051, doc. no. C06798719, August 19, 2019; and S. Pickney Tuck, report on Springer, Paul Le Baron, Cairo, undated.

36. Egyptian-American University Fellowship, "Notice of coming events." February 25–June 1945. Worth Howard, chairman for the Program Committee. Springer Family collection.

37. Department of State to Legation, Cairo, May 31, 1945. Telegram received, stating that the following received passing grades in recent written examinations for foreign service: Vernon D. Hedin, Paul L. Springer. Springer Family collection.

38. Department of State, incoming telegram, Gauss to Department of State. State Department Personnel Records, 123 Springer, Paul L., NARA, College Park, MD.

39. Paul LeBaron Springer, special passport no. 21262, issued October 22, 1942.

40. Postcard, Paul Springer to the Springers. Sarnia, Ontario, Canada, August 19, 1945.

41. Mitter, *Forgotten Ally*, 361.

42. Josette H. Williams, "The Information War in the Pacific, 1945," *Studies in Intelligence* 46, no.3 (2002).

43. Mitter, *Forgotten Ally*, 362.

44. Ibid.

45. "The Surrender of Japanese Forces in China, Indochina, and Formosa," Taiwan Documents Project, www.taiwandocuments. org/japansurrender.htm.

46. Mitter, *Forgotten Ally*, 363–65.

Chapter 15

1. Chapman and Plumb, *The Yale-in-China Association*, 55.

2. Pettus, *A Life for China*, 9–10.

3. Ibid.

4. This supplement was known as "General Order No. 1 of Generalissimo Chiang Kai-shek."

5. David Askew, "Surrender in Nanking," www.endofempire. asia/0909-surrender-in-nanking-3/.

6. Yoloshan is today's Yuelushan, Changsha, Hunan Province (湖南长沙岳麓山).

7. Pettus, *A Life for China*, 11.

8. Ibid., 11.

9. Ibid., 12.

10. Ibid., 12–13.

11. Ibid.

12. Hume, *Dauntless Adventurer*, 189–90.

13. Pettus, *A Life for China*, 12.

14. Ibid., 14.

15. Chinese national currency.

16. Pettus, *A Life for China*, 14.

17. Ibid., 15.

18. Hume, *Dauntless Adventurer*, 200–01.

19. Ibid., 204. Pettus does not mention whether the electric generator Jim Elliott left in Changsha was US Army surplus.

20. Peishiyi was a command and control base, used late in the war as the headquarters of the 68th Composite Wing. In addition, transport aircraft used the airport to fly

troops and supplies into the area, as well as combat wounded to rear areas. The Americans remained at the airport after the war ended, the facility becoming the headquarters of the China Air Service Command, which supplied equipment and other logistical support to American and Chinese forces, along with being headquarters of 14th Air Force. Today, it still exists as Baishiyi Air Base, a People's Liberation Army Air Force base and formerly the main civil airport serving Chongqing, China, located about 13 miles northwest of the city center. It reverted to military use after the opening of Chongqing Jiangbei International Airport in 1990.

21. Hume, *Dauntless Adventurer*, 208–11.

22. Laowhangpin is now known as (Pinyin: Huangping, 黄平), and Kweichow is now known as (Pinyin: Guizhou).

23. 1st Lt. Herman L. Armstrong, *Report on Death of Doctor William Winston Pettis*, AC 6-822606, 530th Fighter Squadron, APO 285, November 27, 1945.

24. Remarks by R. Brank Fulton at the Pettus memorial service, held in New Haven at Dwight Hall on June 23, 1946.

25. Hume, *Dauntless Adventurer*, 225.

26. Ibid., 223.

27. Remarks by Dr. H. C. Chang, director of Hunan-Yale College of Medicine, upon learning of the death of Dr. Pettus, November 23, 1945.

Epilogue

1. Chapman and Plumb, *The Yale-China Association*, 68.

2. Ibid., 69.

3. Ibid.

4. Mitter, *Forgotten Ally*, 365–70.

5. Ibid.

6. Hart, *The Making of an Army* "Old China Hand," 41.

7. Ibid., 70.

8. Ibid., 70–71.

9. Ibid., 73.

10. Ibid., 74–75.

11. Ibid., 74.

12. Elder, *The Oriole's Song*, 186.

13. Ibid., 187.

14. Transcript of a recorded interview with Kenneth Moreland on February 20, 2002, 35.

15. Ibid., 1.

16. "United States Information Agency," https://en.wikipedia.org/wiki/United_States_Information_Agency#cite_note-elder-5.

17. Robert Elder, *The Information Machine: The United States Information Agency and American Foreign Policy* (Syracuse, NY: Syracuse University Press, 1968).

18. "James Ackerman Elliott," https://www.legacy.com/obituaries/pressconnects/obituary.aspx?n=james-ackerman-elliot-jim&pid=87891196.

19. "Hopkins, Arthur H. Jr.," in *Twenty-Five Year Record*, ed. John N. Deming (New Haven, CT: Yale University, Class of Nineteen Forty-One, 1966), 138.

20. Paul Springer to the editor, *Foreign Service Journal*, October 15, 1975.

21. John S. Service, "The Man Who 'Lost China,'" part 1, Association for Diplomatic Studies. Transcript of an oral-history interview with John Service, https://adst.org/2014/02/john-s-service-the-man-who-lost-china-part-i/.

22. Bart Barnes, "Old China Hand John Service dies at 89," *Washington Post*, Feb. 4, 1999.

23. John S. Service, "The Man Who 'Lost China,'" part 2, Association for Diplomatic Studies, https://adst.org/2013/12/john-s-service-the-man-who-lost-china/.

24. Ibid.

BIBLIOGRAPHY

ARCHIVAL SOURCES (PUBLISHED)

Franklin D. Roosevelt Day by Day. A project of the Pare Lorenz Center at the FDR
    Presidential Library.
Saudi Arabian Guests, February 12–14, 1945 aboard the USS Quincy. David L. Byrd
    papers. East Carolina Manuscript Collection, military records, repository, special
    collections, reference.
Senate Internal Security Committee. *The Amerasia Papers: A Clue to the Catastrophe of
    China*, January 26, 1970.

ARCHIVAL SOURCES (NONPUBLISHED)

Springer Family Collection: The Papers of Paul LeBaron Springer
A private collection. Compiled, scanned, and indexed by James P. Bevill. Manuscript and
    typed documents, letters, pamphlets, tickets, photographs, maps, etc. . . . documenting
    Paul Springer's childhood; years at Yale University, 1937–41; Yale-in-China, 1941–42;
    the US Department of State, 1942–48; and the CIA from 1949 until his retirement in
    1968. The papers also include postretirement letters, notes, correspondence, speeches,
    and commentary on the previous periods up to and including 2012.

**Arthur H. Hopkins Jr. Veterans Records, National Personal Records Center, St. Louis,
Missouri**

**Yale University Library Collection, Yale-China Association Records, ID #RU 232,
The Journal of James Elliott**
Series Number III, box 97, folder 762

**Yale University Library Collection, Yale-China Association Records, ID # RU 232,
Paul LeBaron Springer Papers**
Series Number III, box 97, folder 762

**Yale University Library Collection, Yale-China Association Records, ID # RU 232,
Arthur H. Hopkins Jr. Papers**
Series III, box 69, folders 268–70

Yale University Library Collection—William Winston Pettus Papers, ID #MS 786
Series I, box 1, folders 20, 21, 23–28
Series I, box 2, folders 29–38
Series IV, box 3, folders 80–86

Claire Lee Chennault Papers 1941–1967, Hoover Institution, Stanford University
Box 8, folder 47. 14th Air Force, Chinese American Composite Wing, 1943–1945
Box 8, folder 48. 14th Air Force, 68th Composite Wing, 1943–1945
Box 9, folder 7. 14th Air Force, 1943–1945, Military Intelligence

David Dean Barrett Papers, Hoover Institution Archives, Stanford University
Envelope A, photographs
Envelope E, photographs

Joseph Warren Stilwell Papers, Hoover Institution Archives, Stanford University
Box 108, scrapbooks

National Archives and Records Administration (NARA), College Park, Maryland
State Department Personnel Records, 123 Springer, Paul L. / 5
State Department Central Files, Record Group 59, Nationalist China, 1943–1944

National Archives and Records Administration (NARA), College Park, Maryland
Records of the Office of Strategic Services (Record Group 226)
OSS Personnel Records, NARA, College Park, Maryland. Arthur H. Hopkins Jr.
Examples, explanations, and directions for codes and ciphers, ca. December 1943–June
    1944, ca. 50 pp. [WN#04580], box #114
Minutes of a conference in Chungking, China, "held as a result of instructions by General
    Tai Li and General Donovan," December 9, 1943, 5 pp. [WN#07428], box #179
Memorandum on British Intelligence Services in China, January 5, 1944, 18 pp.
    [WN#09823], box # 217
Memorandum providing background information for X-2 activities in Kweilin, China,
    March 25, 1944, 7 pp. [WN#09822], box #217
Office of Strategic Services, Cairo, Cable #555, Action: Special Funds to Panos
    Morphoposos, Aug. 11, 1943. US National Archives. Box # 340.
Memo on *Future Plans for Cairo Intelligence Headquarters*, Stephen Penrose, chief SI,
    July 22, 1944. OSS Records, box 340, US National Archives.
Office of Strategic Services, Cairo, Cable #555, Action: Special Funds to Panos
    Morphoposos, Aug. 11, 1943. US National Archives.

Unclassified US Department of State, FOIA Case No. F-2019-00051, 08/19/2019
American Foreign Service Annual Efficiency Report, Paul LeBaron Springer, Cairo, by S.
    Pickney Tuck, American minister, Dec. 1, 1944. Doc. no. C06798601.
Report on Springer, Paul Le Baron, by S. Pickney Tuck, Cairo, Undated. Doc no.
    C06798719.

BOOKS

Anderson, Scott. *The Quiet Americans: Four CIA Spies at the Dawn of the Cold War—a
    Tragedy in Three Acts*. New York: Doubleday, 2020.
Chang, Iris. *The Rape of Nanking: The Forgotten Holocaust of World War II*. New York:
    Basic Books, 1997.
Chapman, Nancy E., and Jessica C. Plumb. *The Yale-China Association: A Centennial
    History*. Hong Kong: Chinese University Press, Chinese University of Hong Kong,
    2001.
Deming, John N., ed. *Twenty-Five Year Record*. New Haven, CT: Yale University, Class of

Nineteen Forty-One, 1966.

Elder, B. J. *The Oriole's Song: An American Girlhood in Wartime China*. Norwalk, CT: EastBridge, 2003.

Elder, Robert. *The Information Machine: The United States Information Agency and American Foreign Policy*. Syracuse, NY: Syracuse University Press, 1968.

Grimes, Lee, ed. *50 Years from '41: Yale University Class of 1941 50th Reunion, 1991*. New Haven, CT: Yale Alumni Records Office, 1991.

Groom, Winston. *The Allies: Roosevelt, Churchill, Stalin, and the Unlikely Alliance That Won World War II*. Washington, DC: National Geographic, 2018.

Gulick, Edward V. *Teaching in Wartime China: A Photo-Memoir, 1937–1939*. Amherst: University of Massachusetts Press, 1995.

Harris, Sheldon H. *Factories of Death: Japanese Biological Warfare, 1932–1945, and American Cover-Up*. Rev. ed. New York: Routledge, 2002.

Hart, John N. *The Making of an Army "Old China Hand": A Memoir of Colonel David D. Barrett*. Berkeley: Institute of East Asia Studies, University of California, 1985.

Helms, Richard A. *A Look over My Shoulder: A Life in the Central Intelligencer Agency*. Novato, CA: Presidio, 2004.

Hicks, Andrew, ed. and comp. *Jack Jones, a True Friend to China: "The Lost Writings of a Heroic Nobody."* Hong Kong: Earnshaw Books, 2015.

Hume, Edward H. *Dauntless Adventurer: The Story of Dr. Winston Pettus*. Xiangya Culture Inheritance. Wuhan, China: Wuhan University Press, 2016. Originally published in 1952 (New Haven, CT: Yale University Press).

Jackson, Daniel. *Famine, Sword, and Fire: The Liberation of Southwest China in World War II*. Atglen, PA: Schiffer, 2015.

Kahn, E. J., Jr. *The China Hands: America's Foreign Service Officers and What Befell Them*. New York: Penguin Books, 1975.

Liu Weichao, ed. *Qun Ying Hui Cui* (群英荟萃). Yali Middle School in Her Centennial Anniversary, 2006.

Mitter, Rana. *Forgotten Ally: China's World War II, 1937–1945*. Boston and New York: Houghton Mifflin Harcourt, 2013.

Okerstrom, Dennis R. *Dick Cole's War: Doolittle Raider, Hump Pilot, Air Commando*. Columbia: University of Missouri Press, 2015.

Pettus, Sarah. *A Life for China*. Biographical sketch of William Winston Pettus. Berkeley, CA: China Council, n.d.

Reilly, Michael. *Reilly of the White House: Behind the Scenes with FDR*. As told to William J. Slocum. Chicago: Phocion, 2017. Originally published in 1947 (New York: Simon and Schuster).

Ward, Geoffrey C., and Ken Burns. *The Roosevelts: An Intimate History*. New York: Alfred A. Knopf, 2014.

Whittlesey, Marjorie T. *The Dragon Will Survive*. Ft. Lauderdale, FL: Ashley Books, 1991.

Winks, Robin. *Cloak and Gown: Scholars in America's Secret War*. London: Collins Harvill, 1987.

Yu, Maochun. *OSS in China: Prelude to Cold War*. New Haven, CT: Yale University Press, 1996.

PUBLICATIONS

"Christmas Trip 1940." In *Yale Glee Club Program*. New Haven, CT: Yale University.

"The Freshman Boxing Season." In *The 1938 Yale Banner*. Vol. 97. New Haven, CT: Yale

University.

A History of the Class of 1940. New Haven, CT: Yale University.

A History of the Class of 1941. New Haven, CT: Yale University.

Reynolds, W. A. "Operation and Maintenance of a Road Transport System in West China, 1942–46." *Journal of the Hong Kong Branch of the Royal Asiatic Society* 16 (1976): 135–61.

Yale in China: Report of the Thirty-Seventh Year. New Haven, CT: Yale University, 1942–1943.

Newspaper sources

Courier-Post (Camden, NJ), September 2, 1937.

Moore, Don. "He Took President Roosevelt to Malta to Attend the Conference at Yalta." *Charlotte Sun*, February 13, 2003.

New York Times, August 25, 1917.

New York Times, June 4, 1943.

South China Morning Post, October 15, 1941.

South China Morning Post, December 7, 1941.

Weekend China Daily, July 7–9, 2017.

Yali News, September 22, 1941.

Magazine article

Johnson, E. R. "World War II: Fourteenth Air Force; Heir to the Flying Tigers." *Aviation History*, November 2005.

The Association for Diplomatic Studies and Training, Foreign Affairs Oral History Project (ADST)

Transcript of a recorded interview with Cecil B. Lyon, consular officer, Cairo (1944–46). Interviewed in 1988 by John Bovey (ADST).

Transcript of a recorded interview with Ambassador Everett Drumright, diplomat and consular officer in China (1935–62). Interviewed on July 27, 1989, by Hank Zivetz (ADST).

Transcript of a recorded interview with Thomas W. Wilson, Combined Economic Warfare Agency, Cairo (1942–45). Interviewed by Charles Stuart Kennedy on October 30, 1996 (ADST).

OTHER ORAL HISTORIES

Various conversations with former Bachelor Paul LeBaron Springer, Yale '41.

Transcript of a recorded interview with former Bachelor Kenneth Moreland, Yale '43, on February 20, 2002.

ONLINE SOURCES

Askew, David. "Surrender in Nanking." www.endofempire. asia/0909-surrender-in-nanking-3/.

"Battle of Singapore." https://en.wikipedia.org/wiki/Battle_of_Singapore.

"The China Air Task Force and 14th Air Force." U.S. Embassy & Consulates in China.

https://china.usembassy-china.org.cn/china-air-task-force-14th-air-force/.

"Chongqing Baishiyi Airport." https://en.wikipedia.org/wiki/Chongqing_Baishiyi_Airport.

"The Civil War in China, Part II—the Dixie Mission and Losing China." Moments in US Diplomatic History. http://adst.org/2013/12/the-civil-war-in-china-part-ii-the-dixie-mission-and-losing-china/#.WhTk5LpFyM8.

"David D. Barrett." https://en.wikipedia.org/wiki/David_D._Barrett.

DevizesPeaceGroup. "Exit from Burma: A Conscientious Objector's Story." WW2 People's War (an online archive of wartime memories contributed by members of the public and gathered by the BBC). www.bbc.co.uk/ww2peopleswarbbc.co.uk/history/ww2peopleswar/stories/71/a6913271.shtml.

"The Greek Civil War." https://en.wikipedia.org/wiki/Greek_Civil_War.

"India and Pakistan Win Independence." History.com, 2010. www.history.com/this-day-in-history/india-and-pakistan-win-independence.

"Jassy–Kishinev Offensive (August 1944)." https://en.wikipedia.org/wiki/Jassy%E2%80%93Kishinev_Offensive.

Patay, Matt. "King Farouk." IMDb Mini Biography. www.imdb.com/name/nm1531603/bio.

"SACO: The Sino-American Cooperative Organization." DelsJourney. www.delsjourney.com/saco/saco.htm.

"Sorry Mao: It's Pronounced 'Truman,' not 'Too-Lu-Mun.'" Association for Diplomatic Studies & Training. https://adst.org/2013/11/mao-asks-who-is-this-too-lu-mun/.

"Stinson L-5 Sentinel." https://en.wikipedia.org/wiki/Stinson_L-5_Sentinel.

"The Surrender of Japanese Forces in China, Indochina and Formosa." Taiwan Documents Project. www.taiwandocuments.org/japansurrender.htm.

INDEX